Urban Underworlds

Urban Underworlds

A Geography of Twentieth-Century American Literature and Culture

THOMAS HEISE

Rutgers University Press
NEW BRUNSWICK, NEW JERSEY, AND LONDON

Visit our Web site: http://rutgerspress.rutgers.edu

Manufactured in the United States of America

LIBRARY OF CONGRESS CATALOGING-IN-PUBLICATION DATA

Heise, Thomas, 1971–

Urban underworlds : a geography of twentieth-century American literature and culture / Thomas Heise.

p. cm. — (American literatures initiative)

Includes bibliographical references and index.

ISBN 978-0-8135-4784-8 (hardcover : alk. paper)

ISBN 978-0-8135-4785-5 (pbk. : alk. paper)

1. American literature—20th century—History and criticism. 2. Social classes in literature. 3. Literature and society—United States—History—20th century. 4. Group identity in literature. 5. Difference (Psychology) in literature. 6. Place (Philosophy) in literature. I. Title.

PS228.S63H45 2011

810.9'355—dc22

2010004657

A British Cataloging-in-Publication record for this book is available from the British Library.

THE AMERICAN LITERATURES INITIATIVE

A book in the American Literatures Initiative (ALI), a collaborative publishing project of NYU Press, Fordham University Press, Rutgers University Press, Temple University Press, and the University of Virginia Press. The Initiative is supported by The Andrew W. Mellon Foundation. For more information, please visit www.americanliteratures.org.

For Christine

Contents

Acknowledgments

Urban Underworlds was conceived in The Hole, a grimy, graffiti-covered bar in the East Village with no sign advertising its secrets and no locks on the bathroom doors. What drew me there on Friday nights when I was a PhD student was the promise of strong drinks in plastic cups, threadbare couches, and video projections of art-house films over a dancing crowd that almost always included an indie star whose career I followed and the bassist for a popular post-punk band whose CDs I owned. Not far from The Hole was an illegal, unlicensed, amazingly cluttered bar operated by a low-level member of the Italian mafia, to whom I had been introduced one memorable evening in 2002. Inside an apartment building, away from prying eyes on the street, the bar's door was guarded by a bouncer who one night showed me the "Saturday Night Special" he kept tucked inside the puffy winter jacket he wore in all seasons. Such places taught me that much life in the city transpires not only out of view but also "off the map," hidden from the official channels of publicity in order to protect itself from curiosity seekers, as well as the police. I like to think that many of the writers in *Urban Underworlds*, whose novels travel through places far more seedy, would have felt at home in these clandestine locales of twenty-first-century New York.

The Virgilian guides for *Urban Underworlds* have been many, but I would like to thank first and foremost Ross Posnock for his high standards. He has been a source of constant inspiration and a model intellect, one whose rigorous scholarship and clear, crisp writing I hope to emulate. This project is also indebted to Phillip Brian Harper, who helped steer me through graduate school and prepared me for the world beyond it. I would also like to thank Bryan Waterman for his enthusiastic support, which kept me from going under. Alan Williamson, who taught me to ignore the voices that said one could not be an academic scholar and a writer, has left his imprint on my career in ways that I cannot quantify. My close friends John Beckman, Andrew Strombeck, Robert Balog, and Chris Hosea, with whom I often commiserated, lent their companionship, support, and wisdom on our high and low escapades through the city in the late hours of the night. My wonderful research assistants, Stephanie Dixon and Max Karpinski, proofed and fact-checked *Urban Underworlds*, thus saving me time and eyesight. I want to offer my appreciation to my many excellent colleagues and students at New York University and McGill University for the smart, challenging, and invaluable feedback I received in the form of conversations, seminars, and papers over the years. Without the fellowships, grants, and research hiatuses I received at both schools, this book might have never seen the light of day.

For permission to reprint photographs and figures, I have several individuals and organizations to thank. The Museum of the City of New York has been kind to allow me to reprint images from the Jacob Riis collection. I want to thank Frank Oppel for his permission to reprint illustrations and photographs from *Tales of Gaslight New York*. The photograph "Cabaret Dancers, ca. 1937," by Aaron Siskind, appears here courtesy of the Museum of Contemporary Photography, Columbia College Chicago and the Bruce Silverstein gallery, which holds the rights to the photographs of Aaron Siskind. The University of Chicago Press has granted the right to reproduce Ernest Burgess's figure "Urban Areas." I would like to thank the UCLA Charles E. Young Research Library Department of Special Collections, Los Angeles Times Photographic Archives, for its photographs of Bunker Hill and Pershing Square; and I would like thank Yves Rubin for allowing me reprint his photograph of the Bonaventure Hotel in downtown Los Angeles. I am grateful to Margaret Morton for allowing me to reproduce one of the striking images from her book *The Tunnel* (Yale University Press, 1995), a photographic record of underground homelessness in New York City. Part of chapter 2 appeared in a slightly different form in *Twentieth Century Literature* (55.3, Fall 2009) and is here reprinted with permission of the journal. My editor at Rutgers University Press, Leslie Mitchner, has lent me her expert stewardship and insightful commentary, for which I am deeply indebted. Anonymous readers for Rutgers offered astute suggestions for revision that have made this a better book through and through.

I have been working on this subject for nearly as long as I have known Christine Minas, my wife and partner in life's loves and miseries. She has followed me into the cold and, once there, kept me warm. I could never repay her for what I owe in moral support, love, and unwavering patience.

Urban Underworlds

An Overview and an Underview: Uneven Development and the Social Production of American Underworlds

This book is a journey into the depths of human misery and perversity, but it begins where you would least expect it: on top of one of the loveliest buildings in the world. In 1905 the journalist Edgar Saltus stood aloft Daniel Burnham's Fuller Building at Twenty-third Street and Fifth Avenue in Manhattan in order to see for himself "the most extraordinary panorama in the world—a survey of the American metropolis."[1] The twenty-three story, triangular building, popularly known as the Flatiron, was the world's first skyscraper and a stunning harbinger of America's emergent modern capitalist economy. The Flatiron captured, according to Alfred Stieglitz's sanguine description, "a new America still in the making."[2] Saltus, too, recognized that the building signaled a change in the city and the nation, but perhaps an ominous one: "Its front is lifted to the future. On the past its back is turned. Of what has gone on before it is American in its unconcern" (210). The hull of the Flatiron seemed to confidently announce "full steam ahead" into the future. When it was unveiled to the public in 1903, however, there were widespread fears that the narrow building might topple over and crush its spectators, and thus for a time its upper floors remained empty. But by 1905, when Saltus climbed to the top for *Munsey's Magazine*, concerns over its structural unsoundness had been laid to rest. From an Olympian height above New York City this is what Saltus saw, or perhaps it is better to say, this is what he imagined:

> Meanwhile, on those toppest floors, the eager sun, aslant, shuttles the mounting roar. In the noise and glare you need but a modicum

> of imagination to fancy yourself contemplating a volcano in active operation, one that is erupting gold, coining dollars in its depths, and tossing them in the crystalline air—whence they fall, as rain falls, on those who know enough not to come in, who get in the way, fight for a place, and hold it until they have made their pile. It is not of course from such as these that gods shall come, rather a race similar to the curious dwarfs of whom Pliny told, pygmies that passed their lives fighting with phantoms for coin. So, too, fight those that *you behold* from the toppest floors. The struggle is the impetus of their little lives, the substances of their loves and hates; it is the magnet that draws them from regions quasi-polar, wholly tropical, from zones remoter yet, from those nethermost planes where Dante went. (209; emphasis added)

After this epic description, Saltus turned southward—turning "you" with him—and looked to "the lower East Side" and to "the Chinese quarter," and described the first as "a caldron [*sic*]" and the second as "a sewer" (210).

The new vertical architecture of corporate capitalism made possible a way of seeing that the older, horizontal civic architecture of court houses and city halls could not. It simultaneously allowed Saltus a totalizing vision of the city and it turned loose his urban imagination in the "nethermost planes." From on high, Saltus could not only see far but he could also see deep, or at the very least he could intimate depth in the form of an exotic volcano of production spewing gold for the "curious dwarfs" who turned raw material into profit. From on high he could see "Upper Fifth Avenue" where the "gods" of industry lived and the downtown immigrant "sewer" where the "pygm[y]" workers huddled, and he also could see that they were bound to each other (208, 210). "Dante told of the inferno," Saltus wrote, "He told, too, of paradise. Manhattan may typify both" (201). In short, Saltus grasped capitalism's dynamic and polarizing logic of uneven geographical and social development. On a clear day, high above the world, Saltus could discern how the ideology of unequal development had been inscribed into the geography of the city.

Saltus's petition for us to look recalls Karl Marx's invitation to the reader in *Capital* to accompany him and "Mr. Moneybags" below "the surface . . . into the hidden abode of production, on whose threshold there stares us in the face 'No admittance except on business.' Here we shall see, not only how capital produces, but how capital is produced. We shall at

FIGURE 1. A view from the Flatiron Building in 1905. Reprinted from Edgar Saltus, "New York from the Flatiron," *Munsey's Magazine*, 1905. Courtesy of Frank Oppel, *Tales of Gaslight New York* (2000).

last force the secret of profit making."[3] The difference, however, between Marx's Dantean journey and Saltus's is that Saltus never left his perch. For Saltus, the binary geography of modern capitalism was made visible by ascending the emblem of its triumph, a journey up rather than down. From this privileged position of visual mastery, he could discern that the magnetic lure of industrialization drew surplus labor from equatorial nations, transforming the colonial subject into something subhuman. But what he could not perceive was how his ascent had transformed him as well, how it had lifted him out of the welter of the city's street life and out of its lived spaces. In short, he could not understand how it had transformed him into "you," the abstract, disembodied viewer who was liberated from the struggling little lives in the inferno below.

Fast forward roughly eighty years, and we find the French philosopher Michel de Certeau reenacting Saltus's journey just a couple miles south by ascending what was then the world's tallest building: the World Trade Center, the premier embodiment of finance capitalism and "the most monumental figure of Western urban development."[4] In the decades since Saltus, the buildings had grown taller and the canyons deeper. From the 110th floor, de Certeau looked out over the undulating "wave of verticals" and immediately observed two things. First he noticed that his elevation above the bustling world of New York had changed the city into an aesthetic object that he called "a texturology" of extremes, "extremes of ambition and degradation, brutal oppositions of races and styles, contrasts between yesterday's buildings, already transformed into trash cans, and today's urban irruptions that block out its space" (91). And the second thing he noticed was that he himself had been converted by his ascension, had been changed into the "*universal* and anonymous *subject*," a person now free from the burden of racial and gender embodiment, free from the constraints of geography, free to imagine the world (94). "To be lifted to the summit of the World Trade Center," the always self-reflexive de Certeau wrote, "is to be lifted out of the city's grasp. One's body is no longer clasped by the streets that turn and return it according to an anonymous law" (92). "The pedestrian . . . is for an instant transformed into a visionary," he claimed; and continued, "When one goes up there, he leaves behind the mass that carries off and mixes up in itself any identity of authors or spectators. An Icarus flying above these waters, he can ignore the devices of Daedalus in mobile and endless labyrinths far below. His elevation transfigures him into a voyeur. It puts him at a distance. It transforms the bewitching world by which one was 'possessed' into a text that lies before one's eyes. It allows one to read it, to be a solar Eye, looking down like a god" (92).

In this magical passage, de Certeau sees himself seeing and understands that his privileged position in space has transfigured everything upon which he has set his panoramic eye. From up above, the late twentieth-century city's brutal contrasts between "ambition and degradation" and between new "styles" and the almost immediate "trash[ing]" of yesterday's architectures are reduced to a sensual texture and transformed into a text to be read—or at least looked at—from a distance. Yet it is crucial to note that the dialectical opposites—those "extremes" and "oppositions"—that come into view are just as quickly obscured. What obscures the politics of this vision is one's desire for seeing and the seeing of one's desire unfold, or as de Certeau puts it: "this pleasure of 'seeing the whole'" (92). Looking at the city in this way, frankly, is erotic, "a voluptuous pleasure," an "ecstasy" (92). Yet just as crucially, de Certeau knows that from the summit's view so much remains hidden: "Escaping the imaginary totalizations produced by the eye, the everyday has a certain strangeness that does not surface, or whose surface is only its upper limit, outlining itself against the visible" (93).

For Saltus and de Certeau, the modern metropolis was turned into an underworld by the simple fact that their privileged elevation allowed them to look down on the city. The gesture was complex, to say the least. By standing atop the very plinth of capital that had forever altered the world around them, they were able to see how much had changed. The vertical architectures that made this knowledge possible were also the concrete embodiments of a system that both men indicted for the havoc it had wrought. In both cases, the clarity and "all-seeing power" of the bird's-eye perspective turned out to be a mere fiction that obscured more than it made visible. For each, the grimy realities of urban political economy—labor exploitation, struggle, trash, poverty, slums, uneven development—were mystified and mythologized as Dante's hell and Daedalus's labyrinth. The questions swirl. What does it mean to think of those who live in poverty as living in hell? Or to think of poverty as a texture, part of the urban fabric you might run your fingers across? How is it that someone else's degradation has become our "strange new hallucinatory exhilaration," "a delight to the eyes," as Fredric Jameson once suggested when staring over a perpetually decaying downtown Los Angeles from the upper floors of the upscale Bonaventure Hotel in the 1980s?[5] And why is it that the practices of everyday life, sex, work, leisure of the city's socially and spatially marginalized residents—those "'down below'"—have been thought of as part of "a vast secret world," part of the "underground side of social life"?[6]

These complicated questions haunt *Urban Underworlds* from beginning to end. I start with Saltus's and de Certeau's acts of looking because they bookend the historical trajectory we are about to embark upon, a journey that will take us from the Progressive Era into the postmodern in search of the "real" city, the lowdown dirty world below the veil, into the slums and sewers of urban America. It will be a journey through urban decay and urban unrest, into fetid cellar apartments and red-light districts. As the Harlem Renaissance writer James Weldon Johnson put it, we will "nose down into the lower strata of life," into an "underworld . . . of illicit love and illicit liquor, of red sins and dark crimes."[7] This book ventures into America's underworlds not out of a taste for lurid sensationalism, but as an attempt to understand how urban space has been read from the top down by sociologists and planners and how it has been written from the bottom up by writers who speak about the experience of social and spatial isolation, about the experience of being an object of scrutiny, suspicion, and fear.

The underworld has long exerted a pull on the imagination of U.S. writers, as well as on sociologists and planners in search of knowledge of the submerged classes and on urban spelunkers in search of nighttime fun. In the pages that follow, I present a range of writings to give a full account of this enduring cultural fascination: we will find the underworld in popular urban slumming guides for voyeuristic tourists, in expert studies of crime, ethnicity, race, and poverty, in urban planning initiatives, and in modern and postmodern literary narratives, some of which descend down into the underworld from above and some of which claim to originate within its clandestine geographies of underground apartments, sewers, toilets, and rundown parks. Since the concept of an underworld is formulated "up above" in the discourses of sociology, urban planning, and criminology, and deployed "down below," *Urban Underworlds* is by default an exercise in looking from two opposing perspectives.

The literature of the twentieth century will be "canal-dredging" about "submerged peoples and social strata," Max Nordau, the physician, journalist, and author of the positivistic tome *Degeneration* asserted in 1892.[8] Looking over the horizon into the new century, Nordau voiced a vehement polemic against modern art, which he considered unspeakably low in its attraction to perversity and madness, a symptom of a degenerate future that was about to be unleashed. Nordau's moralizing screed over cultural decadence, which he tied to widespread genetic decline and urban living, sounds histrionic to us. Though Nordau's perspective was European and the art he feared was being penned by Charles Baudelaire, Emile Zola, and Oscar Wilde, among others, his commentary strikes a nerve in the American context. The underworld of "submerged peoples" is everywhere in urban American literature and culture from the late nineteenth century to the late twentieth. It is at the center of the distressing assessments of urban life by the diverse array of authors I consider in the pages to follow.

We find the underworld as a source of pervasive unease across the century in expert writings on urban culture by Jacob Riis, Ernest Burgess, Lewis Mumford, Robert Park, Gunnar Myrdal, and Jennifer Toth. We discover it, as well, rearing its head in narratives by Henry James, Djuna Barnes, Claude McKay, Richard Wright, Ralph Ellison, John Rechy, Thomas Pynchon, and Don DeLillo that chart a pathway through America's lowest geographies. But what exactly is the underworld? A phantasm and a specter, the product of a paranoid disposition that sees disorder and cultural and biological decline around every corner? A real territorial culture in the crumbling urban architectures of ethnic slums and racialized ghettos, in the theaters and on the street corners of America's vice zones, and in the rotting spaces of subterranean living? A romantic figment of a literary imagination looking for signs of authentic life in the modern age? The answer is "yes." And to these questions we might ask ourselves, why has the underworld had such a hold on the American imagination? It is not just the object of our scrutiny—the putative underworld and its denizens—that we must look at, but we must examine our own act of looking and ask what it reveals about our culture, our fears and desires, our standards for citizenship, our urban policies. The list goes on. Twentieth-century sociology, criminology, biomedical discourse, and urban planning have not been shy about labeling poor, queer, ethnic, and racial communities in rundown sectors of cities as underworlds of cultural pathology, sexual perversion, and delinquency. The characterization has occurred too many times to dismiss it as mere prejudice by individual experts in particular fields. One approach this book might have taken would have been to dispute the accusations handed down from on high by valorizing the urban demiworld through an assertion of its "right to be different," to paraphrase a strain of contemporary multicultural discourse. To do so would have been to argue for an understanding of it through the lens of late twentieth-century identity politics that has advocated for the rights and recognition of the marginalized. But this book will take another approach: it will map an American cultural fascination with the underworld decade by decade, from 1890 to 1990, reading it back into a critique of urban political economy itself. This book will show that the underworld is a contradiction, a real-and-imagined space, culture, and population.

To understand the origins of this contradiction requires us to uncover the logic of capitalist uneven development, the active production of social and physical degradation. Simply put, uneven development is the geographic polarization of capital and labor and wealth and poverty. As

Neil Smith pointedly declares, it "is social inequality blazoned into the geographical landscape, and it is simultaneously the exploitation of that geographical unevenness for certain socially determined ends."[9] Marx himself graphically described capital's bifurcation of the world by noting that the "accumulation of wealth at one pole of society" is matched "at the same time [by the] accumulation of misery, agony of toil, slavery, ignorance, brutality, mental degradation, at the opposite pole."[10] These are not unfortunate accidents of capitalism, he suggested, but byproducts of its very logic. At periods of rapid industrialization, surplus populations—Marx's term for a motley mixture of "vagabonds, discharged soldiers, discharged jailbirds, escaped galley slaves, swindlers"—have been centripetally gathered by the whirlwinds of change and dropped into the city's center, into its slums, ghettoes, and vice districts as a reserve supply of excessively cheap, overabundant labor.[11] Insofar as urbanization and industrialization produced a new "social scum, . . . a passively rotting mass thrown off by the lowest layers of the old society," sociology, urban planning, and criminology sought to analyze this new contaminating blight on the city to see what it was made of, to see what was truly in the mold culture.[12] One way of understanding and controlling surplus populations was by pathologizing them, turning their difference into deviance, thus deeming denizens of the so-called underworld as unfit for full participation in the upper stratum's institutions of public life. Another, related way was by quarantining surplus populations through zoning and segregation, which were procedures for stabilizing the city in the midst of tumultuous upheavals caused by industrialization. And yet another was by re-norming the abnormal, a century-long project of the liberal and administrative state to make productive citizens. When amoral processes of urbanization collide with normative value systems that define and regulate socially acceptable forms of identity and community, the result has often been a panic over the putatively libidinal and degenerate underworld in the foul architectures of the city. It is in the underworld that we can see how the unruly, anarchic outcomes of capitalist development clash with the morally regulative expert discourses that try to manage the city's spaces and people.

The story that I tell in the chapters to follow is of how and why particular populations in specific geographies—ethnic Americans (chapter 1), gays and lesbians (chapters 2 and 4), the black underclass (chapters 2 and 3), and the new urban poor (chapters 4 and 5)—have been singled out at different moments across the century and classified as members of the underworld. Top-down perspectives—like a "solar Eye, looking down like a god"—have used the trope of an urban underworld as a means of organizing a whole swath of social anxieties that arise at moments of large-scale socioeconomic transformations. Panics over immigration, crime, contagious disease, fluctuations in standards of moral conduct, shifts in the racial composition of urban space, and increasing income inequality are among the many fears that have been displaced and subsumed under this lurid term. To phrase it another way, sociologists, urban planners, and criminologists have employed this trope to congeal manifold, complex social phenomena into a sensational and monstrous figure that allows us to see the strange byproducts of capital—nonnormative cultures living in insalubrious slums, ghettos, and vice districts—and to misrecognize them at the same time. This is to say that the polarizing rhetoric of an urban underworld redescribes the real material outcomes of uneven geographical development through the value-laden, moralizing language of high and low, clean and unclean, paradise and hell. The concept of an underworld is by definition spatial ("under") and social ("world"). As a figure of derision, it collapses social and spatial marginality into each other like a clamshell, creating a newly compacted site of cultural waste, abjection, and exclusion where myriad fears and fantasies can be located. What has been the social function of this? The recrudescence of the underworld in the urban imagination over the course of the century has deflected away analyses of capital and, instead, has led to an essentializing rhetoric over the cultural differences produced by capitalist development. Additionally, labeling, quarantining, and managing poor, queer, ethnic, and racialized populations as underworlds has stabilized white, middle-class privilege in the midst of change and crisis. It has done so by authorizing and legitimizing the production of unequal geographies that isolate disruptive subjects in the city's most blighted spaces.

Literary narratives of the underworld beg to differ with the pathologizing and moralizing authorities that have shone bright lights down where they are unwelcome. Yet the literature that I consider assumes no single, unified stance toward its perplexing subject. At times these narratives claim to speak from the underworld, at others times, they gaze down into it as into a social abyss; sometimes they shield it from further scrutiny, and sometimes expose it as an unconscionable mystification. *Urban Underworlds* does not assign heroic status to American literature and recognizes that the writers in the pages to follow have been motivated by voyeuristic curiosity about the city's lower orders that at times borders on the unseemly. Hardly immune to their culture's contradictions, James, Ellison, DeLillo, and other writers in this book have experienced the farrago of tenements, inner-city ruins, and subway tunnels as hellish, bewildering, overcrowded, and alienating. Yet almost in the same breath, they treat these same spaces as hidden domains that afford community and pleasure forbidden above in the realm of atomistic, bourgeois individualism. American underworld fiction is itself a discourse which, like all urban literature, has "helped to produce 'the city' as an experiential category for a reading public," "disseminat[ing] certain ways of seeing the urban landscape, certain perspectives on the life of its citizens, and . . . institut[ing] certain structures of imagination" that recreate the city as a visceral experience on the page.[13]

American narratives of lower urban geographies, from James's *The American Scene* (1907) to DeLillo's *Underworld* (1997), lead readers into places that they might otherwise fear to tread, teaching them how to move through shadows and claustrophobic spaces, and how to negotiate the strange mores and cultures that made the city seem like a foreign land. With verbal maps and prose rooted in a tradition of empirical verisimilitude, some of this writing has the flavor and pedagogical function of a gritty guidebook. My interest is not in the accuracy of this literature's claims or representations, but in how it has produced an affective geography by encoding for readers very abstract processes of capitalist development as dramatic stories of embattled communities that are struggling to redefine themselves. This literature thus gives form to the confusing storm of modernity and postmodernity by turning to a powerful cultural trope—the underworld—and placing it in the eye of that hurricane.

American literature of the underworld transmits a history of territorial politics—a politics over the right to the city, its streets, its parks, its neighborhoods—that has been obfuscated by discourses that have tended to treat spatially marginalized groups as incapable of organized, rational, and sustained positive agency. This history, what DeLillo calls an "underhistory," is sometimes wholly imagined, or sentimental, or self-aggrandizing, but its importance lies less in its verifiability (how does one "verify" a narrative?) than in the way that it articulates a story that stands in contradistinction to an expert discourse that has often muted the voices of urban actors who have been deemed minor players on the urban stage.[14] A history of agency and change from the bottom up is doubly lost because it has been carted away or buried by the bulldozers of urban renewal that have cleared underworld sites like piles of rubbish to be disposed of. The result has been, in Norman Klein's evocative phrase, a "history of forgetting," a loss of cultural memory with the erasure of marginal or "blighted" urban communities.[15] We can begin to recover this memory through stories of makeshift and neglected populations adapting to and resisting their emplacement, remolding urban space in ways that foster a sense of belonging, safety, and justice. Through finely granulated depictions of urban life, American city literature articulates and preserves in print—through all of the rhetorical artifices of character, point of view, narrative drama, and figurative language—what was being carted away off the page. To this end, American underworld narratives have often served as a repository of unofficial or repressed memories, where, as Ralph Ellison notes, "our unwritten history looms as [the] obscure alter ego" to "what is left out of our recorded history."[16] Djuna Barnes called such underground narratives "the stories that do not amount to much. . . . that are forgotten in spite of all man remembers . . . merely because they befell him without distinction of office or title."[17] Ellison's and Barnes's work is part of a strain of American literature that articulates a history of how those who are "left out," those "without distinction," manufacture their own identities and locales, rather than passively receiving them as already determined. In the narratives considered in this book—by gay, Chicano, and African American writers—the underworld is not the space of the irredeemable Other, but a contested terrain where citizen-subjects try to take possession of their own history and spaces, and ownership of their representations in the wider cultural arena.

In contrast, leading figures in urban sociology, planning, and criminology historically have understood sub rosa populations to be characterized by gender, sexual, and racial disorder, a mélange of prostitutes, queers, black delinquents, the homeless, and heathens. Managing its social threat and contagion required pinpointing the underworld's coordinates. For example, in the anxiety-fueled voyeurism of Jacob Riis's 1890 study of poverty, *How the Other Half Lives*, "the boundary line of the Other Half" ran through the tenements where an ethnic "under world" threatened to shake off its fetters.[18] In the 1920s, Chicago sociologist Ernest Burgess located "underworlds of crime and vice" "in the zone of deterioration encircling the central business section," where he said "are always to be found the so-called 'slums' and 'bad lands,' with their submerged regions of poverty, degradation, and disease."[19] Burgess labeled such urban areas as "the purgatory of 'lost souls.'"[20] At roughly the same time, New York City police commissioner Richard Enright warned of a "new underworld" of "depraved tastes" in the emerging gay and lesbian neighborhood of Greenwich Village, a central nightlife district and vice zone where the queer writer Djuna Barnes worked as a journalist.[21] In 1918, she interviewed Enright, taunting him about the alleged criminality of her clandestine queer community in what amounts to one of the most interesting but overlooked confrontations with power in twentieth-century American literary history.

Efforts in the 1920s and 1930s to map the city's "submerged region[s]" reflected a brewing moral panic over the spaces of working-class nighttime leisure—dancehalls, saloons, cabarets. Before the 1910s these disreputable venues, which in the eyes of many were nothing more than havens for prostitution and a nascent queer urban culture, were often located below street level, where they were visible only to those "in the know." But as they turned fashionable, and as they were cleaned up for middle-class audiences, they literally rose to the surface. To the chagrin of civic authorities who wanted to keep moral boundaries within a framework of high and low, upper and underworld geographies, "indulging in these pleasures no longer required venturing beneath the street," as Lewis Erenberg writes in his study of early twentieth-century commercial pleasure.[22]

The consternation over a subterranean world of erotic leisure, which lasted into the 1930s and beyond, cannot be written off as mere hand-wringing prudery. This version of an urban underworld was thought of as a real threat to the foundation of patriarchal family structures. Some sociologists theorized that the intensely stimulating effects of urban living in general, and nighttime leisure in particular, led to personal confusion and a scrambling of one's internal moral compass. The next step in a fast decline was the erosion of gender and sexual normativity, resulting in an apocalyptic catalogue of social ills that Burgess delineated as "juvenile delinquency, boys' gangs, crime, poverty, wife desertion, divorce, abandoned infants, vice."[23]

But by the middle of the century, these social anxieties were supplanted by new ones that were located in rapidly expanding urban ghettos. Gunnar Myrdal, in his monumental study of race relations, *An American Dilemma* (1944), warned of "a Negro 'underworld'" in "the big cities" where a culture of "petty thieves and racketeers, prostitutes and pimps, bootleggers, dope addicts, and so on" had sprung up in the ruinous environs of the inner city.[24] For Myrdal, urban black culture was understood to be a product of cultural pathology, a pitiful reaction to racism and urban anomie. Ralph Ellison countered these charges in a review of *An American Dilemma* and then penned a more extended refutation of mid-century sociological discourse on the black underclass by way of his novel *Invisible Man* (1952). Ellison's basement-dwelling narrator in *Invisible Man* was not the only one to speak from the underground. Perhaps it is eye-opening to learn that in the 1950s, according to one reputable report, "more than 30,000 families in New York [were] living in illegal cellar apartments 'under the most horrible conditions' which [were] a constant threat to the health of the community."[25] Harlem's housing crisis, which had been festering since the 1920s, helped to fertilize the discontent that led to riots in 1935 and 1943. Sociologists diagnosed the uprisings as mass outbreaks of underclass delinquency stemming from aberrant urban cultures, rather than from uneven development and exploitation. The belief that spatial abjection produced strange mutations in culture continued to have currency late into the century, as evidenced by Jennifer Toth's early 1990s nonfictional study of the fantastic world of "the mole people," rumored communities of tunnel dwellers who have withdrawn from surface life into the dirty interstices of New York City's transportation network.[26] The urban underclass are not only below the bottom rung of the class hierarchy, they're literally—so we are told—below our feet.

What I am noting in the preceding remarks is the material production of nonstandard forms of sexual, gender, and racial conduct by uneven development and moral regulation. Industrialization and urbanization lured different kinds of labor to the city regardless of whether or not this labor matched conventionally valorized descriptions of identity. The agglomeration of racial, ethnic, class, and sexual difference in sectors of the city that were thought to be miasmas of disease and moral ruin produced "new social arrangements, identities, and practices."[27] New sexual and familial assemblages and new forms of leisure and work were created through the juxtaposition and concentration of socially marginalized differences in underserved areas. It is in this sense that the twentieth-century urban underworld was "real," a real product of an economic logic that "does not rely on normative prescriptions to assemble labor" or organize patterns of consumption.[28] To take just one example, consider what historian George Chauncey has characterized as "an extensive sexual underground" of queer men in bars, bathhouses, cafés, and parks in urban centers in the first half of the twentieth century.[29] The so-called sexual underworld in particular, and gay identity in general, "has been the historical development of capitalism—more specifically, its free labor system," John D'Emilo writes.[30] "The expansion of capital and the spread of wage labor," he adds, "have effected a profound transformation in the structure and functions of the nuclear family, the ideology of family, and the meaning of heterosexual relations. It is these changes in the family that are most directly linked to the appearance of a collective gay life."[31] As might be expected, early and mid-twentieth-century religious authorities, antivice societies, and cultural reformers were quick to label new nonheterosexual arrangements as a perverse contagion and were equally swift to clampdown on their public expression. In John Rechy's sexual noir *City of Night* (1963), the queer underworld still flourishes, but only in "subterranean" fashion.[32] The clash between a modern economy's profoundly disruptive capacity to create vice zones that commodified sexual difference (almost all the characters in Rechy's novel are prostitutes) and a puritan mindset's investment in conventional familial and intimate relations that forced homosexuality into the bushes and into the underground, continued late into the century.

Capitalism's raison d'être is the maximization of profit, an aim it achieves through the development of new territories and markets that often destabilize cultural and religious pieties. Under its revolutionary energies, Marx wrote, "all that is solid melts into air, all that is holy is profaned."[33] Not surprisingly, its blasphemous tendencies have given rise to a histrionic vocabulary of urban spaces as infernos, underworlds, and purgatories that have been pinpointed to zones experiencing tumultuous disorganization and transformation. For sociologists, impoverished inner-city locales were real-world laboratories for studying what happens when socially abject labor pouring into the center of cities is met with an outflow of middle-class whites. The fear was that those in the city's depleted zones would suffer from urban anomie, mental breakdowns, and free-floating anger that, proving to be uncontainable, would spill across de facto and de jure boundary lines. In other words, what was feared was the spreading toxicity of slum culture or, worse yet, outbreaks of inner-city collective discontent. To stave off this possibility, urban sociology, as well as planning and policing, reinforced and reinscribed sexual, racial, and moral geographies to contain aberrant populations, as well as to limit the mixing of races and classes as much as possible. Lewis Mumford, in an essay on "urban degeneration" in the congested city, worried over interracial and interclass fraternizing: "connections between the 'respectable classes' and the underworld, by way of pleasure, amusement, and sexual release . . . tend to undermine the morale of the body politic," he wrote.[34] Not only was the body itself in danger of being weakened by too much enervating "release" in the urban underworld, but the body of the nation was at risk of infection.

The moral well-being of the country aside, the real politick behind the isolation and pathologization of underworld zones was to protect middle-class property that would suffer a precipitous decline in value if the slum crept closer, if it jumped the fire line or the bank's red line, so to speak. The quarantining of contaminated red-light districts—which was Mumford's concern—was another version of the middle-class NIMBY (Not In My Back Yard) petitions that later in the century confined waste-treatments plants and garbage dumps to poor communities. The legacy of such tactics has been the association of toxicity with black, queer, or ethnic Americans and immigrants, a point that Richard Wright's novella "The Man Who Lived Underground" (1945) complexly makes by literally submerging its African American protagonist into the city's sewer system, flushing his criminalized body out of sight.

The repression of the underworld is only part of the story, perhaps its least interesting part. It is important to understand that historically the underworld was actively created by zoning that controlled unruly processes of urbanization by compartmentalizing the city by land use. Zoning laws—which were first implemented in the United States in 1916 as part of the über-rationalist City Practical planning movement—did not simply seek to stamp out deleterious urban spaces, they sought to regulate them, too. Inside zoned districts in the Lower East Side, Greenwich Village, Harlem, the Bronx, and Bunker Hill—neighborhoods that I will consider in the chapters to follow—black market economies that served illegal "needs" in the city, such as prostitution, gambling, and drugs, sprouted up for consumers who as often as not have resided elsewhere. A salacious literature of sexual slumming, ranging from guidebooks on where to find women of the night to literary narratives about where to find the city's queer lowlife, responded by promising to help readers, curiosity seekers, and would-be patrons navigate through the clandestine geographies of the city. Across the twentieth century, the underworld has been an imaginative space that middle-class residents have sought to enter, not just run in fear from, a space in which to fantasize about other ways of living and being or to seek refuge from the stultifying domesticity that otherwise occupied their lives, a space in which middle-class men (and sometimes women) might go on secret moral vacations in search of intimacies (or contraband) that they imagined did not exist in their own pure neighborhoods.

The demarcation of the city into moral and immoral geographies thus presupposed transgression. Barnes writes in her novel *Nightwood* that the city's zones are divided—the clean from the unclean, the straight from the queer—but stresses that the two halves are "related by their division."[35] The divided city brings people together in charged terms and in an electric atmosphere. Underworld literary narratives showcase how the relations established between insiders and outsiders in underworld bars, clubs, theaters, and parks were mediated by voyeurism and exploitation and were rarely on equal terms. Historically, middle-class residents and tourists could and did use the underworld as a site of abjection against which to define themselves while still indulging in its sins. But they were not the only ones. As the writer Samuel Delany reveals in his frank memoir of Times Square's seedy adult theaters of the 1980s, gay men of color also sought refuge in the city's dilapidated architectures of queer desire.[36] In the glare of Times Square's neon, Delany writes that he developed an erotic knowledge of the city and himself. To think of the underworld as holding a wholly negative cultural value then is to miss how this vital, though not officially recognized, sector of the urban economy helped men and women on both sides of the divide discover and remake their identities.

Sociological, criminological, and urban planning discourses did not merely "discover" the underworld. They brought it into being by hauling it to the surface like an exotic fish pulled up from the deep. They helped to constitute the underworld by looking for and at it through epistemological frameworks that were predisposed to read densely populated and impoverished spaces as sites of transgression, violence, and disease. "Hegemonic power," geographer Edward Soja states, "wielded by those in positions of authority, does not merely manipulate naively given differences between individuals and social groups, it actively *produces and reproduces difference* as a key strategy to create and maintain modes of social and spatial division that are advantageous to its continued empowerment and authority."[37] Far from being a natural fact of urban life—a result of biologically or environmentally induced depravity, as Jacob Riis argued, or the outcome of self-selection among hermetic, ethnic populations who willingly clustered themselves in slums, as Ernest Burgess postulated—the American underworld arose from political and material determinants. Throughout the twentieth century, it emerged into national consciousness at a nexus of three forces: 1) dominant systems of knowledge production (sociology, criminology, urban planning, and American literature) that bifurcate space and assign values to its divisions, even while interrogating those divisions, as is the case with several of the novels I study; 2) the material production of unequal geographies by flows of capital and labor into and out of different slums, ghettoes, and vice districts; and 3) the making of geographies by

FIGURE 2. "Large apartment complex, 'co-op city' in the Bronx overlooks municipal dump. The refuse continues to be piled up in this already overflowing dump, 03/1973." Courtesy the Still Picture Branch of the National Archives and Records Administration.

inhabitants themselves. In *Urban Underworlds*, I endeavor to recognize the dynamic interrelations between these three levels—the discursive, the material, and the lived—and to understand how and to what ends writers have intervened into the real-and-imagined spaces of America's lowest geographies.

The intention of *Urban Underworlds* is to help return American literature to the microlevel geographies (neighborhoods, parks, streets) in which it originates, to situate these geographies within macrolevel social and spatial transformations (industrialization, migration, changes in technology), and at the same time to attend to the mechanisms of control (zoning laws, policing, ghettoization) that have worked to delineate and manage the spaces in which the writers in this book imaginatively and physically lived and wrote. A multi-scalar reading of American literature of the urban underworld renders visible the contradictions of American culture. It allows us to read the sociospatial production of delinquency and perversion back into a critique of uneven development that produces the very communities and identities that are deemed monstrous.

The reorientation of U.S. literary and cultural studies around the centrality of the critical concept of space is a project that has already begun through fine studies on urban literature by Betsy Klimasmith, Carlo Rotella, Catherine Jurca, and others.[38] Attracted to another body of literary texts, these scholars tell a set of stories of twentieth-century urban life different from each other and from the relatively narrow one I am telling here. Klimasmith traces the evolution of home life in the city and outlines the poetic geography of domestic architectures against a dynamic backdrop of fears of racial and ethnic disorder and familial breakdown. Jurca suggests in her monograph on the suburban novel that the urban anxieties captured in Klimasmith's *At Home in the City* are the same ones that led many white middle-class city residents to feel precisely no longer at home. Rotella's analysis of mid-century fiction, for its part, provides three exemplary case studies of literature from Chicago, Philadelphia, and Manhattan to articulate narratives of urban decline and redevelopment in America's creaking Rustbelt. What these scholarly investigations share is the recognition of space as an arena where social relations are enacted, expressed, and curtailed, and a recognition that social relations (which perhaps find their most complex articulation in literary fiction) dialectically reshape the spaces in which we act even as they are transformed by the shocks of urban renewal and migration.

The literary works I read in this study similarly foreground the crucial but still under-acknowledged role that space has played as an instrument of control, a site of action, and a locus where cultural fears, as well as sexual, racial, ethnic, and class identities, are articulated. "Differences are constructed in, and themselves construct, city life and space," the urbanists Gary Bridge and Sophie Watson argue, "They are also constituted spatially, socially, and economically sometimes leading to polarization, inequality, zones of exclusion and fragmentation, and at other times constituting sites of power, resistance, and the celebration of identity."[39] This insight is found on nearly every page of the literary narratives I consider. Rechy's autobiographical novel *City of Night*, for instance, tracks its anonymous narrator—a gay hustler—through almost every major American urban center in pursuit of a queer underworld. Struggling with his sexuality, he alternates between the domestic and public spaces of straight life and the "submerged" world of gay bars and parks.[40] "Thus the daulity [*sic*] of my existence," he says, "was marked by a definite boundary."[41] This point—that identities are distinctively spatial, that they are constituted and materialized in uneven social and physical urban geographies—I will return to frequently in the chapters that follow.

Recent work in geography and urban studies has sought to theorize the turbulent ways in which social and spatial practices are interwoven through time to create the geographies of cities and regions, states and nations, as well as the geographies of the human bodies that are formed at the intersections of space and desire, power and resistance within these terrains. Henri Lefebvre's magnum opus *The Production of Space*, published in 1974 but not translated into English until 1991, was instrumental in advancing critical understandings of space, which had long been stalled on the notion of space as a transparent medium or an a priori order that merely contains human practices, relations, institutions, and products. Prior thinking on space, Lefebvre stressed, had resulted in "inventories of what *exists in* space," or, at best, a "*discourse on* space," but not "a *knowledge* of space."[42] This was the case in part because space seemed like a given—a natural and immutable category like the ether through which we move and the air we breath. The "illusion[s] of natural simplicity" and "of transparency," which conceived of space as a luminous realm that gives free reign to action, but which itself cannot be altered or manufactured, needed demystification.[43] According to Lefebvre, these misconceptions needed to be exposed for the manner in which they simultaneously occluded and fortified the operations of historical and political forces, the networks and pathways of a society's relations of production and reproduction by which goods are created and exchanged, identity materialized, and the city divvied into normative and nonnormative zones. "Space itself, at once a product of the capitalist mode of production and an economico-political instrument of the bourgeoisie," he stated, "will now be seen to embody its own contradictions."[44]

Lefebvre's theorizations helped resuscitate the nearly moribund disciplines of geography and urban studies by lending them a critical edge that replaced their primary orientation toward empirical description. Since the 1990s, geographers responded to Lefebvre by expanding upon, critiquing, and particularizing his ideas. In doing so, they followed his materialist perspective in order to understand "how human geographies become filled with politics and ideology."[45] "What is the geography of capitalism?" Neil Smith bluntly asks in *Uneven Development* (1984), a question that Soja also poses and answers by returning to Lefebvre's seminal work: "We must begin again with Lefebvre's generative assertion that capitalism has been able to survive and achieve 'growth' by producing and occupying a space."[46] The city spaces capital has occupied (what spaces has it not, one might ask?), have tended to be polarized in antipodal rhythms that the writers in this study have glimpsed firsthand. The downtown tenement slums of New York and the magnificent uptown Beaux-Arts and neoclassical mansions of the Gilded Age's robber barons where expressions of what Henry James pithily termed "the economic idea," the binarizing logic that manufactured immense wealth and poverty simultaneously.[47] The early twentieth-century city's uneven social and geographic development was physically evident to anyone with curious eyes and legs strong enough to walk the city.

In the time since James footed it through New York, capital has left its mark on urban space in ways that are more dispersed and harder to read, but the hieroglyphic signs tell the same story. In a seesaw process of over- and underdevelopment, money in the city moves to where rates of profits are greatest, developing those areas at the expense of others, exhausting them, and then moving on in a cycle of overaccumulation, followed by crisis, and then by economic and spatial restructuring which in turn creates new types of spaces (or redefines existing ones) to advance further accumulation. The wheel spins. Another cycle of boom and bust invariably grows out of the prior cycle's failure to address the fundamental contradictions governing urban political economy in the prior period. As capitalist urbanization creates unequal geographies (ethnic slums, racial ghettoes, and vice districts), over time it erodes them, too. Developers periodically turn to impoverished terrains, selling them as new markets for middle-class housing and consumption, spurring urban gentrification. In dense urban environments where new space is severely limited, capital frequently seeks high profit margins in seemingly depleted spaces with low ground rents, retilling them like a machine turning the soil. As early as 1916, Djuna Barnes in a newspaper article informed her readers that the underworld of opium dens, gambling parlors, and houses of assignation in New York's Chinatown that they might have been hoping to find had been cleaned up, reduced to a "flat tone and a flat surface."[48] The city was becoming as "soulless as a department store," she later commented, a sentiment that New Yorkers would again express at the end of the century when all of Manhattan appeared to be given over to upscale shopping.[49]

But the imposition of geometrical and legible spaces of commerce and middle-class living often only leads to more waste and a new clean-up campaign in a different part of the city. The "'waste products' of a functionalist administration" are, de Certeau remarks, "abnormality, deviance, illness, death," rather than their elimination (94). For the towering Robert Moses, New York's famed and much-feared developer and advocate of highway construction (who pushed an expressway through DeLillo's birthplace, the Bronx, hastening its decline), the costs were worth it. He once nonchalantly asserted, "When you operate in an overbuilt metropolis, you have to hack your way with a meat ax."[50] As a result of urban planners such as Moses, American cities have been streamlined, but a sense of historical time and an experience of rootedness have been disrupted, expunged, or displaced. Thomas Pynchon's *The Crying of Lot 49* (1966) and Don DeLillo's *Underworld* endeavor to understand this disconcerting effect. These novels are as much about highways and suburbs as they are about the inner-city urban underworld that has been left behind. "History is experienced as nostalgia, and nature as regret—as a horizon fast disappearing behind us," Lefebvre somberly observes.[51] Lefebvre's rearview mirror perspective suggests he is speeding away from the city on one of Moses's superhighways that fundamentally altered "the space-time feeling of our period" by destroying city streets, local neighborhoods, places of memory.[52] White flight out of the wilderness of the city and into the paradise of the Levittowns of America traveled along Moses's freeways. In Pynchon's novel, the route is reversed, the arrows point in the other direction. His heroine travels the highways out of her suburb into an urban underworld of eccentrics, queers, immigrants, and rattled war vets that Pynchon tellingly labels W.A.S.T.E. She unearths what America had thought it had disposed of and buried.

The perpetual churning of the city over the course of the century has resulted in the collision of opposing spaces: the lived spaces of marginalized communities built upon "bonds of consanguinity, soil and language" and the conceptualized spaces of planners that rub out distinctions arising from nature, the body, history, sex, and ethnicity.[53] Urban spaces are always filled with residual as well as emergent elements, coalitions, practices, and ways of being that are welded together along these fault lines. Below the threshold gaze of planners is found, to use Lefebvre phrase, "the clandestine or underground side of social life," the streets, apartments, and parks of racially, ethnically, and sexually minoritized populations, which U.S. literature and culture has tended to view as sites of authenticity, premodern or primitive societies in which life is imagined to be lived more immediately.[54]

But under the fantasy of America's ethnic, racial, and sexual underworlds—under Lefebvre's "underground"—another world is also concealed, one much more quotidian, which de Certeau hinted at as he peered over Manhattan: it is the reality of work, home life, and everyday endurance that has been rendered nearly invisible by obfuscating perspectives, whether pathologizing or romanticizing. American urban fiction has not been immune to this knee-jerk reaction. Yet even as it has succumbed to some of the urban mythos of hot-blooded urban subcultures sequestered from view, underworld fiction often has noted the banal realities. Consider, for example, the question the queer of color writer Claude McKay poses in *Home to Harlem* (1928), a rowdy novel of proletarian black life, cabarets, and white voyeurism. In the midst of all of the festive merrymaking in black clubs that are routinely busted by the police, one of McKay's protagonists scratches his head, puzzling, "Why *under*-world he could never understand. It was very much upon the surface as were the other . . . divisions of human life. Having its heights and middle and depths and secret places even as they. And the people of this world, waiters, cooks, chauffeurs, sailors, porters, guides, ushers, hod-carriers, factory hands—all touched in a thousand ways the people of the other divisions."[55] McKay's novel is a classic bait-and-switch. The disappointment it delivers to readers is that the lurid black underworld actually is comprised of everyday porters and cooks. For McKay and the other writers I will discuss, underworld fantasies dissolve in the night when we see the working-class labor and leisure behind them.

Historically, contests over the right to space—protests, riots, community organizing—have surfaced during periods of rapid urban growth and declined when the dividing lines between the underworld and the "other divisions" become more fortified. Cities are malleable, their actual shape subject to alteration by large-scale socioeconomic processes, such as the invention of new technologies (skyscrapers, automobiles, assembly line or just-in-time productions, telecommunication and internet systems), by the discovery and creation of new markets for goods through territorial expansion (suburbs, edge cities, Third World countries), and by the importation of new sources of labor through internal migration and immigration (southern and eastern Europeans, Chinese, Southern blacks). "The historical geography of capitalism," Soja observes, "has not been marked by grand turnabouts and complete system replacements, but rather by an evolving sequence of partial and selective restructurings" that enhance capital accumulation as well as facilitate the "control and discipline [of] the burgeoning urban population."[56] The evolution of urban forms occurs over long historical waves that nonetheless follow a familiar pattern that begins with the pains of "recession, depression, and social upheaval," leads to a restructuring of urban space and a reshuffling of the map of class, ethnic, and race relations.[57] Like a phoenix, a new kind of city arises out of a previous one. The intensification of uneven development, immiseration, and widening income inequality at each stage invariably lays the basis for a new underworld, Marx's "social scum," with a different demographic and a different location to emerge as a new social emergency.

Urban Underworld's historical and spatial arc follows the evolution of urban forms and tracks the production and consolidation of new cultural anxieties, the creation of new spatial Others, and the writing of narratives of the city told from below by novelists who have reconstructed, and in some cases wholly invented, the lowest social and physical topographies they could fathom. For the writers I will consider, mapping an imaginary urban geography—a thickly described world of the city's underbelly—has been a way of understanding social upheaval and urban crisis and decline. As it has uncannily resurfaced across the century, the real-and-imagined underworld has morphed, mutating with the city itself. In the late nineteenth and early twentieth century, the urban netherworld was primarily ethnic in character and thought to be localized in the industrial city's downtown miasma of slums. By the first decades of the twentieth century, however, the new underworld was defined by urban experts by its sexual degeneracy and was believed to be centered in mixed-use commercial districts that catered to a new nighttime leisure economy that was indicative of the expanding reach of consumerism in the corporate-monopoly city. By the middle decades of the twentieth century, heightened racial segregation, white flight to the suburbs, and the displacement of large sites of production to the periphery combined to create the Fordist city, a doughnut-shaped regional form with a racially homogenous inner-city ghetto trapped in the center. A new locus of social fear, the inner city seemed to many mid-century planners and sociologists to be beyond hope, a "terrain of violence and despair" and a "collectivity outside of politics and social structure, beyond the usual language of class and stratum."[58] The Fordist city was in turn superseded at the end of the century by the postindustrial or postmodern city with surreal juxtapositions of poverty and wealth replacing the center/periphery model. Surging income inequality and downtown renaissances that have brought penthouse and loft living to the skid rows of America have resulted in kaleidoscopic mixings within majority-minority cities that are the outcome of globalization processes. This latest urban form with its hourglass-shaped class structure has created an ethnically and racially heterogeneous urban poor dispersed across major American postindustrial landscapes.

The industrial, corporate-monopoly, Fordist, and postmodern city—these are top-down classificatory rubrics, generic types of cities in the truest sense of the word. American literature inhabits these abstractions, fills them with pulse and fear, fleshing them out for readers with detail and toil so that these cities feel real. To apprehend the city in all of its various instantiations, American literature has delved beneath the surface into illegal basement beer dives, queer clubs, and inner-city ruins, where it posits life is lived with the greatest sense of urgency and narrative drama. *Urban Underworlds* tracks the cultural fascination with spatially marginalized zones and peoples through American literature in order to disclose how the underworld has evolved historically and geographically and how the writers who embody diverse racial, sexual, gender, and class positions have represented its evolution within cityspaces that were changing with gentrification, segregation, and white flight before their very eyes.[59]

It is my aim to provide a comprehensive geographical description of twentieth-century American underworlds through a range of literary and nonliterary narratives. A study of how the underworld has been represented in American culture allows us to see how disparate anxieties have coagulated into phantoms of flesh and blood. My story of the urban underworld begins on the Lower East Side of New York in the 1890s, a critical turning point in the U.S. spatial imagination, the decade the country seemingly became smaller and more crowded at once. In chapter 1, I note that 1890 was the year that the U.S. census announced that the westward settlement of the continent had reached a point where "there can hardly be said to be a frontier line."[60] The decade also saw the arrival of hundreds of thousands of southern and eastern European immigrants, many of them landing in New York, where they squeezed into the city's tenements in ways that startle the imagination. Published in 1890, Riis's *How the Other Lives* revealed for the middle class what they ignored at their own peril: an angry "Nether Half" mired in poverty and moral squalor in the rapidly industrializing city.[61] Between 1890 and 1910, the American underworld was thought to be poor, ethnic, and isolated in contaminated apartments, back alleys, and hidden saloons in downtown Manhattan.

In chapter 1, I place Riis's text alongside Henry James's travelogue *The American Scene*, and contextualize them with the fascinating but largely forgotten accounts of urban slumming by Ernest Ingersoll, Frank Moss, and William Meloney. The socioeconomic conditions for slumming literature included the formation of concentrated zones of wealth and poverty that were geographically distanced from each other. Slumming literature translated growing income inequality into a dramatic narrative frame in a way that helped a middle-class readership travel in mind and body through a metropolis that had come to feel disorderly, dangerous, and alien. *The American Scene* employs tropes common to the era's slumming literature, but it also destabilizes many of its sedimented ideologies by being flexibly and generously attuned to the rhythms and meanings of lower-class life. James views the underworld, as he forthrightly declares, as an "imposture."[62] Rather than a separate and exotic world, it is very much a part of a city undergoing social and physical revolutions at all levels.

In chapter 2, I follow the underworld to its new homes in Greenwich Village and Harlem in the 1910s and 1920s, sites of new sexual and racial subcultures that sparked curiosity and worry. These putative underworlds materialized in the public imagination with three developments that helped usher in the corporate-monopoly city: 1) labor migrations of single white men and women, largely from the Midwest, and African Americans from the South to urban centers in the Northeast; 2) the mainstreaming and expansion of a formerly disreputable nighttime pleasure industry associated with poor and working-class ethnics; and 3) the birth of urban planning as a professional discipline. By 1915, the Village hosted the largest gay subculture in the United States, comprising a network of clubs, bars, and restaurants that became routine stops on sexual slumming tours through the area. By 1920, Harlem was the largest African American neighborhood in the nation, labeled the Montmartre of America for its scandalous brothels, jazz venues, and buffet flats that, too, were subject to the leering eyes of outsiders.

To understand these developments, I turn to Djuna Barnes and Claude McKay. First I consider Barnes's journalism on the Village, examining it in the context of planners' efforts to zone the district and in the context of police and civic reformers' efforts to place its nonheteronormative communities under surveillance. Barnes's newspaper writing assembles a queer and bohemian geography by advertising its street life, cafés, and dancehalls to an inquisitive readership and then endeavors to disclaim the very geography that it makes visible. Following my reading of Barnes's newspaper reporting, I focus on her novel *Nightwood* (1936). Located largely in a post-Haussmann Paris, it offers a frank defense of the sexual underworld that would have been impermissible in print journalism of the 1910s. In a posturban-renewal context, *Nightwood* dramatizes the clandestine efforts of a queer underworld of American expatriates to repossess degraded, submerged geographies by creating alternative erotic forms of socializing and contact. Turning to Claude McKay, I examine how *Home to Harlem* interrogates the concept of a racial underworld in the context of an expanding nightlife industry that moved north from Barnes's Greenwich Village to Harlem. McKay sees the black underworld of the 1920s as an overdetermined phantasm that suppresses African American cultural heterogeneity into a mystified image of blacks as naturally expressive, sexually profligate, and prone to criminality. But rather than disavowing black underworld primitivism altogether, McKay resignifies it as a targeted protest against the injustices that stymie life and pleasure in Harlem.

Building on my analysis of the geographic construction of racial subjectivity in chapter 2, I scrutinize the representation of the black underworld in Richard Wright's "The Man Who Lived Underground" and Ralph Ellison's *Invisible Man*. The sociological discourse on the black underclass in the 1940s and 1950s frequently aligned racial abjection with the wasted geographies of decaying inner cities. The idea that America's urban black communities were underworlds of deviancy, violence, waste, and percolating discontent, which needed to be contained, helped middle-class city and suburban residents to (falsely) apprehend the tumultuous sociospatial transformations that created the Fordist city. These transformations included the mass in-migration of undervalued black labor from the South to northern cities and an almost immediate white flight to the highways looking for an exit. Neocolonial exploitation of the inner city eventually fueled riots in Harlem in 1935 and 1943.

Wright and Ellison respond to the pathologizing discourse of race and to the spatial transformations in the city by employing a nauseating cloacal imagery of sewers and human excrement to reveal how a racist culture disposed of blackness to secure white identity and property. They also provide a view literally from the underground of mid-century changes in urban form and the urban crises they engendered. Wright's protagonist flees under a manhole into the city's drain when wrongly accused of murdering a white woman, but comes to feel guilty despite his innocence. His crime is being black, Wright suggests. Quarantining him in the most inhospitable environment, Wright seeks to make clear the debilitating effects that follow from ingesting the poisonous rhetoric of black guilt and deviancy that circulated like sewage in the 1940s. I understand Ellison's novel in this discursive context as well, but I also situate it next to a history of underground living in illegal, squalid cellar apartments in mid-century New York, such as the kind Ellison's hero famously remodels as a sign of his "ingenuity" after he flees from the riot in Harlem.[63] Historically, the racial uprising, which Ellison reported on in an eyewitness account, was linked to a lack of quality housing that forced many residents to live below ground. *Invisible Man*, however, disavows rioting as a viable method of contravening racial exclusions. It discounts, as well, sociological reports of black underclass pathology which did not recognize that urban discontent was actually the result of segregation and neglect. Ellison rewrites the social history of black underworld protest with a narrative of retreat into the underground to articulate a positive and empowered image of black subjectivity.

The Harlem riots were a preview of the exponentially more catastrophic urban uprising in Watts, Los Angeles, in 1965, "one of the symptomatic beginnings of the end" of the Fordist city, which I address in chapter 4.[64] I turn to three texts that stage the experience of spatial marginality during the Fordist city's decline and at the moment of the emergence of its replacement, the postmodern city: John Rechy's *City of Night*, Thomas Pynchon's "A Journey into the Mind of Watts" (1966), and Pynchon's *The Crying of Lot 49*. Set in part or in their entirety in Los Angeles, they extend the reach of *Urban Underworlds* to a geography where sociospatial changes that would become endemic to the United States showed up first.

Characterized by extreme social and geographic fragmentation, the postmodern city poses conceptual challenges for residents, urban planners, geographers, and writers. In the estimation of Soja, Los Angeles is "too filled with 'other spaces' to be informatively described."[65] Chapter 4 tells the story of these Other spaces, beginning with Rechy's peripatetic narrative, which assembles a "netherworld" of aleatory pleasure, a makeshift queer urban culture that has taken root in an impoverished vice district in Bunker Hill and Pershing Square, a small park in downtown Los Angeles.[66] With its fetid depictions of queer bars and movie theaters and an agonized and conflicted narrator, it would be easy to read Rechy's book as another example of a queer novel that has swallowed the mid-century understanding of homosexuality as a lurid illness. But such interpretations stay on the surface and fail to see that the novel is actually about how sexual identity is made in urban space within a context of sexual policing and urban renewal.

Building on Rechy's representation of downtown Los Angeles, I turn to the multiplying geographies of Otherness in *The Crying of Lot 49*. Pynchon's text is a postmodern rewriting of the slumming narrative through which Pynchon's white suburban protagonist comes face-to-face with inequalities that her class myopia has concealed. In the novel, the W.A.S.T.E. conspiracy consolidates and organizes a dispersed underworld for Pynchon's heroine at the same time that it dismantles her presuppositions about American life and liberty to the point of paranoia. Perhaps no other narrative so accurately captures how social position and privilege inform how urban space is read and experienced. At the chapter's close, I turn to Pynchon's essay on Watts, a work that underscores the way ideologies of race and space reinforced the isolations that led to the seismic upheavals in the segregated, fragmented city.

I conclude with Don DeLillo's *Underworld*, which endeavors to map nearly a half century of capitalist geography from the bottom up. *Underworld* covers a lot of ground, tracing the tragic decline of an older spatiality into ruins and the rise of the new postmetropolis in America's Sunbelt regions and overseas. Building on the ideas set forth in prior chapters, chapter 5 expands upon my consideration of this new urban form by turning to recent theorizations that see it as coeval with the dominance of global capitalism in the postwar era, a period characterized by the derealization of urban space into a network of global referents, the wide-scale uprooting of indigenous populations, and spectacular urban decay. Through dialectical representations of wealth and poverty, *Underworld* gives narrative shape to this confusing new spatiality. The novel repeatedly links the protagonist Nick's panoptic office tower and insular suburban life in Phoenix to the fire-gutted tenements and trash-strewn streets of the Bronx where he was raised. Nick's desperate longing for "the days when [he] was alive on the earth, rippling in the quick of [his] skin, heedless and real" is a longing for the era of the Fordist city, hardly a paradise for many Americans.[67] In the novel, the underworld appears in manifold places—in underclass slums, in secret queer geographies, in the crawlspaces of homeless camps and subways for the new urban poor. These sites of indigenization, art, poverty, and memory resist, in DeLillo's words, how "capital burns off the nuance in a culture."[68] In 1890, Riis declared that "thousands were living in cellars"; as DeLillo shows, a hundred years later the underworld's depths seem deeper than ever as we continue to look into the underworld for clues to the future of our changing cities.[69]

1 / Going Down: Narratives of Slumming in the Ethnic Underworlds of Lower New York, 1890s–1910s

"On the morning of June 18 last, New York was horrified by the discovery of the body of a murdered girl hidden in a trunk in a Chinese waiter's room over a chop suey restaurant in Eighth Avenue. Within a couple of hours, detectives and newspaper men had established the girl's identity, and the news of the crime went ringing to the ends of the world."[1] So began William Meloney's 1909 sensational exposé "Slumming in New York's Chinatown: A Glimpse into the Sordid Underworld of the Mott Street Quarter, Where Elsie Sigel Formed Her Fatal Associations." Meloney's report had all of the ingredients of a lurid scandal and a cautionary tale: murder, the seduction and corruption of innocence, opium addiction, an exotic locale, and an interracial love affair gone horribly wrong between a working-class, Chinese immigrant and a white, uptown "nineteen-year-old Sunday-school teacher" who was "a granddaughter of [a] famous Civil War general" (229). What began as a well-intended, if naïve "obsession to save 'heathen souls'" ended with chloroform and "death with a cord" wrapped tight by the "yellow fingers" of Leung Lim (229, 230). If anything positive resulted from the Sigel murder case, it was the validation of the quick work of the police and of newspaper men, like Meloney himself, who sounded the alarm about the fatal attractions lurking in New York's "sordid underworld" of immigrants (229).

Elsie Sigel's murder may have been the occasion for William Meloney's report for *Munsey's Magazine*, but the scope of the article was wider and deeper. When Meloney returned to the scene of the crime, he did so not to search for clues to Lim's motives, but to map firsthand a newly emergent geography of criminality that was a threat to more than girls of "impressionable character" (229). In late nineteenth- and early twentieth-century journalism, the Chinese regularly were depicted as hermetic and inscrutable, and Meloney's report, which characterized them as "contemptuous, blandly mysterious, serene, foul-smelling, . . . and implacable," was no exception (230). But if the faces of the Chinese could not be read—as many turn-of-the-century investigative reporters implied—then perhaps their streets, where other murderous desires were assumed to be incubating, could be. Accompanied by police captain Mike Galvin, Meloney led his reader on a walk through the "unfathomed and unknown" "Mongol quarter of New York," an excursion that began, not insignificantly, with a reassuring stroll past "the Tombs and the Criminal Courts Building" in lower Manhattan (230). Meloney thus escorted his reader as if he or she were an extralegal agent or citizen enforcer of public morality. "Let us enter Chinatown from Chatham Square," he stated at the beginning of a tour which, complete with photographs of street scenes and domestic interiors, proceeded to peer into opium dens where Chinese men and white women stared out with "hollow cheeks" under "sputtering lights," on into a cluttered tenement that showed a "true Chinese disregard for the fitness of appearances," and on through the streets of Chinatown that seemed to possess their own agency and twisted logic (231, 233, 237). In the wild terrain of the immigrant underworld, Meloney's reader discovered that the streets themselves "dart . . . at crazy angles," "wind . . . tortuously," and "run . . . full tilt" (231). With its strange odors and tongues, Chinatown was nothing if not difficult to navigate. Physically, as well as cognitively, it was terra incognita.

For Meloney's Captain Galvin, the district's supposed tolerance for drug use, gambling parlors, and dirty streets led directly to greater moral and legal transgressions: interracial commingling and eventually murder. One hundred and thirty white women lived in Chinatown in 1909, by Galvin's own count. To drive whites out of the "yellow quarter," he pushed for the strict enforcement of "the sanitary provisions of the tenement-house law" and his "campaign for cleanliness" was in full swing "when the Sigel tragedy startled the world" (241). The dream of bringing the district to order was to die a double death. Meloney's article concluded with the police captain throwing up his hands in frustration, declaring a wish to "'pile all of it on a barge and sink it in the East River'" (241). In this chapter I consider the meanings of and reasons why a particular urban geography—the downtown wards of New York's Lower

East Side—came be to understood as home to the city's and the nation's underworld. How and why did this particular neighborhood, which historian Christopher Mele has described as "a complex, highly stratified, and rapidly changing web of microcommunities," come to be reduced in the anxious urban imagination through this totalizing spatial concept?[2] The answer is found in a noxious mix of economics, geography, sociology, and sensational narratives that began to congeal many disparate social fears into the lurid social formation known as the urban immigrant underworld. The concept of the underworld, which was formulated in expert studies of poverty, as well as in popular reports on gaslight New York, served this function: it brought into being, expressed, and simultaneously displaced a series of middle-class anxieties over immigration, crime, and contagious disease. As a result, the Lower East Side's intricate and layered social life, where on a block-by-block basis one would encounter different dialects, foods, religious practices, parenting styles, all varying by the homeland region of the recent immigrants from Russia, Italy, China, and many other parts of the globe, was conceptually rendered invisible, hidden behind a fearful specter. The quotidian, work-a-day world of immigrant life was concealed by a mounting middle-class panic over the momentous changes in the city's demography, customs, and culture.

We can begin to enter into and open up the mystifying trope of the ethnic urban underworld by considering more closely popular, turn-of-the-century slumming narratives such as Meloney's and those of many other writers. Slumming literature's origins are to be found in both the geographical context of uneven urban development, which created devalued areas such as the Lower East Side, and in the discursive context of the then newly formed discipline of urban sociology. Slumming literature was a formally and ideologically diverse discourse that was instrumental in constructing a culturally delinquent, morally destitute, and spatially marginalized underworld Other. It was a discourse comprising novels of slum life, such as Stephen Crane's *Maggie: A Girl of the Streets* (1893); turn-of-the-century urban travel guides, such as Ernest Ingersoll's *A Week in New York* (1891) and Frank Moss's *The American Metropolis* (1897); Progressive, reformed-minded exposés of the horrendous living conditions in ethnic ghettos, such as Jacob Riis's *How the Other Half Lives* (1890); more broadly conceived and complex explorations of class, ethnic, and national identity, such as Henry James's *The American Scene* (1907); and countless titillating and denunciatory articles on prostitutes, the poor, and exotic immigrants, which were published regularly in the popular press.[3] In the pages to follow, I turn to this literature in detail in order to account for the important variations within it: the notable differences between the ephemeral quality of scandalous slumming narratives, for instance, and the enduring and complex work of Henry James. But I also want to argue that all of this literature—low and high—shared a project with urban sociology to map the physical, social, and moral geographies of the city for a bourgeois readership that was fascinated and repulsed by the spectacle of ethnic and class difference in the seemingly chaotic, noisome world of the slums.

Topping from Below: Remapping Lower New York in the Late Nineteenth-Century Travel Guide

When William Meloney labeled the Lower East Side a "sordid underworld" in 1909, he was using language that had been in circulation in New York journalism for more than a half century, particularly in the scandal sheets by newspaper writers and muckrakers who made their trade through exposing the city's mysteries to an eager, easily tantalized reading public. As critics such as Robert Dowling and Scott Herring have shown, mid-century New York was papered with stories about the sins of the city, such as Ned Buntline's *The Mysteries and Miseries of New York* (1848), George Foster's *New York by Gas-Light and Other Urban Sketches* (1850), Jose Vose's *Seven Nights in Gotham* (1852), and George Lippard's *New York: Its Upper Ten and Lower Million* (1854).[4] London and Paris—both older than New York—had had their own urban squalor aired out in the years before the New York city-mystery writers started snooping around. In fact, the transatlantic success of Eugène Sue's *Les Mystères de Paris*, following its translation in 1844, was something of inspiration for Buntline, Lippard, Foster, and others who made a cottage industry out of revealing the secret world of New York's mean streets in luridly purple prose.[5] Their "new obsession" was to tell "the story of New York 'as it is,'" to provide the insider scoop on the debauchery and violence festering in the despoiled geographies of the hoi polloi.[6] In this writing, the slums and shanties of downtown, according to Alan Trachtenberg, were understood as places of "fear and anxiety . . . unfathomable darkness and shadow."[7] These writers promised to shine a light on the horrors of gambling, prostitution, alcoholism, interracial marriage, and police corruption, which seemed to be at epidemic levels at the tip of the island and on the waterfront. By exposing the authentic New York in all of its dizzying and deceptive guises and rough-and-tumble ways, they promised to make the wicked city sensible and legible to readers who wouldn't step foot, at least not admittedly, into such neighborhoods. This rhetoric of exposure, authenticity, and piousness was one that Meloney and other urban writers at the end of the century would use, as well.

To appreciate the groundwork that this earlier generation laid for Meloney, Ingersoll, Riis, and James, we can turn briefly to one of the pioneering books in the genre, George Foster's *New York by Gas-Light and Other Urban Sketches*. A writer for the *New York Tribune*, Foster made a name for himself by spelunking in the decadent, depraved depths of the city. Not to be outshone by his French precursors, he proclaimed with an American bravado that the cities on this side of the Atlantic were just as sordid as any in Europe. In fact, the shadowy streets of lower Manhattan had become, paradoxically, more mysterious at the very moment they were illuminated by the eerie flickering flames from the still relatively novel gas lamps. Through his writing, Foster sought to clarify for his audience what must have been a confusing mélange of rampant poverty, criminalized vice, and burgeoning ethnic diversity that had mushroomed in the city seemingly overnight. Foster sought to illuminate the city first by rhetorically dividing it into sunlight and shadow, Christian and heathen, upper- and underworld, and then he sought to redress these divisions simply by publicizing their existence to curiosity seekers, civic reformers, and police who might help clean up the muck.

The language in which Foster carried out his investigations evinced a mix of desire and disgust. His piousness was shadowed by its wicked twin, a perverse craving. His polarized language infused civic policing with barely containable sexual desire, an unacknowledged wish to participate in the very activities that were being condemned. Much of the slumming literature at the end of the century would be similarly split. Foster promised "to penetrate beneath the thick veil of night and lay bare the fearful mysteries of darkness in the metropolis—the festivities of prostitution, the orgies of pauperism, the haunts of theft and murder, the scenes of drunkenness and beastly debauch, and all the sad realities that go to make up the lower stratum—the under-ground story—of life in New York."[8] "Let no prudish moralist condemn us," he announced of his enterprise, "because we go boldly and thoroughly through the haunts of vice and dissipation in our overgrown metropolis, and describe things exactly as we find them."[9] In the words of cultural and literary historian Robert Dowling, Foster and his fellow gas-light journalists inaugurated "a New York tradition" of "venting moral and environmental anxieties by writing about them."[10] They went where others feared to tread, and if they were called immoral for their titillating tales, it was all in the service of weeding out the city's immoral geographies and its improvident habits.

Though Foster may have stood at the beginning of a tradition of slumming in New York's lower stratum, it was not until forty years later, in the 1890s, that the "moral and environmental anxieties"—the climate that made slumming literature possible and the climate that this literature helped to create—metastasized into a full-blown urban panic. The city-mystery writers decried the loosening of public decency and the sins of too much drink and too much sex, but by the end of the century, problems were much more dire. The country seemingly had turned a wrong corner, and especially in urban centers such as New York, the streets seemed overcrowded and increasingly non-American in tongue and in tone. To get a clearer sense of why the decade of the 1890s was so pivotal, why it marked a tipping point which, among other changes, altered the sense of national space in the U.S. imagination, we might begin by noting one succinct but momentous announcement. It was in the year 1890 that the superintendent of the U.S. census declared that the westward settlement of the continent had reached a point where "there could hardly be said to be a frontier line."[11] Three years later, at the World's Columbia Exposition, Frederick Jackson Turner asserted that the superintendent's "brief official statement marks the closing of a great historic movement."[12] The seemingly limitless horizontal westward expansion of the nation, the source of so much American optimism, had come to a close. Though vast stretches of the West were sparsely populated, the country had in one sense run out of room.

At the same time, the notion that the nation's space was finite was becoming increasingly apparent in the everyday lives of urban Americans. By the 1890s, the cities on the Eastern seaboard were awash in a truly unprecedented wave of immigration, which by one estimate would bring to the shores of the United States "two million eastern European Jews, five million Italians, and millions more from Austria-Hungary, Ukraine, Poland, Greece, Syria," and many more from other Mediterranean and Slavic countries.[13] For many of these newly arrived migrants, the western frontier was not California: it was Boston, Philadelphia, and especially New York. Perhaps nowhere more than in lower Manhattan—where America's future citizens were crammed into hastily and shoddily constructed slum housing—was there the feeling that the country was at its bursting point. Its population by 1890 had ballooned to a million and a half people (a 300 percent increase from 1850), and three-quarters of them were squeezed into the city's 42,000 tenements, sometimes ten to a room.[14] At the end of the century, over half of New York's population was living downtown where open gutters, overflowing sewers, polluting factories, and piles of trash and ashes were daily hazards and humiliations.[15] The population in some wards of the Lower East Side in 1890 reached 1,500 per acre, at a time when the average density per acre in the city overall was just over 58 people.[16] Such human congestion is difficult to comprehend. If extrapolated over the island of Manhattan, it would have equaled twenty million people, roughly ten times Manhattan's population more than a century later.

The transformation of New York's social and spatial organization—its unprecedented ethnic diversity, its brutalizing poverty, and its unsurpassed population density—was an effect of macroeconomic changes that had profound implications for life in the city. Sociologist Lydia Morris recounts that the last decades of the century witnessed a pronounced shift toward an economy based on manufacturing: in 1880 2.7 million people in the United States worked in manufacturing, whereas by 1920 the number had more than tripled to 8.4 million.[17] The immensely disruptive shift from an agrarian-based economy to an industrial one resulted in, and was made possible by, the mass migrations of semiskilled and unskilled laborers from rural areas within the United States and from overseas into quickly expanding urban centers. As a primary motor of late nineteenth-century industrial production, New York drew millions of workers and clustered them in poor and working-class immigrant neighborhoods abutting on downtown factories and shipyards.

It was the importation of cheap and abundant labor into America from across the world that helped spur an economic recovery after several financial panics. The fruits of this rapid expansion were hardly shared equally, and despite the quick pace of industrialization, national unemployment remained close to 20 percent during parts of the 1890s and was almost 40 percent in some industries.[18] Cities like New York were overrun with unemployed, single men with too much time on their hands and too much desperation in their eyes, according to observers at the time. The result was not just poverty; it was perversity, too. When Robert Hunter's 1904 study *Poverty* found that the "conditions of work and of living . . . are so unjust and degrading that men are driven by them to degeneracy," the news was hardly shocking.[19]

Hunter's observation underscores a critical link between unemployment, poor housing, and what was perceived as degenerate social and sexual practices in the urban underworlds of America. The reputed pathology of the immigrant underworld was often diagnosed as having cultural roots, but I want to keep its material underpinnings front and center. It was the sheer magnetic pull of an unrepentantly amoral urban-centered American capitalism that drew a diverse lot of men and women, many of them single and many of them poor, Catholic, or "heathen," from around the globe. In doing so, it overrode entrenched white, Anglo-Saxon religious and social pieties that were invested in maintaining the nation's purity. Agglomerated in underserved, undervalued, rundown areas of cities—ethnic slums in the case of New York in the 1890s—these putatively deviant groupings (and the zones in which they lived) were the focus of much interest and fear for the social and sexual arrangements they maintained. Not only did industrial capitalism produce untold wealth but it also produced poverty, deviance, and difference; or more accurately, it produced poverty as an expression of deviance and difference.

On the socioeconomic origins of so-called pathological cultures, Roderick Ferguson recently has argued that the importation of labor in the late nineteenth and early twentieth centuries resulted in eroticized social formations that violated national ideals of family life: "It [capitalism] does not rely on normative prescriptions to assemble labor, even while it may use those prescriptions to establish the value of that labor."[20] Following from this, the supposed moral degeneracy of the underworld poor—which led Meloney to investigate interracial marriage, opium dens, and white slavery—should be seen as dynamically related to "the anarchic possibilities of economic production" at the close of the century.[21]

Changes in gender roles, forms of labor and entertainment, and modes of dwelling in the city were in part attributable to the centripetal forces of urbanization and industrialization which spectacularly condensed difference and inequality in the city with little or no regard to norms of personal or familial conduct. Because money was to be made packing more people into smaller spaces, landlords routinely overfilled buildings. Lodgers themselves would "sublet the closets and hallways within their apartments or adjacent spaces in common hallways, beneath the stairway, in the basement, or even on the rooftop" in order to help pay the rent.[22] Cramped residences meant socializing spilled onto fire escapes, doorways, streets, and into saloons, and meant that women slept in rooms with male lodgers taken on to assist with the family's housing costs. The "permeable architecture" of the tenement in which sounds and smells drifted from apartment to apartment through shared hallways and bathrooms "facilitated extra-familial connections" and violated middle-class standards of privacy and decorum.[23] The middle-class "contagion scares" of the 1890s were borne out of a fear that nonstandard intimacies and connections were incubating like disease inside the tenement.[24] In sum, the quotidian rituals of work, play, and survival reinforced for the bourgeois imagination extant images of poor immigrants as more sexually profligate, given to prostitution and other criminal vices, and as possessing little respect for the social boundaries they could ill afford to establish. The journalist Eleanor Hoyt's visceral distaste for the "new Americans" was typical: "A large percentage of the immigrants are dirty, ill-smelling, repulsive," she wrote in 1903.[25]

Crowded into dilapidated apartments, many of them in lightless cellars, this late nineteenth-century immigrant population came to be known as the underclass by the sociological, biomedical, and criminological discourses of the period and would be repeatedly referred to as the underworld in literary narratives of urban life at the time. For instance, in his novella *Maggie*, Stephen Crane located the violent, ramshackle street of "Devil's Row" not surprisingly in the hellish world of lower Manhattan, "a dark region where, from a careening building, a dozen gruesome doorways gave up loads of babies to the street and the gutter."[26] For many, the tenements were baby-making machines from which the new effluvium of low life spilled, flowing to the gutter, to the sewer—the analogies to waste were not accidental—and eventually to the river (the tragic fate of Crane's own heroine), where police captain Galvin wanted to chuck the whole degraded and degenerate neighborhood like a rotten Atlantis.

New York has always had its slums. By the end of the century, however, New York was qualitatively and quantitatively different from the 1850 version of itself. Massive immigration and a manufacturing economy had turned it into a competitive-industrial city, an urban spatial form characterized by a central business district, downtown shanties for the unemployed and for underemployed workers that Crane wrote about, and magnificent uptown bourgeois residences that Henry James called New York's "splendid structures."[27] The city's uneven social and geographic development thus was physically evident in the dilapidated, fire-prone tenements at one end of town and Millionaires Row, the Fifth Avenue mansions of Cornelius Vanderbilt, Isaac Fletcher, and Henry Cook, at the other. Such antipodes were the visual expressions of what James in *The American Scene* termed "the economic idea," the binarism that manufactured great wealth and great poverty simultaneously (74).

The mercantile city of the early nineteenth century, by contrast, possessed a more compressed spatial and social order in which diverse socioeconomic populations lived in relative proximity to each other. In the mercantile city, class stratification was more geographically condensed, and cross-class exchanges and relations tended to be more immediate and frequent. The "social relations in New York itself were largely 'primary,'" Robert Dowling argues, "before the rise of immigration, mass marketing, and industrial capitalism."[28] Following from the industrializing economy's increasing polarization of wealth was the greater geographical separation of classes into different zones, isolated from each other in what often seemed like different worlds altogether. The industrial city "was the first in which rich and poor did not live cheek to jowl in a mixed-use urban space."[29]

In short, between 1850 and 1890 New York had undergone profound transformations: social life in the city was increasingly segregated by class and ethnicity. As I will show, turn-of-the-century slumming literature, which often recorded the harrowing trip from the rich northern districts into the downtown slums, depended on the city's social polarity. Geographically condensing poverty had many effects. It resulted in periodic, fast-spreading outbreaks of tuberculosis, typhus, and cholera. Whole sections of lower Manhattan were treated as miasmas of cultural disease, as well. Wealth had fled further and further uptown. The city's new divisions marked imaginary and real moral geographies, boundary lines that protected middle-class social and religious mores from the contagious and enervating environments of the downtown underworld. A popular, sociological, and literary discourse on the slums of turn-of-the-century, industrial New York, reflected and hastened these social and geographic divisions by reinscribing and reinforcing the distinctions between uptown and downtown neighborhoods. Characterizing poor and working-class immigrant quarters as nether regions was not just an expression of religious hyperbole or yellow journalism: over time it had actual consequences for whether or not particular quarters of the city would be targeted for economic disinvestment, urban renewal, and gentrification. This is to say, there was always a material, economic corollary to the shrill and panicked discourse. The story of the reshaping and resignification of urban space—its polarization and moralization—is the story I want to tell. It is a story that begins in the depths of the Lower East Side's tessellated enclaves, for it was there that ethnic heterogeneity and pauperization were geographically squeezed in a way that urban historians recognize as "decidedly modern."[30] What was "modern" was by other measures decidedly inhuman.

The depths of poverty in New York could be empirically verified, could be seen in the densely built, even underground, spaces where the poor lived. To imagine these lower terrains as urban underworlds was to cognitively and geographically contain them. And to leave behind the bourgeois comforts of the upperworld to descend into the underworld slums—as Meloney, Riis, James, and numerous tour guides, social reformers, and middle-class urban spelunkers did—was to experience firsthand the disorienting, disturbing pains and pleasures of the modern city.

When Meloney arrived in Chinatown in 1909 with the promise of uncovering the secrets of the neighborhood, he was much too late: its streets were already filled, in his own words, with "big sight-seeing automobiles" unloading "their cargoes of slummers" (231). In fact, in Meloney's Chinatown slumming tourists nearly outnumber the Chinese residents they have paid to observe like colorful birds in their natural habitat, a gaze the Chinese themselves returned. Meloney's report even included a photograph of several Chinese men and women lined up on a sidewalk, their heads turned to some commotion beyond the edge of the camera's eye. As the inquisitive reader stares at the Chinese, the Chinese stare at the slummers who probably stare back in a mutual gaze of incomprehensibility. Working his way through the crowd, Meloney notes that the slummers are led by a "Semitic-faced youth," presumably one ethnic American (the Lower East Side's Jewish community was, of course, numerous) who is pointing out the newest foreign exotica to a largely white audience (231). No wonder "they are bewildered, uncertain. They feel they are on the threshold of a mystery" (231). In an inclusive direct address to the reader, Meloney suggests, "Let us follow them" (231). The investigation that had begun under the premise of understanding how an urban environment could drive one to miscegenation and murder descends into a spectacle, an act of looking at looking at looking. The reader is pulled along on a slumming tour whose first stop is the "garish hole" where, the "youth" explains, a tong war left ten men dead. "His sanguinary tale is designed to catch the interest of just such people as are following him for a dollar or two dollars a head," Meloney writes without the self-conscious irony that the moment deserves. The tale, he proclaims, "is successful" (232).

Knowledge of the ephemeral practice of slumming largely has been passed down through history by documents such as Meloney's. In

FIGURE 3. "The inscrutable and impenetrable Oriental—denizens of Chinatown watching a slumming-party entering the quarter." Reprinted from William Meloney, "Slumming in New York's Chinatown: A Glimpse into the Sordid Underworld of the Mott Street Quarter, Where Elsie Sigel Formed Her Fatal Associations," *Munsey's Magazine* (1909). Courtesy of Frank Oppel, *Tales of Gaslight New York* (2000).

turn-of-the-century urban America, slumming was a stylized form of class descent that was codified into organized, commercial entertainment for middle- and upper-class city residents and tourists who wished to explore the supposed sources of urban crime, disease, and social discontent. As a form of nighttime and weekend amusement, it promised its participants an authentic experience while casting them in the role of would-be investigators and social reformers. In his history of slumming, Dowling argues that in "New York moral regions proliferated at a fantastic rate at the turn of the twentieth century," and that slumming narratives became "a means of unifying, for better or worse, an otherwise fragmented urban environment."[31] Slumming, in other words, was premised upon the idea that the urban experience was invariably piecemeal and disjointed and that parts of the city were nearly unknowable as a result of uneven development's geographic spatialization of ethnic and class difference. Slumming was a means of momentarily overriding those differences. One could "go down" into the underworld to survey what changes to the modern city had wrought.

And yet slummers, paradoxically, reinforced their social distance from the underworld poor by traveling to them—an activity premised on leisure time and disposable income which the poor themselves did not possess. The slumming tour provided middle-class Americans with positivistic knowledge about how the city was spatially organized and, armed with this knowledge, they could resituate and reorient themselves in a physical and social geography that seemed to be shifting under their very feet. Tightly orchestrated and carefully scripted, slumming tours were designed to induce a certain range of reactions for their participants—excitement and revulsion, fear and loathing—as they purported to offer real knowledge of the city and their place in it. More often than not, the tour confirmed the irredeemable differences and deficiencies of the ethnic poor, reinforcing the quarantining of marginalized populations in so-called urban underworld geographies.

The historian M. H. Dunlop explains in her account of Gilded Age New York, "A typical slumming tour began anywhere between nine and midnight at a police station, where slummers acquired an authoritative and protective police escort."[32] As part of their regular duties, police officers and Pinkerton agents went undercover among the lower classes to investigate crime and to infiltrate and disrupt labor activism among immigrant workers.[33] For a fee, these same off-duty detectives would serve as ushers on a picturesque tour through downtown tenements, opium dens, houses of assignation, flophouses, cellar beer dives, gambling parlors, and black-and-tans where white women and black men mingled, drank, and danced. Usually the descent into the terrain of the urban underworld was preceded by a visit to the police station's rogues' gallery, followed by an inspection of seized contraband.[34] These preliminary measures served to dramatically frame the slumming tour's revelations, while assuring its participants that municipal power authorities were actively controlling a disorderly population. Slumming was inextricably bound up with police surveillance, moral regulation, and the merciless enforcement of hygiene. And as it titillated with tawdry rumors of sexual seduction, it promised retribution against those who threatened the normative parameters of sexual, racial, and national identity.

The phenomenon of slumming was an expression of manifold and at times conflicting positions. On the slumming tour, "the city's squalidly poor or exotically foreign quarters," Luc Sante remarks, were transformed into "a playground of the imagination," a stage upon which the middle-class urban explorer could don any number of guises—a heroic interloper, a concerned citizen, or even that of an indigent wearing shabby clothing and a soiled hat.[35] To the extent that slumming guaranteed its participants empirical evidence of the urban underworld, it also asked them to uncover such evidence through dissembling and deception. In short, slumming was a highly performative activity that frequently necessitated "class transvestism," descending the class ladder in the clothing of its lower echelons.[36]

For some turn-of-the-century urban residents and tourists, "class transvestism" was one way of bridging divides, but for others, the refusal to assume the sartorial markers of poverty was a way of keeping those divisions intact. The slummers captured in one of Meloney's photographs, for instance, sport elaborate hats, ties, suits, and white dresses. The lure of going down-and-permanently-out was militated against by their obvious signifiers of wealth. For them, the desire was to look at the "pornography of race" and class rather than to engage in it.[37] In sum, slumming functioned as a performance of class that reinscribed white, middle-class privilege through the enactment of spatial mobility, the freedom to enter and exit a subaltern space more or less on one's own terms. And it reinforced that privilege through a performance of one's sartorial choices: to choose to dress down or not before one went down-and-out was a luxury.

For all of its negative cultural work, the slumming tour also allowed for new forms of social awareness and provided the opportunity to imaginatively experiment with cross-class and cross-racial desire, though on obviously unequal terms. For its participants, it provided a mechanism for recognizing how inequality, morality, and ethnic difference were geographically inscribed into the urban fabric. The practice of slumming made possible the recognition of how the underworld and the upperworld exist in a contingent relation to each other within the same city. In the journey from uptown to downtown, slumming taught—or at least held out the promise of teaching—its participants that down here people appeared to survive and work, live and socialize differently than they did up there. In effect, the tour translated social relations into spatial relations and thus geographically situated knowledge about class and ethnicity. Or as one woman interviewed by Meloney admits, "When I step out of Chinatown, I become a white woman again. When I come back, I become yellow and mind my own business" (238). The tour complemented historical and

FIGURE 4. "A Black and Tan Dive in Africa." Jacob A. Riis Collection, the Museum of the City of New York.

sociological knowledge about urban life with a new spatial awareness. "At a time when poverty was commonly associated with immigrants, and immigration restriction was a sharply debated public issue," going down, the scholar Mark Pittenger suggests, "could promote a tolerant, cosmopolitan stance" as easily as it "could eventuate in nativist and racist exclusionism."[38] The slumming tour perhaps seldom initiated the critical deconstruction of common-sense notions of cityspace and urban life which held that city residents naturally self-segregated and that the dilapidated, dirty housing and streets in certain enclaves were the natural expression of their inhabitants and users. Nevertheless, it substituted for the practice of social avoidance a practice of engagement and encounter in which the potential for an awareness of how upper and lower social and physical geographies are intertwined could be realized.

For those who could not, or dared not, slum physically, there were always the second-hand accounts available in an expanding market of slumming literature. As Christopher Mele stresses in his history of the Lower East Side, slumming literature provided escapism for middle-class readers constricted by an increasingly standardized industrial economy and

FIGURE 5. "A typical party of slummers coming out of a Chinatown restaurant after a midnight banquet of chop suey and chow mein." Reprinted from William Meloney, "Slumming in New York's Chinatown: A Glimpse into the Sordid Underworld of the Mott Street Quarter, Where Elsie Sigel Formed Her Fatal Associations," *Munsey's Magazine* (1909). Courtesy of Frank Oppel, *Tales of Gaslight New York* (2000).

overbearing Protestant morality: "Popular consumption of sensationalist novels and journalistic accounts evinced a form of bourgeois voyeurism—a temporary, if passive, retreat from an otherwise scrutinized, byzantine, and straitlaced world."[39] Slumming literature provided a conduit for exploring the erotic potential of a city in which ethnic and social differences created temporary frissons between densely clustered bodies and buildings. For all of its entertainment value, this literature had a political and pedagogical function. It spatialized Otherness: it drew readers imaginatively beyond their insular social circle, made them aware of others in the city, and it distanced readers from them at the same time. As Mele records, "accounts of fulfilled temptations and unrepressed desires were universally situated within graphic descriptions of a vile place of starvation, mounting debts, and physical and psychological abuse that reinforced bourgeois superiority and social distance above the netherworld."[40] Furthermore, through narratives of seduction and resistance, slumming literature dramatized and valorized bourgeois self-discipline and moral fortitude that contrasted with the "chaotic free-for-all of wanton women, excessive gambling, and an uncontrollable appetite for liquor and drugs" in the Lower East Side.[41] But perhaps this literature's most significant social function was its obfuscation of the economic underpinnings of poverty. By pointing out inassimilable ethnic and class differences and by portraying poverty as imprisoning and geographically localized, the genre helped to secure the uneven distribution of space at a time when battles over the cityspace were growing more heated by the day.

Slumming literature helped a readership travel—in mind and body—through a metropolis that had come to feel, for many middle-class residents by the turn of the century, disorderly, dangerous, thrilling, and alien. This literature, I believe, should be understood as a cultural form that translated the experience of growing income inequality into a dramatic narrative frame. In a period in which "9 percent of the nation's families owned 71 percent of the nation's wealth," as the 1892 Census Bureau calculated, slumming narratives provided a means of imagining what such inequality actually looked and felt like.[42] Predicated on class segregation, this literature also proffered a means of transgressing it through an urban adventure narrative. It worked to do so by deploying a range of complex rhetorical cues that worked to incorporate the reader into the narrative: including first-person, present-tense narration interrupted by sudden eruptions into the inclusive second person "you"; direct addresses to the reader in the form of disclaimers and warnings regarding what he or she was about to witness; the use of the classical topos of descent into the underworld to shape the journey down into the enclaves of the ethnic poor; frequent temporal shifts into the past tense that mark moments of nostalgia for how the city used to be; and finally, this literature almost always concluded with a return to the safety of the upperworld, literalized through a movement back uptown to which the narrator and reader—now educated, frightened, and frequently exhausted—retreats.

To further exemplify some of these claims, I turn to a typical slumming narrative, Ernest Ingersoll's *A Week in New York*, a popular travel guide published by Rand McNally. Almost completely forgotten by historians and literary scholars, the zoologist and travel writer Ingersoll was a prominent researcher in the late nineteenth century, who was known for the several books and essays he had authored, including

Nests and Eggs of American Birds (1880), *Gold Fields of the Klondike and the Wonders of Alaska* (1897), and "Mollusks in General" in G. B. Goode's *Natural History of Useful Aquatic Animals* (1884). Ingersoll's descent into the urban demimonde in his New York tourism guide stands out in a career that, as Clyde MacKenzie writes, earned him fame among "shellfishery biologists as the author of two outstanding monographs on the shellfisheries of the United States and Canada in the 1880's."[43] In most of Ingersoll's writing, the underworld is an underwater world. But when the wonders of New York had to substitute for the wonders of Alaska or the ocean, Ingersoll recommended a nocturnal ramble through the underworld slums. A nighttime slum tour is the highlighted activity for day six of the week-long itinerary he sets forth for his male reader.

Recognizing that readers will physically reenact that journey downward which he describes, Ingersoll offers this advice: "Hire a guide at some one of the many private detective agencies, and . . . pay him to show you the darker parts of the town at midnight."[44] Slumming, he notes, requires some preparation, and so he strongly suggests that "you . . . leave at home your silk hat, diamond studs and kid gloves, and your watch, too, if it is a valuable one; don't exhibit a roll of bills when you pay for your occasional glass of beer or cigar; don't be *too* inquisitive; and don't allow yourself to be enticed into any back yards, or dark doorways, nor up or down any stairways, by man or woman. Above all, keep quite sober—so clear-headed that you not only can take care of yourself, but that you could closely observe and subsequently identify any person who tried to do you harm" (202). Such sartorial self-consciousness reveals how narratives of underworld descent are structured upon paradox: pledging to authentically document lower-class city life, they expose the performativity of class identity. But they do so only to reinforce class as the immutable signifier of worth. Only at the northern end of the social ladder is identity flexible, finding expression in the marketplace of commodities that one can purchase and in the social affectations in which one's purchases serve as props. In this literature, the lurid essentialism of slum residents shines through any clothing they themselves wear. Or as Ingersoll forthrightly asserts, "the Jew remains a Jew," the Chinese "naturally seek one another's society," and "the women [of the Bowery] are seldom good-looking, vulgar as a rule, and ignorant always" (207, 212, 213). The added paradox, of course, was that a modern market economy had imported the foreign labor that Ingersoll was investigating, and it was this same modern economy that produced the luxuries he needed to divest himself of before he could begin his inquiry.

By the 1890s, New York was an imperial metropolis that drew a dizzying array of peoples as much as it did the colorful assortment of commodities elegantly displayed in the new department store windows lining its wealthy, uptown avenues. Browsing downtown was a different experience altogether. Pressing through the streets, Ingersoll says, "the way is more crowded, and as we jostle through it is hard to believe this is not Naples," and comments at another point that "both sides [of the street are] given up to our Hebraic brethren, who appropriate the greater part of [the] side-walk for the display of their various 'bargains.' Swarthy men and sometimes girls entreat you to enter and buy, not only, but seize your arm and will drag you in" (205, 206). These goods are not behind glass, but are out on the sidewalk to be looked at the same way Ingersoll looks at "our Hebraic brethren." A nearly indecipherable space, teeming with signs of ethnic, cultural, and class difference, the industrial city had to be read up close and on foot.

As he bargains his way through the busy streets, Ingersoll's reader takes in the city's stratified social space in what amounts to a breathtaking if anxiety-inducing propinquity as he moves past the "extremely picturesque and foreign scenes" of Chinatown, then turns "rapidly northward" to the "dark corners behind the Bowery" before finally "hurry[ing] eastward" to the Lower East Side, a district that Ingersoll simply labels "Judea" (207, 210, 212, 213). This is no shopping expedition. Shuttling by a living diorama of foreign peoples and cultures, the reader is asked to "closely observe" and "identify" how the city and the nation are threatened from below by those of "the lowest character," "dark-skinned men," opium addicts, socialists and anarchists, and prostitutes who "flit jauntily along under the glare . . . beckoning" (202, 204, 206, 217). New York at night, Ingersoll exclaims, "equals the terrors of any portraiture in Dante's 'Inferno'" (210).

Torn between a rhetoric of attraction and disavowal, slumming literature, as Ingersoll's example makes clear, highlights the urban underworld's offer of erotic enticement, yet militates against it by the strategic deployment of a rhetoric of middle-class Christian decorum and appeals to institutional authorities. When Ingersoll warns against being "enticed into any . . . dark doorways . . . by man or woman," or when Meloney observes two young Caucasian women "looking in a shop window at a display of lingerie" and sees that "a sleek Chinaman, smiling and deferential, is inviting them within," it is clear that the pleasure derived from reading—or enacting—their narratives inheres in just such a temptation into a life of crime or sin (Ingersoll 202; Meloney 234). Ingersoll's contemporary Frank Moss, a writer, attorney, and member of the Society for the Prevention of Crime, who made a similar excursion into the New York underworld in *The American Metropolis*, was even more paralyzed between fulfilling the mandates of Christian piety and exploring the libidinal urges those pieties repressed. His multivolume work, partly a history of New York and partly a guidebook, reproduced two maps of downtown: one locating the 237 saloons in the Lower East Side's Eleventh Ward, and another highlighting the paltry number of churches (just 5) in the same area.[45] In this context, the claim by Reverend Charles Parkhurst (famous for his crusade against prostitution) in the introduction to *The American Metropolis* was unintentionally ironic: "Youths are not fond of disquisitions, but they like to be shown things, which is exactly what Mr. Moss does in these pages."[46] He shows the saloons—many of them concealed in back alleys, down staircases, or behind false fronts—where one might sin and drink, and the churches where one might seek forgiveness.

Vice in late nineteenth-century America was imagined as a communicable disease that infected slum dwellers as readily as cholera, typhus, or tuberculosis. Prolonged exposure to the noxious downtown underworld could result in irretrievable immersion and decline. "The 'white slaves' of Chinatown," Meloney asserted are a "fiction" precisely because they are not slaves: "No bars or strong doors keep them there. . . . Addiction to opium is their only warder" (239). Timothy Gilfoyle argues in his finely detailed study of nineteenth-century prostitution that "subcultures of prostitutes and sporting men, linked to an alternative society frequently labeled the underworld, became important elements in the social structure and public life of the metropolis" between 1870 and 1915, when "a new geography of sex districts emerged in New York."[47] Centered in the city's "leisure and working-class subcultures," commercial sex was considered more prevalent and blatant the further south one traveled in Manhattan.[48] Gilfoyle quotes the "experience of one anonymous male" who described a descent downtown in 1888: the "further down I got, [the] more stepped [*sic*] in sin did these unfortunates appear."[49] Just as part of the attraction of the slumming tour was the possibility of permanently slipping into an underworld of vice, so too was the confirmation of one's moral superiority that came with resistance to unfortunate solicitations. These texts offered readers a platform for their fantasies, while containing those fantasies within a framework of Christian morality. Slumming literature established social, physical, and moral boundaries for the city even as it trespassed through them by way of pleasure in a dark doorway.

Ernest Ingersoll's guided tour follows through on its geographical logic by reaching its nadir in the slum of Five Points. The neighborhood was the city's lowest point both socially and geographically, and was known in the early nineteenth century as the home of the forty-eight-acre Collect Pond filled with castoffs from the slaughterhouses and known as a communal sewer. It is here, furthest down, where Ingersoll naturalizes deviancy, calling the area an "unmanageable crime-nursery" where "the human drainage of the city" is collected (204, 206). What is essential here is how *A Week in New York* anatomized urban space for its 1890s reader, teaching him that space and class (as well as race and culture) are homologous. In the depths of the underworld, they even converge: "the ground [that is] low" corresponds exactly with "the lowest character" (204). Geography is marshaled as primary evidence. Racial, ethnic, and class eccentricity are geographically rooted, and not by accident, Ingersoll strongly suggests. Works like *A Week in New York* and *The American Metropolis* helped to clarify the bewildering social farrago of the city by collapsing all categorical distinctions. Moss, like Ingersoll, concludes from the evidence gathered on his slumming tour that the Chinese "are a dangerous, useless and disgusting lot of people," the Jews are "human parasites," and all residents east of City Hall must contend with a "record . . . full of shame."[50] Everyone in "this evil part of town," Ingersoll remarks, is either a criminal or looks like a criminal, a distinction without a difference (203).

But out of the depths arises the possibility of change in the guise of new businesses taking root under the watchful eye of the police, seemingly two ingredients in any successful redevelopment project. Knee-deep in the muck, Ingersoll observes how at the "*Police Headquarters* . . . two green lanterns [stand] erect and firm," and notes that "great business houses are rising year by year" in the vicinity (203). "Even the devil is being ousted from all this evil part of town," he concludes (203). For Ingersoll, business will drain the swamp of lower Manhattan. Capital investments seeking profit in cheap ground rents will clear a path through the underworld that slummers (and future gentrifiers) will tread as heroic interlopers. Ingersoll sees a future in which the architecture of commerce rises from the human gutter. The perpetual ebb and flow of capital across geographies that builds up some districts as others fall is manifest here. Inch by inch and "year by year," the underworld slum is eliminated by a reinvestment of money that *A Week in New York* characterizes as an act of physical and moral sanitation. If one's safe passage through the underworld rested upon the erasure of the signifiers of class difference, it was even more dependent upon the large-scale restructuring of the urban environment by which business and law enforcement slowly cleared areas of urban blight. And it is on this note that Ingersoll ends: "Long after midnight," he tells his edified sightseer, "let us go home" (217). The middle-class slummer is ushered to safety in what amounts to a modern version of *The Pilgrim's Progress* through the narrow, trash-strewn streets of the City of Destruction to the clean avenues of the Celestial City that is just a few miles north. Day seven breaks fresh in *A Week in New York* with a survey of Sunday worship services.

Slumming literature helped clear a pathway through the "overgrown metropolis."[51] It instructed readers how to walk through the physical spaces of the city. Slumming literature itself is also a space, a textual one. In reading this literature, we make our way through texts that, as we have seen, elicit competing and sometimes opposing responses: desire, disgust, curiosity, and revulsion. Michel de Certeau in *The Practice of Everyday Life* brings these two spaces—the physical and the textual—together when he postulates that narrative functions as a pathway through textual space much as walkers in the city form a path that writes "an urban 'text.'"[52] De Certeau characterizes "walking as writing" as "a process of *appropriation* of the topographical system on the part of the pedestrian."[53] The walker makes spatial possibilities "exist as well as emerge," he argues.[54] And the inverse of the analogy is also true: "Every story is a travel story—a spatial practice" that puts into motion "the alphabet of spatial indication ('It's to the right,' 'Take a left')."[55] "Narrative structures have the status of spatial syntaxes," de Certeau proposes: "By means of a whole panoply of codes, ordered ways of proceeding and constraints, they regulate changes in space (or moves from one place to another)."[56]

Ingersoll, Meloney, and Moss charted the uneven geographies of the city and through their narrative structures provided "ordered ways of proceeding and constraints." They did so as a means of reasserting the right of the white, male citizen to be any place in the city, a right that was often secured through the threat of violence. Moss informs his reader, a fellow "investigator," that his safe passage through the urban underworld is guaranteed by a "heavy revolver in [his] pocket."[57] Slumming literature provided a mechanism by which middle-class readers could map the city's incomprehensible, alien spaces by walking through them and rewriting them into a script that fit the era's social anxieties. It was only by walking through such spaces that the true character of the city's lowest echelons could be discovered. More often than not, middle-class panics over the spreading physical and moral contagion of the slums were translated by the slumming tour into libidinal fantasies in which the lure of the underworld competed with desires to police and repress it. The conflicted narratives of 1890s slumming literature are animated by divergent urges to move in two directions at once, into a dark doorway on the Bowery or a lingerie shop in Chinatown, and to follow an avenue heading uptown to home and church.

Slumming narratives brought a social underworld into being by delimiting a space of social abjection and then trespassing into it. The frontier of narrative space is established by a contact between two points of difference which are also points of shared space, or as de Certeau writes, a boundary is demarcated "only by saying what crosses it, having come from the other side."[58] For Meloney, Ingersoll, and Moss these points of difference are points of class and ethnic mingling in the claustrophobic zones of the city, where white bodies touch or come close to touching different bodies. When Jacob Riis's *How the Other Half Lives* informs its reader "That was a woman filling her pail by the hydrant you just bumped against" and "Come over here. Step carefully over this baby—it is a baby, spite of its rags and dirt," it reproduces the geography of lower New York in a manner that attests to its uncomfortable density.[59] At these points of contact, the poor are rendered illegible and simultaneously made knowable as specters—"That was a woman," "it is a baby." Drawing the boundaries around the socially unintelligible, turn-of-the-century slumming narratives fortified the contours of a discrete middle- and upper-class subjectivity, defining it in contrast to the racial and ethnic mixing of the "teeming masses" (7).

In *A Week in New York* and *The American Metropolis* geographical uneven development is narrated, and subjectivity, in turn, is spatialized. In these works, the uptown fashionable avenues of shopping, theater, upscale residential districts, and institutions of culture exist a world apart from the downtown underworld of brothels, groggeries, and hermetic ethnic neighborhoods. The logic of uneven geographical development produced disquieting new social and spatial formations. Frederick H. Whitin, the chair of the anti-vice society the Committee of Fourteen, recognized as much when he averred that prostitution is "an accompaniment of civilization; that the crowding in the cities, an increase of luxuries and the postponement of . . . marriage, all tend to increase it."[60] In short, there was to be no narrowing of the chasms between the upper and underworlds of New York because both were the singular outcome of a modern industrial economy that gathered surplus populations and expropriated labor from them. The slumming tour allowed its participants to examine "social conditions"—poverty, crime, bad housing—which were to be understood to have become so entrenched and unsolvable that they only could be seen as a nauseating spectacle.[61] Jacob Riis pessimistically concluded as much at the outset of his illustrated tour of the slums: "We know now that there is no way out; that the 'system' that was the evil offspring of public neglect and private greed has come to stay, a storm-centre forever of our civilization. Nothing is left but to make the best of a bad bargain" (6). These urban guides trespass across "the boundary line of the Other Half" and return again to the upperworld with the understanding that "the coming appeal for justice must proceed from the public conscience. Neither legislation nor charity can cover the ground" (5, 7). Through its narratives of descent, slumming literature wedded social exploration with social regulation and political acquiescence. In the process, it absolved readers of any responsibility outside of their support for continued policing and slum clearance as a way pruning the unruly, "overgrown metropolis."

A Race Apart: Poverty and the Physiology of Crime in Underclass America

In the mid to late nineteenth century, sociological, biomedical, and criminological discourse constructed an underclass population as a scientific corollary to the principally literary construct of the mythical, frightening, and enticing urban underworld. Understanding the historic origins and social meanings of the designation "underclass" illuminates the range of polarized responses that are the source of the slumming narrative's drama. This expert discourse's construction of a spatial Other, we will see, was embraced and rejected by Jacob Riis and Henry James, respectively, who each offered his own version of the slumming tour.

The classificatory rubric "underclass" dates to 1899, when it was first used by the criminal anthropologist Cesare Lombroso, though the idea of a dangerous class of social outsiders is much older and was at the heart of Thomas Malthus's theories of poverty and population growth in late eighteenth-century England. From the second half of the nineteenth century to the early years of the twentieth, Lombroso was the most influential theorist of the origins of crime, and his ideas strongly shaped public understanding of lower-class urban life for generations. Lombroso joined criminology to physiology, professing that some individuals were born criminal, and that visible traces of innate criminality could be discerned in the anatomical aberrations of their faces and bodies. What constituted deformity was aligned closely with the perceived common features of southern and eastern Europeans and Africans who, under Lombroso's taxonomy, became permanently categorized as the criminal classes. In the nineteenth century, Lombroso's theories of underclass crime and deviancy migrated to the United States, where they were importantly augmented to include a focus on the effects of geography, particularly the detrimental consequences of city living. Largely a construction of the Progressive discourses of poverty, morality, criminality, and urbanization, the underclass came to designate those who have been forced out of—or were incapable of being a part of—a cohesive, integrated society, resulting in a socially diverse alterity that was defined more by its shared social and physical space than by a shared sense of racial or ethnic identity. To put this another way, in America the social diversity of the underclass was subsumed under the mantle of a common geography. The downtown populations that late nineteenth-century urban travel guides described were nothing if not ethnically heterogeneous. But these social underworlds had one thing in common: they were all clustered in the city's ruinous depths.

In Progressive America, the idea of an underclass played into social phobias while it simultaneously shielded middle-class economic hegemony by conceptually marking a population as Other. As the class beneath class, the underclass was conceived as the waste product or the residuum that remains when all use-value is extracted from a given population. Ingersoll labeled them "the human drainage of the city"; Riis saw them as those who sleep and eat "under the dump, on the edge of slimy depths and amid surroundings full of unutterable horror" (44). The underclass were thought of as "a race of men, small, ill-formed, disease-stricken, hard to kill," according Geoffrey Searle, or, as an early twentieth-century report from the Eugenics Society asserted, "a race of sub-normal people, closely related by marriage or parenthood, not to any extent recruited from the normal population."[62] Progressive discourse conceptually relegated the underclass to a nonplace inhabited by nonpeople, and physically relegated them to the lowest geographical terrain imaginable. In sum, the urban poor were consistently understood as both ethnically heterogeneous and as a race apart, related to each other by sheer proximity, but unrelated to the general population of middle-class urban residents. They formed a submerged society in the "unmanageable crime-nursery" of the slum, the geographical locus of racial and cultural degeneration and urban crime.[63]

Financial panics in the 1890s—those in the years 1893 and 1897 were severe—hastened moral panics over the corrupting influence of spreading poverty. Idleness and vagrancy, in turn, were criminalized in the period and viewed as violations of a Protestant work ethic. In 1904 (the same year that Henry James returned to New York for a visit that he would later chronicle in *The American Scene*), Stephen Chalmers reported on "tramps" in New York City's parks. Chalmers described them as "specimen[s] of underworld humanity," "a sedentary army of dead manhood" who brood in "semi-oblivion."[64] Characteristically for the period, Chalmers was unable to acknowledge or detect signs of agency among the city's economically devastated. The poor were either hard to kill or half-way dead. In either case, the general consensus was that they were poor not because economic restructuring had failed to provide sufficient employment, but because they were unmotivated, or incapable of motivation, and immoral.

In contrast to these commonly held views, Karl Marx argued for an understanding of the genealogy of poverty as tied to the urban spatial economy. He colorfully characterized the underclass lumpenproletariat as the "ragpickers, knife grinders, tinkers, beggars—in short the whole indefinite, disintegrated mass, through hither and thither, which the French term *la bohème*," which he saw as a distinctly urban social formation. The hoi polloi was found, Marx wrote, "in all big towns," specifically in the slum areas, "a recruiting ground for thieves and criminals of all kinds living on the crumbs of society."[65] Nineteenth-century urban sociologists, for their part, recognized the determinative impact of the environment, but they did so, unlike Marx, by essentializing it as a genetically mutating, contagious, and inheritable force. Lydia Morris emphasizes that for these experts the concept of the underclass expressed a relationship between the city and the body. They argued for an environmental determinism that married poor housing to poor genes to breed an inferior stock of humanity. "Long life in the town is accompanied by more or less degeneration of the race," the London-based *Journal of the Royal Statistical Society* claimed in 1893.[66] This "race," the journal asserted, was distinguished by "the narrow chest, . . . the weak eyes, the bad teeth," a diagnosis which echoed Henry Mayhew's that the poor had "protruding jaws," "slang language," "lax ideas about property, "repugnance to continuous labour," "disregard of female honour," and "an utter want of religion."[67] The underclass body was a text to be deciphered. Sexual lassitude and the lack of respect for private property could be read in the angle of a jaw or the asymmetry of a face.

By the turn of the century, new medical techniques for combating crime born from slum life were the vanguard, supplementing older methods such as the incarceration of the poor in workhouses. On August 12, 1906, the *New York Times* published "The Surgeon's Knife as a Check to Crime: Interesting Experiments Being Made with Boys and Girls of Evil Tendencies," which detailed this latest research. The paper reported that the Pennsylvania Society to Protect Children from Cruelty had teamed with the Philadelphia Board of Health in a joint venture to prevent crime by eliminating "evil . . . criminal tendencies" in the children of convicts through "medical and surgical treatment" rather than by "mere police methods." In effect, it brought medical expertise to Lombroso's theories and combined them with an emergent sociology's focus on the consequences of living in an impoverished urban environment. The large, publicly funded social experiment was under the direction of "a board of medical experts, headed by Dr. S. Weir Mitchell," who wanted to understand more precisely the "physiology of crime" in "this dark underworld of our civilization."

Labeled an "interesting experiment in criminology," the study sought to correct physical "abnormalities" such as the "high-arched palate, the twitching of the features, the involuntary laughter," which were viewed as manifestations of "moral and mental evil" among the progeny of the underclass. The experiments involved the close examination—by Dr. Alfred Gordon and the aptly named Dr. Butcher—of the children of poor southern Europeans and African Americans for indications of atavistic traits that were a precursor of a future criminal disposition and warning signs of systemic racial decline. Dr. Gordon showed the *Times* his evidence firsthand. Pointing to three Italian children: "'Notice their low, bulging foreheads, fixed eyes, hanging lower jaw,' he said; 'physical signs of degeneracy. . . . Here are two others, negro children, 3 and 4 years old, respectively. . . . They show defects in the formation of the face—the upper part of the nose is sunken, the eyes are too far apart, the lower lip protrudes abnormally, the forehead bulges as in the case of the three Italian children.'" In Dr. Gordon's incisive inspection, underclass Italian American and African American children are more similar than different. Their real or imagined racial differences were mere effects of pigmentation that could not conceal from the "science of physical psychology" that these children of the underworld urban slums were predisposed to crime, a predisposition which cut across ethnic and racial bloodlines. In most cases, the children "yield readily to surgery," though physical labor was the needed remedy, the doctors explained, for the most "abnormally immoral." Space and race together created "a criminal of the monstrous type." Fear about urban crime and racial decline were inflated into a new category of person, the grotesque child, the creature from the slums.

One did not have to look too closely to see that these anxieties were an attempt to make sense of, perhaps even dissect, and at the same time to conceal, structural changes in the economy that produced indigent surplus populations in urban areas. The faces of the poor were a ruptural site within the culture. They were a site where the clash between economic transformation and traditional ideas of morality, family life, and citizenship were most apparent, were getting worked out, and in some cases, corrected, reverse engineered. And yet the socioeconomic underpinnings of this rupture were obfuscated by an expert discourse that not only moralized poverty but criminalized and pathologized it, as well. In short, the underclass was not found or passively received or empirically verified by this discourse, but was actively constructed, patched together in Frankensteinian fashion by this discourse's preconceptions about environment and heredity.

For Dr. Benjamin C. Marsh, the secretary of the Pennsylvania Society to Protect Children from Cruelty, poverty and vagrancy were crimes that medicine alone could diagnose and treat. His medical studies on the congenital and environmental determinants of deviancy, one is not entirely surprised to learn, involved the observation of homeless men while slumming disguised as a tramp when he was in medical school. "There was only one sure way to do this," Marsh revealed, "and that was to become a 'homeless man' myself." "In this capacity I penetrated the slums of several cities in Pennsylvania. . . . I went to New York," he continued, "and became familiar with the same conditions there, and then to London. . . . I was thrown into contact with the child-life of the poor and criminal classes, especially the newsboys. It was a strange experience, and rich in just the kind of material for which I was seeking." Marsh's "wandering investigations" for "material" among the poor led directly to crime prevention and potentially even to the renewal of the workforce through a surgically induced assimilation that turned "monstrous" immigrant children into workers and citizens. The *Times*' report began by asking about one child, "Had he been made normal in body, through surgical means, would he have turned out to be the moral monster that he is in the criminal annals of this city?" and ended with Dr. Gordon's confident appraisal of another: "I believe that we may make a useful citizen of him by giving him plenty of physical labor and keeping him in a favorable environment."

Moving on Down: Jacob Riis and Henry James in the Lower East Side

Turn-of-the-century slumming narratives were instrumental in framing and circulating sociological, criminological, and biomedical understandings of the underclass to a lay audience. Jacob Riis's extraordinarily influential reformist exposé *How the Other Half Lives* advanced this work by marrying the narrative drama of slumming literature to the empirical verisimilitude of the era's discourses on poverty, crime, and social deviancy. *How the Other Half Lives* is remembered as the preeminent example of Progressive muckraking, which raised the awareness of middle-class Americans to the fearful social and cultural transformations percolating in the human swamp at the city's southern tip. In bringing to light the terrible housing conditions in New York's immigrant neighborhoods, Riis's text also did much to hasten the passage of tenement reform legislation that outlawed the worst abuses by landlords. Yet even as his work improved the plight of the poor, it made them seem stranger, more foreign, and more licentious. It did so in part by framing Riis's encounters with the ethnic poor as an adventure story into the depths of New York. Riis's narrative of underworld descent is made more harrowing by an accretion of documentary evidence: photographs, illustrations, diagrams of tenements, and pages of statistics regarding immigration, population density, robbery, and vagrancy. Riis brings both forms of argumentation—empirical support and high-stakes narrative drama—together so as to organize and consolidate middle-class sentiment regarding the social ills created by the brutal environment of the tenement, the ubiquitous four- to six-story structure that consisted typically of a front building that "measured 25 feet by 50 . . . separated by a 25-square-foot court" from a rear building that was "25 feet square."[68]

An immigrant himself, Riis's transition from the countryside of Denmark to the bustling streets of New York was a rough one. Riis himself was for a spell homeless, at about the same time that Dr. Benjamin Marsh was playing a homeless man for his "wandering investigations" in New York and London. Steady work finally came for Riis at the *New York Tribune*, where he served as a police reporter. Armed with a pen and recently invented flash-cube technology for his camera, Riis sought to change the face of the city, if not, like Drs. Gordon, Butcher, and Marsh, the actual faces in the city. New York by gaslight had been replaced by New York by flash-cube, as the stunned and startled looks of the poor in Riis's photographs attest. One procedure for Riis was to push open the doors of dark tenement apartments and quickly snap pictures of the residents who looked back in confusion at the explosion of light. Riis changed the city by this means and others. He led the charge for housing reform, slum clearance, and greater police intervention into the domestic and public architectures of New York—tenement apartments, lodging houses, saloons, and back alleys—where the immigrant poor lived and socialized and died in unprecedented numbers.

Though concerned with the "fate of those who were underneath" the "half that was on top," from its first page to its last the target audience of *How the Other Half Lives*, was in fact the middle class (5). As the phrasing of its title reveals, middle-class Americans were assumed to be geographically distanced and under-informed about the social menace brewing south of them. Riis initiates his inquiry with an opening sentence that might have been plucked from a fairytale: "Long ago it was said that 'one half of the world does not know how the other half lives'" (5). But he immediately makes clear that while such ignorance may have been common once upon a time, it no longer is, thanks in measure—he predicts—to his own work. "There came a time," he writes, "when the discomfort and crowding below were so great, and the consequent upheavals so violent, that it was no longer an easy thing to do, and then the upper half fell to inquiring what was the matter" (5). "Information on the subject has been accumulating rapidly since," his own text a compilation of such "information" collected out of the fear that class violence might erupt as it had in the disastrous Draft Riots of 1863 (5). The fear of a brewing social revolution, not the amelioration of poverty, Riis implies, is his true subject. *How the Other Half Lives* thus opens by reawakening a nightmare of collective unrest and by auguring the possibility of future "crimes against property" by those without property, and ends by ominously reminding the reader of the militancy of the underworld poor and working class: "The sea of a mighty population, held in galling fetters, heaves uneasily in the tenements" (5, 218).

Riis's distressing portrait of the "Nether Half" tempers the sympathy it musters (191). The tenements are, he asserts, as Ingersoll would the following year, "nurseries of pauperism and crime that fill our jails and police courts" and breeding grounds that radicalize the poor and the working class (6). They have thrown off "a scum of forty thousand human wrecks to the island asylums and workhouses year by year," have "turned out in the last eight years a round half million beggars to prey upon our charities," have given birth to "a standing army of ten thousand tramps with all that that implies," and "above all, they touch the family life with deadly moral contagion" (6). In *How the Other Half Lives*, "deadly moral contagion" was thoroughly politicized and seeded anxieties over social unrest that, like a virus, might spread uptown. One and a quarter million people in New York were tenement dwellers in 1890, Riis estimated, which amounted to "a proletariat ready and able to avenge the wrongs of their crowds" (17, 204). Riis leaves the reader unsure as to whether it is better to liberate the poor or to keep them enfettered.

How the Other Half Lives stoked class fears over social upheaval by warning that the other half might in a disorienting inversion of the social order become the "half that was on top" (5). Remaking the space of the Lower East Side through new land uses and new laws legislating tenement construction was, for Riis, the only way to stymie disorder. For Riis, slum clearance was a form of social disciplining and a form of moral reformation that substituted for the actual reformation of economic and spatial injustice. Riis made his case partly through hard facts, but he made his most direct appeals to an enlightened public by incorporating the armchair traveler into his narrative, bringing him or her along for the ride down into the city's musty and congested spaces on an underworld slumming tour that is the narrative backbone of the text. In 1893, Edward Martin surveyed the Lower East Side for *Harper's*, and recommended that for those who value "new sensations and suggestions, the East Side is an amazingly rich field," adding "the contemplation of the poor [is] a relief after the contemplation of the rich."[69] For Martin, the slumming tour was the mechanism for revitalizing the attenuated, overly civilized middle-class subject and the means to a rapprochement between the upper- and underworlds, an attitude which was, as we will see, not terribly different from James's own. For Riis's slummer, however, "relief" was to be found not in a rapprochement but in realizing just how deep the chasm was between the two halves of the city.

Early in *How the Other Half Lives*, Riis takes the position of an usher on a voyage into the ethnic underworld: "Down below Chatham Square, in the old Fourth Ward, where the cradle of the tenement stood, we shall find New York's Other Half at home," he writes, and then step-by-step guides the reader "down the winding slope of Cherry Street" (26). The narrative unfolds like a fin-de-siècle urban travel guide, especially at moments when Riis points out noteworthy details ("This one, with its shabby front and poorly patched roof"), passes judgment ("These people are not fit to live in a nice home"), reflects ("It was here the mortality rose during the last great cholera epidemic to [an] unprecedented rate"), and predicts the future ("The evolution is gradual, keeping step with the increasing shabbiness of his clothes and corresponding loss of self-respect, until he reaches the bottom in 'the Bend'") (27, 29, 31, 64). In prose that is meant to move the reader both emotionally and physically, static description is turned into a series of moving images: "Here comes a pleasure party, as gay as any on the avenue, though the carry-all is an ash-cart" (36). All the while, Riis locates his middle-class reader with geographical precision ("we stroll along Madison Street"), so that the narrow alleys and ramshackle architecture of immigrant New York become increasingly knowable and the excursion becomes a reproducible experience that the reader can recreate on his or her own (36). While Ingersoll strongly recommends that slummers in the underworld hire a private detective, Riis insists that "there is no public street where the stranger may not go safely by day and by night, provided he knows how to mind his own business and is sober" (26). In chapter after chapter—"Chinatown," "Jewtown," and "The Down Town Back-Alleys"—*How the Other Half Lives* maps out the poor neighborhoods of the "nether life," "a vast human pig-sty," in desperate need of "moral and physical regeneration" (46, 146, 147).

The narrative tour in *How the Other Half Lives* represents social marginality in spatial terms. This representation is at once ideological (a conceptual realm where the underclass could be quarantined) and empirical (a verifiably low topographical space where they physically resided). The degraded social status of the poor was apparent in how the tenement spatially reproduced and compounded abjection at the microlevel of daily life. In late nineteenth-century New York, the poor often resided in pitch-black interior rooms with no windows whatsoever, referred to by Riis as "unventilated and fever-breeding structure[s]," or in cellars, "many of them below tide-water" (12, 17). In fact, much of New York's so-called ethnic underworld lived and slept in underground spaces. The tenement had "two subterranean levels, both fully inhabited: basements . . . lay partly above the ground" while "cellars [were] completely submerged, airless, and lightless," Luc Sante writes in his history of the Lower East Side.[70] "Cellars were the lowest rung of habitation," he continues, and in "1864 there were 15,224" of them, though only "211 were passed by the Board of Health" inspection that was conducted five years later.[71]

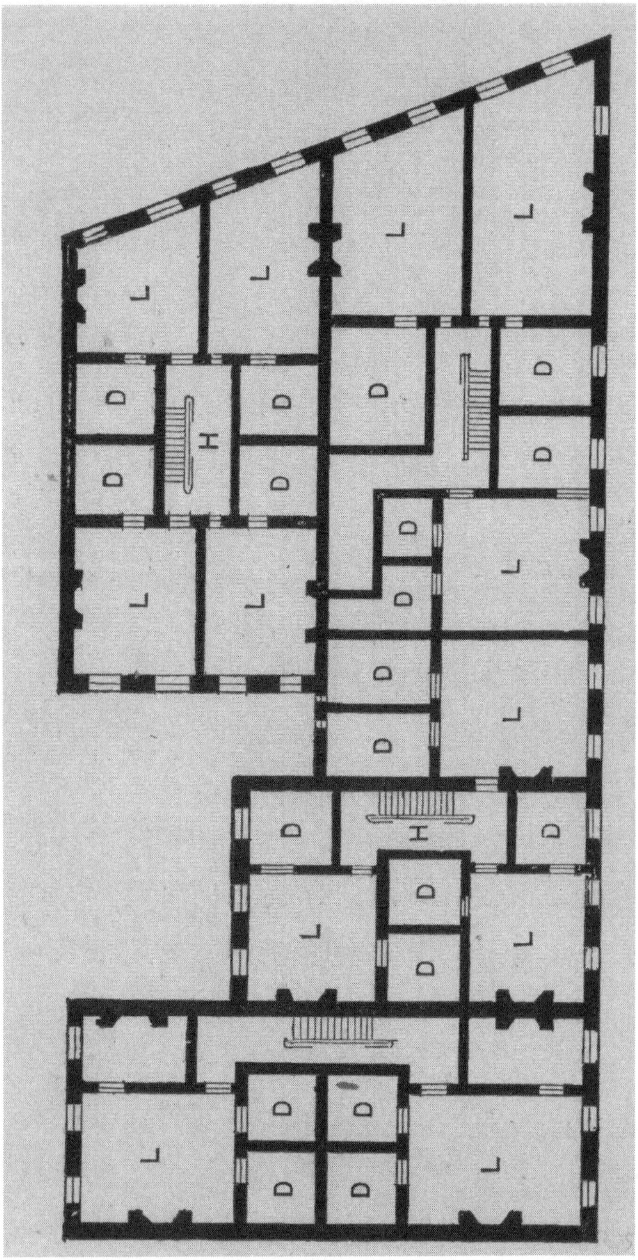

FIGURE 6. "Floorplan of Tenement of 1863." Jacob A. Riis Collection, the Museum of the City of New York. D equals rooms without natural light.

FIGURE 7. "Two officials of the New York City Tenement House Department inspect a basement living room, ca. 1900." Courtesy the Still Picture Branch of the National Archives and Records Administration.

"Thousands were living in cellars," Riis himself proclaimed in 1890, but worse off still were men and women without permanent housing who slept on floors and cots in subterranean hostelries for pennies a night, or at a table in "some foul cellar dive," or, as was sometimes the case, for free in the basement of police stations (14, 119).

Riis publicized the existence of the city's underground population and simultaneously argued that their ghettoization was both fitting and needed to be rectified. His text cut both ways. The destitute inhabitants of the city were, in Riis's estimation, "cave-dwellers" hardly worthy of life on the surface (17). Lending credence to an emerging discourse of environmental determinism that theorized that urban space molded one's character, he asserted that in many instances "the tenants themselves, who had sunk, after a generation of unavailing protest, to the level of their surroundings . . . were at last content to remain there" (17). "That is the one thing that is the matter with the slum—it makes its own heredity," Riis later argued in *The Peril and Preservation of the Home* (1903).[72] When the Tenement-House Act of 1867 was passed—which required one toilet per twenty occupants, ordered the reporting of infectious disease, and banned all dark rooms by requiring external or internal windows in rooms used for sleeping—Riis remarked that "the police had to drag the tenants out by force" (17).

In attending to a situation that could no longer be ignored, the reforms inspired by Riis, such as the 1901 Tenement Housing Act's requirements for improved ventilation, courtyards, and one toilet for every two families, bettered the lives of many. It is also true that the new requirements raised the cost of tenement construction and refurbishment. Such laws displaced onto the streets some of the poor, who turned, as many before them had, to cheaper, temporary, and often more dangerous accommodations. Many undoubtedly turned to trash picking in order to survive. *How the Other Half Lives* presents middle-class readers with the stomach-churning spectacle of a population treated as waste engaged for work in an early form of waste treatment. The rag-pickers sort out "the bones, rags, tin cans and other waste," Riis writes, "that are found in the ashes and form the staples of their trade and their sources of revenue" (42–44).

For those who refused to rifle through garbage for food, clothing, or for items to sell, Riis notes the possibility of a life of crime in an underworld that was often literally underground. Downtown is home to an "army of homeless boys"—pickpockets and beggars—who avoid arrest through "lots of secret passages and short cuts no one else ever found," including chutes and slides under the sidewalks that lead to boiler rooms and subcellars (149, 150). Riis tells also of the fanciful escape routes of the Swamp Angels, a gang of thieves in the Lower East Side, who use the tunnels and sewers to flee from the police and "as a storehouse for their plunder," a detail that momentarily turns Riis's sobering book into a childhood adventure story (32). In "these enormous tunnels . . . a man may walk upright the full distance of the block and into the Cherry Street sewer—if he likes the fun and is not afraid of rats," Riis remarks, adding "Could their grimy walls speak, the big canals might tell many a startling tale" (32). Fortunately, for Riis, such places have been closed off. One of the "first improvements" to the area, he observes, was "the putting in of a kind of sewer-grating" (32). Crime could be controlled by sealing the excremental spaces that New York's most foul residents had commandeered, the "voice" of their hidden city locked up.

Political scientist Richard Foglesong sees the emergence of the discipline of urban planning in Progressive America as the inauguration of new procedures for spatial control. Urban planning endeavored to make cities socially legible by reorganizing public infrastructures, private dwellings, and streets. Riis's work did much to advance this goal, resulting in welcome changes for those who could afford the more expensive new apartments. Foglesong contends that while outwardly late nineteenth-century housing reform sought to improve the lives of the poor, it was also initiated with other goals in mind: first, to stymie the spread of disease to middle-class areas, and second, to pacify the poor and the working class so as to stave off political insurrection. "In all, the housing ordinances of the late 1800s and early 1900s," he posits, "were less a response to the needs of the poor than to the perceived threats—political, sanitary, and social—to the larger community of allowing those needs to go unmet."[73]

Advocates of housing reform did not seek government housing (which would have hinted at creeping socialism) or charity for "the Nether Half": "any charity scheme merely turns [the needy] into a pauper," wrote Riis in *How the Other Half Lives* (191, 201). Instead, they sought new legislation that would work in concert with business to clear congested zones of the city through demolition and through modest improvements in tenement construction. "The business of housing the poor, if it is to amount to anything, must be business," Riis maintained, putting his faith in the market that had created the disaster and in the possible social improvement that would come from living in homes that were "*sufficiently separate, decent, and desirable to afford*" (5, 201). Better homes made better people, Riis implied. On the business side, the aim was to level some of the extreme differences produced by uneven development by allowing for new capital reinvestments: land reclamation and new construction.[74] Urban planning, along with housing reform, petitioned for cityspace that was readable and in which social delinquency would be more difficult to conceal. And it pressed for a remining of urban space that would be both affordable and profitable on multiple levels.

Slumming narratives of the 1890s aided and abetted this goal. They cleared a pathway through the city for their audience of armchair travelers, would-be slummers, and citizen reformers, even as they presented them with an image of the city as impossibly convoluted space. *How the Other Half Lives* went further in this aim. It incorporated both the slumming narrative and the protocols of a quantitative urban sociology that turned the baffling city into "information" that could be studied (5). It wedded the literary construct of the underworld to the social formation of the underclass so as to successfully petition for reforms that would open up and clear out underworld slums—which would, paradoxically, help bring the ethnic slumming tour to its logical demise.

For its part, Frank Moss's slumming narrative argued for the continued existence of the slum, finding in it economies of density that allowed for efficient social monitoring. If the slums of Five Points, Moss calculates, "were broken up into groups and scattered through the cities of our land it would necessitate the doubling of their police forces."[75] It is a sentiment that Riis sometimes shared, especially when he addressed the question of what should be done with the underworld criminal poor who could not be rehabilitated into the fabric of American society. "The under world holds in rigorous bondage every unfortunate or miscreant who has once 'served time,'" and there was nothing in *How the Other Half Lives* that suggested they should be released (195). For "the better class of tenement dwellers," he proposed a "'clean and comfortable home'" in the city, one where "moral and physical redemption" might take hold (7, 199, 205). It was, Riis admitted, the best solution "in the absence of suburban outlets for the crowding masses" (204). The reorganization of existing urban space in the city would be a win-win situation. It would give the working class the semblance of a lower middle-class life that was defined, in part, by the quality of the property in which they lived. And it would ease the conscience of the "half that was on top" by allowing them to believe that industrial capitalism could work for the benefit of almost everyone, that the best really could be made of a "bad bargain" (6). Near the conclusion, Riis surveys the progress to this end: "Two years ago a hundred thousand people burrowed in these inhuman dens; but some have been torn down since. Their number will decrease steadily until they shall have become a bad tradition of a heedless past" (199).

The final narrative that I would like to consider is Henry James's travelogue *The American Scene*, which tells of James's return to New York after "nearly a quarter of a century" of living in England (3). Upon initial consideration, James's rich and difficult text may appear to have little in common with the grubby slumming literature written by Ingersoll, Moss, and Riis. But *The American Scene* should be understood as a component of a broad middle- and upper-class project to cognitively and textually remap the industrial city from the bottom up by descending into its unofficial, subterranean spaces.[76] What makes *The American Scene* an important contributor to the era's slumming literature is the fact that it simultaneously participates in and calls into question two decades of slumming narratives that looked to the Lower East Side's underworld for clues to understanding the massive social, economic, and spatial restructuring that was upending life in urban America. *The American Scene* covers James's travels from New England all the way down to Florida, but almost half of the text concerns New York alone. A significant portion of James's commentary on greater New York City is dedicated to his visit to the Lower East Side. James's journey, we will see, demonstrates *The American Scene*'s investment in slumming literature's conventions and rhetoric, even as the text destabilizes many of slumming literature's ideologies and fears. In the crowded confines of ethnic New York, James is flexibly and generously attuned to the rhythms and meanings of lower-class life in a way that Ingersoll, Moss, and Riis were not. He goes slumming among the underworld denizens only to expose the very idea of the underworld as nothing more than an "imposture" (149). It is not a separate world—and it's certainly not sinister. James contends that what his contemporaries imagined as an underworld is very much a part of the world of New York that was undergoing social and physical revolutions at all levels of society.

By the first decade of the twentieth century, the competitive-industrial city was evolving toward a new urban form. This emergent spatiality was the corporate-monopoly city, and it was distinguished by an increased concentration and centralization of capital in large corporations, an increasingly vertical architecture, the dislocation of industrial production from the urban center to emerging satellite cites, and the movement of a new class of managers, supervisors, and other professionals out to the suburbs. Early in *The American Scene*, James remarks upon the portentous signs of this new architecture's modern alienations: "The multitudinous sky-scrapers standing up to the view . . . like extravagant pins in a cushion already overplanted" have "no uses save the commercial" and they "never begin to speak to you" (60, 61). The growth of "these giants of the mere market" correlated with what James saw as a reification of social and personal life (61). In the modern city, life is becoming so commoditized that citizens themselves were reduced to "property" (104). The increased sense of "the living unit's property in himself [is] becoming more and more merely such a property as may consist with a relation to properties overwhelmingly greater," James comments (104). Surprisingly, it turns out that the vibrant, stimulation-filled milieu of the ethnic poor would be James's antidote to the calcified life that he saw hardening all around him in the city.

The Lower East Side stood in the shadows of these "extravagant pins" that had been stuck in the ground since James had left in the 1880s. And when James traveled down there, he experienced, like slummers before him, competing reactions—curiosity, attraction, repulsion, bewilderment. Against the protestations of his brother William—who in a 1903 letter of "unmixed" advice urged him to stay clear of the mixed "Eastern cities" for there "you will inevitably be subjected [to] . . . the sort of physical loathing with which many features of our national life will inspire you"—James came anyway.[77] He responded that he was returning to New York for "the Shocks in general," for to "simply and supinely to shrink—on mere grounds of general fear and encouraged shockability—has to me all the air of giving up, chucking away without a struggle, the one chance that remains to me in life of anything that can be called a *movement*."[78] Given a pervasive cultural fetishization of poor and working-class life as more natural, spontaneous, and free, as well as more corrupt and contagious, one of the primary and constant enticements for going down was the promise of authentic experience. The "private fascination" with the ethnic poor, Christopher Mele proposes, "may have mitigated an otherwise restless and colorless bourgeois existence."[79] Worries over "encroaching overcivilization," Mark Pittenger adds, led to the truism that "raw, unmediated vitality was both the gift and the curse of those excluded from respectable, middle-class life."[80] Such sentiments surely inform James's desperate bravado and cultural voyeurism, his desire to break out of his own shell. For the aging novelist, slumming, even with all of its lurid connotations and ideological baggage, was his "one chance" at "*movement*."

James's tour was along paths that were already well tramped by others, most famously Jacob Riis. But to distinguish his account from those that had come before, James's opened *The American Scene* with a prefatory rebuttal that implicitly was directed at the appendices of charts and statistics in *How the Other Half Lives*. He claims that his account will provide no useful "information" (4). For James, "information" reifies and abstracts experience, draining from it its noteworthy texture and freezing its movement, granulating it into consumable statistics that have little relation to the geographically and temporally localized human exchanges that James so highly values. At the outset, he states: "There would be a thousand matters—matters already the theme of prodigious reports and statistics—as to which I should have no sense whatever, and as to information about which my record would accordingly stand naked and unashamed. It should unfailingly be proved against me that my opportunity had found me incapable of information, incapable alike of receiving and of imparting it; for then, and then only, would it be clearly enough attested that I *had* cared and understood" (4). It is a declaration that distances James from the quantitative epistemology of turn-of-the-century urban sociology, whose scientific rationalism is structured upon a clear distinction between the expert and his or her subject, and distances James too from popular accounts of the social underworld that reinforced the irremediable difference between the middle-class day-tripper and those who are the object of his penetrating gaze.

The American Scene's extended account of New York begins with James's approach to "the terrible town" through the harbor in a heightened state of intellectual and sensory receptivity, an "open[ness] to corruption by almost any large view of an intensity of life" (57, 58). James speaks here of "a kind of fluidity of appreciation" that in the synaesthetic world of "the serried, bristling city" causes one to "vibrate," to move in tune mentally and corporeally with a stimulating and unpredictable milieu (3, 5, 6). James's work responds to and helps construct a multisensory, polymorphous geography that is tactile, visual, and aural, and which, it is important to note, smudges the distance between the city and its observer. The diction that frames James's entry into the city—"naked and unashamed," "vibrate," "open to corruption"—has an erotic subtextual resonance that is in keeping with urban travel literature in which the city is filled with mysteries to be penetrated and laid bare. But in *The American Scene* James is the one who is "naked," "unashamed," and "open to corruption," and the entire city—not just its designated immoral regions—is a seductress.

Soon enough, James overhears "a voice of the air" that calls out to would-be moralists and implicitly accuses them of hypocrisy (83). While "walk[ing] the streets," he hears "the voice" address, saying: "'it's all very well to 'criticize,' but you distinctly take an interest and are the victim of your interest, be the grounds of your perversity what they will. You can't escape from it, and don't you see that this, precisely, is what *makes* an adventure for you (an adventure, I admit, as with some strident, battered, questionable beauty, truly some 'bold bad' charmer), of almost any odd stroll, or waste[d] half-hour, or other promiscuous passage, that results for you in an impression?" (82, 83). In the nineteenth century, "interest" was not only a term for credit and finance, but was a coded way of talking about prostitution. In this instance, the imagined city-as-prostitute is not mere "property," but a voice that speaks back with gusto. Startlingly, though, we see that James's point of view ("I admit") is actually nested within and indistinguishable from the voice of the "questionable beauty." Where others flee from her for fear of being corrupted (or arrested), James gives himself over to her, treats her as a muse, explaining that "there was enough about her, at all events, to conduce to that distinct cultivation of her company for which the contemplative stroll . . . was but another name" (84). Though a moment of fancy, what is striking here is not that James listens to her siren song, but that he imagines himself as her. The streetwalker is James himself, who is "walk[ing] the streets" not as a piece of property but as a living, desiring agent searching, as he wrote in 1903, for a "possible exotic experience" that he could convert into "vivid and solid *material*" for *The American Scene*.[81]

The American Scene narrates James's flânerie through the prestigious locales of uptown Manhattan—the Metropolitan Club, Central Park, the Plaza, the Metropolitan Museum of Art. James describes what he finds there as a "whole costly uptown demonstration" that smells of "individual loneliness," and he concludes that upper Manhattan holds little magnetic pull for him (120). In contradistinction to the fundamental emptiness that James experiences in the established milieus of Manhattan is "the terrible little Ellis Island," where James, as he watches the newest Americans at their point of entry, expresses both an anxiety over and desire for cross-cultural exchanges (66). For him, the future faces of a new America register an "alienism unmistakable, alienism undisguised and unashamed" (95). At first glance, James seems to characterize the immigrants pouring into New York as irremediably different and perhaps incapable of being woven into the warp and woof of the nation. But on closer inspection, we see that James's diction echoes his own condition upon his return to New York—standing "naked and unashamed" before the city—thus suggesting that the difference between those he sees on Ellis Island and how he sees himself may be narrower than first imagined. The modern mania for precise and stable categorization is on full display on Ellis Island, as new immigrants are, James notes, processed like livestock: "they stand appealing and waiting, marshalled, herded, divided, subdivided, sorted, sifted, searched, fumigated . . . an intendedly 'scientific' feeding of the mill" (66). Turn-of-the-century sociological studies asserted that this population constituted a separate subhumanity. James, instead, posits "alienism" as a temporary, labile category, not an essential or static one. He sees a process of becoming—"the evolution of the oncoming citizen"—rather than a state of being, a fluidity that makes possible surprising forms of identification (97). Such fluidity flows both ways: after twenty-plus years in Europe, James is also an alien. He tellingly and poignantly asks "Which is the American . . . which is *not* the alien . . . where does one put a finger on the dividing line" (95)?

For Riis, "the boundary line"—or perhaps in the end it is just as accurate to say, the new frontier line—between the American and the Indian "savage"-turned-immigrant-alien "lies . . . in the tenements" (5, 6).

When James crossed that putative barrier into the Lower East Side for, as he says, a "'look in,'" he did so with the Yiddish playwright Jacob Gordin at his side, rather than with a guide from outside the community or a moonlighting police officer (149). Rather than a prescribed path, he declares that he will "let each of them [his walks] take its way with me as it would" (89). James's foray through New York as "an inquiring stranger," let us be clear, is made possible by his unmistakable racial, gender, and class privilege. As an extraordinarily wealthy and famous American, James had the leisure to stroll through the city and to take in its cultural and ethnic sites in ways that many of those who were the object of his gaze simply did not. Yet despite these conditions (or perhaps because of them), he resists the impulse to master and clarify the city, to turn into information, or conversely, to turn into a lurid spectacle, a bit of all-too-easy visual entertainment for the effete aristocrat.

If we can think of Progressive-era discourses of underclass urban life as empirical and theoretical grids that ordered and managed the city, then we might think of James's text as written, in part, as a rejection of such an effort. *The American Scene*'s notoriously convoluted, looping, and digressive syntax—which takes its way with the reader as it would—is homologous to the overgrown, crowded city streets themselves. Such formal choices are evidence enough of the umbrage James takes with the cultural imperative for absolute social legibility, the sorting, sifting, and subdividing that he witnessed at Ellis Island. One finds evidence, too, in James's own responses to the city that are qualitatively different from the cramped possessive individualism and racial essentialisms of Ingersoll, Moss, and Riis. James was not always successful in the task he set himself, but in *The American Scene* he endeavors to suspend judgment on what he sees in order to make himself subject to the irrepressible immediacy of the city's ceaseless stimulations, its unending shocks. For James, this was a necessary precondition for understanding the modern metropolitan experience. He tours the city with a negative capability that comes with a "surrendered consciousness" that finds "relief not in the least in any direct satisfaction or solution, but absolutely in that blest general drop of the immediate need of conclusions" (89, 92, 93). If the "relief" that Edward Martin found among the poor was a kind of respite, for James it was something quite different: a strenuous suspension of prejudice and an active search for questions, not answers. What *The American Scene* presented to readers was a personal engagement with the city, especially its lower topographies, which did not seek to impose a set of a priori assumptions about ethnicity, class, crime, poverty, or space. Nor did it seek either, it must be admitted, to solve problems (as did *How the Other Half Lives*) that clustered around these issues.

James's immediate response to life in "the dark, foul, stifling Ghettos" evinces a curiosity about what he might discover and a defensiveness about his own act of staring (101). James uses the language of spatial duality to characterize his descent down "tunnel-like avenues" beneath "the 'Elevated,'" through the streets of "the dense Yiddish quarter" into the Bowery to watch theater, and into "a large semi-subterranean establishment, a beer-cellar" (96, 99, 149, 150). The latter establishments were where the most socially abject populations congregated—the "homeless and hopeless in their utter wretchedness," in Riis's words (61).[82] To be sure, James's "look in" and look under carries as well dominant presuppositions about the life of the underworld poor. In a parallel to Chalmers's description of homeless men, James comments how the area's residents possess "a slow, brooding gravity, a dim calculation of bearings" (97). But even as *The American Scene* makes such assertions, it undercuts its own basis for doing so. Even as it borrows slumming literature's tropes and logic, James's book declares that the underworld is more imagined than real. "Our successive stations were in no case of the 'seamy' order, an inquiry into seaminess having been unanimously pronounced futile," James asserts, distancing himself from the tawdry slummers who came before him (104). And later he underscores the point: "It was definitely not, the question, of any gaping view of the policed underworld—unanimously pronounced an imposture" (149).

James's denials are perhaps too strident, revealing his anxiety about participating in the popular but unseemly activity of slumming. *The American Scene* is a complexly unstable text that refuses to resolve its competing claims into a unified stance. As soon as James makes one assertion or one declaration, he has moved onto another. Even as he asserts the underclass's "slow, brooding gravity," he offers counter impressions of hyperstimulation, lively energy, and stunning overcrowding in which "individual loneliness" is impossible: every "doorstep, pavement, curbstone, gutter, roadway" in the Lower East Side is used, he observes, "for overflow" (100). Underclass life in *The American Scene* is imagined as exceptionally fecund. And its spatial marginalization is treated as a pretext for human creativity, vitality, and ingenuity. Instead of "dead manhood," James pays witness to the sexual vigor of the ethnic poor, itself another common stereotype. Thus we see that despite assurances of no abiding interest in a "gaping view" of "the 'seamy' order," *The American Scene* is enthralled by the Jew's purported seminal potency. "A great swarming . . . had begun to thicken, infinitely, as soon as we had crossed to the East side," James writes (100). "At every step" he is more deeply immersed in "the signs and sounds, immitigable, unmistakable, of a Jewry that had burst all bounds" (100). "The children swarmed above all—here was multiplication with a vengeance," he notes, labeling this as evidence of the "Hebrew conquest of New York" (100, 101). In moments such as this, *The American Scene* gives voice to a white middle-class panic regarding the birthrates of new immigrants, which portend a future non-WASP hegemony that has already conquered parts of the city. James expresses these sentiments and he allows his conflicted responses—his repulsion and attraction—to what he pays witness to without consolidating or simplifying his reactions for himself or his reader.

In one moment he imagines the tenement as an "organized cage," distastefully describing it as "a little world of bars and perches and swings for human squirrels and monkeys," even calling it a "charming little structure" (102). In the next instant, he contemplates "the presiding genius of the district," the capacity of its residents to make do within the geographies they do not own (102). They flourish in the "city of redemption," James remarks, a phrase that rejects the popular characterization of New York as a modern version of Dante's Hell (102). At the same time, James's repugnant metaphor for the tenement as a cage for human animals—"the analogy is irresistible"—seemingly divulges his investment in an architecture of social control that dehumanizes the poor (102). One does not wish to excuse James for voicing prejudices that were all too common in the era. But something beyond simple typecasting is at work here. In this ugly moment and throughout *The American Scene*, it is the irrepressible, uncontainable life of lower New York that is underscored, rather than its association with disease, immorality, crime, and death. On the subject of the human misery caused by the tenement, James veers far from Riis, perhaps too far in the other direction: "On my asking to what latent vice it owed its stigma," he says, "I was asked in return if it didn't sufficiently pay for its name by harbouring some five-and-twenty families" (102, 103). James responds, "But this, exactly, was the way it testified—this circumstance of the simultaneous enjoyment by five-and-twenty families, on 'tenement' lines, of conditions so little sordid, so highly 'evolved'" (103). One moment the tenement poor are "human monkeys," the next they are the measure of human advancement and evolution.

To underscore the "simultaneous enjoyment" of tenement life is a breathtaking disavowal of the punishing material realities that James overlooks. One wishes James had responded differently. Social, spatial, and economic injustice are far removed from James's central preoccupations. What interests him is the aesthetic character of life in dense urban spaces where ethnic differences abut against each other in ways that spark interesting, inspiring frissons that make their way into his own writing. If there is a political edge to James's account of the slums of New York, it is in how *The American Scene* attempts to offset the image of the underworld as a nursery of crime and social deviancy that geographically condenses poverty and desperation.[83] James argues instead that it compounds pleasure, multiplying the instances of human sociability by spatially compressing them. "The gratifications, the aspirations of the 'poor,' as expressed in the shops" and the jostling streets, James states, "denoted a new style of poverty" (103). This "new style of poverty" is not one of economic misery but one in which "every man and woman . . . throbs in the larger harmony" (103). *The American Scene* makes the same argument for the semi-subterranean beer cellar James visits, where everyone and everything is "sociably squeezed together" (150). Throughout his book, James partakes in his own form of social surveillance, which is made more efficient by a debased architecture that crowds together "a collection of extraordinarily equivocal types of consumers" that is "luridly strong" (150). He muses: "There always comes up, at view of the 'low' physiognomy shown in conditions that denotes a measure of impunity and ease, the question . . . of the forms of ability *consistent* with lowness; the question of the quality of intellect, the subtlety of character, the mastery of the art of life, with which the extremity of baseness may yet be associated" (150).

We need not explain away or make excuses for James when his characterizations of lower-class ethnic life bristle against our twenty-first-century sensibilities. His language, though troubling, is mild in its context. What is more important to recognize in our endeavor to understand the social meanings of the urban underworld at the turn of the century is how *The American Scene* offered an appraisal of urban life that stood apart from its peers, even as it relied on some of the dominant tropes circulating in the popular and expert literatures on space, ethnicity, and poverty. Close scrutiny of James's text reveals his refusal to pathologize and criminalize the life of the underworld poor. We see that for James, "lowness" is a geographic marker, not a genetic one. We see his recognition of the "forms of ability" is by necessity honed through the experience of spatial marginalization and by the small, everyday acts of appropriation by the city's impoverished citizens. James envisions—romantically perhaps—a makeshift urban culture of the poor in the process of formation, "a new style of poverty" that makes "art of life."

The American Scene petitions for an understanding of the slum as a richly textured space, one that is directly lived, the domain of inhabitants and users in which one's social being and culture are materialized. Henri Lefebvre called such spaces "representational," describing them as fluid and dynamic and defined by "encounter, assembly, simultaneity."[84] Densely built urban spaces that are the home of history, religion, and nonsanctioned forms of intimacy embody, Lefebvre noted, a complex symbolism, "sometimes coded, sometimes not, linked to the clandestine or underground side of social life."[85] *The American Scene* attempts to turn the "underground side of social life" into physical sensation, rather than abstracting it into mere "information." Though at times James's text represents slum life as an urban tableau vivant staged for his viewing pleasure, we should remember that *The American Scene* presents James not only as a voyeur but also as a participant and an exemplar. James's work argues for a mode of engagement with the city's underground geographies in which "your detachment" combines with "your proximity," in which you "surrender to impressions," resulting in a "relation to New York as, in that manner, almost inexpressibly intimate," and hence making for "daily sensation" (7, 88, 89). The "enjoyment of a real relation with the subject," he contends, is derived from the synaesthetic fluidity of life in condensed urban terrains, which make one a subject of the city, rather than a subject to the city, if one can suspend an "immediate need of conclusions" for the direct apperception of "the signs and sounds" (89, 93, 100).

The decade of the 1890s witnessed a proliferation of slumming literature, from urban travel guides that advocated a form of thrill-seeking entertainment, which doubled as moral surveillance, to Progressive housing-reform literature that appealed to the self-interest of middle-class readers by raising their fears with their consciences. These narratives descended into the social and physical underworlds of the city at a time when the city was undergoing a structural transformation that would alter the geographical anatomy of urban America. The slumming literature of the period created an ideological map of the competitive-industrial city, in which the strange mores of the underworld were exposed in a manner that claimed to verify empirically through firsthand observation what many already suspected: the multiplication of disease, crime, and destabilizing sexual and familial eccentricity. In this sense, the slumming narratives were, in James's phrase, in "immediate need of conclusions," and what they concluded was the superiority of white, middle-class home life that was housed in an architecture, as Riis wrote, that was "*sufficiently separate* [and] *decent*" (5).

From his visit to Ellis Island, James surmises of America's new immigrants, "We must go . . . *more* than half-way to meet them; which is all the difference, for us, between possession and dispossession" (67). The slumming literature that set the groundwork for James's flânerie also went "*more* than half-way," venturing into the neighborhoods of the downtown lumpenproletariat in an exercise of freedom of mobility, but retreating just as swiftly. The slumming narrative was predicated on the geographical segregation of populations by class. Its very existence was evidence for spatial divisions within the city that separated the rich from the poor. While the slumming narrative connected two points in social, physical, and imaginative space—an upperworld to an underworld—it did so in a manner that deduced that these worlds were irrevocably different.

For a turn-of-the-century readership, *The American Scene* attempted to tell a different story. For James the concept of a social underworld was a bourgeois fantasy and a barrier that reinforced divisions that he wished to bridge through a mode of intimate engagement. While Riis sought moral and physical regeneration of the poor, Henry James at sixty-one seemed in search of his own regeneration. When Riis's Progressive theories of environmental hereditism naturalized racial and ethnic difference, James opted to stress the "art of life" and what de Certeau would one day call the "'art of practice'" (67).[86] As cityspace in the first decades of the twentieth century was reshaped by the emergence of large corporate entities, new skyscrapers, and assembly-line production, city life was to become more fragmented, more filled with the alienations of class, race, and ethnicity than ever before. The American underworld would not disappear in these ensuing years, but would evolve in ways that reflected new social anxieties and in ways that would make the "mastery of art of life" and the "art of practice" even more urgent (150).

2 / Degenerate Sex and the City: The Underworlds of New York and Paris in the Work of Djuna Barnes and Claude McKay, 1910s–1930s

In a remarkable but overlooked interview in 1918 with the top law enforcement officer in New York City, Commissioner Richard Enright, Djuna Barnes, writing for *New York Sun Magazine*, made this stunning admission: "some of the nicest people I know are either potential or real criminals," and then noticing that Enright had not taken the bait, Barnes reiterated right before the interview was over, "I have a lot of friends, as I before said, who are either potential criminals or criminals."[1] Barnes's unnamed "criminal" friends were the gays and lesbians who were part of her social milieu in Greenwich Village in the 1910s, where she resided and worked as a journalist before relocating in 1920 to a similar community of American expatriate sexual dissidents on Paris's Left Bank, whose lives she memorialized in her novel *Nightwood* (1936).

As would soon be reported in the *New York Times*, Commissioner Enright, it turns out, was on the cusp of leading a full-blown crackdown on the Village as part of a campaign to stamp out "depraved tastes" in what was termed the "new underworld" of New York.[2] He promised to make the neighborhood "unattractive to the sightseer," by driving out the slumming parties and tour operators, whom Enright labeled "parasites" for the way they profited from the scandalous nightlife that had become synonymous with the Village."[3] And he promised (or was it a threat?) to return the Village "to its previous status as a respectable residential and business neighborhood," back to its mid to late nineteenth-century status as a genteel urban backwater before the likes of Barnes and her friends took up residence.[4] Enright's crackdown, of course, was not intended to protect the district's nascent gay and lesbian community from the prying eyes of unseemly voyeurs. It turns out, the police department was stepping up its prosecution of "parasites" and those they preyed upon, the short-haired women and long-haired men that slummers often came to gawk at. As upper-middle-class professionals began relocating to the Village en masse, Enright, through his clean-up campaign, was trying to make them feel at home.

But these were not the topics of Barnes's interview which, oddly enough, begins by discussing Enright's reading habits and his possession of "the largest Voltairean library" (296). When it had clearly veered off subject and into more dangerous territory, the interview was cut off quickly, with Enright breaking out in a fit of uncomfortable and almost inexplicable laughter as Barnes, apparently, sat silently relishing her minor triumph. In the exchange between the police commissioner of America's largest city and a young queer writer barely eking out a living by writing occasional pieces for the popular press, much more was being communicated than was spoken or acknowledged. To make sense of Barnes's interview (and, it turns out, almost all of her journalism), one has to read between the lines and listen to the silences. Barnes, as she so often would, was playing a game of hide-and-seek that frustrated those who wanted to police or exploit the city's "new underworld."

To understand how and why the ethnic underworld of the 1890s was replaced by a new sexual underworld in Greenwich Village in the 1910s, and then with a racial underworld in Harlem a decade later, requires that we back up a bit and set the scene for the city's swiftly changing immoral geographies. As I illustrated in chapter 1, urban American literature and culture in the last decade of the nineteenth century and the first decade of the twentieth actively constructed an American underworld among the immigrant poor—the lumpenproletariat of trash-pickers, tramps, prostitutes, and underemployed tenement dwellers—as a way of understanding ethnic difference, poverty, assimilation, and crime, the major issues of the time. Urban travelogues, reform-mined exposés, and government-sponsored inquiries into the origins of crime spotlighted the social underworld in the densely built spaces of the Lower East Side's Jewish and Chinese communities, the area just south and east of the Village. By the 1910s the Lower East Side seemed to be losing its grip on the urban imagination. Ernest Ingersoll's 1891 claim that the "great business houses are rising year by year" in lower Manhattan and that "even the devil is being ousted from all this evil part of town" had largely come true.[5] No less a figure than Henry James had in 1907 pronounced the Lower East Side's "policed underworld . . . an imposture."[6] Even Djuna Barnes herself, on a slumming excursion into Chinatown in 1913, would declare "China has given up serving the devil and is serving America" (125). The district, she was quick to observe, had "lost . . . its opium joints, its dens and its terrors, its color and its revelry" that had once made it an exotic and erotic site for many uptown and out-of-town thrill seekers (125, 127). "There is no Chinatown," Barnes concluded, a phrase she repeats three times like a death knell (124, 125, 130). It was just another downtown neighborhood with a "flat tone and a flat surface," a monotonous collection of cheap restaurants and standardized retail establishments that bear witness to a modern market economy's ability to level differences to the common denominator of money (125). When everything is "flat"—when what you see is what you get—there is no space, Barnes suggested, for something so unusual as an underworld.

Beginning with the 1910s, the trope of the underworld was reimagined in American culture. In short, it was sexualized and eroticized. Like an ideological coagulant, the underworld of the early decades of the twentieth century helped gel a disparate mix of emergent anxieties pertaining to the changing nature of sexual life in the city. These ranged from fears over the loosening of Victorian-era prohibitions on sexuality, to the popularization with the middle class of working-class dancehalls, saloons, and speakeasies, to the altered racial composition of the city with the mass migration of African Americans to the North to take part in an industrializing economy. In the 1910s, the fear of a "new underworld" was one means by which social anxieties were luridly melted together and localized in dangerous and degenerate city spaces where everything wrong with modern life seemed to exist. It was fitting, then, that urban American literature and culture would look to the two neighborhoods where these fears were most publicly played out: Greenwich Village, the first "gay enclave . . . to take shape in a predominantly middle-class (albeit bohemian) milieu," and Harlem, a formerly white, middle-class commuter district that within a decade experienced a population sea change that transformed it into the most populous African American neighborhood in the country, a black city within the city.[7]

The story of these changes and the new spatial Others they created is the story of this chapter's neighborhoods. And it is part of a larger story about the geographic ascriptions of sexual and racial identity that I want to tell through Djuna Barnes, the modernist writer who for much of her long life resided in Greenwich Village, and Claude McKay, the Jamaican-born writer whose home, to draw on the title of his most famous novel, was

Harlem. Literary scholars and historians have tended to treat separately the bohemian milieu in Greenwich Village and the cultural flowering of the Harlem Renaissance. But the crisscrossing flows of people and capital across greater New York, America, and in truth the world intertwined these two cultural developments and these two geographies. They were inextricably linked, as well, with the Lower East Side and Paris's Left Bank. Many American bohemians in Paris (including Barnes herself) had migrated there in the 1920s from the Village, and as Christine Stansell records, Village bohemians—envious of the supposed raw vitality of ethnic and proletarian work and life—were among the first to traipse through the Lower East Side a decade before.[8] Italians in the Lower East Side reversed the favor by moving to Greenwich Village, much to the chagrin of upper-middle-class professionals who had followed the bohemians to this piece of prized real estate.

In the midst of all of these dizzying shifts, the face of the underworld changed, first in the 1910s, and then again in the 1920s. Unlike the underworld of the 1890s, the "new underworld" became the locus of a geographically delimited sexual subcommunity in the Village and then of a new racialized class formation, known as the black underclass, in Harlem. The underworld—a trope found again and again in early twentieth-century writings—was a way of making these real-and-imagined territorial cultures visible by constituting them as criminal, socially disruptive, and morally licentious. The queer writers Barnes and McKay reject these aspersions, though they do not lodge simple protests in the name of victimization and oppression. Barnes's Greenwich Village journalism from the 1910s, her Paris-based, underworld narrative *Nightwood* from the 1930s, and McKay's scandalously dirty novel of black lowlife, *Home to Harlem*, published in 1928, track the morphing demography and geography of the underworld as they repossess, deconstruct, and ultimately redefine this bitter epithet.

In this chapter, I understand the spatial significances of the term "underworld" by accounting for the geographic forces that constructed, regulated, and quarantined sexual and racial populations that did not meet normative prescriptions for personhood in American culture of the early decades of the twentieth century.[9] The geographic matrices which built the very spaces that Barnes and McKay inhabited were multiple and overlapping. They included the City Practical urban planning movement (1910s–1930s); the institution of zoning ordinances in New York in 1916; the emergence of a new nighttime leisure economy in the Village and Harlem; campaigns by civic reform societies and the New York Police

Department to prosecute queer subcultural practices in both neighborhoods; the renewed enforcement of urban racial segregation in the 1910s and 1920s; the heated gentrification struggles in the Village between Italians, gays and lesbians, and upper-middle-class professionals; and in Harlem the conflicts between whites and blacks, and between the black bourgeoisie and their poorer counterparts. What we will see is that an investigation of the social meanings of the so-called sexual and racial underworlds from the 1910s to the 1930s reveals important knowledge about how sexual and racial identities are geographically instantiated and how the meanings of those identities, as well as the spaces they inhabit, are contested in the modern city.

Not unexpectedly, the change in the putative underworld's location and demographics transpired as the city itself was being remodeled by new flows of migrant black labor, by new manufacturing technologies that changed the way people worked, and by the greater geographic polarization of wealth with the emergence of a class of corporate managers and supervisors. These changes ushered into being a new urban form that geographers term the corporate-monopoly city. To the extent that New York's social demographics were altered at the start of the new century, its physical spaces were also reorganized, dug up, and zoned by the recently codified discipline of urban planning which, among other goals, sought to eliminate the wasteful inefficiencies and disruptions of nonnormative sexual, racial, and lower-class communities. Urban planning initiated new methods of spatial and social control in an effort to produce a modern city that was legible and stable. In contradistinction to the panoptic, abstract, and implicitly (and at times explicitly) heterosexual spatiality of urban planners, Barnes and McKay textually constructed a secretive city of queer desire and pleasure. They resisted those efforts to discipline the city for the "great business houses" by underscoring instead its erotic possibilities. In Barnes and McKay, the racialized, sexualized, and gendered nature of urban space—cafés, underground bars and speakeasies, blues clubs, brothels, gambling dens, and public toilets—is always foregrounded, and the relays between bodies and architectures create frictions that rub the city's dominant powers the wrong way.

Among Barnes's numerous articles, I concentrate on four devoted to Greenwich Village—"The Last Petit Souper," "Greenwich Village as It Is," "Becoming Intimate with the Bohemians," and "How the Villagers Amuse Themselves," and look at how they articulate from an insider's perspective a clandestine queer subculture. Her newspaper reports form a protective shield to the exfoliating glare of an urban discourse that demanded absolute legibility of bodies and spaces. They were a way in which she both revealed and concealed her Village community. Reading Barnes's articles today can be a puzzling experience. Her evasive and wry style, her elaborate metaphors, and figures of speech, for instance, have led Scott Herring to declare at the outset of his strong reading of these pieces, "I cannot tell for certain" whether or not she gives "the real thing" or merely simulates it.[10] Most scholars of Barnes's work have avoided the problem by avoiding her journalism altogether.[11]

To get at the heart of these time-bound articles, we need to reconstruct a historical and geographic context around them that shows that they are intimately connected to core issues of urban land use, the geographic construction of sexual subjectivity, gentrification, and the street-level policing of gays and lesbians. Stansell rightly observes that while "the Village's reputation for unconventionality and sexual experimentation made it a mecca for gay people across the country . . . in the teens, mentions of gay and lesbian sexuality were heavily coded."[12] Through the tactic of coded signification, Barnes repeatedly alludes to but declines to name her gay and lesbian sub-rosa community. It is by this means that she safeguards it from the slummers and sightseers who voyeuristically traipsed through the new nighttime pleasure spaces that had sprouted up in the Village seemingly overnight.

Had Barnes even wished to pen a frank defense of the Village's sexual underworld, it would have been impermissible in print journalism in the 1910s. *Nightwood* is such a defense, but on another soil. *Nightwood* maps the underworld of queer Americans in Paris in explicit sexual and geographical detail. It dramatizes the quotidian, mythic, sordid, pained, and erotic histories of specific urban micro-geographies in the years before the civic clean-up campaign of Paris's great urban planner Georges-Eugène Haussmann, when, as Barnes writes, "nature had its way up to the knees."[13] And it charts the city's spaces in the years after Haussmann's wrecking and rebuilding crew, when an imperiled and nomadic queer underworld reclaims parts of the twentieth-century city. We find her characters dwelling in the underbelly of modern capitalist geography—pissoirs, slums, and seaports—in ways that produce new forms of interconnection. Barnes's queers remake an emerging urban discourse of sexual pathology and cultural degeneration, which endeavored to bring so-called submerged populations into view in ways that advanced modern clean-up campaigns. Barnes's novel inverts the language of this urban discourse by putting it to use in the service of erotic talk.

When the underworld shifted locations and meanings from the 1910s to the 1920s, it moved from the pleasure zones of Greenwich Village cafés and clubs to Harlem's jazz and blues venues, brothels, dancehalls, and illegal gambling parlors. To track this development, we can turn to the writings of Claude McKay. As Barnes would do for Paris in *Nightwood*, McKay would do for black New York in *Home to Harlem*: he charts its underworld social geographies out of a commitment to depicting the intimate relations of poor and working-class African Americans. Like Barnes, McKay dramatizes how geography—from the places one resides to the places one socializes—constructs one's identity. He does so by reflecting upon the efforts of the black poor to live and survive in the midst of racial segregation, white exploitation, and violence. Accordingly, McKay turns to the trope of the underworld, which in the white urban imagination of the 1920s was synonymous with racial primitivism, the idea that poor African Americans were closer to nature, spontaneous, and culturally inferior. McKay peels back this denigrating label to expose the class realities it hides. The underworld of black primitivism, it turns out, is simply the world of black workers who are out on the town having some fun. Racial primitivism is everywhere in McKay's novel; it's just that it does not mean what white slummers overrunning the neighborhood think it means. If Chinatown has been reduced to a "flat tone and a flat surface," Harlem, McKay writes, still has its few remaining "depths and secret places."[14] In these "secret places," McKay unabashedly showcases a joyous, even primal, underworld. The primitivism he puts on display, however, does not confirm white fantasies of black corporeal excess. Far from it. McKay's black underworld resists and rebukes white economic exploitation and racial voyeurism. It promotes an alternative set of values—sharing, love, sexual desire—as a means, McKay writes, of rising above one's narrow "commercial instincts" in a time when the city was struggling to reconcile the practicalities of business with a new world of pleasure (108).

"Below Bohemia": Zoning, New Urban Amusements, and Djuna Barnes in the Era of the City Practical

As chapter 1 documented, 1890 was an exceptional year in U.S. urban culture. Nearly as momentous in the changes it initiated in the life and culture of cities was the year 1909. "The year 1909 represented a turning point in the history of planning," Robert Foglesong declares.[15] By the end of the first decade of the twentieth century, urban sociological studies and urban planning initiatives strongly argued that U.S. cities were increasingly unmanageable spaces in the grip of crime, poverty, and vice. Urban sociologists and planners responded to two decades of brisk urbanization, economic recessions, and massive demographic shifts by urgently theorizing and implementing a new set of scientific procedures for administering city space. These procedures were rapidly unveiled in 1909 and would continue to shape and regulate urban life for decades to come.

Let me give some sense of 1909's importance for cities. In 1909 the first class in the United States on urban planning was taught at Harvard.[16] That same year, Benjamin Marsh's *Introduction to City Planning* was published, in which he implored cities to actively control peripheral development that was resulting in an unruly sprawl of slums, ethnic enclaves, factories, and suburbs.[17] Daniel Burnham's *The Plan of Chicago*, also published in 1909, fretted about "the chaos incident to rapid growth, and especially to the influx of people of many nationalities without common traditions or habits of life"[18] Burnham's vision of a "well-ordered and convenient city" was not confined to Chicago, but was enacted across urban America in 1909.[19] The year marked the first national conference on city planning, which called for the reorganization of urban space around the values of economy, regularity, and efficiency.[20] And finally, in 1909 the constitutionality of height restrictions for buildings was upheld, granting a legal stamp of approval to the scientific management of space, the means to a new urban spatial economy that through various measures would attempt to bring the city to order through the rational allocation of resources and through the disciplining of potentially disruptive populations.

As a discipline, urban planning arose in response to the corporate-monopoly city's complex new spatiality that was created in part, first, by the advent of assembly-line production (Ford's first plant using this technology opened in 1909), which required larger manufacturing sites that were often located on the edge of the city; second, by increasing class and racial segregation; and third, by the targeted redevelopment of downtown districts, such as Greenwich Village, which had become both a center of commercial nightlife and a burgeoning working-class ethnic enclave.[21] As urban life became more fragmented, planning was one tool for making sense of the puzzle pieces. The theories and policies of expert-led urban management that began to coalesce in 1909 were consolidated under the program of the City Practical movement. City Practical planners and architects envisioned a monofunctionalist city akin to a gigantic depot and distributing apparatus for sorting and circulating people and products. Just as Frederick Taylor's scientific theories of time management raised industrial efficiency by eliminating wasted movement, City Practical experts posited that cityspace itself could be rationally organized to facilitate the efficient circulation of labor and capital.[22] In Manhattan specifically, massive City Practical projects—new highway construction, street widening, the extension of subway and light-rail lines, the separation of commercial and residential areas, and slum clearance—left an indelible mark on the social and physical geography of a changing New York. This emergent discipline was formulated in line with Enlightenment principles of reason, empiricism, and objectivity, which when applied to the study and supervision of the city supposedly resulted in social progress that served the general public. But from its very beginnings, urban planning was also a political activity that advanced a probusiness agenda that reorganized the city through the disinterested rhetoric of scientific rationality. The City Practical movement remade urban geography and shaped a new urban social order to suit the demands of modern capitalism. The class dynamics of these changes were clear when George Ford, a leading City Practical architect, lobbied for planning "which will appeal to the businessman, and to the manufacturer as sane and reasonable."[23]

A central measure for managing urban growth and controlling disorderly neighborhoods were City Practical zoning ordinances, which spread across the United States in the 1920s. These ordinances enacted a spatial and mathematical formulation of power by mapping, gridding, and compartmentalizing the city from a top-down perspective. By its very logic, zoning created geographical divisions and unequally valued spaces by demarcating slums, vice districts, and middle-class residential areas. It created differential land uses by dividing manufacturing districts from residential ones in a manner that was "sane and reasonable" to some and regulative and oppressive to others. City residents who do not meet normative prescriptions of sexual or racial personhood historically have tended to live in the midst of the city's most polluted and impoverished geographies. But this hardly has been an accident of history. The first comprehensive zoning ordinance in New York City was instituted, not surprisingly, in Greenwich Village under the auspices of safeguarding middle-class property in the declining neighborhood. It restricted heavy manufacturing to poorer areas in lower Manhattan or on the waterfront, where industrial runoff could easily drain into the rivers. From day one, the control of urban space through zoning was an exercise of authority over the city's effluvia, its marginalized communities. Zoning's purpose, as early twentieth-century planner Frank Koester bluntly stated, was "the segregation in suitable districts of the different classes of the population."[24] In the process of creating seemingly objective and neutral economic distinctions by land use—some zones for commercial activity and others for private dwellings—zoning inscribed and reinforced the city's uneven geographies of race, class, and sexuality.

But zoning was not the only new trend on the block. The institution of zoning as a modern form of urban management coincided exactly, and perhaps not unexpectedly, with an unprecedented expansion of erotically charged commercialized leisure, a major source of cultural panic and one of the main reasons that the "new underworld" in the 1910s was so heavily sexualized in the pent-up urban imagination. A pleasure industry of cabarets, nightclubs, dancehalls, and jazz bars increasingly seemed on display in New York's Times Square and Greenwich Village, and soon enough in Harlem as well. Such urban amusements had been the pursuit of the working class, but when they were increasingly favored by the middle class with money to spend and energy to burn, the moral alarm in the culture began to sound. Lewis Erenberg argues in *Steppin' Out* (1981) that this development "marked a profound reorientation in American culture."[25] Mixed-sex nighttime amusements that were in 1890 considered the disreputable domain of working-class men and prostitutes had by the 1910s achieved "a legitimacy in urban life unheard of in the Victorian age."[26] Noting in particular the anti-vice Committee of Fourteen and the Chicago School of Sociology—which saw the mainstreaming of illicit entertainment as a sign of "cultural decline and urban pathology"—Erenberg writes that "the changing character of the American city . . . offered new freedoms to people who, the reformers thought, were ill prepared to handle them."[27]

Ernest Burgess, a leading researcher associated with the Chicago School of Sociology, was one of the first to translate the fear of "new freedoms" into a working theory of spatially induced deviancy. In the simplest of terms, Burgess and his colleagues, the sociologists Robert Park and Roderick McKenzie, argued that metropolitan environments were reshaping the character, the mind, and in some extreme cases, even the body of the citizenry, almost always in ways that were negative. "The great city, with its 'bright lights,' its emporiums of novelties and bargains, its palaces of amusement, its underworld of vice and crime, its risks of life and property from accident, robbery, and homicide," Burgess wrote, "has become the region of the most intense degree of adventure and danger, excitement and thrill."[28] The city was not simply the site of social transgression, but it was also an enzymatic catalyst that physically and morally broke down the fiber of the urban citizen. The city induced social transgression, as well as hosted it. "Rapid urban expansion is accompanied," he posited, "by excessive increases in disease, crime, disorder, vice, insanity and suicide, rough indexes of social disorganization," whose roots were traced to "the immigration into a metropolitan city like New York and Chicago of tens of thousands of persons annually."[29] Cut off from their rural or small-town communities in America or from overseas, their families, and their churches, new residents were overwhelmed, Burgess reasoned, with an "intensity of stimulations" that tend "inevitably to confuse and to demoralize the person."[30]

Burgess is remembered most often for his urban models, the maps he constructed in the form of bulls-eyes that tracked the expansion of the city, its different land uses and demographic shifts. As if charting the ripples from a stone dropped in a lake, Burgess followed the waves of population movements through larger and larger rings spreading out from the ground zero of a central business district from which the city's older residents were displaced by the force of new arrivals. Especially interesting for our purposes was the fact that Burgess literally put the urban underworld on the map, locating it within the "zone of deterioration," the area where the new immigrant was most in danger of being overstimulated into promiscuity, vice, or homosexuality. Of this underworld, he wrote: "Within the central business district or on an adjoining street is the 'main stem' of 'hobohemia,' the teeming Rialto of the homeless migratory man of the Middle West. In the zone of deterioration encircling the central business section are always to be found the so-called 'slums' and 'bad lands,' with their submerged region of poverty, degradation, and disease, and their underworlds of crime and vice."[31]

Burgess's zones and rings were a means of conceptually containing and encircling the underworld. But it is important to note that the zoning ordinances that sought to contain the "underworld of vice and crime" on the real world of the streets—to fix it in a certain place in the city—did not work to prohibit it. Quite the opposite was true. Zoning made the underworld's existence possible by setting aside a highly circumscribed and policed space for forms of sociability that did not meet traditional definitions. The city's underworld, hence, was built out of urban planning's binary divisions, which did not eliminate social pollutants but merely quarantined them in a diseased and contaminated ramshackle ward, a moral brownfield. The effects of such a strategy were

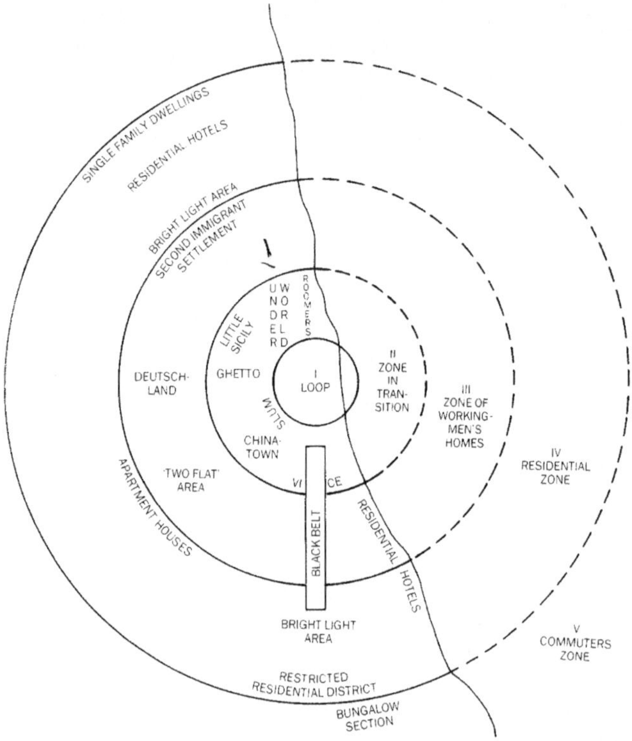

FIGURE 8. Ernest Burgess, "Urban Areas," from Robert Park, Ernest Burgess, and Roderick McKenzie, *The City* (1925). Courtesy of the University of Chicago Press.

twofold. Shunting vice and semi-illicit activities to other zones secured the social value of bourgeois morality and domestic life, while simultaneously creating imaginary playgrounds in other neighborhoods where an expanding class of managers and supervisors could frolic, a reward for the disposable incomes that increased productivity and efficiency helped to accumulate.

Although commercial nighttime leisure was a newly viable sector of the urban economy for well-heeled early twentieth-century revelers seeking escape from the stultifying life of home, it nevertheless failed to meet hegemonic prescriptions for honorable and productive conduct. Since "spatial boundaries are in part moral boundaries," it is not surprising that the popularization of tawdry forms of commercial pleasure was consistently understood in geographical terms by reformers who looked for a way to visualize and contain their anxieties over the changing mores of the time.[32] For instance, moral corruption from the mixing of classes and ethnicities in dancehalls led Belle Moskowitz, head of the Committee on Amusement Resources for Working Class Girls, to fret in 1915 over "an evil condition working upward into other strata of society."[33] There was a spatial corollary to her panicked claim. Working-class basement beer-halls actually began to physically move upward to street level in order to attract middle-class patrons: "Indulging in these pleasures," Erenberg writes, "no longer required venturing beneath the street."[34] As Richard Barry noted in a *New York Times* article on May 30, 1935, the proliferation of nighttime leisure was a mounting problem of the "upper-under-world" where "unguarded daughters of the rich" were lured into sexual and financial ruin in a hot, toxic nest of drugs, alcohol, unscrupulous men, and dancing. The *Nation* also weighed in, noting how "the spirit of caste and convention is disappearing," adding, "a little bit of the underworld, a soupçon of the half-world—there you have the modern synthesis of New York."[35]

The transformations that segregated and divided the city radically transformed the area around Greenwich Village in which Barnes lived. In the eyes of many, the economic and social decline of the Village began when a small African American community settled on its southern edge and when Italian immigrants in large numbers relocated there after moving out of the Lower East Side in the 1890s. By the first decade of the century, a new influx of single, primarily Caucasian, young men and women changed the character of the neighborhood once more. Drawn to the area's cheap rent, the new bohemian émigrés soon established in the midst of this formally upscale neighborhood a thriving arts scene, several journals about politics and writing (including *Masses* and *The Little Review*), numerous cafés and literary salons, and dozens of bars, dancehalls, and restaurants. An emerging gay and lesbian community was nested within this larger bohemian milieu that itself stood apart from the immigrant community in the Village.

From one angle, the influx of new residents set the stage for the formation of new communities and cultures, but from another angle (that of Burgess), it was the catalyst for just the opposite: "disease, crime, disorder, vice, insanity and suicide, rough indexes of social disorganization." The sociologist Caroline Ware wrote in 1935 that in the Village one saw "the thin line between the underworld and legally ordered society, the pervasive hand of the real estate interests pulling the stops on the community's life." Or as Barnes herself described the overlapping, and at times tense, divisions and juxtapositions: "satin and motorcars on this side, squalor and push carts on that."[36]

By 1910, half of the residents of the area were Italian-born. Resentment and conflict between the local Italian Catholic residents and the free-love and radical suffragist bohemians was common: "The local people regarded the Villagers," Ware writes, "as a menace to the decency of their neighborhood," and the newer residents condemned the local Italians for having too many children and for "their noise and dirt."[37] In the context of such social divisions over territory and in the context of Commissioner Enright's clean-up campaign, queer men and women in Greenwich Village and elsewhere in New York, the historian George Chauncey writes, constructed "a gay city in the midst of (and often invisible to) the normative city."[38] In the Village, they did so by inhabiting, without always being welcomed, its bohemian spaces that primarily catered to heterosexual desire. Within a few short years the Village was part of "an extensive sexual underground," "a vast secret world" throughout downtown New York.[39]

But within a few short years, its "secrets" were out and the slumming expeditions that previously had ventured down into the Lower East Side's immigrant communities were heading for Greenwich Village. Staring at class and ethnic difference was passé; the new action was with sex. Relentless sensation-monger, self-promoter, and community newspaper publisher Guido Bruno was only too happy to capitalize on his neighborhood's reputation for being "irregular," a place people went "to hide their secrets."[40] "Here it is after the war, the 'gay corner' of New York. Did you say you wished to 'tour' Greenwich Village? You must come down in the evening," Bruno enticingly and shamelessly petitioned, putting "gay corner" and "tour" in quotation marks as if winking at his reader who might be up for indulging in something more than sightseeing.[41]

The Village's status as sexually outré was instrumental to its marketability, but this reputation had to be carefully managed. Too much dirty subcultural capital limited the neighborhood's long-term appeal as a place of residence and investment, and yet too little might kill off interest. Village denizen Floyd Dell understood the situation personally: "In a magazine article I pronounced a funeral oration over the Village. For this I was bitterly reproached by a Village friend whose real-estate business was, he thought, threatened by my sinister utterances."[42] The Village, Erenberg comments, "had increasingly become a tourist area and nightlife zone for uptown whites" who came to "indulge in wilder forms of sensuality" and to "see lesbians and homosexuals on the streets."[43] One of these lesbians was Barnes, with her short coiffed hair and trademark black coat. According to biographer Phillip Herring, when Barnes moved to the Village in 1915 she was jobless (her freelance journalism work was intermittent and low-paying).[44] "Close to starvation at times," she "considered turning prostitute."[45] Barnes settled on the less respectable, ragged southern edge of Washington Square—at 42 Washington Square South, just below where Henry James was raised and just north of the Village's "Negro Alley."[46] In between one of the city's most impoverished communities and the home of one of its most prominent families, Barnes's gay and lesbian subculture would try to make a space for itself.

Barnes's articles reflect upon all of the issues I have been enumerating—changing demographics, new forms of entertainment, cultural voyeurism and secrecy—through stories about tango dancing, amusements at Coney Island, slumming in Chinatown, squatters in Manhattan, and life in Greenwich Village. And almost without fail, these articles focus on the city's socially marginalized peoples, whose low status Barnes consistently characterizes in spatial terms. For instance, a convict in Brooklyn is described by Barnes as "representative of what [we], in ignorance, think of as the lurid 'underworld" (28). Or of the sideshow performers on Coney Island, Barnes remarks, "You look down upon these people as from the top of an abyss; they are at the bottom of despair and of life" (279).

My primary interest is with Barnes's four articles on Greenwich Village, all published in 1916, the year the Zoning Commission tried to stabilize the Village's tumultuous social and spatial fluidity by setting aside central blocks for residential use. A prohibition on tenement construction had been in effect since 1910, another effort to stem the inflow of lower economic groups. With narrow, tree-lined, crooked streets that disrupted Manhattan's street grid, the Village was somewhat geographically isolated from the rest of the borough, perhaps making it an ideal location for what Chauncey termed the city's "sexual underground." But a series of major construction projects in the 1910s and 1920s—the West Side Highway, the widening of Seventh Avenue, additional subway stations along Sixth Avenue, and the opening of Holland Tunnel—made the Village "one of the most 'passed-through' and accessible sections of the city."[47] To be blunt, these City Practical projects remade the physical geography of the Village in ways that advanced the class interests of its latest wave of colonizers, the upper-middle-class professionals whose relationship with the area's mixed race, ethnic, and sexuality communities was often strained. With the help of new construction and transportation projects, the Village was opened up to the downtown financial district where many of its newest residents worked. A September 29, 1929, *New York Times* report entitled "A New New York Invades 'the Village'" announced that "The Latin Quarter . . . is no more" and observed that "once enclosed dingy alley-ways, full of dingier tenements, have been sliced off at certain corners, opened up at others." The "gay corner" was exposed in so many ways.

The physical exposure of the Village by City Practical reclamation projects coincided with targeted police harassment of public expressions of gay and lesbian sexuality. The Committee of Fourteen and the Society for the Suppression of Vice, for instance, viewed queer sexuality and prostitution as a major cultural disturbance and regularly dispatched agents to cruising areas in the Village—dancehalls on Thirteenth Street, cafés on MacDougal, bathhouses on Lafayette—in order to conduct surveillance and file reports for Enright's Police Department. Accordingly, "the number of men convicted in Manhattan for homosexual solicitation leapt from 92 in 1916 . . . to more than 750 in 1920—an eightfold increase in four years."[48] The police infiltration of spaces of queer intimacy and the City Practical's elimination of much of the Village's geographical privacy were interrelated efforts to "impose a single, hegemonic map of the city's public and private spaces on its diverse communities," one that would eradicate inefficiencies in land use by transforming "unwholesome" districts into high-value upper-middle-class neighborhoods.[49] The appeal to reason and respect was an unsubtle warning to those who had sparked the real-estate boom in the Village in the first place that their presence was no longer needed or wanted.[50]

Barnes's journalism grapples with the meaning and impact of these flows of capital and peoples on queer life. As we turn to consider her journalism in this context, we see immediately that it must negotiate a formidable formal and ideological impasse that might be framed as follows: How does one working in the medium of print journalism avoid further exposing the Village at a time when its physical and social privacy are severely compromised by police and by land developers? What we find is that even as Barnes publicizes the Village, she ironizes the district's scandalous reputation and charges with hypocrisy those who impose their morality upon it. In "Greenwich Village as It Is," a title suggesting that a real inside scoop is forthcoming, the reader finds his or her own lurid wishes unwelcomingly dispelled by Barnes who archly writes: "But where are the records that state that all malefactors and hypocrites have been caught within the limits of what we call our Bohemia? And as for crime, have all its victims been found murdered in the beds of Waverley Place and Fourth Street? Oh! out upon it, this silly repetition about the impossible people living here. Because we let you see us . . . must you play forever the part of the simpering puritan who never heard of sex relations" (227). One detects in her response unease over the publicity—"we let you see us"—to which her journalism is formally committed. Her writing constructs the Village as a real-and-imagined space that is identifiable, even mappable, according to the precise coordinates Barnes sometimes divulges to the would-be sightseer. Yet she militates against this publicity through rhetorical strategies that conceal more than they reveal. Douglas Messerli notes the degree to which "Barnes seems to go out of her way to obfuscate just that material which journalists generally employ to establish who, where, what and when—in short, the facts."[51] For Messerli, Barnes's rhetorical strategies are an expression of her idiosyncratic temperament. Barnes's penchant for obfuscation might be better understood as a response to a specific political and spatial crisis. Her rhetorical choices are freighted with political consequences, for they attempt to restore some of the sexual privacy destroyed by the City Practical and by the concomitant spike in arrests of gay men for "disorderly conduct." Barnes's journalism, we might say, assembles a queer geography and then endeavors to shield and disclaim the very geography that it makes visible.

Barnes engages in a coded, carefully managed, though uneven, portrait of subcultural queer life framed within a discourse of publicity and voyeurism. In "The Last Petit Souper (Greenwich Village in the Air—Ahem!)" she begins: "I have often been amused—perhaps because I have not looked upon them with a benign as well as a conscientious glance—to observe what are termed 'characters' going through the city and into some favorite cafe for tea" (218). Upon the "characters" she espies (are they real or imagined?), Barnes bestows the fanciful names "Vermouth, Absinthe, and Yvette—the last a girlish name" (219). "Yvette was feminine—he could not only look the part, he acted girlish in much that he did," she writes, observing that his "coat was neatly shaped, frayed but decidedly genteel" and appeared to have "what must be called skirts," beneath which his "legs swung imperially" (220, 221). Barnes's vignettes in "The Last Petit Souper" consist of these three, highly stylized gay men flouting the imperatives of productive masculinity by simply spending the day eating, drinking, and daydreaming in the café culture of the Village.

It is a subject she returns to in "How the Villagers Amuse Themselves," in which an unnamed local with a "sullied reputation" and a "manicure set" sings about finding "some yet-unconquered boy" (246, 247). Barnes's typecasting of gay male femininity carries an oblique political charge. Appreciating their soft felt hats, scarlet lips, silver canes, and long fingernails, Barnes foregrounds their beauty, frivolity, and aesthetic richness, which contrast strongly with the rest of New York. In the era of the City Practical, the city has been rendered "soulless as a department store," which only further compounds the Village as a geography of erotic fantasy both for those "characters" who lived and frequented the area and for those who looked upon its inhabitants with less than a "conscientious glance" (225). "It is not permanent, the colors will fade. It is not based on good judgment," the people who are "standing before Greenwich Village" murmur "in pitying tones" (224). "How barren and how dull becomes mere specialization," she writes, "how much do we owe to those of us who can flutter and find decorative joy in fluttering away this small allotted hour, content with color, perfume, and imported accents" (218). In effect, the Village's sexual demimonde is a cultural residuum, a quaint holdover from another era when, before the mechanization of Taylor and Ford, time could be wasted.

For Barnes, the Village's "fluttering" men pose no true threat to the cultural trends toward "mere specialization," which not only subdivided and "allotted" each moment of the working day but also each parcel of cityspace to maximize its use and profitability. What these men in all the figurative richness that she bestows on them represent is an alternative way of being in the city that did not subscribe to the dominant culture's definitions of productive manhood. The campaigns to rid parts of the city of their local textures in which they found "decorative joy" was an impossible task, since these textures were themselves an outcome of industrialization and urbanization. The "color, perfume, and imported accents" that Barnes speaks of were clung to ever more dearly as they seemed to slip into the past. But from another perspective, they did not belong to the past at all. The "imported" sights, sounds, and smells of the city were wholly modern.

The anarchic outcomes of economic transformation in the 1910s and 1920s resulted in a new exotic mix of nationalities, sexualities, and classes in Greenwich Village, people who themselves were a kind of local color for those who gazed upon them. New forms of labor and new forms of consumption made possible Barnes's "girlish" men ornamented with accessories, and they also made possible a more broadly diverse and disorienting mélange that Burnham had a few years prior fretted over.[52] Giving a quick glance down a Village street, Barnes notes "dark-eyed Italian children," "Jewish girls," "Norwegian emigrants," "a colored girl," "a Japanese servant," "beggars," and short-haired women and long-haired men (225–227). In what amounts to a verbal map for the reader—"you of the outer world"—Barnes surveys the inner world of the Village's commercial establishments known for attracting a gay and bohemian clientele, such as the basement restaurant Polly's, the bar called the Mad Hatter, and the Liberal Club salon dedicated to discussions of art, socialism, women's suffrage, and birth control (228–230, 232, 240). Modern capitalism created the conditions for the formulation of a queer commercial infrastructure—the restaurants, bars, theaters, clubs found in Barnes's writing—that simultaneously created same-sex desire and catered to it.[53] As Lillian Faderman argues specifically in regards to women: "urbanization and its relative anonymity and population abundance" were prerequisites to even "the possibility of lesbianism": "It was necessary that institutions be established where [women] could meet women."[54] "We have all that the rest of the world has in common commodities," Barnes proudly asserts, "and we have that better part: men and women with a new light flickering in their eyes" (232).

Any complete erasure of the Village's heterogeneous communities in the name of modernization and efficiency—or in the more immediate name of rising real-estate values—was an impossible task, since it was industrialization and urbanization that produced ethnic diversity and emergent forms of personhood (eroticized hybrid assemblages of sex and gender) in the first place. This didn't stop the City Practical planners from trying, nor did it put an end to the raids on gay establishments, which were all too common in the period. The logic of capitalist urban development in the first decades of the new century thus was highly contradictory. The expansion of the industrial economy drew hundreds of thousands of men and women from across the country and from across the world to New York, who were then clustered in densely built neighborhoods where emergent cultures and ways of being formed out of the clash of old traditions and new realities. At every turn, capitalism and urbanization by this process produced differences (new-fangled commodities, uneven geographies, novel forms of sociability, even new types of people). And yet, over time, these differences and new spaces were leveled out and homogenized through mandates for efficiency and legibility. The so-called sexual underworld was bound up with this logic. Barnes's Village was an outcome of agglomeration economies that generated unstable clusters of populations—"on every corner . . . a new type"—in a space marked as dirty, criminal, and degenerate (226).

In spite of, or perhaps because of, all of the pathologies heaped upon the Village (and later Harlem), the neighborhood was the subject of incredible curiosity and fascination. Looking at these "new types" was the business of slumming by groups of nighttime partygoers from outside of New York City or from uptown who would regularly troll the Village's streets and nightclubs—or stare at them from tour bus windows—in order to espy sexually risqué behavior in spaces marked as sexually Other. When Enright threatened to make the Village "unattractive to the sightseer," he was not just promising to bully the commercial operations that exploited its status into shutting down but he was also pledging to drive from the neighborhood the very communities that slummers had come to find.

What was the social meaning of such lurid inquisitiveness? In the modern, heavily zoned city, slumming in the urban underworld articulated the difference between heterosexual and homosexual practices. For thrill-seekers leaving the putatively straight and socially valorized spaces of home for a temporary descent into the queer or sexually ambiguous locales in other neighborhoods, slumming produced a body of knowledge about the erotics of urban geography at a time when modern sexuality was becoming more complex. Slumming made evident how sexual subjectivity was defined by the architecture and urban geographies in which one lived, played, or fantasized. To be sure, it did so primarily through the lens of voyeurism and exploitation. This certainly was the case for what Barnes describes as the "endless crowds of 'slummers'" through the Village whose presence she records in a humorous anecdote in "Becoming Intimate with the Bohemians": "I stood on the corner of Sixth Avenue where it runs past Greenwich Avenue one night, and as I stood there a fur-trimmed woman, heavily laden with jewels, and two lanky daughters hailed me. . . . 'Where is Greenwich Village?' she asked, and she caught her breath. 'This is it,' I answered, and I thought she was going to collapse" (237, 244). For those wealthy, naïve, and annoying outsiders who come to Barnes looking for evidence of the Village's scandalous and eccentric reputation, she shows them the Village "as it is," coyly deflating their illusions and sending them on their way.

Sometimes those who ventured into the Village to see "the 'gay corner' of New York" were themselves gay men who sought relief from claustrophobic middle-class norms in their own suburban or uptown neighborhoods, or straight men whose sexual slumming in gay clubs was more of the participant-observer variety than just pure observation. Slumming was both escapism and an escape. For Ralph Werther, it was a refuge. The son of a well-to-do family, the college-educated and transgender writer "from the best quarter of the city," Werther (a nom de plume) was a contemporary of Barnes and a fellow writer who authored two "spectacular queer self-studies" filled with "descriptions of urban underworld sex acts" in the slums of New York: the sensational memoir *Autobiography of an Androgyne* (1918) and its sequel *The Female-Impersonators* (1922).[55] Werther's autobiography was published by the professional *Medico-Legal Journal* (sadly, his only publishing outlet) as a case study in sexual pathology that was distributed by mail to doctors of sexology. It offers up a campy, yet at times psychologically and emotionally tortured portrait of his escapades from the early 1890s to 1918. Writing from within a discourse that considered him an extreme sexual curiosity, Werther confesses, his queer flânerie was almost always in the "red-light district[s] of the foreign laboring classes of the city" where he ventured for companionship and rough sex "near midnight" with "the un-Americanized laborer."[56]

The eroticization of working-class ethnics is a long-standing aspect of American sexual culture, in part because sexual commerce historically has been zoned into ethnically diverse neighborhoods. Werther's *Autobiography* makes the commingling of fetishized ethnic and sexual differences explicit. He is up-front about his preference for Italian and Irish "ruffians" who were fond of "fairies" like himself.[57] In a section of his memoir titled "My Then 'Stamping Ground,'" he relates how he often dressed as a girl and descended into the underworlds of the Lower East Side and the Village where "the immigrant element predominates," even going so far to enumerate a list of the exact streets in which the "bacchanalian madness" was at its most fervent.[58] Werther's writings preserve for history a sense of how fully developed, if still confined to the late hours of certain quarters of the city, the queer underworld in New York was before World War I. The "apparent depravity" of moonlight groggeries, "the basement of a ramshackle rear tenement," queer dancehalls, and other "pestilential places," drew him repeatedly from his "intellectual and decent community" by the sheer force of an "overpowering impulse to do what mankind regards as unspeakably low."[59] But in addition to his self-proclaimed sexual compulsion that drove him to frequent bouts of sexual slumming that eventually added up "in [his] career as a fairie [to] about eight hundred intimates," Werther also sought with certain men ("'husbands' *par excellence*") the urgent but lasting bonds of intimacy that are formed out of imperilment.[60] "Do you realize that you and I are united by a closer bond than that which unites you to your most intimate chums and pals? . . . Will you regard our association as not merely for sensuous enjoyment, but also for close friendship, and for mutual help in the trials of life?," he would poignantly ask his partners in what amounted to a de facto queer wedding ceremony.[61] "How easy it is, comparatively, for the normal man to gratify the procreative instinct!," exclaimed Werther.[62] "The 'classy,' hypocritical, and bigoted Overworld considers a bisexual as monster and outcast," he attests, "I was *driven* to a career in the democratic, frank, and liberal-minded Underworld."[63]

As Werther's experience bears out, the sexual geography of New York was split in two. In a defense of his "double life"—one uptown and one down—he was adamant that "the author was not at all to be blamed for having recourse to the slums. For me it was the only way then open to satisfy the most exacting demands of Nature."[64] It was within the divided sexual geography of the city (and within the pages of a study of sexual pathology) that he was to be "the author" of his own complex identity.

A sense of this division is felt, too, in Barnes's 1916 "How the Villagers Amuse Themselves," though it appears that Barnes's (and Werther's) downtown queer underworld was on borrowed time. In the report, Barnes writes about sexual slumming at the Village's Webster Hall, one of the nation's first modern nightclubs and a space used for society events and political gatherings. It is here that Barnes watches as a "boy in white flannels, white face, and rouged lips skipped lightly by" (250). Another transgender boy, Alexis, who has left his "shelves of Rabelais" for an evening of dancing, mourns how recent efforts to regulate nighttime leisure have made Webster Hall too clean for his tastes (250). By 1917, anti-vice societies had shut down most of the illicit establishments in white neighborhoods.[65] Those that remained were forced to present a more respectable face to the public, which they did by becoming increasingly commercialized, watered-down for a mainstream clientele. It is in this climate, Alexis laments, that "one can sit in the gutters of Manhattan and arise covered with nothing worse than the shadow of a star," or hunt through "its most corrupt sewers" and find "nothing but a lot of castoff ethics" (250). His poetic description links queer sexuality with forbidden underworld fecundity and dirty pleasure that Werther had found in abundance in years past but which seem increasingly difficult to find in the modern city, at least in commercial establishments like Webster Hall. For Barnes's Alexis, the moral and physical corruptions of queer sexuality are precisely the source of its hypnotic eroticism that has drawn him downtown to the well-publicized Village, only to discover the kinds of sexual immersions he has sought might best be appreciated in the fescennine novels of Rabelais that we are told he has left on his shelves uptown. The Village already had ceased to be the city's center of erotic transgression. "Localities and atmospheres should be let alone," Barnes declares in another article, "There are so many restaurants that have been spoiled by a line or two in a paper. We are in that same danger" (226).

The scholar Justin Edwards calls Barnes a "mystifier and demystifier" who offers conflicting responses to the spatial crisis her work negotiates.[66] In "Greenwich Village As It Is" and "Becoming Intimate with the Bohemians," Barnes maps the public spaces in which queer subcultural life was transacted, like a guidebook noting the precise addresses of some of its establishments—"at 64 West Eleventh Street," "on MacDougal Street just above the Dutch Oven" (229, 230). But more often than not, Barnes is reticent, surveying the Village from outside—names, addresses, that's all—and letting "you of the outer world" on the inside only infrequently and on her own terms. If anything, the gay dance in "How the Villagers Amuse Themselves" merely confirms her claim that there is nothing much for anyone to see here. Aware that her words will further publicize the Village and subject it to the social and geographic "dangers" of commercial exploitation, Barnes withholds information, thus enacting a logic of nonpublicity that is surprising for journalism. "In the basement is all that is naughty: spicy girls in gay smocks," Barnes is willing to say of the well-known Brevoort (234). Of the less "gay" but more socially abject underworld bar "the Hell Hole," patronized by "the sordid faces . . . of colored women and men," Barnes tells her reader that its "slit in the door" effectively warns would-be day-trippers to stay away (243). And of the "lost places" in the neighborhood—the places where the Village's gay and lesbian community really "amused themselves"—she is less forthcoming still. They exist, though exactly where will remain a mystery, so long as Barnes is writing. The gap between the underworld's material context and its cultural representations—which is to say, the gap between the daily and perhaps somewhat mundane life of gay men and women making do in the city and the fantastical sexual intrigue and oddity reported in the press—remained large, and Barnes preferred it that way. "Becoming Intimate with the Bohemians" ends with the denial of intimacy, a further spurning of the reader: "No, I shall not give them away, but I'll locate one of them. . . . It is a basement this side of Sixth Avenue. . . . This is real—this is the unknown. Even a basement has its basement, and this is one of the basements below Bohemia" (240, 241).

The social construction of the sexual underworld in the 1910s was an outcome of years of economic disinvestment and uneven development. The new queer underworld illustrated the shifting moral valences assigned to space in which some urbanites were "simpering puritans" and others had "sex relations" (227). In transgressing boundaries, slumming reinforced the association of homosexuality with a degeneracy that was reassuringly endemic to a specific locale. When new opportunities for land speculation and residential gentrification arose, the Village's queer spaces were increasingly subjected to the "remorseless enforcement of sanitary regulations" and outright police harassment.[67] Zoning ordinances and police surveillance worked to push queer life further underground, below the new "flat surface."

Barnes responds to this crisis by writing about the Village from a perspective that mediates between the "outer world" and the neighborhood she is hesitant to reveal. For Barnes, authentic queer life was contingent upon being submerged, unknowable, and away from the prying eyes of New York. Her authority as a community insider and her authority over her readers as a reporter on her community derived from her familiarity with the secret world that her readers sought and from her refusal to divulge that world to them. Ultimately the underworld—hidden below the basements of a "depraved" neighborhood—remained concealed within her prose as a means of staving off the erosion of local detail in the community she seeks to shield. Barnes inverted the late nineteenth-century slumming literature that I considered in chapter 1. Those exposés on crime and degeneracy made "real" the lurid subjects they reported. Their colonizing discourse elicited and assuaged middle-class anxieties about urban life by assuring readers that the city's criminal and ethnic underworlds were securely sequestered. Barnes, in contrast, kept the city's sexual mysteries a mystery in order to make them "real," safeguarding her marginalized neighborhood from the modern city's fatal exposures.

"A Detour of Filthiness": Sexual Slumming in *Nightwood*'s Queer City

When Barnes landed on Paris's Left Bank in 1920 on assignment for *McCall's Magazine*, her surroundings must have seemed familiar. An extensive bohemian and gay and lesbian expatriate community had put down roots in the neighborhood, establishing a salon society and a vibrant café scene that Barnes would have recognized from the Village. Paris was filled with a who's who of lesbian or bisexual writers, artists, and patrons: Natalie Barney, Gertrude Stein, Sylvia Beach, and

H. D., to name just a few.[68] Harold Stearns, author of *Civilization in the United States*, wryly commented at the time, "You could have sworn you were only in a transplanted Greenwich Village . . . except for the fact some people stubbornly persisted in talking French."[69] Feeling at home, Barnes bought an apartment on rue St.-Romain, stayed a dozen years, and became a prominent if still relatively marginal figure in the history of American modernism. She was friends with James Joyce, and no less an authority than T. S. Eliot introduced *Nightwood*, the novel that Benstock has called the ultimate "cult guide to the homosexual underground nightworld of Paris."[70] But Greenwich Village and Paris had something else in common that Stearns's quip did not mention: both had been subjected to massive spatial redevelopment, reclamation, and reorganization that directly impinged upon each district's sexual demimonde, its secret underworld.

A little more than a half century before the City Practical movement in America, Paris had been radically and famously modernized by Haussmann at the behest of Napoléon III. In his history of the built space of the underground in nineteenth-century Paris and London, David Pike remarks that Haussmann's plan was for "the total control of the city," a top-down renewal of urban space in order to purge Paris of the ills of poverty, disease, moral depravity, and revolutionary sentiment.[71] One way Haussmann envisioned that he would achieve his aim was through the construction of a modern sewer system that would address Paris's infamous sanitation problems: "The subterranean galleries, organs of the great city, would function," Haussmann wrote, "like those of the human body, without showing themselves in the light of day. . . . The secretions would take place mysteriously and would maintain the public health without troubling the proper order of the city and without spoiling its external beauty."[72] Haussmann imagined the city expunged of its physical pollutants, the daily "secretions" of urban life—the offal swept into gutters, the uncollected excrement of citizens, the garbage piled on streets—all safely, "mysteriously" shuttled away, leaving the surface world untroubled.

If Haussmann was able to dream of a properly ordered surface in which people and products, capital and labor, circulated as smoothly as "pure and fresh water," it was only because he had first dreamed of disturbing the world aboveground, tearing up the narrow streets and crowded neighborhoods of Paris and revamping them into a legible modern system.[73] "The problem," for Haussmann, according to architectural historian François Loyer, "was one of creating a hierarchical, poly-nuclear city whose successive centres were to reflect their respective roles."[74] In short, Paris needed to be "transformed into a rational city."[75] Underneath Haussmann's organic language, in which bodies and urban space were coextensive, was raw, nasty politics. His plan to remake Paris affirmed Michel de Certeau's assertion that the "rational organization" of space "must . . . repress all the physical, mental and political pollutions that would compromise it."[76] To spur economic expansion of Paris and to make the city revolution-proof, Haussmann's urban renewal program called for the wide-scale destruction of working-class apartment blocks and slum housing as well as numerous twisting, congested streets that were easily barricaded by rioters. Furthermore, the city was partitioned into twenty arrondissements to facilitate policing and tax collection. Paris's divisions geographically inscribed class, ethnic, and sexual difference, making them more visible and facilitating their management by governmental power. In Loyer's words, Haussmann's "immediate preoccupations" were "greater legibility and differentiation."[77]

Nightwood is a salvaging operation long after Haussmann has left the scene. Barnes's darkly erotic novel does not clean up after Haussmann, but seeks to dirty up the city once more by imagining it as a site of cultural, sexual, and physical decay, devolution, and degeneracy. In this regard, the ambitions of the text are twofold: to recreate the finely granulated textures, smells, and sights of a pre-Haussmannized Paris "before hygiene was introduced," and to show that even in the modernized, post-Haussmann city there remain sordid, grimy underworld enclaves where city residents amuse themselves (*Nightwood* 17). *Nightwood* achieves both of these aims through the cross-dressing, quack Doctor Matthew-Mighty-grain-of-salt-Dante-O'Connor. His breathless monologues, which are tantamount to verbal slumming tours, preserve the unofficial histories of Paris that were endangered by Haussmann, and map contemporary Paris's queer underworld where intimate practices are quarantined to hidden locales in the late hours of the night. Barnes's ideas about space, sexuality, and cleanliness, which she had begun to formulate in her journalism back in New York, thus find an expanded platform in *Nightwood*.

In both urban planning discourse and in modern sexology, there was a frequent equivalence between dirty spaces and dirty bodies, polluted geographies and polluted body parts. *Nightwood* does not deny these equivalences. Instead it plays them up, exposes them, demystifying their supposed natural linkages. Barnes's novel tracks how sexual difference is spatialized, disclosing how it is materially written into the city by zoning, and how it is discursively instantiated through theories that argue that moral and physical deterioration resulted from prolonged exposure to a hyperstimulating environment. As Dianne Chisholm cogently observes, *Nightwood* never offers a narrative of healthy, vibrant homosexuality that might counter the discourse that categorizes it as degenerate and ruinous.[78] Such a narrative would be only an inversion of the morality and ethic of productivity in the wider culture. Scott Herring argues as much when he insists that Barnes "was suspicious of prescriptive identity categories," gay or straight.[79] What Barnes's narrative does do—and this is what makes the novel such an exceptional read—is lead us downward through the city on a verbal joy ride, at each stop proffering examples of filth and sexual submission, not so that we can moralize them but so that we can see them in new ways: as sources of pleasure and erotic power.

Nightwood is a veritable freak show. In its pages we discover the underworld's denizens in full flower: transvestites, lesbians, gay men, beggars, mentally retarded children, and circus sideshow performers. We might think of *Nightwood* as a narrative analogue to the photographs of the secret world of Paris that made Barnes's contemporary Brassaï famous. With his portraits inside brothels, interracial dancehalls, and gay and lesbian bars ("temples of Sapphic love" in Paris's "Sodom and Gomorrah") he captured the "colorful faces of its underworld" before they totally disappeared.[80] Combining the documentary skills of Jacob Riis with the city-mystery writers' passion for the lurid, Brassaï carried his camera in a quest for an urban ethnography with no broader social aims than the documentation of an urban folk culture that he was certain was becoming extinct. The denizens of the underworld were, in his romanticized imagination, "the real night people," who "live at night not out of necessity, but because they want to. They belong to the world of pleasure, of love, vice, crime, drugs." Paris's urban exotica, "the secret, sinister world of mobsters, outcasts, toughs, pimps, whores, addicts, inverts," Brassaï wrote, was vanishing with "our century's mad rush."

Barnes's underworld, like Brassaï's, is racially and ethnically diverse, transnational, polymorphous, and queer in every sense of the word, but it had a staying power that Brassaï did not recognize. In Brassaï's estimation, the underworld was an entirely residual urban culture from the "most remote past." But the complete erasure of the queer and criminal lumpenproletariat in the service of a bourgeois spatial economy was impossible, because the production of degraded folk cultures itself was an expression of capital's logic of uneven development. Put another way, the city produces more and more waste even as it builds better sewers. The modern city hardly could be said to have flushed away its queer folk culture. The modern era's "infinitesimal surveillances, permanent controls, extremely meticulous orderings of space, indeterminate medical or psychological examinations" were designed, as Michel Foucault has argued, to bring deviance into view for examination, not kill it off.[81] *Nightwood*, we will see, considers how "meticulous orderings of space" partition the city into moral and immoral geographies and how "indeterminate medical or psychological examinations" endeavor to shape the human body to its insalubrious environment.

At the center of Barnes's underworld stand three Americans, the "bearded lady" Doctor O'Connor, the "born somnambule" Robin Vote, and Nora Flood, a woman with the "temperament [of] . . . an early Christian" who is pulled into their orbit (35, 51, 100). The story that *Nightwood* tells of Nora's doomed love for the promiscuous Robin is rather straightforwardly simple, but the manner in which it is told is anything but. If Barnes was trying to work out an aesthetics of privacy in her journalism by balancing innuendo with indirection, with *Nightwood* she opts for a neo-baroque semantic excess that is difficult to see through. The text's opacity is compounded by a narrative of digressions, diversions, arabesques, and false leads that leave many readers lost. The closest equivalent to this verbal impasto might be Henry James's prose in *The American Scene*. Barnes's prose style carries over into her depictions of the people that populate her novel and thus throws into relief knotted questions of how putatively aberrant subjectivities are to be categorized and made legible, a major concern of the period. In the fantastic world of *Nightwood* identity is unstable, blurred, hybrid, indeterminate; the lines between sex and gender are dissolved by men, like O'Connor, who dress as women and by young women, like Robin, who look like boys. Scott Herring argues that the "text is self-consciously antimimetic" and that it "refuses to offer readers any intelligible contribution to the sociological or psychological understanding of the modern homosexual."[82] *Nightwood*'s underworld bodies are not impossible to understand: it's not as if there is nothing to learn from them. They should be read not so much for what they reveal about queer identity as for what they tell us about urban political economy. Barnes's text reads the queer body against the grain. It finds on the queer body traces of historical and material exclusions, the scars of isolation in degraded urban geographies. These bodies with all of their visual confusions are themselves a site where the modern madness for order and for sexual normativity gets scrambled.

Nightwood registers the influence of a historical moment that applied theories of physiology and sexuality to the sanitization of urban space. In the early twentieth century, urban underworld spaces were imagined as Petri dishes that bred "physical disease [and] moral depravity," according to Henry Morgenthau, president of the inaugural conference on city planning in the United States.[83] Such sentiments had their roots in nineteenth-century European theories of cultural degeneration. The leading theorist of this discourse was Max Nordau, a journalist and physician in Paris who authored the massive tome *Degeneration* (1892). Dedicated to criminal anthropologist Cesare Lombroso, Nordau's "dear and honoured master," *Degeneration* posited that urban-centered industrialism was resulting in increased hysteria, neurasthenia, and an "increase in the number of the degenerate of all kinds."[84] Nordau fretted that "the inhabitant of a large town . . . is continually exposed to unfavorable influences which diminish his vital powers."[85] Degeneracy was physical, and could be read in "the unequal development of the two halves of the face and cranium."[86] And it was cognitive, thus heard in the voice and read on the page. In Nordau's diagnosis, the degenerate suffers from a "distracted consciousness" and "surrender[s] himself to the perpetual obfuscation of a boundless, aimless, and shoreless stream of fugitive ideas."[87] Urbanization, he pessimistically concluded, promised "sexual psychopathy of every nature": masochists will "form the majority of men, cloth[ing] themselves . . . in feminine apparel"; women will "wear men's dress"; and then, turning his sights on culture, Nordau claimed that the literature of the twentieth century will be "canal-dredging" about "submerged peoples."[88] It was as if Nordau had seen the future and it was Djuna Barnes.

Degeneration theory made sexual abjection visible by constellating signs of difference into an imaginary totality: "submerged peoples," an underworld inhabiting the lowest social, and in many cases, physical geographies. It would be a mistake to think that such theories were exposed as a product of gloomy homophobia by the more enlightened minds of the twentieth century. The idea that reordering space was coextensive with reordering the social and individual body continued to have currency well into the 1930s and beyond. Lewis Mumford, for instance, worried that in urban areas "connections between the 'respectable classes' and the underworld, by way of pleasure, amusement, and sexual release . . . undermine the morale of the body politic."[89] There was too much sex in the city, and most of it was perverse. A new adrenal gland operation that received national press coverage in the 1930s endeavored to get sex back on the straight and narrow by restoring "femininity . . . and attractiveness" in women who possessed "decidedly masculine traits."[90]

An exhaustive, thousand-page compilation of research into the queer body, *Sex Variants: A Study of Homosexual Patterns* (1941), took such experiments to greater lengths in what amounted to the most comprehensive scientific study of homosexuality in the United States.[91] Presided over by Dr. George Henry, the study recruited approximately a hundred male and female volunteers from New York City—many of whom resided in the sexual subcultures of Greenwich Village and Harlem—and asked them to testify in detail to their sexual activities in the form of first-person case histories and to submit themselves to a series of medical examinations. In addition to conducting a battery of other tests, Henry and his collaborators x-rayed the pelvises of gays and lesbians, concluding that "sex variants" possessed a different "pelvic architecture" which correlated with "psychosexual behavior" and to aberrant sexual development.[92] But more visual evidence was needed, and so in an appendix titled "The Gynaecology of Homosexuality: Illustrations and the Need for Them," Henry reviewed the work of his colleague Dr. Moench, who took records by placing "a glass plate on the vulva, and outlining the external genitals upon it in soft crayon—then tracing this outline on [a] record sheet."[93] Because Moench's method "did not embody any detail of structure," Henry was "compelled" to make use of his "own case-records . . . from life and from measurements . . . exactly to scale."[94] The concluding pages of *Sex Variants* are composed of thirty-one meticulous drawings of the vulvae, nipples, and clitorises of lesbians in various states of excitation. Doctors Moench and Henry literally wrote on top of the queer body, subjecting it to a biomedical discourse that approached pornography in its fascination with rendering sexual difference graphically and anatomically visible.

Early in *Nightwood*, Barnes lays the queer underworld body out on a table for the reader to examine. That body belongs to Nikka, "the nigger who used to fight the bear in the *Cirque de Paris*" and who is "tattooed from head to heel with all the *ameublement* of depravity" (16). Nikka's body is exhibited by O'Connor, an expert turned pervert, a "variant" of Doctor Henry. When Barnes first introduces O'Connor in the novel, he is loudly championing from the end of a table the unofficial narratives of urban culture which are composed of what the official histories, written by those who are properly credentialed, exclude, denigrate, or downplay. O'Connor says these unofficial narratives are "the stories that do not amount to much. . . . that are forgotten in spite of all man remembers . . . merely because they befell him without distinction of office or title" (15). The novel's keeper of underworld history, O'Connor proclaims, "In the acceptance of depravity the sense of the past is most fully captured," adding, "cleanliness is a form of apprehension. . . . Destiny and history are untidy; we fear memory of that disorder" (118). "In man's body are found evidences of lost needs," Barnes writes, the needs for pleasure, history, and community (52). Nikka's body bears this underhistory in its most graphic forms. It is revealing, though, that Nikka is not physically present in *Nightwood*, but rather appears in the form of an anecdotal description delivered by the doctor. In other words, he is less a person than a text. What is inscribed on his body, we are told, is a celebration of sex and filth alongside "the coping of the Hamburg house of Rothschild" and "a terse account in early monkish script—called by some people indecent, by others Gothic—of the really deplorable condition of Paris before hygiene was introduced" (17). On his backside—"just above what you mustn't mention"—flies a bird with a streamer that says "*Garde tout*!" a warning that even excrement must be kept and preserved (17).

In showing us how to read Nikka's body, Barnes, through O'Connor, shows us how we should read her novel. The braided "vine work" of his tattoos, "garlanded with rosebuds and hackwork of the devil," find their formal equivalent in Barnes's contorted, looping sentences filled with allusions to classical literature and folk customs and with sudden detours into history, science, geography, and mythology that might leave one as wonderfully lost as a visitor to Paris before Haussmann plotted it so clearly (16). Nikka's body is a legend without a map, all symbols and no road. He is Shakespeare's Othello with a penis so long that "at a stretch it spelled Desdemona" (17). To be sure, Nikka inhabits the racist caricature of black sexual prowess. But he expands this typecasting into bawdy "subterranean humor" (47). To the hygienic discourses that would declare this body obscene, Nikka's body writes back with a sneering laughter that takes pleasure and pride in dirty jokes and sex. "I asked him why all this barbarity," O'Connor says, "he answered he loved beauty and would have it about him" (17).

Barnes gathers her strange cast of characters around the garrulous O'Connor. Nora, who is in her "late twenties," is "doing advance publicity for the circus" when she meets O'Connor and Felix Volkbein (18). An effeminate Viennese Jew, Felix has come into the world without parents (his mother dies immediately after he is born) and with few notable possessions, among them two portraits of sumptuous Florentine actors that are passed off as aristocratic ancestors (7). "There were few trades that welcomed Jews," Barnes writes, so disguise and deception become strategies for survival for the "wandering" Felix who, also through the intervention of O'Connor, meets Robin in Paris in 1920 (5). Drawn to her "fluid sort of possession" (112), Felix convinces her to marry, only to be abandoned by her—"she took to going out; wandering the countryside; to train travel, to other cities" (45). Their marriage dissolves after the birth of their mentally slow child Guido. Robin then moves in with Nora, only to leave her, too, for the nightworld of Paris's queer social scene. Nora's long and anguished conversations with O'Connor about Robin comprise the remaining bulk of the text. Around this thin narrative skeleton, Barnes fleshes out an entire urban underworld perfumed with the aromatics of decay. Representatives of this world, Robin and O'Connor are Barnes's leading indicators of cultural degeneration. Robin's body "exhale[s] . . . earth-flesh, fungi, . . . captured dampness"; she smells like the underground (34). For his part, the "I'm not neurasthenic" Doctor O'Connor sleeps in "ladies underclothing" in a squalid apartment littered with piles of medical books, "a rusty pair of forceps, a broken scalpel, half a dozen odd instruments," and a "swill-pail" (33, 78, 79). "A vice district in miniature" is Scott Herring's perfect description.[95] The Doctor's vice is "bounded on the one side by the church and on the other by the court" (29). The two dominant powers that write the city's prohibitions try to fence in O'Connor, but within their "bounded" space is "the doctor's 'city,'" from which he tells the "unexpurgated" story of how the urban is divided between day and night, sacred and profane, upper and underworld (15).

Nora's effort to track down Robin sends her to O'Connor's bedside at "about three in the morning," seeking advice (78). A panicked Nora pleads to O'Connor "tell me everything you know about the night," his "favourite topic" (79, 80). What she receives instead amounts to a counterdiscourse to urban planning: he figuratively pieces together the city for her. O'Connor tells her that the city's zones are divided, but stresses that they are "related by their division" (80). "We tear up the one for the sake of the other," he says (82). Paris had been partitioned, of course, into asymmetrical, but interdependent domains. The body too, O'Connor observes, has been bifurcated into clean and unclean realms, practices, and desires, resulting in corporeal alienations that need to be healed. "A man is whole only," he declares, "when he takes into account his shadow as well as himself" (119). In his "appallingly degraded" apartment, he educates Nora by taking her through a verbal "detour of filthiness," a slumming tour not just through space, but backward in history (79, 84). "Have you thought of the night, now, in other times, in foreign countries—in Paris," he tauntingly asks (81). "I've never known it before—I thought I did, but it was not knowing at all," the "Puritan" Nora responds, quivering (51, 82). In spite of her lesbianism, Nora is deeply invested in monogamy, domesticity, and cleanliness. She is estranged from what O'Connor celebrates as "the body and the blood of ecstasy, religion and love" and so to "cure" her, to move her beyond her own internal divisions, he regresses her like a doctor applying electro-shock therapy (118).

The first step forward is in reverse as he takes her to "other times" and other spaces. The initial stop is the underworld slums of the Zone, the terrifying terrain of Montfaucon, the enormous dump and cesspit in northeast Paris where the corpses of executed criminals and the bodies of slaughtered horses were disposed and whose odor was so powerful that it regularly wafted into central Paris.[96] Its revolting "stench . . . plucked you by the nostrils and you were twenty leagues out," O'Connor recalls (81). The queer body spills over normative parameters—Nora's Robin is "a tall girl with the body of a boy," "who lives in two worlds"—and so do "the streets" of the old Zone (35, 46, 81). They "were gall high with things you wouldn't have done for a dare's sake . . . and everything gutters for miles and miles" (81).

O'Connor's stream-of-conscious monologues—a sign of his "shattered nerves," Nordau would say—have a specific pedagogical end (*Nightwood* 154). They anatomize for Nora the city and the bodies within it as part of a bristling critique of the modern fetish for order, legibility, and hygiene. The modern urban economy has no tolerance for the contradictions it generates, for the coexistence of pain and pleasure, beauty and deformity. To unmoor Nora, O'Connor asks her to think through these contradictions and to experience them bodily by descending into them. This descent is an inner bowel movement downward, an examination of the body's internal sewer system which is modeled for Nora in the guise of "the Frenchman" who "can trace himself back by his sediment, vegetable and animal, and so find himself in the odour of wine in its two travels, in and out" (84, 85). "The American," O'Connor argues, "separates the two for fear of indignities, so that the mystery is cut in every cord" (85). Against a bourgeois model of selfhood that treats the body as sealed, discrete, and impermeable, O'Connor underscores a fluid, shape-shifting model of queer identity that understands the body in all of its porosity. Open at both ends, the body is not despoiled, but merely part of the soil.

As she sits at his bedside, O'Connor pressures Nora to take into account her "shadow," but such naval gazing is of limited use if it is not a conduit for shared experience with others (119). O'Connor's verbal slumming tour thus leads Nora and the reader into a contemporary queer underworld where bodily pleasure and bodily fluids are exchanged, where hyperstimulation does not break the individual down but aggregates the social body, joining strangers in sexual contact. Frankly put, the divided city comes together in the degraded queer architectures of the city. Nora knows nothing of these spaces, but O'Connor has become intimate with them from cruising—"I haunt the *pissoirs*," "circular cottages" in the homosexual vernacular (91). Through his sexual flânerie he has mapped the underworld of queer meeting places where he has found not pain, as Nora does, but—and this is key—bliss in the transgression of constricting social codes and discourses.

Consider, for instance, O'Connor's extended parody of theories of environmental determinism and degeneration. The Doctor proclaims in an exercise of obscene storytelling that he can detect "from what district they [his lovers] come, yea, even to an *arrondissement*" by the taste of their seminal fluids (92). Relating past arguments regarding "the particular merits of one district over another for such things, of one cottage over another for such things," he questions: "'Do any of you know anything about atmosphere and sea level? Well,' I says 'sea level and atmospheric pressure and topography make all the difference in the world!' My voice cracked on the word 'difference'" (92). Here is the geographical production of sexual difference at its most base. It's as if Haussmann's spatial divisions have acclimatized citizens in the most intimate fashions. As *terroir* is to French wine, urban topography is to the semen of queer men.

But when *Nightwood* thereafter turns to public sex between women, the tone darkens. Lesbian promiscuity in the urban underworld is the source of Nora's heartache in the way that anonymous sex between men in criminally reappropriated spaces is not for O'Connor. In a scene that greatly disturbs Nora, O'Connor describes "girls . . . in the toilets at night . . . kneeling in that great secret confessional crying between tongues, the terrible excommunication" (95). In language that conjoins the figural downward damnation of the soul with the literal motion of 'going down' during oral sex, O'Connor recites what he has overheard: "May you be damned to hell! May you die standing upright! May you be damned upward! May this be damned, terrible and damned spot! May it wither into the grin of the dead, may this draw back, low riding mouth in an empty snarl of the groin!" (95). At the center of eroticism and death, Barnes depicts the city's queer lovers, who already are damned in this world as well as the next, redundantly cursing each other. Note here what Nora cannot—excommunication is secretly a pleasure: it provides the very language for lesbian sado-masochism. The discourse is turned back on itself and repurposed. For Barnes the crying in tongues at Pentecost twists into an act of cunnilingus mixed with an erotics of verbal domination reminiscent of the Marquis de Sade, Robin's favorite writer. Too much for Nora to hear, she yells "Don't—don't!" (95).

What in God's name is O'Connor doing, we might wonder? The short answer is that the Doctor is attempting to edify Nora about the material existence of the city's degraded geography and its role in constructing sexual personhood. Cruel but necessary, this edification is achieved by wearing her down—"a bitch on a high plane"—lowering her by reducing her to tears (146). Nora is defined by what has been taken from her, but, in reality she "robbed herself for everyone" (51). Which is to say, her profound sense of disenfranchisement stems not from what she has lost (namely Robin), but from her belief in ownership at all costs, her anxiety-ridden possessive individualism that frets over the loss of control. Nora believes that the only way she can secure Robin's love is by preventing her from loving others, taking sole possession of her heart instead of sharing her affection. "Die now, then you will be mine forever," she once whispered in her ear (145). As several chapter titles reveal—"Bow Down," "'The Squatter,'" "Go Down, Matthew"—*Nightwood* commits to the principle of erotic submission and debasement, which Robin enacts when she "goes down" on the floor before Nora's dog, "dragging her forelocks in the dust" (169, 170). But such an "obscene and touching" moment is beyond the pale for Nora (170).

O'Connor persists though in his method of prying Nora from her old attachments, a strategy that moves toward its climax when Nora begs him to divulge the events of the terrible night Robin's new lover Jenny "laid her eyes on Robin," stealing her away (99). Propped in bed under a blanket, O'Connor mercilessly stalls and savors the moment by announcing "I'm coming to something," then after a few more pages of tearful impatience, "it's all of a certain night that I'm coming to, that I take so long coming to it," and finally, "I'm coming by degrees to the narrative of the one particular night that makes all other nights seem like something quite decent enough" (90, 97, 99). O'Connor, we know, has in the past admitted to masturbating in the church of St. Sulpice. I submit that he is here pleasuring himself by turning Nora's sorrow into a masturbatory narrative that is largely a product of the sexual energy that it binds and sustains (99). From Nora's pain he weaves a pornographic story that he tacitly asks Nora to share in, to "come to," as a means of recouping pleasure from what has been lost, taken, or denied. Isn't this *Nightwood* in a nutshell?

O'Connor's twisting and turning "detour of filthiness" makes Nora squirm, but in the wrong way. He has tried to turn pain into ecstasy by asking Nora to exchange what was never hers to begin with—Robin—with what has been hers from the beginning—her body's pleasure. The strategy fails. Robin's radically contingent and uncontainable sexual desires take her beyond the parochialisms of city, nation, and sexual identity. She leaves a trail of lovers on her pan-European peregrinations and returns with songs "sometimes Italian, sometimes French or German, songs of the people, debased and haunting" (57). And though Barnes does not show this transnational queer underworld, we are told that Nora in an effort "to understand her" has retraced Robin's footsteps (156). "I haunted the cafés where Robin had lived her night-life; I drank with the men, I danced with the women," Nora reveals in a quick summary, adding that she has frequented the bars of "the Montparnasse quarter" and "the streets of Marseilles, the waterfront of Tangier, the *basso porto* of Naples" (143, 157). Robin's flight is an opportunity for Nora's political knowledge and a possible condition for her erotic fulfillment, neither of which, it is important to note, are realized. Connecting her with colonized and migrant queer populations, Nora's excursions hold the potential for sexual and political illumination regarding the forms of intimacy, community, and danger faced by a deterritorialized queer underworld moving between cities and across national borders. But potential knowledge of a transnational queer subculture is forestalled by her despair over her individual loss and by her inability to see beyond her own tears. For all intents and purposes, this larger world remains a blank within Barnes's text. "I have been loved . . . by something strange, and it has forgotten me," she cries, "I will find her again" (155, 156). "A broken heart have you!" O'Connor says, calling her a "fool" for "going back to find Robin" as if she is property to be reclaimed (154, 165). In the end "the people of the underworld" are not Nora's people (31).

Beneath *Nightwood*'s surface-level narrative of estranged lovers, O'Connor sees what Nora cannot: the more important story of the modern city's sexual underworld, a product of punitive morality that overlays a fragmented and unequally divided geography. The truth of sexual identity is that it is deeply imbricated within modern capitalist spatiality. In Barnes's narrative the verbal and bodily intimacies of underworld sociability never coalesce into a collectivist vision for sexual liberation or for reorganizing urban space by protocols that promote social equality or even for establishing the kind of territorial enclave that is incipient in Barnes's journalism on Greenwich Village. Instead, *Nightwood* eroticizes the city's divisions that enforce sanitary gender and sexual norms that create untold amounts of anguish. It does so not to confirm queer sexuality as etiolated (or as healthy), which is to understand sexuality within moral parameters, but to spotlight deviancy's social and material origins. "Those who love a city, in its profoundest sense, become the shame of that city, the *détraqués*, the paupers," Barnes writes, "their good is incommunicable" (52). The "difference" that "atmospheric pressure and topography make" is the sexual diversity that heteronormativity and urban planning conceal (92). "To think is to be sick," O'Connor laments (158). *Nightwood* thinks through bifurcated formulations of geographic identity so as to understand how such divisions create the framework for ruptural possibilities within a culture.

Barnes writes a narrative of the urban underworld that underscores flux, instability, and flexibility in opposition to rigid systems of thought, an opposition enacted through disruption and reterritorialization, primary tactics of the marginalized. In *Nightwood*, the terms of exclusion are the terms of shared pleasure. Its underworld of transgressive sexuality poaches the spaces of the city to formulate a critical site where the multiplication of contagious intimacies can be better understood. Back in the United States, that critical site was "Harlem . . . the Montmartre of America," and it is now to that infected and infectious black city that we turn our attention.[97]

"Harlem Is Mine": Taking Back the Night in Claude McKay's *Home to Harlem*

When Lewis Mumford warned against an "underworld . . . of pleasure [and] amusement," what he feared most was cross-class mixing in dancehalls and saloons that would lead to "promiscuous sexual intercourse"; that is, the multiplication of social and sexual exchanges that were nonproductive (such as dancing) and nonreproductive (such as prostitution and queer sex).[98] Claude McKay memorably described this potent cultural anxiety and gave it a location: "the contagious fever of Harlem" (15). *Home to Harlem* takes Mumford's underworld as the libidinal ground zero of cultural rebuilding, not decline. The novel sees the underworld as where, with an almost utopian sentiment, new human geographies are made in the name of love, sex, togetherness, and sharing. The urban planner's solution for combating these "new elements of degradation" was to disaggregate the "commercial exploitation of sexual interests" in the city, to widen as much as possible the geographical separation between "the 'respectable classes'" and "the underworld."[99] That remedy was shortsighted, and in the end it backfired badly. The crackdown on vice districts and semi-illicit nighttime economies in or adjacent to white, middle-class neighborhoods that had being going on since the 1910s scattered the sexual geography of the city, but it hardly erased it. The action merely shifted, out of Greenwich Village especially. The underworld migrated deep into Harlem, and white people simply followed.

When a cleaned-up Village no longer sated hegemonic fantasies of exotic sexuality, slumming parties set their compasses north for Harlem, and at the front of the pack were the Village bohemians themselves. "White mainstream urbanites," historian Kevin Mumford states, were just a few paces behind.[100] The two groups arrived at different destinations, different Harlems even. A "virtually all-white leisure zone" sprouted up that catered to downtown New Yorkers who wanted to get a little taste of the racial underworld within a highly commercialized and utterly unthreatening environment.[101] Cabarets such as the Cotton Club, Connie's Inn, and the Plantation Café had whites-only door policies that were enforced, in what must have been a strange scene, by black bouncers.[102] The black entertainment carried their instruments through the back door. Queer and bohemian slummers who wanted to be part of the action, rather than part of the audience, avoided these watered-down venues and sought out more clandestine scenes. As James Weldon Johnson described them in *Black Manhattan* (1930), "these seekers. . . . peep in under the more seamy side of things; they nose down into lower strata of life."[103] The refined and austere Johnson was forced to admit, "Harlem has, too, its underworld, its world of pimps and prostitutes, of gamblers and thieves, of illicit love and illicit liquor, of red sins and dark crimes."[104] His spatial metaphors were not just fanciful. Prohibition had driven much of the nighttime economy underground: the majority of speakeasies were off the map, "hidden in alleys and basements."[105] With all these Caucasians storming Harlem, the black writer Rudolph Fisher felt the neighborhood was "no longer mine but theirs."[106]

Claude McKay's bawdy novel *Home to Harlem* was one way of taking it back. "Harlem for mine!" and "Harlem is mine!" McKay's working-class protagonist exclaims in the opening pages (8, 17). *Home to Harlem* is an imaginative act of black working-class territorial repossession—a taking back of the night—in the context of white slumming and racial segregation. Where the more adventurous white libertines espied an underworld of "sins" and "crimes" in Harlem, McKay saw something

FIGURE 9. Aaron Siskind, "Cabaret Dancers, ca. 1937." Courtesy of the Museum of Contemporary Photography, the Aaron Siskind Foundation, and the Bruce Silverstein gallery.

altogether more interesting and quotidian: the black poor and working class. Readers who have slummed imaginatively in the novel's many wild cabarets and grimy brothels, buffet flats, and gambling parlors have also missed what McKay in the midst of all the ruckus was pointing out to them. The novel's black underclass got lost in the shuffle. Readers who were not titillated by the book's racial and sexual carnival tended or pretended to be shocked. Wayne Cooper remarks that "in 1928 the existence of such types of black communities, though privately acknowledged, was not publicly advertised in respectable black publications."[107]

The template for this kind of racial exposé had been set two years earlier with the scandalous novel *Nigger Heaven*, by Carl Van Vechten, the white nightlife impresario and queer patron of African-American art and literature. Van Vechten's subject was the explosive confrontation between African American middle-class cultural aspirations and what he called the "love of drums, of exciting rhythms," and "warm, sexual emotion" which were every African American's "primitive birthright."[108] With its "sociological realism" and its appended "Glossary of Negro Words and Phrases," it was a "modern guidebook" to the hoi polloi.[109] *Nigger Heaven* raised hell in Harlem. Upon reading it, W.E.B. Du Bois felt a "blow in the face" and he accused its author of exploitation and a betrayal of confidence.[110] But *Home to Harlem* was no *Nigger Heaven*. It was worse. It was worse because it was an insider job that wrecked the carefully managed public image of middle-class black life that was part of Du Bois's strategy for what he called the Talented Tenth, those members of the upper echelons of black political and cultural life who were charged with advancing the black cause in positive ways.

Du Bois's reaction? "After the dirtier parts of its filth I feel distinctly like taking a bath," he famously quipped about *Home to Harlem*, adding, McKay "has used every art and emphasis to paint drunkenness, fighting, lascivious sexual promiscuity and utter absence of restraint in as bold and as bright colors as he can."[111] Instead of taking back Harlem, McKay had given away the store. Instead of keeping quiet about what was "privately acknowledged," he fed, in Du Bois's eyes, "that prurient demand on that part of white folk for that portrayal in Negroes of that utter licentiousness which conventional civilization holds white folk back from enjoying."[112] That "prurient demand" did not hold back either: the book sold almost 50,000 copies immediately and was rushed through five printings in its first six months, making it the first bestseller of the Harlem Renaissance.

But Du Bois had gotten the novel all wrong. *Home to Harlem* is no narrative of racial or class descent for outsiders, but the story of those who call Harlem home. There is no denying the novel's unashamed investment in presenting a highly libidinal version of urban black life. "Dark dandies," "pansies," lesbians, bisexuals, straight men on the hunt for "the best pickings": these are not marginalized voices in the novel, they *are* the novel (30, 31, 35). Yet against this catalog of human types, McKay places another one. Or, to be more accurate, I should say, McKay repeatedly and consistently redescribes these same human types as types of labor. Something of its erotic charge is defused when the black underworld is re-presented, as McKay does, as "pot-wrestlers, third cooks, W.C. attendants, scrub maids, dish-washers, stevedores" (29). But one surmises that this is exactly the point. Such lists of lower and working-class occupations are enumerated at the very moments the novel indulges in racial primitivism. This is a calculated strategy, one that Du Bois entirely missed. McKay's insider account of Harlem's nightlife, we will see, demystifies the phantasm of black underworld primitivism that drew many whites to uptown to gaze upon a race considered to be naturally expressive, sexually profligate, spontaneous, and prone to deviancy. This reputed naturalness is shown to be all smoke and mirrors by the novel, which links the origins of modern primitivism to urban political economy, segregation, and to the spaces of lower- and working-class leisure. Just as Barnes's *Nightwood* does not entirely disavow queer underworld promiscuity, *Home to Harlem* does not entirely reject racially primitivist typecasting. Instead McKay's imagination puts it to use to build a clandestine black community that endeavors to stay out of the reach of white exploitation.

What I am suggesting is that in order to properly understand McKay's steamy portrait of Harlem's "low night life," we need to account for the geographic determinants and class inflections of the real-and-imagined racialized underworld in the 1920s (*Home to Harlem* 82). Racist images of black cultural nonnormativity are long-standing in American culture, but in the first decades of the twentieth century such beliefs entered the new spatial context of the highly segregated corporate-monopoly city, an urban form that filled these stereotypes with urgent fear and allure, a sign of how deeply the city was divided by race. Douglas Massey and Nancy Denton maintain that "the era of integrated living and widespread interracial contact was rapidly effaced in American cities after 1900."[113] The frequency of interracial contact declined at the same time northern cities became more racially diverse. Upwards of a million African Americans left the South under the impact of World War I, and another 800,000 to 1 million left during the 1920s, many migrating to the Northeast.[114] The result of these mass movements of people was a boiling urban crisis, at least in the minds of many planners, sociologists, and white homeowners.

The arrival of southern blacks in northern cities in unprecedented numbers spurred new methods of containing a perceived threat. To ensure the property value and moral integrity of white neighborhoods, the federal Home Owners' Loan Corporation's Residential Security Maps drew red-lines around black areas, more restrictive housing covenants were written up, and white violence along the perimeter of the new color wall spiked.[115] What was the fallout from all of these strategies? It was nothing less than a seismic population shift that signaled a wholesale failure to preserve the dream of Harlem as a white ethnic neighborhood: in the 1920s over a hundred thousand whites left, most for the suburbs, as almost ninety thousand African Americans arrived.[116]

Segregation partitioned the city by skin color. But this was only part of the story. McKay's novel of the "streets!" presents a more finely granulated portrait from behind the color line (26). It is impossible to redraw racial borders without reshuffling the boundaries of class and sexuality, a fact that McKay was well aware of. In restricting access to employment and capital, segregation was "the principal organizational feature . . . responsible for the creation of the urban underclass."[117] By severely constraining the spatial expression of class difference, segregation collapsed and concealed the multiplicity of black life when viewed from outside, leading to anxiety inside the neighborhood by middle- and upper-class African Americans who dreaded being grouped with their social inferiors simply because of a common racial heritage. About this, McKay would later comment in *Harlem: Negro Metropolis* (1940): "There is no other minority group in New York having such an extraordinary diversity of individuals of achievement and wealth who are compelled to live in the midst of the mass."[118] "Inexorably the individual is identified with the mass," he claimed, "and measured by its standards. The efforts of the Harlem élite to create an oasis of respectability within the boundaries of Aframerica is strenuous and pathetic."[119] Or as one character in *Home to Harlem* characterizes the situation: "Wese too thick together in Harlem. Wese all just lumped together without a chanst to choose and so we nacherally hate one another" (285).

I want to turn to *Home to Harlem* in order to suggest that it interrogates the geographies of class in early twentieth-century New York as a way of disrupting the cultural fantasy of a black underworld. This disruption is achieved, in part, by McKay's reinterpretation of what it means to be primitive. Set in 1919, McKay's episodic narrative through a nearly all-black, overcrowded Harlem relates the story of Jake—a semi-illiterate war deserter, longshoreman, and railroad cook—and the loves and friendships he makes while reintegrating himself into the neighborhood after two years overseas: "Harlem! Harlem! Little thicker, little darker and noisier and smellier, but Harlem just the same," Jake rhapsodizes on his return home (25). The storyline around which *Home to Harlem* is constructed is Jake's love for a prostitute named Felice whom he meets at a saloon on his first day back, but whom he loses track of the next morning when she slips away without revealing her name. Their reunion at the end brings the novel full circle, but it is what happens in the middle that matters. Jake settles in with Rose, a cabaret singer who earns extra money through prostitution. When Rose expresses a desire that Jake "beat her up a little" to prove that he was not a "sissy" but a "*ma-an* all right," he leaves her (113, 117). Visible signs of domestic abuse are a status symbol in McKay's Harlem, a proud indication that a woman's intimate life is heterosexual and patriarchal. Jake escapes to the all-male preserve of the Pennsylvania Railroad. There he befriends Ray, an upper-class, effeminate Haitian who is himself the victim of another form of violence: America's imperialist occupation of his country. When Ray sails off on a freighter at the end of part two—reversing Jake's route home by boat—Jake decides that he will make Harlem his home once more. In the closing pages of the novel he is reacquainted with Felice, now the lover of his estranged friend Zeddy. When Zeddy publicly reveals that Jake is AWOL, Jake and Felice make arrangements to leave for Chicago, another migration in a book filled with them.

This storyline is largely beside the point. Its main function is to provide a narrative space for the voices and lived architectures of the black poor and working class, both straight and queer. What Djuna Barnes once said of her "basement below Bohemia" is echoed by McKay: "This is real—this is the unknown." *Home to Harlem* is the story of Harlem told from below, below the ideological fantasies of lower-class black deviancy that circulated freely in the culture. Early twentieth-century fantasies of black sexual and cultural eccentricity are unintelligible outside of the context of segregation. By making the points of contact between whites and blacks rarer, segregation infused interracial exchanges with a fearful and erotic charge. The color line was heavily sexed because, in addition to demarcating racial difference, it also marked a so-called deteriorating zone of perversion: Harlem was New York's largest black neighborhood and its largest vice district. Roderick Ferguson remarks that the confinement of "prostitution, gambling, and drug and alcohol use to black neighborhoods" were among "the material conditions that located Harlem outside the proper boundaries of the heteropatriarchal household."[120] There are white slummers running through the pages of *Home to Harlem* in search of Harlem's local brand of racial perversion, but the novel is not for them or for their real-life counterparts. Nor is it for those whom McKay elsewhere called the "head-ossified Negro intelligentsia."[121] Unlike *Nigger Heaven*, McKay's narrative expends little energy in guiding the reader through the neighborhood. One would be ill-served in using it as a guidebook. Chapters break off abruptly. Conversations are held without dialogue tags. Instead of engaging in careful realistic description and scene setting, McKay's prose is a highly impressionistic swirl of colors. For readers looking to have their racial stereotypes confirmed or critics looking to combat those stereotypes through a highly selective portrait of black urban life, *Home to Harlem* responds simply and forthrightly, "there is no such thing as a typical Negro" (63). To make his case, McKay records the full palette of Harlem's diversity, describing African Americans as "putty-skinned," "black," "potato-yellow," "dull-black," and "heavy brown" (33).

If this debunking strategy is true, what are we to make of the fact that McKay plays the trope of the racial primitive for all it is worth? Open any page in *Home to Harlem* and you are likely to find Zeddy described as an "ape" with "gorilla's feet," another character as a "cock," Jake as a "handsome hound," his loyal friend Billy as a "wolf," and dancing women in cabarets as "abandon[ing] themselves to pure voluptuous jazzing" and the "primitive joy of Harlem" (53, 54, 87, 108, 109). With the exception of the cultivated Haitian Ray, there is hardly a character who is not at some point likened to an undomesticated animal. Occasionally voices of dissent emerge, such as a Susy, the girlfriend of Zeddy who in an exercise of her "proprietary sense" clamps down on his "enjoyment of Harlem's low night life" (82). Labeling Harlem a "Nigger hell," "a stinking sink of iniquity" "where niggers nevah go to bed," she insists (unsuccessfully it turns out) on reining in Zeddy (79, 99). Such voices are drowned out by the sound of saxophones, blues songs, stomping feet, and laughter. All the noise gives "niggers brain-fevah," Billy says (285). Infectious racial primitivism was every African American's "birthright"—part of the black cultural DNA, Van Vechten implied—which only made whites feel that much more unnatural, even as they sought to "enjoy a little regression back to jungle life."[122] White fascination with urban African-American culture was expressed by the "white publishing world's demand for realistic narratives of the black underworld," Robert Dowling observes.[123]

This fascination—whether celebratory or disapproving—was opportunism mixed with racial ignorance and, sometimes, racism plain and simple. But it needs to be seen through the lens of the socioeconomic transformations that, as suggested earlier, endeavored to make the city practical. In other words, modern black primitivism as a literary and cultural trope was an unexpected and paradoxical outcome of planning that appeals "to the businessman, and to the manufacturer as sane and reasonable."[124] Primitivism was a compensatory white fantasy that ameliorated the "unnatural" mechanization of labor and the unrelenting stress upon efficiency in the modern city. "If the factory, campus, office, and corporation were dehumanizing, stultifying, or predatory," David Levering Lewis stresses, "the African American, largely excluded because of race from all of the above, was a perfect symbol of cultural innocence and regeneration."[125] None of this, of course, makes the fantasy of black underworld primitivism any less sour in the mouth. But if we were to view McKay's novel as catering directly to the publishing market's sordid demands, which rewarded black authors who were willing to sell out their communities for a buck, we would have to turn a blind eye to the novel's many subtleties. And we would have to ignore McKay's unabashed rejection of "the worthless standards of the whites."[126]

To understand McKay's handling of black underworld primitivism, you have to understand the spaces in which it is located. Jake says as much to the "delicate-fibered" Ray, who is largely ignorant of the black underclass: "There's all kinds a difference in that theah life. Sometimes it's the people make the difference and sometimes it's the place" (202, 222). Ray is introduced in part two of the novel, but it is in part one that McKay most thoroughly maps the racial and class divisions within Harlem, observing how they are spatialized in the new nighttime leisure economy, the some 125 nightclubs that were operating in Harlem in the mid-1920s.[127] Reflecting upon the ownership and clientele of the area's cabarets, McKay remarks that "Barron's was still Barron's, depending on its downtown white trade," while the newly redesigned Goldgraben's, a former basement cabaret that has been brought up to street level and thus to respectability, is also white-owned, but caters to the black bourgeoisie, the "ladies and gentlemen of the [Black] Belt" (28, 29). Such establishments are "distinguished for their impolite attitude toward the average Negro customer, who could not afford to swill expensive drinks" (316). In contradistinction stands the demiworld of Jake's black underclass, such as the "garish gold" and "screaming green" Sheba Palace, "entirely monopolized for the amusements of the common workaday Negroes . . . longshoremen, kitchen-workers, laundresses, and W.C. tenders" (294, 295). Behind the masquerade of "rouged maroon" lips at Sheba's are the city's black workers not working (295).

But the preeminent locale of underclass primitivism in the novel is "the Congo," "a real throbbing little Africa in New York" that manages to stay in business in the face of "formidable opposition and foreign exploitation" (29). The Congo functions as the Other space in the night's pleasure economy: "When you were fed up with the veneer of Seventh Avenue, and Goldgraben's Afro-Oriental garishness, you would go to the Congo and turn rioting loose in all the tenacious odors of service and the warm indigenous smells of Harlem, fooping or jig-jagging the night away" (30). When James Weldon Johnson stressed, "There is a large element of educated, well-to-do metropolitans among the Negroes of Harlem who view with indulgence, often with something less, the responses of the masses to these artless amusements," one imagines he had a venue like the Congo in mind.[128] Heedless of such prohibitions, McKay "indulges" the Congo with thick subcultural description; in its "hot soup," couples, dancers, and strangers meld together in "rhythmical abandon," a collective sexual embrace on "hungry nights" (37). As its name suggests, the Congo is Harlem's heart of darkness in the modern city. Yet McKay turns the colonial epithet upside-down: whites are barred from entering. Thus the "you" whom McKay addresses in his description of the club is not simply anyone, not simply any reader, as he immediately makes clear. "You would [go to the Congo] if you were a black kid hunting for joy in New York" (30). Caucasians storming Harlem in search of the savage at the Cotton Club are missing the real excitement—"the Congo was thick, dark-colorful, and fascinating"—but their presence at the Congo is unwanted and denied (36). The racially exclusive door policy (no whites allowed) shields Harlem's black underworld by creating a safe zone where African Americans can seek pleasure away from rampant racial and sexual voyeurism. At the Congo, "You kain always find something that New York ain't done made a fool of yet" (35).

In McKay's hands black underclass primitivism is a targeted protest by blacks for blacks against the injustices that stymie life, love, and bodily pleasure (44). Far from transforming poor and working-class African American life into an image of abstract freedom for economically privileged whites seeking to escape oppressive social codes, the novel stages the primitivist fantasy for an African-American audience and readership. "A jungle atmosphere pervaded the room, and, like shameless wild animals hungry for raw meat, the females savagely searched the eyes of the males," McKay writes in one typical description of the heated atmosphere of black visual eroticism (68). In another "scene of blazing color," he observes that "there is no human sight so rich as an assembly of Negroes" "all rioting together in wonderful harmony" (320). Out of "their melancholy environment" African Americans "create mad, contagious music and high laughter," McKay writes, adding that whites cannot understand this because "the instinct of comprehension" has been "cultivated out them" (267). Jake is characterized as possessing a "primitive passion for going against regulation," a telling description in the age of the corporate-monopoly city (44). This passion is for his benefit, not for any white person's visual delight. It is what urges him on, keeps him light on his feet in this peripatetic novel where improvisation characterizes both Harlem's music and its way of life (44). As the often out-of-work Zeddy puts it: "niggers am made foh life. . . . I wanta live and I wanta love. And niggers am got to work hard foh that" (49). In McKay's Harlem, the black underclass works hard at being primitive, and their primitivism sometimes depends upon, in Jake's words, "the place."

McKay's Harlem may be home, but it's no utopia. His Harlem is divided by internal rivalries and violence, as witnessed near the close of the novel when Zeddy pulls a razor on Jake, shouting that Felice is "*my* woman," and Jake counters with a gun leveled "straight at his heart" (326). The encounter nauseates Jake, who immediately chastises himself for acting white. He is "disgusted . . . to think that he had just been moved by the same savage emotions as those vile, vicious, villainous white men who, like hyenas and rattlers, had fought, murdered, and clawed the entrails out of black men over the common, commercial flesh of women" (328). This is a reversal of the primitivist motif if there ever was one. McKay reassigns the racial meaning of primitivism and denatures it by locating its origins not in biology but in modern political economy that demands beastly competitiveness and violence. In marked contrast, the transformative power of "pure voluptuous jazzing" inheres in the fact that it causes "you" to rise above your "commercial instincts" (108).

What the novel exposes in the end is that the fantasy of black primitivism does not exist outside of a (white) market economy that reduces human exchanges to exchanges of monies, bodies, and services. Black primitivism exists inside this dynamic as an exemplification and a critique of dehumanization and commodity fetishism. McKay's novel pries open the meaning of black underworld primitivism, assigning its negative associations with animalistic violence to whites and reserving its positive associations with pleasure and love for poor and working-class African Americans. *Home to Harlem*'s black leisure spaces are at one and the same time part of the new nighttime economy created by modern capitalism and a territory where black bodies are free from the symbolic and real labor they perform for white eyes. Following from this, McKay's black underworld should be understood not as a sign of cultural decline or degeneration, but rather as a repository for an alternative value-set in the face of a rapacious and acquisitive market. In this context, Felice's decision at the beginning of the novel to place Jake's fifty-dollar note back in his pocket after they make love takes on new meaning (16).

In *Home to Harlem*, the black primitivist fantasy is an anti-racist critique of black dehumanization. It must be admitted, however, that this fantasy is itself a mystification of poor and working-class life. Attempts to textually represent any class, race, or sexuality seem laden with problems of typecasting that reduce the nuances and complexities of groups and individuals. This is the case even when, as is the case with McKay, it is done in the service of progressive, positive cultural work. Despite his privileged status as a bestselling author, McKay himself—queer, black, and the son of peasant farmers—experienced multiple forms of social domination throughout his life. Yet his celebration of the culturally denigrated black underclass seems to overreach when it imbues its primitivist ethic with transformative powers. The result is that the black poor become romanced yet again, this time as a heroic alternative of a modern, overly civilized world.

We should see *Home to Harlem* as a textual space in which the fraught and contradictory meanings of the black underworld are registered, explored, and worked out. McKay attempts to address the problem of fetishization through Ray who, in a key moment in the novel, struggles to understand "what they called in print and polite conversation 'the underworld.' The compound word baffled him, as some English words did sometimes" (224). Ray's mediation on "the underworld" reveals the class underpinnings of this pervasive cultural mystification. At first blush, the friendship between Jake, whose "life had never before touched any of the educated of the ten dark millions," and Ray, whose university education has led him to think poor blacks are "simple earth-loving animals," seems like an odd coupling (155, 164). Ray's elevated class position has denied him access to sensual pleasure, leaving him "isolated and helpless" and dependent upon literature for his imaginative life (200). Ray is envious of

Jake's vigorous masculinity, but finds his language uncouth. In their initial conversation on the Pennsylvania Rail Road, where both of them are working, Ray is reading about Sappho when Jake approaches. "Sapphic and Lesbian . . . beautiful words," he says, to which Jake responds with a blues lyric that Ray calls "damned ugly": "there is two things in Harlem I don't understan' / It is a bulldyking woman and a faggoty man" (129). Jake's knowledge about queer life stems from the lowdown clubs that he frequents, Ray's from the literature he reads. Extending the chiasmus, Jake brings Ray down into the underworld—introducing him to "little white packets" of cocaine and to brothels and bars "crowded with black steelworkers in overalls"—and Ray lifts up Jake by educating him about the "civilized tradition" (148, 151, 263). In this exchange, Jake remains fundamentally unchanged; he leaves the novel (in preparation for moving to Chicago with Felice) much as he came into it. Ray, on the other hand, swears off "modern education" and declares "civilization is rotten" before he exits the novel as a "mess boy" on a freighter sailing to Australia and then to Europe (243, 275). Ray, McKay implies, is retracing Jake's voyage in hopes of living the "free life" (207).

What Ray has learned—and which necessitates his reeducation in "fertile reality"—is that the conceptual rubric that he had used to organize his knowledge of race, class, and geography is radically incommensurate with the multiplicity of black urban life (228). As if the veil has been lifted from his eyes, Ray ponders: "Why *under*-world he could never understand. It was very much upon the surface as were the other . . . divisions of human life. Having its heights and middle and depths and secret places even as they. And the people of this world, waiters, cooks, chauffeurs, sailors, porters, guides, ushers, hod-carriers, factory hands—all touched in a thousand ways the people of the other divisions. They worked over there and slept over here, divided by a street" (224, 225). In the final analysis, it turns out that the myth of the black urban underworld is nothing more than the ugly reality of segregation compounded with class politics and white desire. The corporate-monopoly city is a city divided and yet, as Doctor O'Connor adds in *Nightwood*, its geographies are "related by their division" (80).

In the period that I have covered here, zoning ordinances and racial segregation cut the city horizontally on "the surface." For anxious urbanites these divisions were, in turn, verticalized into markers of degeneration and racial primitivism. In response, the work of Barnes and McKay turns the underworld into a critical site for reimagining the unequal spatial economies of the modern era. Their writings militate against the division and segregation of the urban fabric and underscore the degree to which white privilege depends on the disorder, madness, and cultural impoverishment of minoritized populations that are caught within terrains undergoing decline, gentrification, and urban redevelopment. "We let you see us," Barnes writes, even though, McKay adds, you, the "white visitors. . . . see the grin only."[129] In Barnes's queer nightworld, transgressive sexuality amplifies the terms of exclusion, transforming them into an erotic discourse of bodily release. Something similar happens when McKay's characters get "carried away by the sheer rhythm of delight" and become "gorgeous animals swaying there through the dance, punctuating it with marks of warm physical excitement" (108). The city's racial segregations—its divisions on the surface—are momentarily offset by the fusion of black bodies in the "depths" of "secret places" that these divisions force into being.

As socioeconomic conditions in Harlem worsened through the 1930s and on through the war and postwar decades, McKay's vision of everyone "rioting together in wonderful harmony" gave way to black underclass riots or "uprisings," as the inner-city disturbances in 1935, 1943, 1964, and beyond were often called. These radical acts of territorial repossession were seared into the memory of the following generation of writers. As I show in the next chapter, the literature of the black underworld in the 1940s and 1950s continued to plumb the underworld—going literally underground in the work of Richard Wright and Ralph Ellison—to unearth the origins of white fantasies of lower-class African American delinquency.

3 / The Black Underground: Urban Riots, the Black Underclass, and the Work of Richard Wright and Ralph Ellison, 1940s–1950s

"Have you ever stopped to think what the future Harlem will be?" James Weldon Johnson brightly asked in 1920.[1] The question was posed in good faith, but the answer may have brought tears. As we saw in chapter 2, "black Manhattan" had developed a reputation as a scintillating nightlife underworld in the 1920s, much to Johnson's chagrin, but this itself was a minor blot, a mix of racial embarrassment and white opportunism that would pass like any other fad in a modern economy given to distractions. The upward arc of the neighborhood, like the stock market, seemed all but guaranteed. The black libidinal underworld would vanish into the past as Harlem's Talented Tenth expanded and as more and more Harlemites cast off the low-down culture of primitive jazzing that McKay's *Home to Harlem* had helped codify, and reached instead for the heights of Striver's Row or Sugar Hill. These desirable middle-class neighborhoods within Harlem were perched above the Valley lowlands of the "slum dwellers" as a kind of racial mountain and inspiration.[2]

By some measures, Johnson's 1920s optimism could not have been further off the mark. The under-acknowledged but simmering racial antagonisms in Harlem and other black communities were becoming more heated by the day. Rates of juvenile delinquency, infant mortality, and disease were on the increase.[3] The housing crisis was worsening. Uneven geographical development and racial segregation was a disaster for the residents of Harlem and of the other inner cities that were rapidly forming in Chicago, Detroit, Oakland, and elsewhere. Within black neighborhoods, housing stock was limited, primarily white owned, rundown, and upward of 20 to 50 percent more expensive than in other parts of the city. In the urban imagination of the 1930s and 1940s, the rip-roaring black underworld of speakeasies and blues clubs largely disappeared and was being replaced by a new, altogether harsher and absolutely real underworld that recalled the Lower East Side's basement apartments in the 1890s, which Riis exposed as a source of fuming class anger. "Down into the ground they have gone," those "families which cannot pay the high rents," Adam Clayton Powell declared in 1935 in the *New York Post*.[4] Deepening poverty was being concretized in the built spaces of New York City in ways that portended new crises and new social antagonisms. "People were said to be living in 'coal bins and cellars'" Gilbert Osofsky writes in his history of the neighborhood.[5] As the "people"—the black underclass—went down, they came up more angry. In 1935 Harlem finally burst into riot. In 1943, it did so again.

In this chapter I tell the story of the material space of the black underground in the decades bracketing World War II through the work of Richard Wright and Ralph Ellison, two writers who fathomed the psychodynamics of living in the most condensed, degraded urban terrains. The trope of black underworld in urban American literature of the 1920s was used primarily as a spatial metaphor for black cultural pathology and primitivism which some writers, such as Claude McKay, sought to resignify. In McKay's *Home to Harlem,* Ray wonders, "Why *under*-world he could never understand. It was very much upon the surface," as were the other "divisions of human life."[6] McKay's novel sought to demystify the metaphor and at the same time attempted to affirm and honor poor and working-class black life for the boisterous alternative that it presented to what McKay pithily termed "regulation."[7]

Whereas McKay contended that the black underworld was actually "very much upon the surface," Wright and Ellison in the ensuing decades would take another tack, would try to understand how black life actually had come to be very much below the surface, and how underground space had become infused with race in the most literal of ways. In Wright's novella "The Man Who Lived Underground" (1945), it is into the abominable space of the sewer that his protagonist flees from the police for a murder he did not commit; in Ellison's *Invisible Man* (1952), it is into one of Osofsky's coal bins that his anonymous narrator plunges as he is chased through Harlem during the night of a fiery riot that consumes the final chapter of his text.[8] Insofar as African American districts were once synonymous with cabaret life, the new sociological realities of the 1940s and 1950s cemented another set of underworld associations: actual underground living as a response to a housing emergency rooted in racial segregation. In turn, these changes demanded a new response from black writers. Wright and Ellison, in different ways, took up this mantle with a new literature of the black underground.

What we will see in the pages that follow is that Richard Wright and Ralph Ellison anatomize the intensified racial geographies of the Fordist city, the mid-century urban form that emerged out of the socioeconomic and spatial restructurings of the Great Depression. They do so through narratives of descent that immerse them in the squalid geographies of racial denigration—sewers, cellars, trash-strewn streets, and even underground psychotherapy clinics. “To live in Harlem,” Ellison declared, “is to dwell in the very bowels of the city.”[9] Repeatedly, these two writers turn to a nauseating cloacal imagery to strongly suggest that the ghetto had become the excrement of urban America, which a dominant white culture had deposited underground as a way of safeguarding psychologically the sanctity of white identity and materially the value of white property. In short, Wright and Ellison face head on the cultural conflation of blackness with waste, a gesture reminiscent in strategy to McKay's willingness to embrace black primitivism in order to restage the racist fantasy for progressive cultural work. Their strategy was risky in that it had the potential merely to confirm white fears and fantasies, rather than to deconstruct the politics of this ugly association.

But the risks were worth it, and needed. In the urban imagination of the 1930s through the 1950s, the image of black underworld waste was everywhere, and its function was to solidify and mystify a series of tightly interconnected issues and anxieties over property, collective violence, and delinquency. “When [people] approach me they see only my surroundings,” Ellison's cellar-dwelling narrator claims at the very opening of *Invisible Man* (3). Images of squalid, waste-filled geographies became a way of talking about poverty, racism, and black non-normativity while avoiding these issues at the same time.

As I will detail in the pages to come, the riots of 1935 and 1943 (the latter reported on firsthand by Ellison) were a collective political response by the black community that was in part a reaction to the decrepit, unsanitary state of housing in Harlem. The riots were, in short, a radical exercise in the remaking—or perhaps destroying as a precursor to rebuilding—human geographies in the context of racism. The popular press and municipal authorities, however, understood the riots not as conscious exercises of will, but as signs of cultural and psychological degeneration.

The struggle over the origin and meaning of the riots was a heated debate that would shape understandings of collective action for decades. Sociological studies of race in the period intervened in the debate by arguing that delinquency and cultural pathology were both the outcome and the cause of the squalid living conditions of black urban Americans. This circular logic—that living in the ghetto resulted in random, senseless acts of black normlessness, mental illness, and delinquency, and that these same acts made the ghetto a mentally and culturally debilitating environment—left urban African Americans trapped, their heads spinning.

In much of the discourse on black poverty and black cultural eccentricity in this period, the trope of waste was made to be isomorphic with the sordid realities of African American life. And since delinquency was both an origin and a symptom of squalor, no amount of protest otherwise would change anyone's mind. Wright and Ellison tried to dispel this poisoned reasoning. They waded into this sewer of the white imagination in order to unpack the gross corporeal excesses it heaped upon black Americans. Wright's descent in "The Man Who Lived Underground" exposes how such racial ideologies of black uncleanliness were internalized by African Americans in ways that turned them into complicit, pacified, self-regulating subjects. Ellison, for his part, deployed the image of black waste in his essays from the 1940s in order to spark moral outrage that he hoped would end an era of benign neglect and lead to greater state intervention into Harlem: more money, more affordable healthcare, and the like.

Ellison spent a good deal of the 1940s and 1950s thinking through how Harlem's housing crisis, its riots, and its problem with delinquency were interrelated. His novel *Invisible Man* is the culmination of that thinking. The novel literalizes the underworld, but turns it on its head so that it stands not for pure libidinality (which the novel recoils from) or even black collective violence (which it rejects), but instead stands as the space of individual privacy, heroic self-recreation, and writing. In essence, Ellison's underworld is a site where his protagonist pieces together a different narrative of black identity and racial embodiment in the context of the Fordist city's violent exclusions. What I have been suggesting throughout this book is that in order to grasp the geographical imagination of American literature we need to understand the spatial context of its production. And so now it is to another part of that story we turn, the strange twentieth-century history of black subterranean living.

"Down into the Ground They Have Gone": Subterranean Living in the Fordist City

In the years immediately preceding and following the Second World War, tens of thousands of African Americans lived underground, a fact largely erased from historical memory but preserved in complex and allusive ways in the black literature of the period. When Ellison disclosed that his anonymous narrator "had been forged in the underground of American experience," the resonance was not only metaphorical but also literal in a way that is lost on most of today's readers.[10] The history of underground living is a history of racial segregation and migration, the history of a people's movement northward in search of work and greater freedom that ended with a new set of racial boundaries. In *The Gold Coast and the Slum* (1929), the influential sociologist Harvey Warren Zorbaugh described black migrations into Chicago (Richard Wright's adopted home) in military terms, making clear how unwelcome the newcomers were: "Into the heart of Little Hell [a Sicilian area] has come, since the war, a fourth invasion which has gradually darkened its streets: the Negro from the rural South."[11]

Urban forms are malleable, and fears of such malleability were underpinning Zorbaugh's observations and commentaries. Urban forms expand, are reshaped, become denser, or depopulated with technological innovations in production, consumption, and transportation, with the in-migration of new (black) labor and the out-migration of whites, and with the movements of capital, taxes, and government expenditures. These spatial changes tend to occur over medium to long-term historical waves, though they are accelerated with local, national, or even global crises of overaccumulation. From the restructuring spurred by the Great Depression and the war effort emerged the Fordist city, characterized not only by the triumvirate of mass industrial production, commodity consumption, and expansive government power in the form of new social welfare programs but also by its hardened ethnic and racial lines.

The often-noted benefits of the postwar economic boom—an expanded middle class and rising wages—were unequally distributed by race. In fact, in northern cities several of the racialized spatial trends that had been in motion in the prior generation's corporate-monopoly city were intensified: more undervalued black labor poured in, seeking an escape from Jim Crow and a chance to participate in the militarized industrialism of the 1940s, and more whites moved out to the new planned communities along the highways. The result was further white suburbanization to the periphery and greater residential racial segregation. The growth of new suburbs resulted in new markets for consumption and new investments in infrastructure, while the redivision through segregation of existing urban spaces (the inner city) was a way of absorbing surplus labor and a means of extracting additional profit from a trapped market. Hence, racial segregation was both a spatial exercise of power and a means for urban capitalism's expansion in a post-crisis atmosphere. The city actually became more racially polarized as a result. Mid-twentieth-century segregation limited the available space for New York's burgeoning black population, which had increased over 600 percent from the beginning of the century. Following from this, housing in black neighborhoods was significantly more expensive than comparable housing in other urban areas.

The situation was worsened by the fact that African Americans were routinely locked out of unions in the manufacturing economy or employed as scabs to break those same unions. Newly invigorated residential segregation thus combined with an out-of-reach labor market to create a concentrated geography of poverty that was without precedent. While racial segregation was a fact of life in the 1920s, it was in "the years after World War II," Douglas Massey and Nancy Denton remark, that it "became a permanent structural feature of the spatial organization of American cities."[12] "Areas of acceptable black residence became more and more narrowly circumscribed" as the century wore on.[13] More than ever, Du Bois's dream of black "freedom for expansion and self-development" seemed like a dream deferred.[14] In 1948, James Baldwin described the problem in terms of barely containable anxious fear: "Harlem is pervaded by a sense of congestion, rather like the insistent, maddening, claustrophobic pounding in the skull that comes from trying to breathe in a very small room with all the windows shut."[15]

Powell urgently penned his 1935 *Post* article on underground apartments in Harlem in response to the riot of the same year. The collective disturbance of public space was immediately keyed to the despoiled conditions of private space. Powell was explicit on this point: "Fully ten thousand of the Harlem citizenry now live in cellars: dark, damp, cold dungeons" which he labeled "breeders of crime" and "embassies of death and sickness."[16] "Here they exist in squalor worse than that of the sharecroppers," Powell said, adding "Families 'live' in these basements . . . floors of cracked concrete, walls of whitewashed rock, slits for windows, no toilets except the tin can in the corner with a sheet hanging over it."[17] Further west, in Wright's Chicago, where McKay sends Jake and Felice at the end of *Home to Harlem*, reports stated that "Sixty per cent of the Negro families live in rear flats or basements."[18]

For African Americans, living underground materialized a sickening ideology of uneven spatial relations, making noxiously manifest what Powell described as "a new social scheme or rather a new social 'odor' that should smell pretty bad."[19] Half-hearted efforts to ameliorate this harsh existence in the 1940s—such as the construction of new low-income housing within Harlem—failed to provide relief or clear the air. By the 1950s, the situation was still dire. The Citizens' Housing and Planning Council (CHPC) of New York addressed the crisis multiple times in its newsletter *Housing News*. In 1952, the year *Invisible Man* was published, the CHPC in an article titled "The Cellar Menace" cited the commissioner of health's finding that "The illegal use of cellars as living quarters is increasing steadily in Manhattan and some sections of Brooklyn and the Bronx," causing a "serious and difficult problem."[20] "In Harlem, 840 buildings were inspected" by the Health Department, the CHPC stated, and found "325 cellars, or 39 percent were in use as homes," a rate double that of other parts of the city.[21]

Later that year, the Housing and Planning Council again reported on the matter, this time in "Cellar Occupancy Attacked." The numbers were astonishing. The assistant district attorney, Edward Silver, estimated, according to the CHPC, "that more than 30,000 families in New York are living in illegal cellar apartments 'under the most horrible conditions' which are a constant threat to the health of the community as breeding places of contagious disease."[22] "Some of the caves, not worth a dollar," he stated, "rent for $60 to $65 a month," far in excess of standard accommodations in white, working-class neighborhoods.[23] "Every effort will be made to relocate the ousted tenants in decent apartments," the CHPC concluded, but observed that "the housing shortage would make this difficult."[24]

The association between collective unrest and squalid living was an old one. In the 1890s, Jacob Riis had proclaimed that "thousands were living in cellars" and hundreds of thousands more were living above ground in the carceral architecture of tenements.[25] Riis estimated that "at least" 80 percent "of crimes against property and against the person are perpetrated by individuals who have either lost connection with home life, or never had any."[26] When the "crowding below" in the unwholesome tenements is "so great," the "consequent upheavals" will be "so violent," he warned.[27] Riis's spatial imagination was almost Newtonian, for every action there was an equal and opposite reaction. Such spatial dynamics carried over into the Fordist city, which even more than Riis's metropolis was marked by urban decay and unrest centered in neighborhoods that suffered a lack of jobs, a dearth of employment agencies, hospitals, mental health institutions, and a declining tax base.

The most spectacular outbreaks of unrest in New York were the Harlem riots of 1935 and 1943. The uprisings were a reaction to the Fordist city's spatial inequalities, but time and again they were interpreted by New York Mayor Fiorello LaGuardia as a sign of black cultural pathology mixed with leftist political activism. The specific catalyst for the 1935 riot was the false rumor that a teenage boy had been beaten to death in the basement of E. H. Kress and Co. on 125th Street after stealing a knife from the store. The rumors touched off storms of angry protest against long-standing grievances. But these grievances were dismissed when LaGuardia labeled the uprising the work of "a few irresponsible individuals"—black hoodlums and delinquents—who were spurred on by the kind of Communist propaganda that Ellison would later incorporate into his novel: "My purpose," the Mayor announced, "is to let the Communists know that they cannot come into this country and upset our laws."[28] His appointed commission, whose conclusions he fought to suppress, rebutted this theory in the strongest terms: the "Communists . . . deserve more credit that any other element in Harlem for preventing a physical conflict between whites and Negroes."[29]

In viewing the riot as the work of alien and atypical elements in the urban population, LaGuardia sought to minimize the extent to which his own policies were culpable. Powell, however, leveled the blame squarely on the mayor: "it was an open, unorganized protest against empty stomachs, overcrowded tenements, filthy sanitation, rotten foodstuffs, chiseling landlords and merchants, discrimination on relief, disfranchisement, and against a disinterested administration."[30] The following year, Alain Locke characterized the riot as "a Ghetto mutiny" and, in recommending a program "to improve the Harlem situation," proclaimed housing as "the most serious special community problem."[31] The African American is "the man farthest down," and "he tests the pressure and explores the depths of the social and economic problem," Locke eloquently stated.[32]

The riot of 1935 was a shattering event in the African American community, its causes and effects discussed for years. But the riot that followed on the first of August 1943, at the end of a long and scorching summer weekend and after sensational newspaper stories about a "Negro crime wave," painfully demonstrated that the root of black discontent remained unaddressed.[33] The riot was sparked by an incident at the Braddock Hotel on West 126th Street, in which a white police officer shot and wounded an unarmed black solider, Robert Bandy, who had intervened in a scuffle between the officer and a woman who was demanding a refund from the hotel. A reputed haven for narcotics and prostitution, the Braddock had been under surveillance for over a year when Bandy was shot. The police had a standing policy of barring racially mixed couples from staying at the hotel, regardless of marital status, which they enforced by entering rooms in the middle of the night to eject tenants.[34] Rumors spread that a black solider had been killed, leading thousands to protest, loot, and set fires throughout Harlem by nightfall. The riot, which left six African Americans dead, 550 arrested, and property damage in the millions, was quantifiably twice as destructive as its predecessor.[35] In the aftermath, LaGuardia again blamed "hoodlums and criminals."[36] With greater foresight and greater historical memory, Harlem's *Amsterdam News* on August 7, 1943, explicitly linked the two uprisings in an article titled "1935 Riot Causes Started '43 Riot." The paper's editorial board that same day issued a statement that "Mob violence never helped anybody," and warned that if legal and civil rights weren't soon forthcoming then "similar disturbances should cause no surprise."

Ralph Ellison himself weighed in on the 1943 riot in a newspaper report. Standing at Eighth Avenue and 127th Street at three A.M., Ellison surveyed the disquieting scene. "There was the sound of gunfire and the shouting as of a great celebration," he began the article, which captures the night's surreal atmosphere with images of "broken clocks" littering the streets and little boys walking around in the early hours of the morning with stolen candy bars and penny whistles.[37] Similar images would eventually make their way into the last pages of *Invisible Man*. But these ludic scenes give way to Ellison's moralizing commentary, which unlike Powell's and Locke's response, redirected blame back onto the community: "Going through the crowd, it was very noticeable that this whole incident was a naive, peasant-like act of revenge."[38] Ellison dismissed the riot out of hand and blamed it on the delinquent behavior of recently migrated African Americans from the rural South ("peasants") who were unable to cope with the psychologically deleterious and anomic conditions of urban life. The report was capped with a withering rebuke: "Much will depend upon how well Mayor LaGuardia, working with Negro elements who would rather not see this type of thing, is able to reach the people of Harlem."[39]

Ellison's views of collective violence would change over time, becoming more complex, but never radicalized. In *Invisible Man*, he would link black underclass protest to underground living, but in a way that reversed the causality between the two. For now, what I want to underscore is how interpretations of the riots by African American leaders and writers of the period showed remarkable similarity in their rejection of them as misguided and detrimental to the project of racial advancement. On this point, Ellison was not alone. It is worth noting in this vein how the riots were described through spatialized class dynamics as underworld uprisings by lower-class blacks "farthest down," as Locke wrote, a "deep undertow . . . against the surface advance of the few bright years of prosperity."[40] Or as McKay, referring to the 1935 event, suggested, it was a "frenzied orgy of destruction" that "finally 'blew the lid off'" of the community.[41] The spreading slums of the masses had long threatened to submerge "the Harlem élites," and with the riot had been nearly successful in doing so.[42] Because racial segregation condenses the geographical expression of class difference—"visually, Harlem creates the impression of a mass of people all existing on the same plane"—the riots were for middle-class African Americans particularly anxiety inducing.[43] In the public eye, Harlem's black bourgeoisie was lumped with criminal elements and the poor. Conflated with putatively atypical populations on the basis of shared skin color, middle-class African Americans were at pains to make the social and class heterogeneity of their neighborhoods evident. One way they did so was through ascribing moral value to material inequality. Hence Ellison's distinction between "Negro elements who would rather not see this type of thing" and those engaged in a "peasant-like act of revenge."

From another perspective, however, the riots signaled the will of the city's poorest residents to remake their geographies actively at the very emergence of the segregated Fordist city by burning it down in hopes of beginning again. The rioters recognized that space is neither inert nor immutable, but an arena for struggle. In rioting, they redefined the space of the margin into the space of defiance. The cellar apartments of Harlem were not just incubators of crime and disease but also breeding places of contagious affinity and political consciousnesses that quickly multiplied when sparked by white violence. At no point in the subsequent discourse of the period, however, were the riots understood as legitimate protests against white neocolonialism, or as instances of counterviolence to the historical and daily violence of segregation, or as examples of property redistribution in light of ongoing economic disenfranchisement. Out of political expediency some saw the riots as exemplifying the putative non-normativity of black culture and then left it at that, but others dove deeper. The question of how the man "farthest down" would respond to living in claustrophobic, segregated northern urban communities preoccupied urban sociological literature, as it did Ellison and Wright, who were often in conversation with this literature. In the years after the riots, Ellison and Wright both waded down into the murky waters of the underworld to see, as Ellison once put it, whether "geography was fate" after all.[44]

"Abysmally Obscene": The Cloacal City in Ralph Ellison's "Harlem Is Nowhere" and Richard Wright's "The Man Who Lived Underground"

For African Americans, the ghetto indexed the depths of race-based economic exploitation. For many sociologists, the abject living conditions of black, as well as ethnic, slums were an outcome of environmentally determined pathologies. Zorbaugh remarked in his study of Chicago's bohemian "half-world," "Little Hell," and "black belt" that "the slum sets its mark upon those who dwell in it, gives them attitudes and behavior problems peculiar to itself."[45] The space was contagious. Stay in it too long and it would change you. The inner city, for Zorbaugh, was a cosmopolitan underworld where what passed for freedom and individualism was really anonymity and deviance. Such zones were diverse, but only in the sense of the detritus and waste they naturally precipitated: "men and women derelicts, users of opium, drunkards, the 'queer,' criminals and outcasts."[46] Even in more racially homogenous zones where, in Zorbaugh's words, "a whole people is segregated by virtue of color," "one finds more grades of people living together than in any other area within the city."[47] Gunnar Myrdal, in his expansive study of race relations, *An American Dilemma* (1944) (a work that Ellison professionally reviewed), would later refer to these zones as "a Negro 'underworld'" in "the big cities" where a libidinal culture of "petty thieves and racketeers, prostitutes and pimps, bootleggers, dope addicts, and so on" had taken root.[48] Under this libertarian underworld was a harsher reality. "Malnutrition, bad housing, and lack of schooling actually deform the body and the soul of people," Myrdal remarked, and noted that the correlation between these conditions and "tuberculosis, venereal diseases, prostitution, juvenile delinquency, and crime" had been "demonstrated so often by American experts that we do not have to add anything to the evidence."[49]

The city concentrated cultural, racial, ethnic, and class differences, but this pressure did not cause communities to form. It caused the body and the social fabric to fall apart. In Zorbaugh's estimation, the slum was the antithesis of community, an "area of disintegration and disorganization," the home of "psychopathic personalities," "foreign colonies," and a "submerged population" whose "only contacts with the conventional world are through the social agency and the law."[50] Reading Zorbaugh's *The Gold Coast and the Slum* and Myrdal's *An American Dilemma* leaves one with the impression that the Fordist inner city had wholly degenerated into a derelict zone of dazed peoples shuffling past pawnshops and shuttered businesses. The impression stuck, and it helped define the response to the riots in the period. Surely a population so broken and addled could not act en masse or could only do so in the case of a mass outbreak of mental illness.

The theory that the political problems of the inner city could be addressed by treating individual behavioral problems through therapy had real currency in the 1940s. Ellison himself ascribed to it in "Harlem Is Nowhere," a 1948 essay (later collected in *Shadow and Act*) which addressed the psychologically debilitating and demoralizing effects of living in a crowded, unclean geography. Its title suggested that Harlem was cut off from the rest of the city. The definitional "nowhere" of Utopia was inverted in Harlem into a dystopian reality of lost souls. Harlem was "a ruin," Ellison went on to admit, and it was the city's "bowels" (295, 296). The excremental imagery was Ellison's way of trying to attract greater state intervention into the mental well-being of black communities that had suffered so unjustly.

The history of slavery and humiliation and the ongoing trauma of segregation lay behind Ellison's thinking, but the immediate occasion for the essay was the founding of the Lafargue Mental Hygiene Clinic, a low-cost psychiatry facility that was the first of its kind in the neighborhood. Its director, Dr. Fredric Wertham, who later was made famous in the 1950s for his crusade against depictions of sex and drug use in comic books, opened the clinic in Harlem in order to address racial inequalities in health care in New York and to help stem juvenile delinquency arising from racial anger. In particular, the explosive mix of delinquency and putative psychopathology in Harlem were thought to originate in the neighborhood's housing emergency. On April 13, 1946, the *Amsterdam News* ran a front-page story, "Harlem's Mental Clinic Doing OK," declaring that Harlem desperately needed mental health services because of the deleterious effects of the housing crisis: "Harlem, with its crowded, filthy tenements . . . has been a fertile ground for growth of mental ills."

Living in the pressurized terrain of the ghetto had its psychic cost—mental breakdown and anger—which in the aftermath of the riots many of Harlem's leaders feared might spark more explosions in the streets. Yet the *Amsterdam News*'s claim was bitingly ironic. As a result of the lack of affordable space in Harlem and no public funding, the clinic itself was compelled to open underground, in the basement of Saint Philip's Church on West 133rd Street.

Ellison played up these ironies. Biographer Lawrence Jackson notes that Ellison originally intended the essay to be accompanied by startling photographs that would "show crowded areaways and tunnel-like passages overflowing with garbage, peopled by figures hustling through doorways and streaking across the picture frame."[51] When the magazine that was to publish the essay folded, Ellison relied upon the drama of his own words to press home how frightening underworld Harlem had become: "One must descend to the basement and move along a confusing mazelike hall to reach it. Twice the passage seems to lead against a blank wall," Ellison wrote at the start of his essay (294). Just trying to find the clinic showed one how disorienting life was in Harlem, how the community had lost its bearings and become walled in, and how the people to whom the black bourgeoisie were supposed to reach out were unreachable. "Here, in the basement," Ellison stated a few pages later, "a frustrated science goes to find its true object; the confused of mind who seek reality. Both find the source of their frustrations in the sickness of the social order" (302).

For Ellison, Harlem was the city's dark unconscious where all the nightmarish dreams that whites had of black urban squalor were materializing. "The most surreal fantasies are acted out upon the streets of Harlem," Ellison observed, and then as if to prove the point, he catalogued a highly sexualized and entirely fantastic pastiche of teenage deviancy in which "a boy participates in the rape-robbery of his mother; . . . two men hold a third while a lesbian slashes him to death with a razor blade; boy gangsters wielding homemade pistols . . . shoot down their young rivals" (297). The younger generation offered an ominous warning. Many older African Americans, especially recently uprooted southerners, were also lost in a landscape cluttered with "garbage and decay" and lost, as well, in the more insidious and often invisible machinations of northern racism, Ellison implied (295). How they would cope was Ellison's life-long creative interest. The "character that arises from the impact between urban slum conditions and folk sensibilities" was the subject he would pursue through nearly all his writing (296). In "Harlem Is Nowhere," Ellison was careful to locate the pathology he ascribed to the black underclass to macroeconomic forces, the tumultuous clash between two modes of development: a residual southern agrarianism and dominant northern industrialism, each regulated by different regimes of racial and spatial control. In the Great Migration from the South to the North, southern blacks experienced a disorienting onrush of time, telescopically speeding through history by moving through space. They had come through a maelstrom only to find themselves "wanderers dazed in a ghetto maze, a 'displaced person' of American democracy" (300).

Doctor Wertham diagnosed Harlem with "free-floating hostility," an anger that was not bound to any singular cause. But the phrase underscored, too, the worry that black delinquency might be geographically uncontainable, might float past the de facto racial boundary at 110th Street, Harlem's southern border on Manhattan's West Side (301). In response, the clinic established itself as a regulatory institution that sought to renormalize the black underclass who were, Ellison stated, "enraged with the world" and whose anger sparked "the spontaneous outbreaks called the 'Harlem riots' of 1935 and 1943" (301). For Ellison, who placed his faith in the assimilating structures of liberal democracy, the larger project was not one of curing the black underclass of mental problems, but rather of integrating the poor into "the main institutional life of society" (299). America's political, educational, familial, and cultural institutions, and the performative rituals and celebrations around them, helped incorporate citizens into the dominant and stabilizing ideologies of the nation. Ellison went so far as to call these institutions and the practices they administered "therapy" for white Americans. The fact that blacks were excluded from them, or were included on unequal terms, was a painful reminder of their second-class status (300).

Wertham's work in his "Harlem basement" was important, but it turned out to be much too limited in scope: "a thousand Lafargue clinics could not dispel the sense of unreality that haunts Harlem," Ellison concluded (302). Ellison's diagnosis of Harlem recognized that the ailment was national, not local. In deploying potentially inflammatory language that metonymically associated the ghetto with urban sewers, he sought to argue that the genealogy of the black underworld was to be traced to the geographical expression of racism in a modern capitalist economy. In Ellison's view, living in the pressurized, segregated terrain of the city did not result in a feeling of boundedness, the sense of belonging to a besieged territorial culture that might serve as a foundation for a collectivist politics tied to place. Just the opposite was true: to live in

Harlem was to live "nowhere." For Ellison, the origins of the "sickness of the social order" lay in the nation's exclusion of black Americans from its symbols, rituals, and institutions (302). Thus it was into the transcendent spatiality of the racially heterogeneous national community that black Americans would need to aspire for their well-being and for the health of the country.

Ellison would eventually bring together his ideas about segregation and subterranean living, individual and civil disobedience, and the psychological function of liberal democratic institutions in *Invisible Man*. But the first to map out this terrain was Ellison's mentor and sometimes-rival Richard Wright, who was himself a patient of Dr. Wertham, and whose novella "The Man Who Lived Underground" served as a model for Ellison's novel.[52] "The Man Who Lived Underground" relates the story of Fred Daniels, an African American who is wrongly accused of murdering the white female neighbor of his employer. After he has been beaten into signing a confession of guilt, he sneaks out of a police station's window and heads down into the city's sewer system through a manhole cover. Though its geographical coordinates are ill-defined, we might read Wright's story in the context of Chicago's black-belt slum that had come under such intensive sociological scrutiny in the recent past.

At the outset, Wright reduces Daniels's world to two stark choices: "hide" or "surrender."[53] Under extreme duress, Daniels opts for the former and spends the bulk of the novella traversing the maze-like sewer, collecting tools, stealing electricity, and sleeping and dreaming. But ultimately he is compelled ("chooses" would suggest too much agency) toward the latter, toward "surrender," as he resurfaces and seeks out his interrogators. He does so not to enact revenge or even to declare his innocence, but to attest to his guilt, even though he himself maintains he has murdered no one. When the police hear of his fantastic story of living underground—"I was down in the basement"—they are hesitant to believe him, and so they follow Daniels back to the sewer, where they shoot him in the chest (74). "You've got to shoot his kind. They'd wreck things," a cop says as Daniels's body sinks into the sewage (84). Wright closes with his black protagonist as "a whirling object rushing alone in the darkness, veering, tossing, lost in the heart of the earth" (84). Hiding or surrendering turn out to be one and the same: the black man who is not fit for life above lives and dies in the garbage below.

The sewer, the literary historian David Pike argues, is not only a literal depository of "excrement and offal . . . [and] cast-off and outmoded remains of things," but a metaphor for social anxieties about civic disorder, disease, and madness.[54] As we saw in Djuna Barnes's *Nightwood*, the sewer symbolically resonates as the city's "most organic, primitive, and uncontrollable part," and yet it is also instrumental in the smooth functioning of the city.[55] Quite literally it is an underworld of urban pollutants that without proper management threaten to percolate upward onto the streets. In Wright's hands, the sewer's fetid atmosphere is freighted with political and racial dimensions that stand in for white fears of the disorienting, unclean world of the riotous urban ghetto whose anger was free-floating. To put it another way, the unequally divided geographies of the Fordist city and the different values attached to them (rationality versus madness, cleanliness versus filth, law versus disorder) are made strikingly visible by Wright's sewer. The link between these two geographies is Daniels. From beginning to end, Wright's African American male subject is caught within the disciplinary regimes of white power. Hunted by the police, Daniels descends into the sewer, thereby confining himself—willfully imprisoning himself—to a terrain that is only a more degraded version of the de jure and de facto segregations that built the twentieth century's racial ghettos. In Wright's imagination, the sewer is where the criminalized African American who has been accused of violating the space between black male bodies and white female bodies is forced to surrender. It is not just the place where an individual black subject is incarcerated, but where a "kind" of person who "wrecks things," the black underclass, is disposed of in the riotous 1940s. It is where the "free-floating hostility" of the delinquent underclass subject finally sinks.

Wright reimagines this noxious link between blackness and waste to give an anti-racist charge. In line with this argument, Pike observes that Wright uses the underground to "analyze the place of African-Americans in postwar society," implying that the underground is "the only place left to live" and that living underground is an "inherently untenable situation."[56] The sewer is both a place of foul materiality and a refuge, a substitute prison and a dwelling place. Early on, Wright establishes the sewer, as we might expect, as an "abysmally obscene" place filled with the "odor of rot," "gray-green sludge," "horrible disease," and even a dead baby with a "mouth gaped black in a soundless cry" (21, 22, 24, 26). The "streaking water" of the sewer tugs violently at Daniels's body, continually threatening to pull him further down into gross debasement, to immerse him—if we are to read these scenes politically—in the images of racial degradation that freely circulated in the period (65). But Daniels quickly transforms the sewer into "a sort of cave," a shelter, a temporary respite from the policed geographies above ground. In the underworld, Wright's protagonist forages for food, scavenges for tools, and rigs up a light bulb like a modern-day campfire (23). He reverts, in effect, to the state of a primitive hunter-gatherer. Yet at the same time and in his own strange way, Daniels is a homemaker. He lives underground, as Wright stresses in his title. In an era when the poorest of the poor lived in what amounted to urban "caves," Daniels makes something from his spatial marginality, though this act of making do, we must admit, is dripping with irony among many other things.[57] His abode has a working radio, and his cave, "not worth a dollar," is wallpapered with money he has taken from a jewelry store's safe. He steals it not so he can spend it, but so he can use it. In short, for Daniels, this appalling home is turned into a showcase for his inventiveness, self-sufficiency, and empowerment. Momentarily at least, Daniels shows himself neither to be a mere ward of the state's expanding social welfare net nor a convict handled by prison wardens.

In the end, however, this may be more of a delusion of grandeur than real agency, as is evident by Daniels's premature celebration: "He had triumphed over the world aboveground! He was free! If only people could see this!" (54, 81). From one angle, Daniels might be thought to enact Michel de Certeau's idea of the "tactic," a disruptive poaching on the space and property of the dominant culture as an exercise of a stealthy, localized counterforce.[58] But understanding the novella in this way, I would suggest, is to misread it. Daniels's secretive actions—his prowling through the sewer and the spaces interconnected with it—are solitary, profoundly alienated, and in no way collective. The clandestine isolation that makes these acts possible also renders them negligible.

Nor does the makeshift dwelling of Wright's protagonist rise to the order of what the scholar bell hooks posits as "the subversive value of homeplace" in African American history.[59] Hooks stresses the black home as "a private space where we do not directly encounter white racist aggression," "a crucial site for organizing, for forming political solidarity."[60] In contrast, Daniels's quasi home is a permeable space into which the pollutions of racism are continually poured. It is literally saturated. The rain that seems to be falling through the entire novella overflows into the sewer, blending the upper and underworld and perhaps portending a storm of racial protest that Wright obliquely hints at in closing. Hardly exempt from the world above, Daniels's sewer is an awful repository for all that white society casts off. Though Daniels feels like he has "traveled a million miles away from the world," he is never that far from the surface where the police cars race through the wet streets (23). Throughout the narrative, police pry open the manhole cover, shout down into the sewer, and fire their weapons into it in what amounts to a surreal variation of the routine violation of African-American privacy by police in hotels like the Braddock or DEA agents with battering rams. The critic Michel Fabre correctly observes that "alone in his cave," Daniels may try to remake "his universe in an ironical antithesis to what is considered the normal world. . . . But whether he takes apart or reconstructs, Daniels is nonetheless prisoner of the preexisting relationships, because reversing a signification implies accepting its priority."[61] Wright's protagonist may refashion his space—or at least redecorate it—but he never fundamentally changes it.

How, then, might we think about Wright's protagonist in a way that does not confirm white fantasies of black degradation or disempower attempts at black agency? I would argue that Daniels is a vehicle for thinking through the psychodynamics of racial domination in a spatial context. He stages questions for the reader to ponder, questions that he himself is incapable of answering. Wright is quite specific on this account. Daniels's descent into the city's material underworld is an escape to a kind of polluted Walden where he can think through "a series of questions: Why was this sense of guilt so seemingly innate, so easy to come by, to think, to feel, so verily physical?" (60). Spatial withdrawal at first appears to afford the critical distance that is impossible in the more threatening climate above. Or as Fabre comments, for Daniels subterranean living is "an opportunity to scrutinize his culture from the outside."[62] Fabre's reading, however, misses Wright's most important irony: in the underworld Daniels cannot think straight, cannot get his bearings. As in Ellison's "Harlem Is Nowhere," the bowels of the city are latent with psychological distress. Rather than the clarity of critical distance, Daniels experiences amnesia, mental fragmentation, and the release of repressed desires in a space that produced a new "intensity of feelings" (25). The sewer does not liberate his mind; it rots it. "Some part of him was trying to remember the world he had left," Wright comments about Daniels, who at one point even wonders "what was his name" (40, 53). "He stared, trying to remember," Wright says, "He stood and glared about the dirt cave, his name on the tip of his lips. But it would not come to him. Why was he here? Yes, he had been running away from the police. But why? His mind was blank. He bit his lips and sat again, feeling a vague terror. But why worry?" (53). Living in the racial underground regresses the subject to a nearly infantile state. By the time he crawls his way back to his captors, Daniels speaks in "childlike" tones, incapable of stringing together a coherent narrative of his time underground (74). If he is not to be an imprisoned subject in America's penitentiaries, he might be a patient in one of black America's underground psychiatric institutions.

"The Man Who Lived Underground" does not contest but rather confirms the psychic costs that arise from extreme marginalization. It is important to recognize that it does so as a rebuttal to contemporary urban ecological theories that insisted slums and ghettoes were the product of natural selection, not the raw sewage of racism. Wright agrees with the contention that the "slum sets its mark upon those who dwell in it" and that within it "cultures lose much of their identity" and "mores tend to lose their sanctions."[63] But he is at pains to point out that the slum's seeming enzymatic destruction of cultures and personalities is the result of how space and race combine to produce a compounded site of domination. What we witness in Wright's narrative of decline is the systematic erasure and redescription of black identity. Daniels's life prior to his entry into the penal system is a memory displaced beyond the book, but snippets of it appear in references to a job and a wife. His time in the sewer's "dank space" transforms him, fills him with "an irrational compulsion to act," makes him walk "aimlessly" while wondering "*What was the matter with him?* . . . It was these walls; these crazy walls" (20, 57). The foul environment reformulates the former law-abiding subject into the stereotypical black underclass criminal-in-waiting whose psychotic blood lust grows in the ghetto. And as he spends more and more time incarcerated in the underworld, he begins to slowly chip through its walls—"He hewed softly for hours at the cement"—until he carves out holes large enough to squeeze through (35). In Wright's novella, the black man is on the loose beneath the city.

Much of the middle section of "The Man Who Lived Underground" is composed of Daniels crawling in and out of holes in the sprawling clandestine network of the urban sewer. Wright's sewer links fragmented parts of the city—a church, a movie theater, a mortuary, a fruit and meat market, a jeweler—all of which have walls that abut the underground tunnels. Crawling in and out these spaces, Daniels becomes the escaped convict and the voyeuristic predator who can seemingly be anywhere at any time. As if conducting an experiment, Wright uses these adjacent sites to test his character's reaction to new environments. Each test confirms Daniels's deepening psychopathology. When he tunnels into the back of a meat locker at "Nick's Fruits and Meats," for instance, his eyes light upon the mesmerizing sight of a blood-covered butcher whacking at a "hunk of steer" (38, 39). The underground manufactures impulses that are inexplicable to Daniels himself and that mark an increasing alienation between his own body and mind. He stares "fixedly at the cleaver" and examines "the sharp edge smeared with cold blood . . . fascinated and repelled by the dried blotches": "He wanted to fling the cleaver from him, but he could not. . . . He was determined to keep it, for what purpose he didn't know" (38, 39, 41, 42).

Wright's protagonist next crawls into a jewelry store, where he discovers his blood lust evolves into a desire for objects of a higher order: money and a "fair-haired white girl" (42). As he ogles her from the shadows, the intimations of an interracial rape fantasy are present, if never articulated. The "girl" screams upon spotting Daniels, but is quickly dismissed by her male coworkers as "dreaming" (42). Alone with a safe full of money, Daniels is tempted by "the mere fact that he could get it with impunity" and convinces himself that taking it is not stealing since his motive is not to materially benefit from the theft, but rather to thrillingly exercise his will (43, 47). In other words, money has no value for Daniels and stealing is only a perverse demonstration of self-aggrandizement. He doesn't "loot" because he needs to, but because he wants to: "He wanted to steal the money merely for the sensation involved in getting it" (45). The implication is that theft by the black ghetto subject has little do with material inequality and everything to do with psychological abnormality. Later he holds a pistol to the sleeping night watchman's head and smiles "indulgently" at how "he could send a bullet into that man's brain" (50). Whispering "Boom!" with "silent laughter," Daniels in his own mind becomes the murderer others fear him to be (50). Subsequently beaten by the police, who hold him responsible for the theft, the watchman commits suicide. The "cold blood" that fascinated Daniels is now on his hands.

Under the duress of institutionalized racism and violently enforced spatial isolation, Wright shared Ellison's fear that the "confused of mind" might act out their "surreal fantasies . . . upon the streets" or, in Wright's case, under them.[64] Both were writing in the wake of the 1935 and 1943 riots, and though Wright does not allude to the riots, the meaning of his novella is complexly bound up with them. The riots were viewed as "spontaneous outbreaks" of impulsive and non-purposive anger by looting "hoodlums and criminals" in LaGuardia's estimation, or, in Ellison's, by those who felt "some racial or personal guilt."[65] They were not, as Ellison says following Wertham, targeted toward "any specific object," namely, structural racism.[66] Whether such diagnoses were offered by white psychiatrists or black novelists, interpreting the riots in this manner robbed their participants of agency. And it had the potential to transfer the notion of guilt back onto the victims of spatial isolation and racialized violence. Wright's novella was an attempt to prevent the latter from occurring by locating racial guilt in the structures that perpetuated it.

In the final movement of Wright's narrative, Daniels resurfaces and, with "his mind filled with the image of the police station," he is hypnotically compelled through the streets, drawn by his internal sense of guilt as he searches for a way to turn himself in (68). Fabre writes that "In the framework of the narrative, we discover that this guilt is not within the province of the police or the law; on the contrary, it is such a basic psychological fact that it represents (in the Kantian sense) one of the forms of the human mind, the mark of our condition."[67] This, I must say, is hardly the case. Fabre's misunderstanding, it must be stressed, is Daniels's as well. Wright is not so much exploring, as Fabre indicates, a "metaphysical anxiety" stemming from universal guilt as he is dramatizing how dominant racial ideologies are internalized and then cloaked in the guise of being self-originating.[68] Mid-century urban sociology and social psychology constructed a black underclass subject who was guilty—guilty of immorality, guilty of pathological familial structures, guilty of drug abuse, guilty of poor work ethics, and guilty of having no respect for property. Daniels is mistaken about his "great sense of power," to be sure (62). But he is also mistaken about his own sense of guilt and its origins. What he says of the jeweler's guard, he says of himself—"he was not guilty of the crime of which he had been accused, he was guilty, had always been guilty" (62). This kind of universal "metaphysical anxiety" is not the secret truth of Wright's text, but the very problem it seeks to expose, insofar that the problem short-circuits alliances which bind together larger political identities. Daniels misunderstands his guilt to be "innate," when in truth it is localized in the state apparatus of the police and in the built space of the city's lowest and most degraded domains where poor African Americans were expected to live (60). In short, he is unable to see the racial specificity whose burden he is forced to endure: "He had signed a confession. Though innocent, he felt guilty, condemned" (41). He sees himself only as others see him, and what he sees he takes as true. Wright's protagonist cannot perceive that his own racial anxiety might be the very thing that connects him to other marginalized subjects in the slums.

Urban sociology and social psychology—which considered the slum a "world apart"—formed a vital part of a strategy of containment, a means of quarantining an unruly population.[69] The rhetoric of debasement, squalor, and disease that ran through this discourse served to disarm and discount the possibility that lower-class African Americans might rise from their submerged state. This body of knowledge on socio-spatial debasement was structured around a descriptive vocabulary that bifurcated space into uneven geographies to show how far below national ideals some populations fell. David Pike has addressed the social function of these formulations: "The world above—the world of law, order, economy, conformity—is given structure and order by what it excludes beneath it as unfit," he argues, going on to assert that "needless to say, this is a symbolic gesture, reinforced by myriad linguistic pairings and tropes: high and low, up and down, upper and lower, light and dark, north and south."[70] Yet in discursively producing a condemned and polluted geography where the dregs and the outlaws accumulated, urban sociology also produced a new critical site for thinking through the social effects of spatial inequality. This last point needs to recognized, for it holds the key to understanding how Ellison and Wright stepped through this fraught terrain. The rhetorical site of debasement created an opportunity to "shift from metaphor to analysis when we speak of the language of the city," an opportunity to demystify the obfuscating language that impeded social change.[71] "Filth is the contradiction that assails the *idealized* principles of equality," anthropologist Michael Taussig asserts, to which David Pike adds, "Whatever exposes the contradiction . . . is consigned to the underworld as unclean."[72]

In sum, the sewer as a site of African American habitation in "The Man Who Lived Underground" spatializes the social relations of racism in the Fordist city. It congeals images of black deviance, delinquency, and squalor. By materializing the ideology of racial abjection, Wright's sewer makes this ideology visible to us, if not to his own protagonist. The putative unclean fecundity of the black underworld in Wright's fiction exposes the material production of social and cultural marginality. But when inner-city residents defied their decades of material impoverishment and economic and political exploitation through an exercise of collective agency, this same discourse diagnosed their actions as evidence of cultural pathology and as a sign that recent migrants could not acculturate to urban living. Ultimately both explanations blamed the riots on atomized elements adrift in the inner city, and thus helped to forestall the formation of a black territorial politics for at least another generation. What we witness in "The Man Who Lived Underground" is the production of a racially dominated consciousness which obviates its own liberation. Wright's work fittingly concludes with Daniels taking his last breath of air, "his mouth full of thick, bitter water" as the "current spun him around" (84). "The Man Who Lived Underground" shows how inner-city African Americans in the 1940s ingested the "bitter water" of racism to the point that they held themselves guilty for challenging their confinement in the underworld sewers of urban America.

"Man Lowest Down": Ralph Ellison's Underground Harlem and "the Pathology of American Democracy"

Follow me out of the sewer and into the cellar, the "hole in the ground" where the title character of Ralph Ellison's *Invisible Man* happens to be living (13). It may seem that in the seven years between Wright's novella and Ellison's epic novel, we have not traveled very far—from worse to bad, at best—but this is not the case. Through *Invisible Man* Ellison sought to change the mid-century cultural conversation about black abjection. The invisible man's famous hole is a real material space in the segregated Fordist city and a metaphor for the invisibility, unwantedness, and suppression of black life. But in the hands of Ellison, this hole is turned into an underground counterspace where critical distance on the hierarchy of class and race relations is gained and where self-liberation, forged out of the experience of spatial marginalization, is strategized in terms that reject the massive collective delinquency of the Harlem riots.

In *Invisible Man* the first step to self-liberation is through writing into historical memory "what is left out of our recorded history," what Djuna Barnes's O'Connor once labeled "the stories that do not amount to much."[73] Underworld fiction has often taken on this salvaging function, preserving and reimagining the everyday endurance and transformation of neglected communities. For Ellison, however, the micronarratives that the novel records are not the stories of O'Connor's foul slums, but rather the racial struggle for dignity and freedom of movement. In his essays, Ellison frequently reflected upon the social role he envisioned for imaginative fiction. In "Going to the Territory," he remarked that America's "unwritten history looms as [the] obscure alter ego" to the officially sanctioned narrative of the nation like an uncanny racial shadow. "Although repressed from our general knowledge of ourselves, it is," Ellison assures, "always active in the shaping of events."[74] That "unwritten history" is what the invisible man is writing, and he writes it underground in the cellar apartment he quite unexpectedly finds himself in at the novel's conclusion. When Wright's Daniels finds a typewriter, he manages to peck out his name on the keys and laughs to himself that "he would learn to type correctly one of these days."[75] Ellison's protagonist beats him to the punch, typing out what he himself calls "a whole unrecorded history" of Harlem, which turns out to be a whole other version of America, a country "as chaotic and full of contradictions, changes of pace, and surprises as life itself."[76]

Invisible Man's prologue and epilogue, which are spoken in the present tense and from underground, frame the trials and tribulations of the narrator's time up above, the past-tense narration that he has written during his internal exile. Well known to many readers, the episodic events of Ellison's bildungsroman can and have been read as allegories with mythological and folkloric resonances that recall the layers of James Joyce's *Ulysses*. But a brief review demonstrates that each episode also arises from the real-world politics of migration, unemployment, racism, housing, and collective violence.

The novel's upper- and underworlds, in other words, are as much historical and sociological as they are mythological. The college the invisible man attends in the early passages of the novel, for instance, is modeled on Ellison's own all-black vocational Tuskegee Institute. For a time, the Chicago School sociologist Robert Park worked for the Institute, organizing conferences and managing the school's publicity. Park was considered by many to be the real power behind Tuskegee, a school whose mission was to turn out black students whose training prepared them for work in northern factories. Co-written with Ernest Burgess, Park's *Introduction to the Science of Sociology* (1921) was a standard text in sociology courses at the school, including the one in which Ellison was enrolled. As a student, Ellison read Park's infuriating claim that "the temperament of the Negro. . . . [is] a genial, sunny, and social disposition" that shows "an interest and attachment to external, physical things rather than to subjective states and objects of introspection."[77] In the educational context in which he himself worked, Park was denying African Americans the capability for self-awareness and philosophical rumination. As one might expect, Ellison found such sentiments deeply offensive for their patent racism.

An inability to distinguish between individuals and larger group identities, which are ascribed to each unique member of a race, was sociology's second failure for Ellison.[78] Lawrence Jackson writes that "the sociology debacle had broader consequences for Ellison's intellectual growth. He decided that he would approach intellectual issues, literature, and the arts as an individual."[79] In *Invisible Man*, the college, like Tuskegee, is a massive project in social engineering to acculturate African Americans as a group. The college's internal racism and power politics display little sympathy for the plight of individual students, such as Ellison's smart hero, and as a result, the invisible man is expelled when he jeopardizes the school's relationship with a wealthy white benefactor.

By sending his protagonist to New York to look for work while dreaming of returning to college at a later date, Ellison in effect makes him part of the massive migration of poor, southern African Americans to northern cities in the 1940s. And yet he also casts him as a future member of the college-educated, upwardly mobile, Talented Tenth that would be the backbone of the black urban middle class. The tension between these two poles of identification push and pull at the invisible man throughout the novel. The labor dispute at Liberty Paints that soon follows the narrator's arrival in New York further traps him between two collective entities: management that uses him for menial labor and the union that rejects him as a management spy. The invisible man, in turn, rebuffs the purported benefits of trade unionism, petulantly remarking that "they were forcing me to accept things on their own terms" (218).

The blast at Liberty Paints, which the narrator accidentally sets off, drops him in the hands of the factory's doctors. The nightmarish scene that follows is a redescription of black identity by white "scholarly looking" experts that recalls a whole history of invasive medical practices to normalize putatively aberrant populations (235). The physicians attempt to rewire Ellison's hero through electro-shock, promising "as complete a change of personality as you'll find in your famous fairy-tale case of criminals transformed into amiable fellows" (231). The scene signals Ellison's rethinking of psychotherapy as coercive renorming, the terrible infantilization of blacks in the service of eliminating delinquency and excess anger. In the closing chapter of the novel, after detailing the invisible man's rapid rise and fall through the ranks of the stultifying Brotherhood, a thinly veiled version of the New York Communist Party that takes him under its wing and trains him to be a spokesperson for the group, only to cast him aside for insubordination, Ellison sets fire to Harlem with a reenactment of the riot of 1943. He does so by dramatizing it as partly the result of the communist exploitation of Harlem's grievances, a charge floated in the popular press and by Mayor LaGuardia. In a panicked flight through the streets as Harlem burns behind him, the invisible man falls into an open manhole where he "plunge[s] down,

down" into a cold coal cellar (553). In the sociological and journalistic literature of the period, the housing crisis precipitated the riot, but Ellison reverses the causality: the riot causes the narrator's housing crisis. In the blur of time between his Icarus-like fall and the first words of the prologue, he steals into a basement—a gesture that accrues new potency in light of the CHPC reports—and defiantly decides to "take up residence underground" in a basement of a "building rented strictly to whites" in "a border area" near Harlem (5, 558). But what the narrator ultimately discovers "beneath the surface" is that he "must come out, . . . must emerge" from his isolation because he "has a socially responsible role to play," a role in which writing will play the main part (12, 567, 568).

Ellison's novel has generated shelves of scholarly criticism, but it has yet to be placed within what I think is its most immediate historical and spatial context: Harlem's housing emergency and riots, which inform nearly every episode.[80] In the pages that follow, I want to underscore the geography of Ellison's imagination by noting how his novel rewrites the cultural narrative of underworld black squalor and delinquent pathology. But first it is useful to recognize the story that Ellison is not writing. As a rebuttal to condemnatory narratives of black lowlife perpetuated by W.E.B. Du Bois, McKay offered the celebratory *Home to Harlem* in which the irrepressible black underworld took center stage, to the embarrassment of many. Readers searching for an updated version of McKay's libidinal architecture of cabarets, brothels, saloons, and jazz clubs in Ellison's Harlem will soon find their efforts turn up little that is salacious.

As Paul Anderson documents, Ellison considered such "literary decadence" to be wholly counterproductive. In Ellison's opinion, "the supposedly unrepressed psychic abandon energizing black popular music," such as is heard shaking the pages in McKay's novel, too often resulted in "racial romanticism" and exoticism for whites.[81] Ellison himself was a talented trumpet player and a student of jazz and the blues—writing with a deep appreciation about both in *Shadow and Act* and *Going to the Territory*—but he found the frantic jazz of mid-century bebop to be cold and mathematical. "A new and disturbing development" is how Ellison described it.[82] The foremost exponent of the new discordant, avant-garde sound was the saxophonist Charlie Parker, who operated in, as Ellison memorably put it, "the underworld of American culture."[83] The tragic irony of Parker's short life, in Ellison's estimation, was that in seeking to escape the role of minstrel entertainer through his aggressive playing and his disdain for his audience, he wound up appealing to rebellious white, middle-class hipsters engaged in fashionable nihilism and drug abuse while slumming in jazz clubs in search of the neoprimitive. Despite his best efforts, despite his "calculated surliness and rudeness," "Bird was indeed a 'white' hero," Ellison writes.[84]

Of course, the older jazz tradition of Count Basie, Duke Ellington, and Louis Armstrong was also subject to exoticization, appropriation, and misunderstanding by whites; nevertheless it expressed for Ellison the richness, complexity, and hardship of the black experience. When, in the opening pages of the novel, Ellison's narrator places a jazz record on the phonograph in his underground lair, it is Armstrong's lyrical "poetry [made] out of being invisible" (8). Listening to Armstrong opens a hole in perceptual reality through which the invisible man plunges "like Dante . . . into its depths," moving through an "underworld of sound" (9, 12). The descent is not into a world of pure libidinality, but into a submerged racial history of pain and a search for freedom that leads the dreaming and hallucinating narrator back to another site of African American community and endurance: a post-Emancipation black church that is haunted by the legacies of slavery.

Ellison's choice largely to avoid the communal pandemonium of McKay's proletarian underworld is freighted with class implications. And as we will see shortly, it is also bound up with Ellison's rejection of his own narrator's period of irresponsible delinquency—the invisible man's breaking and entering, drug use, and assault, which the narrator learns as well to cast off as short-sighted, indulgent, and born out of unproductive anger and resentment. Ellison's novel briefly peers into "the gin mills and the barber shops and the juke joints and the churches" of Harlem, but its protagonist does not linger in this poor and working-class milieu (460). Significantly, when the narrator late in the novel steps into "Barrelhouse's Jolly Dollar, a dark hole of a bar and grill" patronized by "men in working clothes and a few rummy women," he is viewed with suspicion as if he doesn't belong (413). McKay's working-class Jake would have been at home here, but Ellison's more fastidious narrator is a stranger in a strange land. His efforts to ingratiate himself by referring to other men in the bar as "Brothers" are rejected and come off as forced: "Shit, he goddam sho ain't no kin of mine!" a patron yells (413).

The figure in the novel who comes closest to emblematizing what Gunnar Myrdal in 1944 termed the "Negro underworld" of "petty thieves and racketeers, prostitutes and pimps, bootleggers, dope addicts, and so on" in "the big cities" is Ellison's slippery Rinehart (330). Rinehart is a confidence man, hustler, numbers runner, and preacher all under one white hat. Known to almost everyone on Harlem's streets, he is at the hub of the underground, black-market economies of policy and prostitution that in the mid-century period proliferated behind the walls of segregation. Historically, underground economies were a response to labor market exclusions and to underserved consumer demand, a means of survival and profiteering through homegrown exploitation of women and men looking to get lucky by local lotteries or by other means. In the sociological literature on race and urban living by Myrdal, Zorbaugh, and others, such illegal markets were theorized as disintegrating and disorganizing communities and their residents. Rinehart is to be taken as symptomatic of the enzymatic erosion of values and traditions into mere criminal self-interest. He is a sign of urban anomie that Ellison, in "Harlem Is Nowhere," linked to centrifugal disorientation and severe psychic distress caused by living under a new regime of racism in claustrophobically condensed northern cities.

Rinehart, like Harlem itself, is nowhere. He does not even so much as make a cameo in the novel. This boogey man of white sociology is more invisible than the invisible man, though like the racial specter he is, he's believed to be everywhere. When the narrator is pursued by gang members of Ras, the black separatist radical whose incendiary rhetoric is setting minds on fire in Harlem, he dons the disguise of a hat and sunglasses to duck out of view. By doing so, he accidentally impersonates Rinehart, bringing to life the figure who exists off stage. Immediately taken for this delinquent subject by people on the streets, the narrator ponders Harlem's criminal underbelly that is suddenly revealed to him: "I had heard of it before but I'd never come so close," adding, "I thought, I'm upset because I know I don't have to know him, that simply becoming aware of his existence, being mistaken for him, is enough to convince me that Rinehart is real" (486, 487). Rinehart is a racial phantasm, a congealed set of social anxieties about race and space that assumes the status of being real through discourse and rumor, much like the black underworld subject we find in studies of sociology and urban planning. One hears about or becomes aware of the likes of Rinehart and then one sees him, or, worse yet, is mistaken for him. This is to say, the discursive fantasy of a racial underworld is indistinguishable from its reality because the discourse helps create the environment for this world's emergence. Or as the invisible man wonders, "Perhaps simply to be known, to be looked upon by so many people, to be the focal point of so many concentrating eyes, perhaps this was enough to make one different; enough to transform one into something else, someone else" (328). Has a more poignant description of how voyeurism produces new types of abjected personhood been written? Rinehart haunts because he is not only what Ellison's abused and alienated protagonist might become if not called to play "a socially responsible role" but also because he is what Ellison's narrator is already understood to be—and thus in some way already is—a black delinquent subject who, isolated and angry, skulks in the basement of a white house, the very domestic architecture of racial purity that segregation sought to preserve (568). Having caught "a brief glimpse" of Rinehart's world, the narrator eventually learns to turn away from what he represents: normlessness, cynicism, and self-interest (488). The black underclass subject, however, remains the ghostly Other, the "chaos against which" Ellison will articulate a positive image of black masculinity.

If Ellison's novel steers away from the illicit black underworld, it also largely avoids representations of urban black squalor. Images of black impoverishment circulated in popular and sociological discourses of the period not as signs of poverty, but as markers of physical and moral uncleanliness. Such discourse depoliticized material inequality through the figure of waste and transferred the onus for its production back onto its victims as an unbearable social weight. Though poverty is rooted in a toxic mixture of race, class exploitation, and geography, its origins often have been obscured under the shocking spectacle of garbage-filled streets and crumbling, rat-infested buildings that this mixture produces. Images of "crowded, filthy tenements," to quote the *Amsterdam News*, have circulated with little restraint in all kinds of writings on impoverished urban areas. To the extent that Ellison's novel depicts black urban degradation, it does so to illustrate the class and geographical divisions within Harlem. To put it more bluntly, *Invisible Man* treats waste as a metonym for a certain class of African Americans with whom Ellison's narrator is sometimes lumped, to his own consternation. For instance, roaches crawl down the pipes in an apartment where he stays, but they are from the upstairs neighbors who "live in filth" and who are not "a credit to the race" (249, 318). When the invisible man later gets scolded for dropping his garbage into a neighbor's receptacle, when walking through Harlem, he is taken aback. Naïvely thinking that "garbage is garbage," he is unaware of its incendiary political content (320). The neighbor screams, "We keep our place clean and respectable and we don't want you field niggers coming up from the South and ruining things" (319, 320). "Blazing hate," the neighbor blames underclass garbage with trashing the streets. The irony, of course, is that the narrator is conscientiously not littering. But he is guilty of the greater transgression of not respecting another's property, the crime central to all rioting. Though he considers "this woman crazy," the association she draws between him and "field niggers" who ruin things deeply unnerves him (320). He is from the South, but his fields are (or were) his college's landscaped "hedges and wild roses" (34). When he reaches his "clean hand" into the "rotting swill" to retrieve his package, the odor wafts into his nose, a troubling permeability between self and environment (320). Ellison describes him as repeatedly using a handkerchief, desperately trying to remove the stain of this gross association.

The full force of Ellison's strategic decision to downplay the black underworld of pleasure and squalor only becomes clear when we realize what Ellison was writing against. Ellison was compelled to carefully unlink the connections that had been soldered in the period between a deleterious urban environment, black pathology, and collective unrest. As I have noted, in the 1940s and 1950s these causal linkages had been welded into an imprisoning loop: cultural pathology was an outgrowth of living in the ghetto, and the Harlem riots were an unmistakable sign of that pathology manifested as mass delinquency, which only buttressed the argument for further isolation. As Joe R. Feagin and Harlan Hahn argue in *Ghetto Revolts: The Politics of Violence in American Cities* (1973), the diagnosis of urban rioting as "unhealthy" and "abnormal"—"a manifestation of a pervasive sickness"—prompted the conclusion that urban discontent could "be corrected by strong palliatives, quarantined by repression, or dismissed as atypical."[85]

Ellison certainly agreed with the widely held opinion that the underclass uprisings of 1935 and 1943 were not only ineffective but also misguided and counterproductive. But the circular logic that linked the riots to individual and cultural pathologies that were themselves ecologically determined was a devastating disenfranchisement of black communities and a castigation of all urban African Americans as eccentric. In response, Ellison needed to do two things: first, reassert the fundamental, but easily concealed, political nature of space, and second, redescribe black asociality not as psychopathology but as a conscious choice, though a choice he himself would choose to reject. Doing so did not mean ignoring the dirty realities on the ground (or under them), and neither did it entail pretending that white fantasies of black nonnormativity held no power. Rather, Ellison set for himself the task of writing through these historical and discursive contexts in order to recoup a vision of African American agency that did not succumb to the enervating effects of the slum. Turning now to *Invisible Man*'s representations of the housing crisis and riot in Harlem, we will see how Ellison worked toward a new notion of spatial politics, which finds its fullest articulation in the novel's conclusion.

As a resident of Harlem, Ellison witnessed daily how the politics of racism were inscribed into the city's public and private spaces, and he adapted these historical realities for his novel. The street-level rumblings that eventuate in the riot are heard from the moment the narrator steps foot for the first time into an already jittery Harlem. Fresh from the South, he is discombobulated by the neighborhood's noise and congestion, and before he knows it, he wanders into the middle of a gathering of the inflammatory Ras. "I had never seen so many black men angry in public before," the invisible man says to himself, observing that "it was as though a riot would break any minute. . . . I was careful not to look back lest I see a riot flare" (157, 158). Nearly halfway through the novel, street-level skirmishes flare up again after Ellison's protagonist happens upon an elderly African American couple who have been evicted in the winter and whose "broken-down chairs," "cracked dishes," "a faded tintype of Abraham Lincoln," and "junk" are piled like rubbish on the sidewalk (265, 271). Sensitive to injustice, his eyes burn and his throat tightens (264). He subsequently learns that "they're agrarian types. . . . being ground up by industrial conditions. Thrown on the dump heaps and cast aside" (286). Clustered around them are fuming local residents, police, and white members of the Brotherhood who see the housing crisis as one of the causes around which to rally Harlem to class conscious. When the officer pushes the elderly woman as she tries to reenter her apartment, the narrator is "outraged and angered," both desiring the crowd's percolating violence against the cop with his "blue steel pistol," and fearing it (269, 272). Suddenly finding his voice, the invisible man speaks up, encouraging the crowd to organize as a "law-abiding" people who will not tolerate the indignities of segregation that have kept "two old folks . . . cooped up in a filthy room" (269, 271).

Mocking the language of urban renewal, Ellison's hero calls the crowd's repatriation of the couples' discarded belongings back into their apartment a "clean-up campaign" (276). But the victory is short-lived as several additional police officers arrive and, brandishing weapons, threaten to "clear the streets" of both garbage and people (277). Dramatizing an occurrence that unfolded daily throughout Harlem, the eviction scene underscores how public action is defined as a question that pits state-sanctioned violence against the people's right to assemble for collective protest in public space. When an officer places "a riot call," the crowd responds "What riot?" (277). "If I say there's a riot, there's a riot," he declares, then zeroing in on members of the Brotherhood, demands "what are you white people doing up here in Harlem" (277).

"We're citizens. We go anywhere we like," they respond, a revealing exchange that equates citizenship with spatial mobility that is tied to race but not wholly dependent on it. Some whites, such as the police, can go anywhere they like by exercising territoriality, by using the machinery of the state to establish newly bounded spaces in which they can operate more securely. The movement of other whites, such as radical leftists, and nonwhites are curbed in the process.

The curtailment of white access to Harlem in the 1940s stymied interracial solidarity among the very kind of radical groupings Ellison depicts. Later the 1960s, Ellison would testify before the Senate Sub-Committee on Executive Reorganization, convened to address the mounting social disorder in American inner cities, that "it was not until the War . . . that whites started staying away, and often this was done through the Police Department. White visitors were stopped at 110th Street and told they shouldn't go to Harlem."[86] Historically the kinds of combinatorial alliances that police sought to shut down included those built between the Communist Party, left-leaning unions, the National Negro Congress, and the Consolidated Tenants League, who joined forces to petition for rent control in Harlem. In the midst of the wartime economy, the lack of affordable housing became a defining issue, a rallying site where groups exercised power in the segregated city as part of a larger civil rights agenda. Only after the riot in 1943 did the Office of Price Administration—which had been imbued with the authority to set limits on rent increases, but had refused to impose them—open a branch in Harlem to nervously monitor the housing situation. By the end of the year, it relented and mandated rent control.[87] In Ellison's novel, the seething anger over abuse and neglect reaches a breaking point near the end, when the police shoot a wayward black member of the Brotherhood named Clifton. Clifton's mass funeral procession winds through "the poorer streets," growing longer and longer on a "hot and explosive" day when Harlem is a tinderbox (439, 440). "A much broader group was stirred up over the shooting than I had imagined," the narrator reflects, "Crowds formed at the slightest incidents" and "several clashes erupted" (468, 502).

The depiction of full-scale rioting, which consumes the final chapter of the novel, begins with the narrator sprinting to Harlem in the middle of the night after receiving a phone call about the riot. The scene amounts to a reenactment of Ellison's late-night jaunt to the neighborhood to cover the 1943 uprising for the *Post*. Over the course of the chapter, Ellison's representation of the riot modulates wildly. The riot is a Communist plot to destroy the neighborhood ("the committee had planned it" [541]); the beginning of militant pan-African revolution ("Come away from this stupid looting. . . . Come jine with us to . . . get guns and ammunition," Ras demands [544]); and an underworld carnival with no political aims whatsoever ("a huge woman in a gingham pinafore" on top of a "Borden's milk wagon" swills "beer from a barrel" [532]). That the riot might be all of these testifies to the narrator's inability to formulate a stable response to it and testifies to the social and political climate in which interpretations of inner-city violence were hotly debated. Ellison's novel intervenes into this debate by dramatizing black urban unrest in a manner that destabilizes its meaning and discloses, in turn, that how collective action registers personally and socially is an effect of ideological positioning. *Invisible Man*, however, is not merely a disinterested effort to underscore the production of meaning. Rather the text does, as one might say, take sides. Ellison's novel in the end works vigorously to discount the efficacy of collective violence as a tool for advancing social and spatial justice by rewriting the social history of African American mass protests with a narrative of a retreat underground that imagines civil disobedience in individualized terms. But before the novel concludes in this manner, it posits a much more radical understanding of the riot as a collective act of territorial politics by marginalized residents to exert control over their community. This vision of the riot, which I would now like to consider, is seared into the pages of the book and is not easily forgotten.

The narrator's first impression of the riot as he stands on the outskirts of Harlem is that it sounds "like a distant celebration of the Fourth of July" (523). Consider how this analogy surprisingly intimates that the riot is both a modern black colonial revolt to declare and demand equality and independence and a commemoration of a historic, white, colonial uprising that is being updated so as to guarantee full citizenship rights to African Americans. The narrator's first response, in other words, is the radical implication that the riot is a justifiable localized insurgency to counter decades of economic and governmental subjugation. As the rioting increases, so does the narrator's identification with the everyday residents of Harlem who are carrying it out—he felt "a surge of friendship," he says (526). As the night unfolds, the narrator—feeling betrayed by the Brotherhood and feeling no kinship with Ras's racial separatism—forms part of a small band of rioters, led by "a little hard man" named Dupre (527). "I felt no need to lead or leave them," the narrator confesses, as the group collects buckets, flashlights, and kerosene, making sure to avoid stealing from "Colored stores" as it journeys across the neighborhood to a "huge tenement building," a disease-ridden monstrosity that looms as a totem of injustice (529, 530, 533). "My kid died from the t-bees in that deathtrap," Dupre reveals with anger (534). "This the place where most of us live," one of the other men in the group says, but he is hardly sanguine: "You call *this* living" and as he contemplates setting it on fire, assures "it's the only way to git rid of it" (533).

The riot as an instance of radical spatial praxis culminates in the tenement's torching, the destruction not of a black home, but of a machine of white exploitation (533). What is crucial to note is that the invisible man actually helps set the building on fire. After all of the women and children are carefully removed from the tenement, he remarks that "We slopped the kerosene about, upon an old mattress, along the floor; then moved into the hall" before the fateful lightning of matches (535). Imagine for a second if Ellison's narrative were to conclude with this moment, if its last and lasting image was this towering inferno lit up against the dark Harlem sky and the group of men "silhouetted against the red flare, looking into the flames, shouting" (535).

If Ellison had ended here, his novel would have assumed a much different stance about the nature and value of collective spatial politics than it ultimately does. But the unthinkable or inadmissible possibility of positive radical and purposive action against injustice is undermined by the chaos that Ellison finds latent in the riot and by his narrator's rejection of his own participation in the burning of the building. The novel's treatment of the revolt is underwritten by a pervasive unease that tempers and ultimately negates its efficacy. The novel's shift in ideological perspective is most tellingly revealed when Ellison switches in his narration of the arson from the collective first-person plural to a third-person point of view, a move that internally distances the narrator from the very work in which he participates: after the "*We* slopped" follows "From all through the building came the sounds of footsteps. . . . *The men* worked in silence now, like moles deep in the earth," followed in turn by "*They've* done it. . . . They organized it and carried it through alone; the decision their own and their own action" (535, 536, emphasis added). The narrator here praises the men for planning and following through on their intentions without relying upon the top-down party politics of the Brotherhood or any other institutional framework. But the added effect of Ellison's pronominal shift is to shift culpability away from the invisible man himself, whose hands are reeking of kerosene. His need to rapidly distance himself from the maddening crowd accrues new urgency as they flee through the streets with the burning edifice behind them. "I was one with the mass, moving down the littered street over the puddles of oil and milk, my personality blasted" (537). The psychically shattering effects of collective action are as great as the psychopathological outcomes of racial exploitation. "The violence was pointless," the narrator claims, "It was suicide" (502, 540).

In *Invisible Man* every attempt at collectivist politics—the college's racial accommodationism, trade unionism at Liberty Paints, Ras's racial essentialism, the Brotherhood's historical consciousness—ends in disaster. The riot suffers no less a fate in Ellison's hands. The novel disavows the black underclass uprising as a viable method of contravening the Fordist city's racial exclusions and economic exploitations, seeing in its mass action an unruly crowd hell-bent on breaking windows. The riot does not compel one to rise up from below; rather it makes one go down and hide where one can "think things out in peace, or, if not peace, in quiet" and where, over time, one can turn the "recognition of necessity" into "the recognition of possibility" (488, 558).

The key moment that initiates the invisible man's withdrawal from surface life not insignificantly follows from his rejection of the black underclass's social struggle on the streets of Harlem. While running through the neighborhood, the narrator is stopped when someone he thinks may be a "Cop" yells "'Hey, you!'" (552). In this precise instant, he steps through an open manhole, "plung[ing] outside history" that dissolves him into invisibility, a non-subject who has vanished from the earth (368).[88] The invisible man's plunge into the underground removes him from history and from the surface, where history is being made on the streets, a retreat that sets the stage for his transformation from a recruited subject—a Brotherhood spokesperson or member of a mob—into an individual subject who authors his own story outside of the domain of institutional or collective politics. Like Wright's protagonist, Ellison's narrator is chased into the underworld, but once there he heroically decides to stay. The action of the invisible man's past-tense narration comes to a halt with him in the complete darkness of a hole where he says, remarkably, "I was whole" (558). Burning for light the papers in his briefcase—his diploma and the scrap with his Brotherhood name on it—he reenacts the torching of the tenement, reimagining social protest as a personal act of defiance that destroys the identities foisted upon him. "They were all up there somewhere, making a mess of the world. Well, let them," he states, and then later, with greater clarity of mind, remarks "I learned in time . . . that it is possible to carry on a fight against them without their realizing it" (5, 558).

In the socio-spatial context that I have been elaborating, Ellison's forthright declaration that he wanted "to avoid writing what might turn out to be nothing more than another novel of racial protest" is infused with a newly charged understanding.[89] Let us consider for a moment what Ellison proposes instead of protest in the post-riot aftermath of the prologue and epilogue. In the prologue, the narrator hardly can be said to be a model citizen. In fact, in the "shut-off and forgotten" basement where he is holed up, he is a delinquent, living off stolen electricity, drinking gin and smoking "reefer," and slinking angrily above ground at night (5, 8). With LaGuardia's declaration still ringing in the air that the riots were started by a "few irresponsible individuals," the invisible man pointedly boasts "I am one of the most irresponsible beings that ever lived" (14). The meaning of his delinquency should be understood in terms of—and ultimately in contrast to—the riot. In other words, his radical asociality marks a repudiation of the collective delinquency and mass sociality of the Harlem uprising which was, in the mayor's estimation, led by hoodlums and criminals for whom the bitter narrator might be mistaken. The crucial point here is that for Ellison delinquency does not hasten the riot, as popular and sociological discourse argued. Instead, delinquency follows from the riot's failure to address the problems of socio-spatial injustice in a lasting manner.

Underground, the invisible man takes matters into his own hands. In the final analysis, his actions turn out not to be symptomatic of environmentally induced pathology. Rather, they are a conscious, tactical manipulation of space and the social codes of race that are inscribed in space. *Invisible Man*—like other underworld novels I have considered—brings to life a poetics of the antidiscipline. The diametrical opposite of mass public protest, the invisible man's tactical subversion is contingent, off-the-cuff, and covert. The zoot-suitors whom Ellison's narrator watches on a subway platform after Clifton is killed are the first to enlighten him to this possibility. These urban toughs of the so-called black underworld are dressed in "their well-pressed, too-hot-for-summer suits, their collars high and tight, about their necks, . . . their coats long and hip-tight with shoulders far too broad to be those of natural western men" (429, 430). In his critique of Gunnar Myrdal's study of America's racial conundrums, *An American Dilemma*, Ellison singled out the claim that "Negro culture and personality" were "the product of 'social pathology.'"[90] But "it does not occur to Myrdal that many of the Negro cultural manifestations which he considers merely reflective," Ellison wrote, "might also embody a *rejection* of what he considers 'higher values,'" "the traits held in esteem by the dominant white Americans."[91] It was not that Ellison approved of this rejection, embodied by the zoot-suitors; he just disapproved of the way Myrdal failed to see it as a sign of human will. As his narrator muses over the meaning of their outfits, he recalls "what had one of my teachers said of me?—'You're like one of these African sculptures, distorted in the interest of a design'" (430). The key word here is not "distortion," which is a result of ideological, environmental, or biological deformation, but "design," which is a result of human creativity. The invisible man flips the claim into his own question: "Well, what design and whose?" he now asks, noting that the zoot-suitors' "costumes" originate not in an ancestral African homeland, but are "surreal variations of downtown styles" (430, 432, 433). They have reworked the modern sartorial codes available to them, not as an irrational response to racism but as a creative expression of their ingenuity. They appropriate the white, middle-class business suit, transforming it into a type of armor, a lesson that the narrator will bring with him underground.

But adopting the cool disaffectedness of the zoot-suitors (or of Charlie Parker) is not Ellison's answer. For Ellison, the answer was to be found in rewriting how race had been inscribed in the city. The literal underground in *Invisible Man* is a space off the map, a clandestine realm in which Ellison redefines denigrating images of black underworld abjectness. The squalid black underworld will turn out to be the opposite of what whites imagined it to be. The narrator's ingenious poaching on Monopolated Light & Power company's electricity transforms one of the thousands of "dark, damp, cold dungeons" of New York that Powell spoke about in 1935 into a warm hole, "*full* of light" (6). His Promethean theft of light foregrounds how white space can be creatively reappropriated and consumed from below—rather than destroyed above. His underground appropriation of power is more than a source of self-congratulatory boasting: "I've wired the entire ceiling, every inch of it," he tells, going on to provide the exact number of bulbs he has installed: 1,369 (7). This act of interior redecoration crucially underscores how uneven flows of power produce the visual fictions of race at the heart of mid-century sociological discourse. This becomes clear when we learn that the meaning of the precise number of his light bulbs can be decoded when cross-referenced with the Harlem dream books that residents regularly consulted when trying to select numbers for the neighborhood's illegal lotteries.[92] One such dream book is among the evicted couple's belongings piled on the curb. The 1,369 figure turns out to be a code for "shit," a humorous, if secret, mocking of the culture's images of black squalor and sewage.

The invisible man's hot-wired ceiling makes a mockery of what Ellison chides as "that pseudoscientific sociological concept . . . 'high-visibility,'" which partly held African Americans responsible for the hardship they endured because of visible racial difference.[93] Ellison argued that "'high visibility' actually rendered one *un*-visible" despite "the bland assertions of sociologists" to the contrary.[94] Myrdal had advanced the notion that "the Negro's 'social visibility" was an effect of "dark skin, woolly hair, broad nose, thick lips and prognathism," along with a "cranial capacity slightly less" than whites, a consequence of the deformations of the body from poor diet and bad housing.[95] As we have seen, such diagnoses of the putative underworld body have a long history in American culture. Mid-century urban sociology was a spectral regime of racial truth that taught whites how to see blacks and blacks how to see themselves as different, as worth less. Insofar as African American "high visibility" was a problem that Myrdal in part traced to material impoverishment, it was a problem that Ellison thought could be addressed in part discursively. In other words, it could begin to be rectified through a novel that would help change the social meaning of African American embodiment and, in its small way, chip at the walls of segregation that quarantined blacks as social pollutants.

To this end the narrator steals what is not his—figurative and literal power—in order to produce what also is not his: the right to his own image, a kind of property more valuable than physical property. The blinding light of white voyeurism produces the social meaning of the materially exploited black body by setting it in contradistinction to whiteness and all of its positive connotations. But now with power in his grip, the narrator deploys it so that blackness indexes a "certain ingenuity" (7). Ellison lamented that black characters in American fiction were too often "figures caught up in the most intense forms of social struggle" and "were without intellectual depth."[96] In response, he places his protagonist "in the great American tradition of tinkers," making him "kin to Ford, Edison and Franklin," a child of the Enlightenment (7). "Call me . . . a 'thinker-tinker,'" the invisible man asks (7). The narrator sets out to belie the racist claims for black intellectual inferiority that Robert Park and other sociologists had perpetuated. Ellison's wily narrator does so by tinkering with the very basis of Cartesian Enlightenment ontology by reinserting its excluded variable, the African whose social invisibility has guaranteed unfettered white selfhood. Instead of Descartes's "I think, therefore I am," Ellison's hero announces both "I am an invisible man" and "I . . . possess a mind" (3). His ability to think has been denied, has been rendered invisible in American literature and culture.

Being invisible is not the horror story it might otherwise be, if we redefine invisibility as the disembodiedness that comes through writing, a shrugging off of the terrible corporeal excesses that have been foisted upon the invisible man for the world of print where only his mind matters. This is exactly what Ellison does. In announcing that he is "an invisible man," Ellison's narrator makes clear that he is both an individuated masculine subject and, as he says, "'a disembodied voice,'" a writer and thinker whose body is invisible but whose discourse is eminently legible (568). "Why should I be the one to dream this nightmare . . . if not to at least *tell* a few people about it," the narrator declares (566). "So why do I write, torturing myself to put it down," he asks, answering, "Because in spite of myself I've learned some things" (566). In the end, spatial exploitation is recreated into a privileged, private terrain for contemplation and writing, a place to "put it all down" (566). Having metaphorically harnessed control over his own image through his acts of tactical delinquency, he begins the harder work of writing as a practice of social responsibility (566). In *Invisible Man* the "freedom" to think is instantiated through the technology of writing, and it is through writing that Ellison's narrator abstracts himself into black and white, which will allow him to travel to spaces beyond where his black body can take him, contravening the Fordist city's racial boundaries and its repellant discourses of racial inferiority. As much as his words cannot be geographically circumscribed, the writing of those words presupposes his spatial marginalization. The riot between blacks and whites is transformed into words in "black and white" in a book that bears the invisible man's ironic name (13, 14).

Returning to Ellison's concept of an "unwritten history" of the nation, we might ask just what kind of history this is. Certainly the history of black Americans living in inhumane, illegal spaces is a history that has been left out of the official record, but this is only a part of the story *Invisible Man* tells. The story of the Fordist city's geographic and racial polarizations ends in urban crisis. The story that Wright's Fred Daniels types out while underground begins and ends with the single sentence, "It was a long hot day" (53). Like long, hot days in the ghetto in which police shoot black men, we can surmise that if Daniels were to finish his story it probably would end with chalk outlines and another uprising. The invisible man's claim that "I am not complaining, nor am I protesting either" is a pointed declaration in an era of burgeoning racial discontent, as is his assertion that "the fact is that you carry part of your sickness within you, at least I do as an invisible man. I carried my sickness and though for a long time I tried to place it in the outside world, the attempt to write it down shows me that at least half of it lay within me" (3, 562). Urban sociology and social psychology pathologized African American difference and argued that full-citizenship status was contingent upon normalization or Americanization, and that this in turn could be demonstrated through a conscription to patriarchical family structures, a submission to social authority, and, if need be, through therapy. Though the black underclass was a material and social formation with a specific historical emergence, this discourse postulated that the material evidence (disease-ridden tenements and littered streets) of its emergence signified a sickness within, an inner poverty, as opposed to inner-city poverty.[97]

Myrdal's text facilitated the normalization of black Americans, while Ellison's *Invisible Man* resisted it by petitioning for nonconformity: "Whence all this passion toward conformity anyway?" (563). Yet Myrdal and Ellison are not as far apart as they might seem to be. By nonconformity, Ellison's hero does not mean delinquency or racial and sexual eccentricity; rather, he means diversity—"diversity is the word" (563). The narrative that the invisible man writes is "nonconformist" only to the extent that it conforms to the true principles of liberal American pluralism that racism has subverted but which the epilogue continues to celebrate: "affirm the principle on which the country was built and not the men, or at least not the men who did the violence" (561). Insofar as urban sociology constituted a black underclass that resisted the mandates of "the American Creed," Ellison brought to life a black subject who resisted violations of that "Creed" and called for the expanded application of its principles to all Americans.[98] Ellison posited that "in order for democratic principles and ideals to remain vital, they must be communicated not only across the built-in divisions of class, race, and religion, but across the divisions of aesthetic styles and tastes as well."[99] In this light, Ellison's use of the word "diversity" assumes a new inflection that has as much to do with an aesthetically heterogeneous cultural field as with a socially diverse demography. In defining "essential 'Americanness'" as a "freewheeling assault upon traditional forms of the Western aesthetic," Ellison turns to culture as a domain for conflict and makes *Invisible Man*'s blend of black folk culture and classical allusion quintessentially American.[100] What Ellison's narrator records when he writes America's "unwritten history" is not a history of material and social oppression so much as a cultural history of adaptation told from the point of view of a racialized subject who is batted about by forces greater than himself. In this sense, what Ellison called the "man lowest down" (a recontextualization of Locke's description of the 1935 rioters) is "vital" to the liberal state's legitimacy. The "man lowest down"—the black underworld subject—is a challenge to the state's ability to integrate its diverse subjects and the culture's ability to integrate the aesthetic diversity that arises from them. Following from this, America's "unwritten history" is not what the culture needs to exclude, but what it needs to incorporate as "progress toward the fulfillment of the democratic ideal."[101]

In spite of *Invisible Man*'s closing celebration of democratic principles and its call for their renewed application in the field of culture—the place where we fight it out, rather than fighting it out on the streets—the striking images of Daniels's body sinking into the sewer and the Harlem tenement ablaze remain, refusing to fade. These arresting scenes of the sheer brutality of racism and the collective violent protests against it signal the inability of cultural practice alone to correct the failed implementation of those very principles. The underworld narratives of Wright and Ellison wade down into the dirty waters of American racial abjection, and they both salvage something valuable from waste. Ralph Ellison and Richard Wright harnessed widely circulated images of black underclass degradation and transformed them into opportunities to critically deconstruct how space and race had become conceptually and literally conflated. Rather than discounting such images out of hand as mere racist distortions, they confronted them, interrogating the material and discursive origins of African American debasement.

Insofar as Wright exposes how the abominations of racism are internalized, Ellison shows how they might be rewritten from below through a narrative that presses America to live up to its own ideals. This is important work, to be sure. But in light of the new geographies of poverty produced by racial segregation and long-term sectoral restructuring of the economy toward low-wage employment, Americans would continue to fight it out on the streets, not just in the discursive realms of print. A decade after *Invisible Man*, the terminal decline of the Fordist city and the subsequent emergence of the postmetropolis were hastened by the mass rioting of the 1960s, most spectacularly in the Watts riot of 1965, which made the Harlem riot of 1943 look like a brushfire. "How had it ever happened here, with the chances once so good for diversity?" Thomas Pynchon would ask at the end of *The Crying of Lot 49* (1966), another narrative of underworld waste.[102] In this context, a focus on more "diversity" may seem increasingly insufficient. Unlike Ellison, we might understand the continued existence of men and women "lowest down" in America's undergrounds not as exceptions to democratic principles but as constitutive of the dynamic and polarizing logic of capitalism's production of uneven geographies and unequal social formations. The underworld would hardly disappear in the subsequent decades. In the literature of the 1960s, as we will see in the next chapter, the underworld would again be a site of fascination and fear as American writers continued to struggle to reconcile the proliferation of social diversity in an urban form cut by divisions that were deeper than ever.

4 / Wasted Dreams: John Rechy, Thomas Pynchon, and the Underworlds of Los Angeles, 1960s

In September 1964, William Wilcox Robinson published a small, curious booklet titled *Tarnished Angels: Paradisiacal Turpitude in Los Angeles Revealed*, which offered a thumbnail sketch of the history of prostitution in downtown L.A. beginning with the city's founding in 1781. In this long history, offered up in no more than thirty tiny pages, the 1890s stand out as the peak years of "open and gaudy" prostitution in Los Angeles, the same decade, as we saw in chapter 1, that Jacob Riis and Ernest Ingersoll fretted over the possibility of being tempted by the inviting eyes of a woman into the dark doorways of the Lower East Side's brothels.[1] If one bookend of *Tarnished Angels*'s history was 1781, the other was equally specific: 1909. It was the year, according to Robinson, "when the Los Angeles vice district was wiped out" (23). "Until eventful 1909 prostitution had been taken for granted by officialdom, with underworld orders recognized, also, by most of the local judges," Robinson, from the distance of the 1960s, seemed to lament (24). The story of urban vice in 1909 was a tale of two cities. As I argued in chapter 2, 1909 was the exact year that urban planning was formalized as a discipline and the City Practical movement was initiated to administer cityspace around the mandates of efficiency and the rational allocation of land. New clampdowns on sexual delinquency in so-called underworlds of prostitution and queer sexuality in lower Manhattan and in Greenwich Village were immediate, while in L.A.'s downtown "the parlor houses, the brothels, the cribs were padlocked and the girls were scattered" (24).

The selling point of Robinson's little book was not its sketch of local history. It was instead the even tinier booklet wrapped inside it like a surprise: a facsimile of an 1897 brochure titled "LA Fiesta de Los Angeles, Souvenir Sporting Guide." The brochure was a brief Baedeker for men visiting the city who might wish to mix sex-tourism into their time at the annual festival, "a joyous interval of parades, band concerts, and street gayety lasting several days and nights" (3). The brochure's anonymous editors adopted a late Victorian posture of feigned innocence in their prefatory note as a set-up to the salacious information that their 1890s reader was seeking: "In presenting this little book to the public, we desire to have it understood that it is not for glory or renown, but for the sake of those strangers who visit our fair city and incidentally for the few shekels we get out of the advertisements."[2] With these niceties out of the way, the guidebook's authors proceeded to facilitate their reader's sexual slumming tour by providing advertisements for brothels in the downtown area, many of them clustered along rough-and-tumble Alameda Street, where a taste for racial fetishism ran thick. At "The Octoroon," one advertisement promised, there awaited "a lively, good looking set of girls who will create sport enough to last for a year to come."

Hidden behind the scandalous contents of the brochure was a larger truth about the Janus-faced nature of sex and cityspace, which Norman Klein has remarked upon in *The History of Forgetting: Los Angeles and the Erasure of Memory* (1997), "Cities for tourists often have twin images: one for families, one for the underground weekend. L.A. was famous for its underground world, including red-light districts set up by the city itself during the boom of the 1880s. But these shady services," he adds, "had to be isolated carefully from the real estate promoted to white, prosperous tourists. The raunchy businesses were best left in, or near, non-white areas that tended to be permitted in the north and east of downtown, away from residential real-estate expansion, if at all possible."[3] The real history of the American underworld, as I have been arguing all along, is a real estate story.

But what did Los Angeles's carnivalesque 1890s world of urban sexuality have to do with the 1960s? What were the parallels that Robinson was trying to imply, but which he left unarticulated? Robinson furnished no explanation for his decision to reprint in its entirety what he called "a rare sociological item for the collector of Los Angelesiana," but the nostalgic tone of his prefatory history provides some clues (4). One might speculate that it was not the "eventful 1909" that was on his mind when he contemplated a history of the vanished underworld, so much as it was the anxieties over current events unfolding in downtown L.A. His wistfulness for a grittier Los Angeles of another era spoke volumes more than his reprinted "pocket-size advertising brochure" that would allow readers to momentarily step back in time (4). Klein remarks that for the nostalgic urban imagination, "the past is not the issue at all; it serves merely as a 'rosy' container for the anxieties of the present."[4] A travel history like Robinson's should be understood (to quote Michael de Certeau) as an "exploration of the deserted places of . . . memory," a walk through an expunged urban history in downtown L.A.—empty lots, stone staircases leading nowhere, traces of an old light-rail line, remnants of a lost community—which perhaps never so much existed as it was dreamed in the light of the present.[5] What was being erased from view and from memory in the 1960s were the spaces, voices, and everyday textures and details of so-called underworld communities in Los Angeles. Once "set up by the city itself," the city was clearing them away in the name of progress and urban renewal.

In this chapter, I turn to two very different novels of the 1960s that forestall the history of forgetting, John Rechy's *City of Night* and Thomas Pynchon's *The Crying of Lot 49*. Rechy's novel tells the story of a makeshift community of sexual delinquents in the parks and street corners of downtown L.A., a group of men (and some women) who steal pleasure while always on the run from the police seeking to clean up the area. Pynchon's novel, for its part, uncovers a newly diverse—racial, sexual, ethnic, and simply eccentric—underworld in Los Angeles and elsewhere across California which, far from being rubbed out of existence, seems to be hiding under every figurative rock once one learns how to look for it. But before we can understand the social and physical geographies of these novels, a lay of the land is needed, a sense of how the city was reshaped and reimagined not only from the bottom up but also from the top down in this recent historical period.

In the early 1960s, when *Tarnished Angels* was printed, downtown Los Angeles was being dug up and rebuilt by the longest-running act of slum clearance in U.S. history, the Bunker Hill Redevelopment Project (1955–2015). From the late years of the nineteenth century through the early years of the twentieth, Bunker Hill had been home to many of L.A.'s elite families. Perched above the basin, the neighborhood's prominent Victorian mansions looked over a downtown area where people still farmed, though as worries over spreading prostitution made clear, other, even older, professions were in view. But by mid-century much had changed: those same Victorian windows stared out onto streets of liquor stores, saloons, cheap hotels, and on to a mix of Mexicans, Italians, Chinese,

African Americans, and a growing gay and lesbian population. According to one estimate, by 1961 the city was home to a 140,000 gay men and women.[6]

The narrative of middle-class white flight, urban decline, and future redevelopment in this formerly respectable neighborhood was all too predictable. A chapter of the same story had been written already in Greenwich Village, and a new chapter was about to be inscribed into the sun-blasted topsoil of LosAngeles. As wealthy Bunker Hill residents relocated to the city's suburbs, their Victorian painted ladies were cut into rooming houses for low-income renters, and some were divided into brothels as well. In 1957, the Department of Building and Safety condemned much of Bunker Hill as a fire hazard, declaring that 60 percent of its buildings were unsafe for habitation.[7] Reports pinpointed the district as the epicenter of L.A.'s mounting drug, crime, and health problems, essentially giving a green light to the wrecking crews that would raze the old Victorians and to the building crews that would raise the corporate office towers in their place. The redevelopment of Bunker Hill was coordinated with an extensive transformation of the surrounding narrow, curved, and inclining streets (some of which were literally straightened out) and with a relandscaping of Pershing Square, the small city park and social miasma where John Rechy's gay underworld had taken root. "The number of faggots cruising around here is legion," the poet Hart Crane once quipped about the park.[8] With the aim of luring upscale shoppers back downtown, the urban renewal of the area proceeded in conjunction with a vigorous targeting by police of prostitution and homosexuality. Each step in downtown L.A.'s forward-looking development was matched by an act of rearguard social containment. Los Angeles's "vice district was wiped out" for the second time in half a century.

Any top-down imposition of a space of commerce and social discipline necessarily reshuffles, upends, and remakes human geographies—the territories of life, love, and resistance—which urban literature has turned to in order to think through the politics of class, race, ethnicity, and sexual identity. In the case of the dramatic but local transformations of downtown Los Angeles, this last development was a harbinger of a much broader process of social restructuring from which the urban form known as the postmodern city was born. I will address the postmodern city more extensively in the next chapter, where it is the subject of Don DeLillo's epic novel *Underworld* (1997), but I note here that the prosecution of sexual delinquency and the renewal of urban space in and around the Bunker Hill area in the 1960s were indicative of systemic

FIGURE 10. "Victorian houses on Bunker Hill with steel frame of 42-story Union Bank building rising behind them, Los Angeles, Calif., 1966." Courtesy of UCLA Charles E. Young Research Library Department of Special Collections. Los Angeles Times Photographic Archives. Copyright © Regents of the University of California, UCLA Library.

changes to American work and leisure that would become clearer as the century drew to a close.

What would happen later in other cities was showing up first in the mesocosm of L.A. Like most American cities after World War II, its Fordist economy was based on heavy industry and manufacturing, and its geography was a mix of residential suburbs, black ghettoes, and a downtown in decline. Yet near the peak of its Fordist period in the 1960s, L.A. "simultaneously developed as a prototype for what is now commonly described as 'sunbelt' forms of industrialization and urban growth."[9] It was as if L.A. became a post-Fordist or postmodern city ahead of schedule. The nation's future was coming true in its dystopic western promised land: a sprawling fragmented patchwork of suburbs, exurbs, and satellite cities connected by highways reaching to the horizon, a new computer and weapons economy, and the creation of underground black markets for the new urban poor. These postwar urban transformations were explosive and did not come without a fight, as riots in the mid-1960s in Harlem, Detroit, Newark, and Chicago attest. Even in a decade punctuated by frequent urban revolts, the five-day black underclass uprising in the impoverished Los Angeles neighborhood of Watts was on another scale. The most traumatic inner-city disturbance the country had yet witnessed, the Watts riots fundamentally altered the redevelopment of Los Angeles's proto-postmodern downtown by sparking further retrenchment: in its wake "resegregated spatial security became the paramount concern" for businesses and white homeowners.[10] In retrospect, it did much more. "If there is just one event," the geographer Edward Soja writes, "to choose from to signal the initiation of the contemporary restructuring process all over the world, it may very well be the Watts riot of 1965."[11] "Ignored for so long as aberrant, idiosyncratic, or bizarrely exceptional, Los Angeles, in another paradoxical twist, has," Soja also observes, "more than any other place, become the paradigmatic window through which to see the last half of the twentieth century."[12]

Succinctly put, Los Angeles in the 1960s witnessed an assault on public expressions of sexual non-heteronormativity, the country's most catastrophic racial uprising, a dramatic reconfiguration of one of the city's most historic neighborhoods, and the emergence of the city as the epicenter of Pentagon spending and corporate infrastructure. I turn to the work of John Rechy and Thomas Pynchon because they compel us to understand these changes and upheavals from the perspective of the city's spatially marginalized populations. On the surface, Rechy's earnest, semiautobiographical, first-person narrative of an unnamed gay prostitute, and Pynchon's postmodern, pastiche-filled text about the strange holdings of a dead real-estate developer may make an odd couple. But despite differences in tone and form, *City of Night* and *The Crying of Lot 49* are both stories of underworld Los Angeles. They are stories about the micro-geographies of exclusion of those left out of hegemonic postwar narratives of economic expansion, suburbanization, and heterosexual domestic fulfillment.

The settlement of Los Angeles by white Anglo-Protestants from the Midwest in the half century between 1880 and 1930—"the largest internal migration in United States history" and "the least heroic," as one historian has described it—was fueled by an extraordinarily successful booster campaign to market the region's Mediterranean climate, reputedly a cure for all sorts of physical and mental ailments.[13] The redevelopment of L.A.'s downtown in the 1960s was the latest effort to let in more disinfecting sunshine. *City of Night* repudiates this rhetoric by demythologizing Los Angeles as the fabled land of rebirth and renewal. "*You can rot here without feeling it*," Rechy writes.[14] The musty gloom of Rechy's homosexual noir counters the city's surfeit of sunshine and reproductive sexuality with a narrative of gay men who hide in "long shadows" until forced into daylight by the police who descend regularly on Pershing Square (141).

The novel captures the queer world of Pershing on the eve of its destruction, textually preserving it for future readers.[15] The turpitude revealed by Rechy is not queer sexuality and prostitution. It's the relentless harassment of gay men and drag queens—L.A.'s angels—and the spaces they inhabit. Though *City of Night* lingers longer in southern California than it does anywhere else, its peripatetic narrative's geographical reach is in fact national. The diasporic queer community that Djuna Barnes hinted at in *Nightwood* is here in full color, though within a decidedly American context. With a forthrightly spatial vocabulary, Rechy's novel charts a migratory sexual "netherworld," a "boiling subterranean world," a world of "submerged lives" that is always on the move, momentarily inhabiting parks, street corners, theaters, and the "shadowed world of dim bars . . . extending like an underground from New York to Hollywood with fugitive stops in other cities" (31, 99, 185, 236). Through the trope of the sexual underworld, *City of Night* produces a political and erotic knowledge of national geography that shows how sexual identity is spatially contingent, how sex becomes ghettoized, and how moral geographies are constructed by policing and urban redevelopment.

Three years after *City of Night* was published, Thomas Pynchon followed with *The Crying of Lot 49*, another peripatetic novel, though from a much different point of view. Pynchon's novel records the peregrinations of a middle-class housewife, Oedipa Maas, whose suburban isolation has made her unaware of the kind of urban queer "streetworld" found in Rechy's novel.[16] Maas's journey by car, which leads her through L.A.'s thoroughly corporatized and militarized landscape of aerospace manufacturers, expensive housing developments, and cloverleaf freeways, ushers her into haunting proximity with W.A.S.T.E., an acronym for We Await Silent Trystero's Empire, a secret, centuries-old organization that communicates through an alternative postal system which uses garbage cans as mailboxes. But the real-and-imagined underworld of Trystero turns out to be one of the biggest red herrings in postwar fiction. The true waste that Oedipa encounters during her investigation of her ex-lover Pierce Inverarity's estate is a newly diverse and atomized urban underworld of the poor. Forced to reckon with the knowledge that this disinherited population is "the legacy" that she has discovered and that this is "America," she nearly loses her mind.[17] However, Oedipa's paranoid fantasy of the Trystero conspiracy is not simply a senseless delusion. It is an important ideological screen that allows her to continue to function as a bourgeois subject by permitting her still to believe in a narrative of national innocence. If America is home to a secret cabal of W.A.S.T.E. rather than a world of wasted populations for whom the nation has no use or place, then the life of Pynchon's protagonist—its suburban quietude and middle-class comforts—remains unindicted.

The structuring ideologies of bourgeois existence, Pynchon shows, do not, indeed cannot, account for the realities of social and spatial exploitation. Those realities were nowhere more evident than in Watts, a neighborhood concealed from view by what Pynchon describes as a white fantasy of black cultural delinquency. *The Crying of Lot 49* never mentions Watts, though one suspects Oedipa may have passed it during her many drives on the freeway. The cataclysmic riot of 1965, however, was the subject of Pynchon's one instance of published journalism, "A Journey into the Mind of Watts" (1966). In a nearly perfect inversion of Oedipa's perspective, Pynchon writes that from the vantage point of Watts, the "white culture" surrounding it is a "well-behaved unreality" that is difficult to understand. In the end, what Pynchon and Rechy both articulate through the trope of the social underworld is a critical human geography of how marginalized identities and imperiled communities respond to their emplacement in the midst of seismic upheavals in the fragmented, segregated city that affected everyone, including suburbanites and inner-city residents.[18] The tumultuous emergence of L.A.'s postmodern sprawl and deepening inequality were an "exaggerated case of more general national trends."[19] The restructuring in Los Angeles in the 1960s heralded developments that were, to paraphrase Pynchon, the legacy of America.

Subterranean Worlds: Urban Redevelopment, Queer Spaces, and John Rechy's *City of Night*

John Rechy's underground queer novel *City of Night* is a salvaging operation in the historical context of police persecution and urban renewal, two deeply intertwined exercises of spatial power. Through the eyes of an anonymous male hustler, Rechy's narrative crisscrosses America, from El Paso, to New York City, Los Angeles, San Francisco, Chicago, New Orleans, and back to El Paso, where the exhausted and emotionally distraught narrator finally, if only briefly, settles down to write the history of "the nightworld," plumbing the meaning of his experience of sexual alterity in a homophobic country (377). In the tradition of much American urban fiction, *City of Night* thematizes the abiding loneliness and anonymity of the newcomer in the big city, in this case a young man driven from the dusty, windswept plains of Texas by his Scottish father's violence and his Mexican mother's suffocating love. But Rechy also radically reshapes this perennial theme by spinning it into a frank counternarrative of an emergent queer citizenry, "citizen" used here in the older sense of one who freely inhabits the spaces of the nation, and more specifically, the spaces of its cities. From the start, Rechy frames his narrative as national in scope and urban in focus, with an opening sentence that looks to a future national space of one sprawling queer megalopolis: "Later I would think of America as one vast City of Night stretching gaudily from Times Square to Hollywood Boulevard" (9).

For Rechy, the promise of the nation is to be tested through the experience of what has been termed "a queer counterpublic," a community of gay, lesbian, and transgender Americans residing, surviving, and moving through the crucible of its cities.[20] *City of Night*, much like Djuna Barnes's *Nightwood*, repudiates traditional models of identity—reproductive, consumerist, patriarchal—and their mirror image in same-sex domestic monogamy, and agitates instead for a radically public sexual citizenship that is understood in spatial terms. This repudiation is built into the dialogic structure of the novel. Its episodic narrative advances through a rhythm that alternates between chapters titled "City of Night," which are dedicated to the narrator's account of his hustling, harassment, and loneliness in despoiled urban terrains, and chapters simply titled with the names of men and women ("Mr. King," "Pete," "Miss Destiny," "Neil," "Jeremy") who represent the plurality of the nation's nonstandardized sexualities (gay, bisexual, transgender, fetishistic) that the narrator comes to know firsthand. In this way, *City of Night* weaves together the spaces of the city and the voices of the city's sexual outlaws. By showcasing a national sexual diversity that was hidden and denied in the period, the novel demonstrates for readers that geography is instrumental to how human sexuality is categorized and lived under duress.

Upon publication, *City of Night* was roundly castigated by critics, and even today it has not received the scholarly attention it warrants. Robert Kirsch in a *Los Angeles Times* review (June 16, 1963) described it as "mawkish," and claimed that it was "the end of the line, so far as I'm concerned, of the subterranean literature of shock." "At best," he acidly quipped, "it is a raw document in social pathology. It is a book, but let's not dignify it by calling it a novel." Peter Buitenhuis of the *New York Times* in a review two weeks later felt also that it exhibited little in the way of craftsmanship and that its subject, the disturbing "half-submerged world of homosexuality," was one he would "prefer to ignore." As these remarks make plain, early reviewers read the novel as an instance of unmediated realism ("a raw document") whose subject was a clandestine geography ("half-submerged world"). For Buitenhuis, *City of Night* was not so much an example of "social pathology," as it was a study of perversion: "Mr. Rechy," he claimed, "is the Kinsey of the homosexuals, and it may be that 'City of Night' will do for the United States what the Wolfenden Report did for Britain."

What the Wolfenden Committee (officially the Home Office Committee on Homosexual Offences and Prostitution) did for Britain was draw up, with the assistance of the Metropolitan Police commissioner, "a homosexual map of London," which circled in red "the places where police arrests for importuning and gross indecency were most frequently made."[21] On the eve of Queen Elizabeth's coronation in 1953, London was in the grip of a sex panic over "the twin vices of male homosexuality and female prostitution," which were thought to be centered in specific zones of the city that were along the queen's parade route.[22] Authorities feared that a national celebration of the British Commonwealth might be derailed by displays of transgressive sexuality by less than ideal citizens. Through its maps, the committee sought to bring depravity into view in order to remove it from sight, something that Buitenhuis, strangely enough, thought that Rechy's novel of the queer underworld would also accomplish. The Wolfenden Report advocated the partial decriminalization of homosexuality at the same time that it understood homosexuality to be to a public disturbance that needed to be geographically administered and regulated, a project that was not unlike the City Practical's goals with regard to Greenwich Village forty years earlier. In the words of British cultural historian Frank Mort, the Wolfenden Report mobilized "a panoptic vision of the city and its subjects," a bird's-eye perspective, which like all such panoramic claims to mastery, was "invariably exterior to the practices it seeks to classify through processes of inclusion and exclusion."[23]

Peter Buitenhuis's comparison of *City of Night* to the Wolfenden Report was correct on one account, but still fundamentally misguided. Led by its footloose narrator from the East Coast to the West, Rechy's novel charts a mobile urban queer subculture across the nation, but it does so from the perspective of the "streetworld," not from the aerial view implied by maps of the city or country. When viewed from a position above or "invariably exterior," sexuality is unequally and falsely bifurcated into hetero- and homosexual. *City of Night*, however, is written from a ground-level perspective that reveals the manifold complexity of urban sexuality, which it does by bringing the reader into intimate proximity with the lives of drag queens, lesbians, rough-trade practitioners, and leather and BDSM fetishists who try to outwit the very kind of surveillance operations Wolfenden employed. Rechy, who himself worked as a street hustler, recognizes the numerous internal distinctions within the queer community when he, in an expository parenthetical aside in the novel, exposes the diversity concealed by the label of gay prostitute or hustler: "malehustlers ('fruithustlers' / 'studhustlers': the various names for the masculine young vagrants)" (92). Inasmuch as the committee turned its attention to the conceptualized spaces of sexuality—the quantifiable, mapped locations in the city where public sexuality was treated as a menace—Rechy's novel zeroes in on the lived spaces of the body and the practices of desire, fantasy, dress, coded gestures, and speech that only can be known by an insider or confidante. The edificatory function of this intimacy was important to the book's reception, its meaning, and its effect upon uninitiated readers. If for some reviewers, *City of Night* spotlighted activities that needed to be policed or were better left in the dark altogether, for some gay readers it not only mapped a queer world but it also taught them how they might be in that world. As the novelist Felice Picano, author of *The Lure* (1979), remembers, "I was 19 years old and trying to become a homosexual . . . I didn't even know what there was of the gay world. And *City of Night* was my entry into it."[24]

City of Night's pedagogical function is to anatomize for the reader urban queer spaces, to define the terms of the underworld sexual economy's argot ("queen," "queer," "trade," and "scoring," and to bring to light the taxonomy of niche sexualities produced within the terrains of the disciplined city (97). "The shape of the world I had chosen emerged," Rechy's narrator says a third of the way into the novel as his familiarity with the queer underworld becomes fully realized (120). As if in a parody of a sociologist or a cultural anthropologist conducting field research, he states, "I had learned to sift the different types that haunted those places: "the queens . . . eyeing the youngmen coquettishly" and the "mostly uneffeminate" "scores" that "I could spot . . . easily" (31, 32). "You learn to identify them [the scores] by their method of approaching you," he explains, adding "they will offer a cigarette, a cup of coffee, a drink in a bar: anything to give them the time in which to decide whether to trust you during those interludes in which there is always a suggestion of violence" (32). As the narrator himself learns how to be a hustler—turning his research into practice—he teaches the reader, passing along vital information he has gleaned firsthand.

In *City of Night* the manufactured "realness" of the queer underworld, which was essential to readers such as Felice Picano, is constructed from the novel's decipherment of subcultural codes, its setting in geographically determinate city spaces (Manhattan's Times Square, L.A.'s Pershing Square, New Orleans's French Quarter), its use of "real," historically verifiable gay bars (the Waldorf and the 1–2–3 in downtown L.A.), as well as its straightforwardly chronological first-person narration of naked confession. The novel's sifting and spotting of the underworld sexual picaresque, energized by a dramatic narrative of imperiled sexuality, casts the narrator as an interested investigator, what Henry James termed, as I noted in chapter 1, a "restless analyst" in search of knowledge about life in the city.[25]

This knowledge is directly transmitted to the reader, who is incorporated into the text as a would-be gay prostitute when the narrator suddenly and frequently imagines the reader in the universal second-person. "You and he complete strangers again after the cold intimacy. You may move from the dungeon into the cavern of the moviebalconies and try to score again," Rechy writes (31).[26] Hypermasculine and religious (even if no longer a believer), the narrator is deeply conflicted over his homosexuality, which he repeatedly denies. Rechy's protagonist thus speaks to himself when he speaks to the reader as "you," doing so in an effort to produce himself as a queer subject. His confession is a confession to himself, a painful admission that he is gay. With its verbal maps and its moments of expository prose, the novel functions as a guidebook to the queer urban subcultures of the nation, a guidebook that also works to produce queer readers by teaching them, in the words of Picano, how to "become a homosexual."[27] The text thus constitutes a community of readers who fill the void of an agonizing loneliness in the narrator and in "you." The "boiling subterranean world" of queer desire, the novel seems to say, is self-reflexively the novel itself, and your immersion into the text is an immersion into queer life. Rechy's book is a narrative of queer America and is itself America. "America as one vast City of Night" is *City of Night* which has "fus[ed] its darkcities" into a textual space that the reader can imaginatively inhabit (9).

Beginning with its first stop in Times Square, *City of Night* escorts readers through the immoral geographies of the nation. The narrator's departure from El Paso to New York, however, is preceded and informed by two deaths, of his beloved dog Winnie and his tyrannical father. The latter is the condition of his liberation and the former is the source of a terrifying knowledge about death, which he will spend his entire journey trying to disavow. When Winnie dies, the narrator's mother tells him with "crushing tenderness" that "dogs dont go to Heaven. . . . the body just disappears, becomes dirt" (11). In the days that follow, he can "smell the body rotting" in the blistering Texas summer sun, so he and his older brother dig up the decaying carcass and bury it deeper (11). Its gross materiality confirms the mother's assertion and forever haunts her young son, who responds with adolescent self-pity and anger at the sad, awful fact that death is meaningless. Early on he stops going to Mass, gives up praying, and in defiance of his Catholicism, he has sex with a girl under a statue of Christ on Cristo Rey. He imagines reaching up to God and, in an act of queer oedipal violence, "punctur[ing] Heaven" (10). When he flees to New York, he discovers that his individual blasphemous intention is multiplied and aggrandized into a whole urban ethos: New York's phallic "knifepointed buildings stretching Up" are desperate to break free and "soar in . . . to the Sky" (21).

For the sixteenth-century Spanish mystic Saint John of the Cross, the dark night of the soul is a painful purging of the self for the wanderer who suffers from a profound attachment to a world that must be left behind as the soul is transformed into a vessel for God's light. *City of Night* reworks this mystical experience, inverting its terms by making

New York's, and later L.A.'s, transgressive sexual subculture a site of transformation where a knowledge of bodily pleasure and community is ascertained. As is Barnes's *Nightwood*, Rechy's novel is a celebration (though at times a painful one) of the queer, the dark, and the forbidden, a celebration that is often done through the inversion of religious terms. In the novel, the queering of the sacred is the project of the ailing "Professor," whom the narrator meets not long after he begins hustling in Times Square. He preaches from his bed in a sumptuous but disorderly apartment filled with books, statuary, and paintings, where beautiful young, untarnished male "Angels" attend to him. The baroque scene recalls the bedroom of Doctor O'Connor in *Nightwood*, but without all of the fungal abominations. From the Professor, the narrator learns a heretical theology in which "Death is merely the absence of life," "God is evil," and "the world [is] completely good" (64, 65). A brilliant monologist, but emotionally demanding and a little frightening, the Professor voices the question that is at the heart of *City of Night*: "The only immorality is 'morality'—which has restricted us, shoved into the dark and most beautiful things that should glow in the light, not be stifled by darkwords, darklights, darkwhispers. Why is what I do Immoral when it hurts no one?—no one! an expression of: . . . Love . . . Yet this unreasoning world ignores the true obscenities of our time: poverty, repression, the blindness to beauty and sensitivity" (70).

Though Rechy's protagonist is "mesmerized by the words" of the Professor, who soon passes away, they sink in only after a long series of searing events (76). Insofar as Rechy's novel allowed future readers imaginatively and literally to enter a queer subculture that was, in the Professor's phrase, "Heaven . . . on earth," it promised nothing of the sort for its own tortured narrator, who is stricken by a deep sense of shame for his bodily desires (76). The entire narrative drive of the book might be described as a prolonged effort, as the narrator says, to avoid having to "face myself" (340). His paroxysms of guilt send him periodically back to the "straight" world, shuttling between hetero- and homosexual geographies. But his sense of shame should not be understood to stem from his participation in a homosexual urban underground. To read the novel in this manner is to profoundly misunderstand it as a document of sexual pathology, rather than as a queer narrative. The narrator's guilt arises precisely from his failure to fully integrate himself into the queer nightworld. What is the source of this failure? In the first instance, it is money: for sexual exchanges between gay men the novel substitutes monetary exchanges between male hustlers and their male clients, in which sex becomes work. In order to read the novel correctly, we have to read past the unreliable narrator, who ameliorates his sexual guilt by redescribing his homosexual desires through the lens of prostitution. From the narrator's perspective, prostitution is not an expression of his homosexuality but is actually a denial of it. In the complex sexual economy of the novel, gay-male prostitution produces one's sexual orientation and one's gender as heterosexual and masculine.

In *City of Night*, masculinity and heterosexuality are inseparable and mutually constitutive. In other words, when the narrator is at his most masculine he is at his most heterosexual, and vice versa, no matter what activities he might be engaging in. Even when, or especially when, he is hustling as an emotionally unavailable, reticent ("I would never talk to anyone first"), and rigidly masculine top, he is at his most straight (53). "Whatever a guy does with other guys, if he does it for money, that dont make him queer. Youre still straight," his friend Pete teaches him (40). The definitional margins of the narrator's own masculinity and putative heterosexuality are fortified by strenuous repression and "devouring narcissism," which sends him seeking "more reassurance, in numbers," a "further irony" that is not lost on him (54). The more men who have sex with him, the straighter he becomes. Prostitution is strictly a "one-way desire" (54). The point is forcefully underscored in a key passage in which the narrator stresses that "it was *I* who would be the desired in those furtive relationships, without desiring back. Sex for me became the mechanical reaction of This on one side, That on the other. And the boundary must not be crossed" (54). Throughout the novel gestures of mutual intimacy, such as by Dave, a gay man who challenges the narrator to give up hustling, or by Jeremy, the man who offers love and friendship in the novel's emotional climax, are rebuffed.

In *City of Night*, queer identity and the psychodynamics of repression have thoroughly geographic dimensions. The novel sexes geography, much like *Nightwood* and *Home to Harlem*. As Rechy reminds us, sexuality is always geographically situated within bounded urban terrains: "This on one side, That on the other." "The arbitrary stamp of 'differentness' [is] imposed," the narrator insists, "by the world that creates it and then rejects it" (223). In the novel, the experience of "'differentness'" is a creation of regulated spaces of intersection and convergence in which different modes of life collide, architectures and artifacts of the past and the present are juxtaposed, and habitual and fixed ways of seeing the world are interrupted by a sensory onslaught. Capital, the literary scholar Patrick O'Donnell argues, produces sites "where libidinal energies are negotiated and exchanged," where all kinds of people are clustered in critical mass and thus where "raw libidinal energy is converted into unitary selves, political systems, language, writing, national bodies, memory."[28]

In the novel, the exchange of monies, bodies, and bodily fluid transpires first in Times Square, where the narrator lands after leaving home, and then in downtown Los Angeles, where he migrates to after leaving New York. These are figurative and literal crossroads where all sorts of rough and regular trade take place. Within these two paramount capitalist cityspaces, Rechy locates the underground sexual economy of the gay prostitute. Arising out of these spaces, moreover, is the memory of Rechy's lonely narrator, who is tortured at the novel's close by the possibility that his urban alienation might have been assuaged had he only allowed himself to be part of one of the rag-tag queer communities he encountered. The narrative of this failure is precisely the narrative that Rechy seeks to undo by constituting queer subjects (Rechy's characters and his readers) and by joining them in a national body (America as one sprawling city of night). But this utopian horizon is simultaneously countered by the gritty realities of the black market economy that both makes the formation of a queer community possible and forestalls it, at the same time. Money lubricates sexual exchanges by bringing people together, and it keeps people apart by reducing sex to alienated labor and a fetishized commodity. In *City of Night* both alienation and fetishization are evidenced in the narrator's accrual of countless anonymous partners who are drawn to a chiseled physique and a feigned semi-illiteracy that signify as all body and no head. All of his partners are mere numbers, numbers that never add up to a community.

As Rechy shows, the male prostitute is a transgression of social edicts that valorize reproductive heterosexuality at the same time that he is the personification of the market's logic, which turns the body and its labor into a commodity. Rechy's narrator thus operates in the space of misalignment between dominant sexual regimes and an amoral mode of capitalist production that draws diverse forms of sexualized labor and consumption into urban spaces. This space is as much ideological as it is a real sexual underworld. To say that the sexual underworld was (and is) "real," is to highlight the fact that in certain urban zones, semi-licit commercial sexual activity was localized and regulated. New York's and L.A.'s vice districts of adult bookstores and theaters, strip clubs, and single-room-occupancy hotels were (and still are) zoned as sexual markets outside of middle-class residential neighborhoods. These vice districts serve a need in the city, and thus are tolerated within limits. Those limits are usually reached when transgressive sexuality spills across boundaries or becomes a public disturbance, or when the lure of market gains from urban redevelopment of these under-capitalized spaces is too rich to ignore. Efforts to quarantine queer sexuality to specific districts in both New York and Los Angeles historically buttressed the normative sexuality of heterosexual residents by geographically distancing "differentness." As we saw in chapter 2, zoning helped to guarantee the purity and privacy of heterosexuality by isolating other forms of sexual practice in an "Othered" space which heterosexuals could either avoid entirely or enter into with the security of knowing that they could use the space without being defined by it. In "The City of Desire" (1991), Pat Califia describes such zones as mixed-use commercial districts in "deteriorating neighborhood[s]" where, with "a token invisibility," "sexual minorities" are gathered alongside poor residents and tourists who—crossing moral and physical boundaries—slum there for sex.[29]

Rechy presents these zones with a level of empirical detail that implies a high degree of intimate familiarity. His narrator observes that in New York the sexual underworld is composed of the "world of Times Square . . . from 42nd Street to about 45th Street, from grimy Eighth Avenue to Bryant Park," and also includes 34th Street and "Third Avenue, the East 50s" (20, 30, 56). For its part, "the West-Coast Times Square" is "the area about Los Angeles Street, Main Street, Spring, Broadway, Hill—between about 4th and 7th streets," as well as the "teeming" Pershing Square into which "the world of Lonely-Outcast America [is] squeezed" (87, 88, 91, 93). Downtown L.A.'s "three-feature moviehouses, burlesque joints, army and navy stores; gray rooming houses squeezed tightly hotly protesting against each other" comprise a red-light district that, long after Robinson's 1909, has reconstituted itself (88). Like the calling card of the "girlish Negro youngman" handed to the narrator as soon he exits the Greyhound station in Part 2 of the novel, the Bunker Hill/Pershing Square vice district announces "WELCOME TO LOS ANGELES" (88). "Those first days in Los Angeles," the narrator states, "I was newly dazzled by the world into which my compulsive journey through submerged lives had led me" (99).

Rechy's finely granulated depiction of the social spaces within the erotic topography where queer men meet underscores this sexual geography's socially devalued status. It is the space of the culture's detritus, a castoff sexuality making do in a fetid atmosphere. He notes, for instance, the queer underworld's "*walls greasy from days of cheap cooking, cobwebbed lightbulbs feebly hiding in opaque darkness, windowscreens if any smooth as velvet with grime*" (100). In the novel, the built spaces of queer desire are often in the dark (in the balconies of Times Square's theaters and in Pershing Square's "long shadows" that "protect the exiles, shelter them soothingly") and literally underground (in "the toilets in the subways—with the pleading scrawled messages") (31, 141). And most especially, Rechy's sexual underworld is a world of mildewed bars hidden from public view and frequented by prostitutes, such as Ji-Ji's, a "malehustling and queen bar" off a "tunnel-like opening" in "a hidden underground shelter," or the "1–2–3," "a cavern of trapped exiles" where "tough-looking masculine hustlers, young fugitives from everywhere and everything" and the "sweetest-looking queen[s] in L.A." form a "thick crowd," or the aptly named "Hodge Podge," an "outcast bar" "a block from Pershing Square" that "you descend into . . . as if into a cellar" and find "Negroes and vagrant whites, heads and hypes, dikes and queens" on the dance floor (101, 109, 169, 171).

These descriptions reveal sexuality as a geographic production, the outcome of urban spatial divisions that externally divide people (hetero- and homosexual) and that internally divide individuals. The mental compartmentalization of the narrator's sexual identity is enacted spatially as he repeatedly enters into and retreats from underworld districts. He steps into these spaces to hustle and then guiltily retreats to their margins. He literally lives "on the fringes of that world but still outside of it." "Thus the daulity [*sic*] of my existence," he says, "was marked by a definite boundary" (99). In Rechy's downtown L.A., these divisions are geographically specific: the dividing line between "the Other World" (the guilt-free middle-class world of work and privacy), and the "different world" (the world of "submerged lives" and public sexuality) is discernibly located at Hill Street and Olive (31, 91, 99). The narrator rents a room in a hotel on the edge of L.A.'s sexual underworld, yet at some distance from it, a marginal position that affords him comfort and plausible deniability (99). "Pershing Square," he remarks, "east of there when the desire to be with people churned within me; west of there to the hotel when I had to be alone" (99). Outside of the patriarchal domain of his father's household and his mother's overbearing love, the foundation of his masculine heterosexuality turns fragile, destabilized by the penetrating stares of male desire he sees everywhere in the city undressing him. His sexual identity is a "wavering and ephemeral" "structure" which he anxiously performs and reproduces (even mass produces) in "numbers" (54). But at times the strategy backfires "sharply" (54). When that occurs, he temporarily leaves "the Street" for "the Other World," a pendulum swing that sends him searching for some resemblance of a barely remembered heteronormative life (91).

Rechy's queer underworld offers a margin of sexual freedom and the chance for companionship for the men who are a part of it. The opportunity comes with the high cost of having one's sexuality metonymically aligned with the "waste of modernity" in the degraded architectures of the city's underbelly.[30] Companionship comes, too, with the immediate risk of arrest, which is ever more prominent as urban renewal procedures seek to eliminate the very spaces a prior generation's zoning had erected. In Rechy's New York, "the newspapers are full of reports of raids: UNDESIRABLES NABBED" (53). And in the Los Angeles chapters of *City of Night*, the police are everywhere—in gay bars, on the streets, and in all-night coffee shops (the "meeting and exhibition place[s] for the nightworld") (180)—rounding up gay men, questioning and fingerprinting them. The local headlines "gleefully announce: RAID IN PERSHING SQUARE" (123). The police maintain a command center in "the depths of the subterranean garage" beneath the park (123). Not long after the narrator starts hustling in L.A., the police haul him into the underground station and make it clear to him that he has been under surveillance. Sergeant Morgan menacingly warns, "Ever-one's hearda Pershing Square, and I figure thats why youre here. . . . We got plainclothesmen all over, watchinya. You wont get away with nothin! Now maybe I cain tell you stay outta the park cause it's public—but I sure as hell can make it Rough for you" (122). The urban policing by Rechy's tough-talking L.A. cop quarantines peripheral citizens, defining them, at least in part, by their emplacement. In the words of Steve Herbert in *Policing Space* (1997), police "mark and enact meaningful boundaries . . . to restrict people's capacity to act by regulating their movements in space."[31] Since "space is important to the identity and power of a variety of social groups," Herbert notes, this "ensures that a complicated politics of spatial control persists across the variegated landscape of cities such as Los Angeles."[32]

Historically, disciplinary procedures for monitoring sexually offensive urban populations derived from section 674 of the California Penal Code. Convictions for 674 lewd and lascivious conduct offenses required violators to register as sex offenders for the rest of their lives.[33] It is in this climate that Rechy asserts that southern California is notorious for entrapment—"theyll even offer you money and bust you later" (222). Under the zealous leadership of the Los Angeles Police Department's William Parker (the police chief when Rechy was writing his novel), "arrests for 'sex perversion' crimes, involving primarily male homosexuals, jumped dramatically."[34] The spike in arrests was the result of sweeps for prostitution, vagrancy, and cross-dressing, which often led to public shaming and to the loss of employment for men caught in the dragnet. "The mid-twentieth century was the bleakest period in L.A. history for homosexuals," claim Lillian Faderman and Stuart Timmons, historians of gay life in Los Angeles.[35] "When I first realized I was homosexual," a character in *City of Night* confesses, "I felt guilty, as if I had committed a crime" (360).[36]

The policed space of Pershing Square organizes L.A.'s sexual plurality. While making for more efficient monitoring, it paradoxically creates a space of potential public disturbance. The city's centralization and condensation of differences manufactures new forms of experience in locales that are at once at the center of the city's anxieties about public disorder and sexuality and a meeting place for the marginalized. Overflowing with signifiers of history, religion, sex, and culture, and filled with discordant voices, Pershing Square is the richest textual space in *City of Night* and its most disturbing. In a passage that runs over two pages, Rechy immerses the reader in the park's welter of noise and bodies, a fluid, hybridized space of multiple deviancies.

> I walk about the teeming park for the first-time—past the statues of soldiers, one on each corner of the Hill Street side—past an ominous cannon on Olive, aimed defiantly at the slick wide-gleamingwindowed buildings across the streets: the banks, the travel agencies (representations of The Other World, to which I will flee recurrently in guilt and feel just as guilty for having abandoned if never completely, the world of the parks, the streets)—past the statue of Beethoven with a stick, turning his back fiercely on the Pershing Square menagerie.
>
> Throughout the park, preachers and prophets dash out *Damnation!* in a disharmony of sounds—like phonographs gone mad. . . .
>
> And while the preachers dash out their damning messages, the winos storm Heaven on cheap wine; hungry-eyed scores with money (or merely with a place to offer the homeless youngmen they desire) gather about the head hunting the malehustlers and wondering will they get robbed. . . . And the heat in their holy cop uniforms, holy because of the Almighty Stick and the Almightier Vagrancy Law; the scattered junkies, the smalltime pushers, the teaheads, the sad panhandlers, the occasional lonely exiled

> nymphos haunting the entrance to the men's head; more fruits with hungry eyes. . . . Mostly later at night, youll find, when the shadows will shelter them—queens in colorful shirtblouses. (91, 92)

One of the goals of Rechy's novel is the conversion of socially rejected "'differentness'" into a culture of different spaces. Far more often than not, the cacophonous space of difference—such as Rechy's Pershing Square—is understood as a zone of deviance, a dangerous, noxious mixing of classes, races, sexualities that has been the worry of social ecologists since the 1920s. In the hegemonic view, difference is equated with decadence, cultural decline, and degeneration. Urbanists Gary Bridge and Sophie Watson have argued for an alternative view that recognizes that marginalized identities are positively articulated in space in ways that may be invisible or misunderstood by outsiders.[37] Efforts to renovate and smooth over disruptive locales in the name of urban renewal have paved over spaces of "resistance and self-definition" for marginalized groups.[38]

Many different populations congregate in Rechy's park. It is the haunt not only of hustlers but also of "dismal old tramps" who use it for shelter, the elderly who socialize on its benches, preachers who hold forth from soapboxes, and "a few stray girls" who are looking for handouts, food, and cigarettes (133, 144). And most important, the park is a space where members of a diasporic queer community from across the nation first enter upon arriving in Los Angeles, a space where individual alienation is overcome and where knowledge about the police, apartments for rent, and prostitution is circulated. In brief, the park is not just a place for solicitation but is also a place of public and personal memory in the face of assault and erasure. The so-called lowlife atmosphere of downtown L.A. is a multilayered space of collective memory, a space where an alternative history of the city is inscribed by subjects whose communities are under siege from the moment of their founding (131). The negative solidarity of its many users and inhabitants derives from the spaces they share as a result of multiple axes of exclusion: economic, sexual, age-oriented, and ideological. It is as if this diverse group which could hardly be said to have much in common, was collectively, if only symbolically, oriented around the park's cannon.

What Rechy's alienated protagonist discovers in the musty underworld of Pershing Square and elsewhere, but does not always act upon because of his own internalized sense of guilt, is something as simple and mysterious as contact—the earliest stages of community building, the base from which underworld intimacies will grow. Rechy writes that it "was of course in Pershing Square" that the narrator first meets the flamboyant Miss Destiny, "a slim young queen with masses and masses of curly red hair" (94). She is his impresario to "that ratty world of downtown L.A." and a "real" historical personage (and friend of Rechy) who, on more than one occasion, was arrested for wearing gender-inappropriate clothing (97). And it was in the park that the narrator befriends Chuck, a hustler from Georgia, "one of [downtown Los Angeles's] best-liked citizens" whose blasé attitude is a quality the narrator tries to emulate in order to survive on the streets (126). "He seemed to live his life untouched by turmoil—yet the turmoil surrounded him constantly," the narrator observes, later musing that "he seems like a kind of symbolic anchor," one who "would become a part of my memory of Pershing Square" (126, 128, 134).

Contact, as I am using it here, is the intersection of racial, sexual, ethnic, or other kinds of differences within space, an experience of exchange made possible by the urban phenomena "of encounter, assembly, simultaneity."[39] The queer science-fiction writer Samuel Delany reflects upon the meaning of urban contact in *Times Square Red, Times Square Blue* (1999), a book of memoir and essay that is useful for understanding both the utopian horizon of underworld sociability in Rechy's narrative and the historical threats (policing, urban planning, and renewal) that the so-called queer underworlds in both New York and Los Angeles suffered. Distinguishing contact from the motive-driven prerogatives of "networking," which are dependent upon membership in exclusive clubs, societies, or institutions, Delany writes that "contact" is "more broadly social and appears random" and is "associated with public space and the architecture and commerce that depend on and promote it."[40] Delaney reflects upon the early 1990s massive redevelopment campaign in Times Square, which began with the area's rezoning and which precipitated a displacement of a public sexual culture that had been located there since the 1960s. The New York City Council's Zoning Text Amendment of 1995 aimed to purge Times Square by prohibiting the operation of adult businesses within five hundred feet of a school, house of worship, residence, or another adult business. Like similar efforts a half century earlier in Greenwich Village, it did not stamp out the putative sexual underworld: it scattered its geography. Given the density and mixed-use nature of New York City, the ordinance pushed adult bookstores and theaters to the largely industrial, poor, and ethnic western edge of Manhattan and across the East River into the neighborhood of Long Island City. "An imagined community is being planned by the business leaders, and *New York Times* editors and owners," Mark Sussman wrote in response, "an imagined moral community that has little to do with the real needs of New Yorkers. . . . Another imagined community, a fantasy of an Underworld, is moved elsewhere."[41] A windfall for bourgeois homeowners in the surrounding area, the corporate revitalization of Times Square was contingent upon driving out the semi-licit economy of sex, sanitizing the space, and installing the family-friendly commerce of Disney. A fantasy world indeed. The uprooting of sexual nonconformity was a major step forward in a resurgent real estate market that made New York, for some, a livable city once again.

As we saw with Robinson's *Tarnished Angels*, the erasure of urban spaces of difference produces nostalgia for a livelier, more sensational city and produces anxiety over the possibility that something vital will be irretrievably lost in the ceaseless push for modernization. To be sure, many of Times Square's adult businesses were seedy, exploitative, reputed to be controlled by New York's underworld crime families, and a blight to many who lived in their neon shadows. For some queer men, however, these vice zones were where they developed an erotic knowledge of the city, an awareness of queer sexuality's policed boundaries, its socially devalued status, and its possibility to transgress the economically exploitative architecture that housed it. Rechy's and Delany's understanding of public sexuality as nested within the space of the market, which it both relies upon even as it seeks to exceed its strictly monetary ends, is at least as old as Walt Whitman's sentiment in "City of Orgies." Whitman rhapsodizes, "as I pass O Manhattan, your frequent and swift / flash of eyes offering me love, / Offering response to my own—these repay me, / Lovers, continual lovers, only repay me."[42] Likewise, Rechy (if not his narrator, for whom sex remains a strictly monetary transaction) understands sexual desire as a mechanism for overcoming the city's anonymity by uniting strangers through public intimacies that surpass the alienated economic exchanges made through commodities. In *City of Night* repayment comes in the form of sexual pleasure—"body fusing with mouth," "mutual, nightlong, unpaid, sexsharing"—which affirms life and draws men together out of the swirling crowds. As Rechy keeps his anguished narrator locked in an economy he calls "sexmoney," he multiplies around him examples of a more radical culture of sex by gay men whose embodied practices unlink money and pleasure (348). In other words, even as the narrator continues to see himself as a hustler who cannot be intimate with other men on equal terms, he is also painfully aware of an underground world of bars where men congregate not as hustlers and scores, but as lovers, "bars [that] attracted large numbers of youngmen who went there to meet others," places "where males danced with males, holding each other intimately" (56). Such "bars made me nervous," he admits, remarking that "largely, I avoided them" (56).

But the utopian promise of contact in the public spaces of the city is still available to the reader who perhaps can see what Rechy's own narrator cannot. What is formed in these socially and economically devalued terrains are knowledges and intimacies that are public, political, potentially collective, and not tethered to the domestic space of monogamy and reproductive ideals.[43] In short, such spaces underscore that one's right to the city is not (or should not be) dependent upon first attaining normative sexual standards and that one's way of being in the city does not derive first and foremost from consumerist exchanges or a defense of property values. It is the promise of forms of sociability (sexual and nonsexual) that are interclass and cross-racial, the promise of an emergent urban collectivity that is conscious of how space and power define and limit how we move and love, how the daily struggles for territory create opportunities for allied networks beyond the boundaries of the city's differences.

Thirty years before Times Square's reconfiguration, the Bunker Hill Redevelopment Project, in combination with stepped-up policing, sought to forestall just such alliances. The Redevelopment Project scrubbed Pershing Square into a new abstract space devoid of the history, texture, and the sweat and stain of human bodies. Both the park and the adjacent neighborhood were subjected to transformations that locally reconfigured the boundaries of the public and the private. Urban planners worked to eliminate the "subterranean," "submerged," and "lowlife" world of queer sexuality through policies and practices that would raise ground rents, pushing the putative underworld out of the area (Rechy 31, 99, 131). The decaying Victorian houses of Bunker Hill were physically carted away and deposited in another part of the city, where today they remain as displaced curiosities. Like the land itself, history in L.A. was capable of being moved. In what amounted to a modern version of California's environmentally disastrous policy of dynamiting and hosing down mountaintops for gold prospecting, the top of Bunker Hill was shorn off and its slope was regraded to integrate the neighborhood with the rest of downtown. Its community was pushed to the other side of the Harbor Freeway.[44]

On September 3, 1964, at roughly the same time that Robinson was

FIGURE 11. "William Frederickson Jr., Robert Howe, and William T. Wright examining a model of the planned redesign of Pershing Square, Calif., 1964." Courtesy of UCLA Charles E. Young Research Library Department of Special Collections. Los Angeles Times Photographic Archives. Copyright © Regents of the University of California, UCLA Library.

printing *Tarnished Angels* and *City of Night* was still shocking its readers, the banner headline in the *Los Angeles Free Press* declared "Pershing Square Defoliated: City Says 'Get Out' to Eccentrics, Pensioners, Non-Conformists." In the words of the *Free Press* columnist, Ridgeley Cummings, the Square was "debenched, bull-dozed, torn-up." The developers uprooted many of the park's shade trees that Rechy described as "*the trees [that] hang over it all*," which had provided cover for innumerable clandestine encounters (93). What was once a space inhabited and used by a downtown subcultural community of queers, pushers, and hoboes became a space for office workers and shoppers who would pass through it without lingering. The "pleasant tropical garden-like oasis in the center of the city" was being paved, the *Free Press* observed, into "a routine concrete park that would be duplicated anywhere." Any remaining doubts that the redevelopment of the park was a bald exercise of power were laid to rest when John Ward, an executive in the Parks Department, was asked if the Square had been altered so as to discourage assembly, answered in Cummings's article, "'I think you can fairly say that is a design premise.'"

According to one estimate, since the start of the Redevelopment Project upward of "50,000 residents—Chinese, Mexican, and Black—[have been] displaced" in the course of the numerous "improvements" to Los Angeles's central business district.[45] And "over the last twenty-five years more than thirty skyscrapers (most foreign financed and owned), several apartment buildings, and a contemporary art museum have been set in place on the hill."[46] Purging the area of "blight" that "interrupted real-estate values between the new City Hall and the great department stores on Seventh Street," urban renewal helped to reconsolidate downtown and slow the seemingly inexorable sprawl of the city to the west and east, where money and power were increasingly located.[47] In the process, the project sought to rehabilitate a normative vision of sexuality and a consumerist model of citizenship by attracting businesses and shoppers (if not residents) back to a newly cleansed central Los Angeles, a revitalized hub of a postmodern city in the making.

This is the spatial history of *City of Night*. Rechy's novel intervenes into this fraught time and place by textualizing the sights and sounds of a community of "mangled American outcasts of every breed" in downtown L.A. on the eve of that community's erasure, forestalling a history of forgetting that is endemic to Los Angeles (127). After his long journey crisscrossing the country and after having collapsed from pills and exhaustion in New Orleans, Rechy's narrator returns to El Paso. As he rests and recuperates, he reflects, though his reflections are merely a gathering of broken fragments: "The undiscovered country which may not even exist and which I was too frightened even to attempt to discover. Life conspiring to trap us! And I feel trapped by the world which I know now has sought me out as ineluctably as a shadow seeks its source in the bright sunlight. . . . That world which Ive loved and hated, that submerged gray world; this world which is not unlike your own. . . ." (372). His hesitant, elliptical monologue suggests an insight just beyond the threshold of language or admissibility. He cannot shore these fragments against the ruins of the urban wasteland. They fail to coalesce into a vision of another future. A few pages later, the book appears to end on a note of pure negativity: "And what has been found? Nothing" (379). And yet the "undiscovered country" that the narrator has been "too frightened even to attempt to discover" and which "may not even exist" is the country that the reader finds and which the narrator himself has written back in El Paso: "America as one vast City of Night stretching gaudily from Times Square to Hollywood Boulevard" (9).

In the postwar period what Rechy's narrator has discovered but denies finding is a thoroughly urban nation, sprawling from coast to coast, with beleaguered queer communities in each of its cities. Or more accurately, this is how he "would *think of* America," as in, this is how he would imagine it to be (9, emphasis added). What kind of national space is this, we might ask? At the edges of its narrator's panicked vision, *City of Night* sees a subterranean queer citizenry linked both by its rootlessness (a lack of a place to call its own) and its forced emplacement in imperiled urban districts. These spaces are inhabited and lived with a degree of provisionality and urgency that marks them as radically different from the stable, domesticated spaces in which heterosexual subjectivity is formed. The aleatory, transient, and fugitive nature of the queer underworld engenders a nomadic subject, who is always passing through spaces on "the grinding journey to—. . . Where?" (82). Such spaces are forever "in the process of becoming *and* disintegrating," forming communities and dispersing them.[48] Or as Rechy's narrator ponders: "New people would replace me on Times Square and in the park. . . . You touch those other lives, barely—however intimately it may be sexually. . . . Their lives will continue, youll merely step out" (81, 82). He adds, "I'll search again through the labyrinthine world I had found on Times Square, in downtown Los Angeles, Hollywood, Market Street . . ." (272). Rechy's narrative articulates an imagined geography composed not of fixed sites, but of flows of desire in which queer urban subjects, sexual "outlaws," as he calls them, are literally on the run.[49]

The Stonewall Inn riot in 1969 is generally credited with launching modern queer collective action by joining gay, lesbian, and transgender men and women, homeless youth, and other Greenwich Village residents in an exercise of territoriality to protest daily harassments, humiliations, and to fight for a place of their own. Historically, the suppression of spaces of difference through urban renewal policies has worked not only to manage the past but also to control the future by uprooting queer, poor, ethnic, and racial communities and counter-hegemonic solidarities, and by cutting short incipient narratives of urban life that are—paradoxically—a product of spatial marginalization itself. In other words, marginal narratives that protest social domination and uneven development seek to eliminate the very conditions of discrimination that brought them into being in the first place. But they do so on terms that call for equality and recognition, terms quite different from the urban renewal practices that often have been implemented without input from the communities that have the most at stake.

City of Night imagines no such act of communal defiance. Instead, in the years before Stonewall, it preserves in print a memory of queer life as the rush and the push of "short, short, short interludes," "restlessly pausing before rushing," and "the relentless flow of life" of men who make do in the midst of larger prosecutorial forces (81, 82, 120). Instead of defending a space of their own, Rechy's queer men move from place to place, in and out of bars and parks. Like the underworld of *Nightwood*, queer subjects in *City of Night* are mobile, but not mobilized. What Rechy's novel distilled from this provisional world was a thickly detailed textual space where gay men could find themselves and discover others like them, a space inside the pages of a book that was perhaps more durable than the spaces it described (372). Rechy's novel makes these spaces and ways of life available to readers as alternatives, unrealized futures, paths not taken. In the early 1960s, Los Angeles reinvented itself as a post-Fordist city, at once recentralized and sprawling, a city filled with sexual, racial, and ethnic differences that were being erased and shunted to the margins. On the cusp of a new era of urban atomization, fragmentation, and battles over the right to space, *City of Night* preserves the diverse voices the city would rather forget and captures a glimpse of another kind of city in which Americans "of every breed" are momentarily and intimately fused (127).

Highway to Hell: The Underworld, Urban Sprawl, and *The Crying of Lot 49*

In the early and mid-1960s, John Rechy's contemporary Thomas Pynchon also was mapping the delirious postmodern geographies of California. But he was doing so through a very different set of eyes: those of a suburban housewife, Oedipa Maas who, confused and on the edge of despair, finds herself late one night prowling "among the sunless, concrete underpinnings of the freeway, finding drunks, bums, pedestrians, pederasts, [and] hookers" while looking for a garbage can with the acronym W.A.S.T.E. stenciled on its lid (129). The story of how Pynchon's middle-class heroine winds up in this predicament is a story of one woman's descent into the social underworld, a disorienting journey through lower and lower strata of the urban class structure. It is a story of how ideologies are inscribed into the very spaces in which we live and work, how ideology determines what can and cannot be seen, and how the movement from a space of privilege into a space of social blight causes one's ideology (in this case, Oedipa's belief in the fundamental social inclusiveness and shared economic prosperity of America) to become sundered.

Over the course of the novel, Pynchon mercilessly pushes Oedipa—a twenty-eight-year-old Young Republican, Tupperware-party attendee—into the city's waste until, like Barnes's Nora, her cloistered existence and her myopic worldview are profoundly troubled. Brian Jarvis rightly comments that she "undergoes a disembourgoisement."[50] Her protected life in Kinneret-among-the-Pines (where protective shade trees surely serve another purpose than those in Rechy's Pershing Square) is forever changed when she receives a letter informing her that her old boyfriend and "California real estate mogul" Pierce Inverarity has died and that she has been named "to execute the will" (9, 10). A surprising if apparently innocent request, it soon immerses her in Inverarity's vast real estate and asset holdings and may implicate her in what could be a massive conspiracy involving Trystero, a clandestine organization that communicates through specially marked garbage cans (9, 10). Oedipa's quest to understand W.A.S.T.E. is Pynchon's request that we understand the historical and geographical determinants of social waste, the myriad discarded and dislocated populations of the racialized, the sexually pathologized, and the poor who have been excluded from the sunny, cheerful narratives of postwar American triumphalism. *The Crying of Lot 49* maps this period's social and physical geography through a sprawling, labyrinthine narrative from the top down and the bottom up, a narrative which, we will see, is always attuned to the dialectical relations between real-estate speculation, a new weapons economy, increasing suburbanization, and what Pynchon calls "a whole underworld" (116).

Set entirely in California, *The Crying of Lot 49* is more geographically narrow than *City of Night*, but its scope, like Rechy's novel, is resolutely national. Oedipa's peregrinations carry her up and down the state, from the small, middle-class Kinneret on the central coast, to San Narciso (a satellite city "near L.A." and "Pierce's domicile" and "headquarters"), to the San Francisco Bay Area and back to Los Angeles, but as the narrative draws to a close Pynchon expands the horizon of her search's implications (24). "She had dedicated herself, weeks ago," he writes, "to making sense of what Inverarity had left behind, never suspecting that the legacy was America" (178). What Oedipa unearths are the new urban poor: the newly diversified and multiplying poverties that are the underacknowledged legacy of the last three decades of the American century. They are the novel's underworld. To understand Oedipa's discoveries one has to understand the myriad built spaces of California that she traipses through and understand how these spaces (to quote Barnes) are "related by their division" within a highly fragmented social geography.[51] In the novel, the suburban enclave of Kinneret, the militarized sprawl of Los Angeles, and the micro-geographies of W.A.S.T.E. are linked to each other by means other than California's famous freeways. What connects them is one simple fact: the processes of urbanization that have brought the postmodern city into being has resulted in an intensification of inequality at every point on the urban spectrum. This knowledge has escaped Oedipa, and she pays dearly for it. In Pynchon's novel, the city is a postmodern wasteland and Oedipa, upon glimpsing in her strange encounters nearly every instance of its socially diverse marginalized populations, will understand little of what she sees.

Los Angeles's "metropolarities"—Edward Soja's term for a newly complex geographical shape of power, status, and inequality—are scattered throughout the huge, broken city.[52] The familiar bipolar geographical expression of wealth and poverty fails to represent the new urban realities of a city fractured at every turn. In an effort to mentally piece it back together, Soja in his book *Postmodern Geographies* has circumscribed Los Angeles with a "Sixty-Mile Circle."[53] Think of it as one of Ernest Burgess's concentric diagrams from chapter 2 widened to the breaking point. Like a target on a radar screen, the "Sixty-Mile Circle" is a visual abstraction of a vast landmass stretching from the Pacific into the desert, across three counties, several military bases, and over more than a dozen cities, and many tensely juxtaposed ghettos, barrios, and spectacularly wealthy, walled-off enclaves.[54] Trying to describe postmodern L.A.'s confusing spatiality pushes the geographer to the edge of "linguistic despair": "It is difficult to grasp persuasively in a temporal narrative for it generates too many conflicting images, confounding historicization, . . . limitless and constantly in motion, never still enough to encompass, too filled with 'other spaces' to be informatively described."[55] "What is this place?" Soja wonders.[56]

The question is Oedipa's. The answer is Pynchon's, whose novel endeavors to map at the very moment of its emergence the postmodern city that so befuddles its expert observers. In a key moment early in the novel and on the first leg of her investigation, Oedipa sees the outer-Los-Angeles area of San Narciso while "look[ing] down a slope" from inside her rented Impala (24). Her perspective is akin to that of the geographer or the urban planner who from above the city tries to apprehend it, in hopes of discerning some kind of intelligible pattern. "Like many named places in California," Pynchon writes, "it was less an identifiable city than a grouping of concepts—census tracts, special purpose bond-issue districts, shopping nuclei, all overlaid with access roads to its own freeway" (24). The offspring of a recent postwar infusion of money ("the plinth course of capital") and "land speculating"—its oldest building is from just "before World War II"—San Narciso is typical of unregulated Sunbelt expansion that stretches as far as the eye can see (24, 182). "San Narciso had no boundaries," Pynchon pointedly declares (178). This type of city, so unfamiliar to Oedipa, is a jumble of industrial manufacturing, weapons plants for the new post-Fordist economy, and postwar planned residential communities. It is a mishmash, Oedipa observes, of "beige, prefab, cinderblock office machines distributors, sealant makers, bottled gas works, fastener factories, warehouses," "the Galactronics Division of Yoyodyne, Inc." with its "wide, pink buildings, surrounded by miles of fence topped with barbed wire," "guard towers," and "two sixty-foot missiles," and "a vast sprawl of houses which had grown up all together" (25, 26). San Narciso is a place that most people simply pass through, a nodal point where labor and capital are exchanged and commodities are assembled and shipped out, a place where if one pauses it is to buy gas or stay for a night at a cheap motel like Echo Courts before heading elsewhere. But for those who actually live there—at "Fangoso Lagoons, a new housing development" and "one of Inverarity's interests"—the rupturing of any conventional notion of space and history is built, Oedipa learns, into the experience of the place itself (31). Its "artificial lake" is lined with "restored galleons" from the "Bahamas; Atlantean fragments of columns and friezes from the Canaries; real human skeletons from Italy; giant clamshells from Indonesia—all for the entertainment of Scuba enthusiasts" (31). The world comes to San Narciso in fragments and the dead-form of lost cultures transfigured into commodities which residents discover at their leisure.

For Oedipa, southern California is a "hieroglyphic" that she will seek to decode to tell a national story, an idea that Soja himself will later put forward when he positing that in L.A. "each piece of the restructured socio-spatial mosaic can be seen as a kind of social hieroglyph representing and revealing all the complex dynamics of the postmetropolitan transition" (24).[57] Oedipa's attempt to decipher San Narciso's secrets is strongly shaped by her ideologically informed experience of geography.

What Pynchon's novel shows us through Oedipa is how space and class are correlated with what we are capable of seeing—and not seeing, for that matter. Oedipa's elevated physical position on the incline surveying the sprawl is one of desired visual mastery in which the city is abstracted into shapes and swirls crisscrossed by lines of freeways like a Mondrian gone haywire. From this "high angle," she is neither in nor of the city but soaring over it in her Impala (24). Later in the narrative, when she travels across the Bay Bridge, we note that Pynchon places her again in exactly the same position: "Looking down at San Francisco . . . from the high point of the bridge's arc" (108). Momentarily spellbound in a "'religious instant'" above San Narciso, Oedipa detects a "sense of concealed meaning," "an intent to communicate" (24, 25). Its militarized desert-scape, which reminds her of a printed circuit in the back of a transistor radio, is on the precipice of revealing something to her about recent radical changes to mid-twentieth-century American life that have transpired while she has been ensconced in Kinneret with its herb gardens and cute downtown markets where non-threatening Muzak is piped in to push products (10, 24).

The all-seeing panoramic point of view is blind to the fine granulations of the lived spaces of the city that we have encountered up close in James, Barnes, McKay, and Rechy. What Oedipa cannot see is greater than what she can. Her blindness, Pynchon implies, is a direct effect of her literal and conceptualized space above the city, combined with the fact that her suburban life has concealed from her the gritty realities of the huge metropolitan area that is just an afternoon's drive south for her. Soon enough the city's strangeness—its "squatters" "drifters," its "God knew how many citizens" who have chosen "a calculated withdrawal"—will surface when she comes down to their level (124, 180). Despite her elevated perspective's promise of knowledge, it ends up revealing little to her, except her own renewed capacity to be wowed. An inkling that there is, to put it colloquially, more to life than her middle-class domestic boredom lets on, is strongly present, but any wider insights into the social and material forces that have created San Narciso, to say nothing of everyday life in the city, remain occluded behind the smog, the hazy filter of her middle-class worldview. With her sense of space and social life adapted to the ordered homogeny and privacy of suburban living, and ill-equipped for making sense of the new space she finds herself in, she finds that Los Angeles's "revelation[s] . . . tremble just past the threshold of her understanding" (24). It is, Pynchon writes, as if, "on some other frequency, or out of the eye of some whirlwind rotating too slow for her heated skin even to feel the centrifugal coolness of, words were being spoken. She suspected as much" (24, 25).

Oedipa knows that she cannot see what she cannot see, a self-conscious lack that has as much to do with her gendered experience, we should recognize, as it does with class. Pynchon's protagonist is meant to emblematize middle-class, white American women in the 1950s and 1960s whose enforced domesticity and limited career prospects Betty Friedan famously analyzed in *The Feminine Mystique* (1963), and whose plight she sought to rectify by helping to establish the National Organization for Women in 1966, the same year *The Crying of Lot 49* was published.[58] The myth of women's domestic fulfillment runs counter to the reality that Oedipa's life is "a fat deckful of days which seemed (wouldn't she be first to admit it?) more or less identical" (11). But Oedipa is no feminist crusader. As Pynchon makes evident in the early pages of *Lot 49*, the only way that Oedipa imagines her escape from this trap as a "captive maiden" in a "Rapunzel-like role" is for a man to climb up her tresses and rescue her (20, 21). She wants to believe that the codes of chivalric romance—which have encapsulated her in Kinneret's bedroom community—will be the same ones that will save her. Any suggestion otherwise literally reduces her to crying. Early on, she recalls the haunting time when she and Pierce once stood in front of Remedios Varo's triptych *Bordando el Manto Terrestre* depicting "frail girls" in a tower who are embroidering a tapestry that spills out the window. In Varo's painting, female containment is doubled: the tapestry the girls are weaving entraps the entire world, "all the other buildings and creatures, all the waves, ships and forests of the earth," rendering any escape, any flight to a place of freedom beyond the strictures of gender imaginatively impossible (21). Oedipa's "dark green bubble shades" instantly fill with tears (21). She sees the world through the watery distortions of her own personal sorrow. When she leaves behind the safety of Kinneret (which she tellingly says does not need "redemption," though in her mind Los Angeles does), and leaves behind her husband Mucho to strike out on her own (admittedly in the service of another man), a new sense of adventure rushes in (55). Only it is not the one she imagined.

Much of Oedipa's time is spent in her car, shuttling from one locale to the next. The fact reflects the new realities of postwar American life, but Pynchon's novel wants us to recognize the car as a tool that changes urban space even as it carries us through it. Los Angeles was the first major world city to be designed with the automobile in mind, an urban prototype for the "large areas of the globe" that "now consist of car-only environments—the quintessential non-places of super-modernity."[59] By the 1960s the city had the highest number of automobiles per capita in the country and one of the lowest percentages of street areas navigable on foot.[60] The British historian of architecture Reyner Banham once quipped that he "learned to drive in order to read Los Angeles in the original."[61] As Oedipa descends into L.A.'s fictional San Narciso at "70 mph along the singing blacktop" on an access road that she describes as a "hypodermic needle" in "the vein of a freeway, a vein nourishing the mainliner L.A.," her attempt to read it "in the original" garners the reaction: "It seemed unnatural" (25, 26). Banham failed, like Oedipa, to recognize that the automobile is a symptom of our lack of connection to the city, not a solution to it. While it has allowed us to compress time and space and hence to visit friends and family far away, it is also the vehicle that has made our separation possible. It is both the means of Oedipa's escape from Kinneret and one of the reasons why she lives there.

There are no suburbs without the invention of the automobile. The massive highway construction projects of the mid-century aggressively altered the shape and constitution of American cities by draining money and people out of older urban cores and driving them to the periphery. The new freeways in the 1950s were, in many cases, plowed through inner city neighborhoods after exercises of eminent domain and slum clearance. For suburbanites working in the city or simply visiting it, impoverished districts became an ocular spectacle, a sight glimpsed at high speeds through a window or a rearview mirror. By inserting a private space into the public areas of the city, the car has further reduced opportunities for intergroup contact. Pynchon tellingly likens Oedipa's automobile to her husband's soundproof DJ booth: she cannot hear the "words . . . being spoken" to her because she is hermetically sealed in a self-contained atmosphere. What is missing from her knowledge of the city is that very thing that the car's reconfiguration of the urban fabric has worked to destroy, the very thing that is present in abundance in Rechy's novel of streetwalkers: the streetworld. Pynchon's aim in *The Crying of Lot 49* is not only to get Oedipa out of Kinneret but also to get her out of her car and onto the streets, where she is certain to discover strangeness in a world where "pedestrians," Pynchon writes, have been lumped with "pederasts" and "hookers," violators of an unspoken social code in which walking the streets for any reason is cause for censure (129).

As does *City of Night*, *The Crying of Lot 49* maps urban American life in the 1960s from the bottom up, while noting how the socially marginalized have been aligned with spaces of waste and uncleanliness. In Rechy's anguished novel, "the pleading scrawled messages" in "toilets in the subways" are desperate attempts to overcome gnawing loneliness by calling into the dark for some response, some contact (31). Oedipa's knowledge of the city's "separate, silent, unsuspected world" also begins, surprisingly, in a bathroom (125). At "the Scope, a bar out on the way to L.A., near the Yoyodyne plant" she reads "on the latrine wall, among lipsticked obscenities . . . the following message": "*Interested in sophisticated fun? You, hubby, girl friends. The more the merrier. Get in touch with Kirby, through WASTE only, Box 7391, L.A.*" (47, 52). "WASTE? Oedipa wondered," copying the Trystero's symbol of a muted post horn that accompanies the advertisement, which like a key to Pandora's box will unleash all kinds of secrets (52). A good deal cheekier than anything found in *City of Night*, Kirby's message seems to take the Whitmanian promise of a "City of Orgies" literally, but does so not with Rechy's angst but out of a desire for merry fun. Kirby's "engineering lettering" gives away the fact that he is technician at Yoyodyne, one of the "electronics assembly people" who haunt the bar (47, 52).

The juxtaposition of the fortified space of Yoyodyne (a space of exclusion, über-rationality, and death) with the space of "waste" indicates that they are not antithetical to each other, but are expressions of a single logic. The juxtaposition calls to mind Ralph Ellison's *Invisible Man*, in which the narrator's all-black college is a massive experiment in social engineering that is just up the road from the Golden Day, a bar with a bedlam-like atmosphere popular with prostitutes and psychically addled veterans. The rational ordering of space produces the very waste that must be excluded to ensure its purity. This is true whether it is material or social waste in cesspits on the outskirts of Barnes's Paris, in sewers below Wright's Chicago, or in tenement cellars in Riis's Lower East Side. In Pynchon's case, the waste and madness are inside the system itself, as seen in the general lunacy of Yoyodyne stockholders, who sing hymns to Minuteman missiles while "Negroes [carrying] gunboats of mashed potatoes" serve lunch (82, 83). The madness seemingly extends to Stanley Koteks, too, the engineer who tells Oedipa during her fact-finding mission at the plant that certain people, the "Sensitives," can sort fast and slow moving molecules with their minds (87). Oedipa quickly learns that Koteks is "part of . . . an underground of the unbalanced" (88).

Oedipa's discovery of the muted horn symbol on the bathroom wall initiates her investigation of Trystero, which consumes the remainder of the narrative. Through her research into original, if corrupted, editions of the Jacobean play *The Courier's Tragedy*, her interviews with the eminent L.A. philatelist Genghis Cohen, and through her conversations with the literature professor Emory Bortz, she pastes together a history of the secret organization dating back to sixteenth-century Europe, when it was a counterforce to the imperial postal service of the Thurn und Taxis family. Using violent stealth attacks and employing the tactics of "silence, impersonation, [and] opposition masquerading as allegiance," it was a true threat to the monopolistic control of mail routes and the distribution of information (174). But in the mid-nineteenth century, a split within Trystero led a number of its members to emigrate to the United States and seemingly to become involved in every major chapter of American history—from "back in the gold rush days" when its agents masked themselves as Native Americans and attacked the Pony Express, to the federal government's suppression of independent mail routes (the real reason for the Civil War), to trafficking in the skeletal remains of World War II American GIs (91).

This alternative national (and world) history—a mix of rumor, fact, and innuendo—which Oedipa labors to piece together is hardly reliable and never amounts to "the central truth itself" (95). More than anything, it indicates a will-to-believe, the need for an organizing principle in the face of doubt, a desire for a representation of agency in the midst of one's own bewilderment and lack of control when faced with incomprehensibly complex historical and geographical possibilities. Oedipa herself writes in a note under the muted horn she copied at the Scope: "*Shall I project a world?*" (82). Inundated and overwhelmed with random amounts of data pertaining to the Trystero, "she would," Pynchon writes, "give them order, she would create constellations" (90). But this will-to-believe is a will-not-to-believe something else. And this something else is what was revealed without her knowing it when she first discovered the "WASTE symbol" in a public restroom. Whatever insurgent, resistant force it might have been in the past, the Trystero conspiracy in contemporary America is an obfuscating screen, an ideological ruse. Looking for Trystero's silent empire, Oedipa misses what is staring her in the face. The real Trystero—by which Pynchon means America's surplus populations—are the excreta of late capitalism's "WASTE system." America's real waste is its human effluvia, a diverse, dispersed, and largely powerless castoff people who circulate through the nation without direction, voice, or purpose (124). This knowledge, we will see, is too much for Oedipa to bear.

The real-and-imagined underworld stands as Pynchon's indictment of America's failure of its own "citizens" (124). To be more exact, it is an indictment of the reckless post-Fordist development that was especially egregious in Los Angeles, but which was indicative of national trends. Richard Lehan writes in his consideration of Pynchon's novel that L.A. is a "space filled but not ordered."[62] It is a space in which unfettered capitalism has run amok. In Pynchon's novel, post-Fordist capitalism is embodied in Pierce and his numerous corporate partnerships, whose need "to possess, to alter the land, to bring new skylines, personal antagonisms, growth rates into being" obliterates any sense of history and traditions that would anchor the formation of community in the area (178). Nothing stands in its path: even the local cemetery seems to have been exhumed "for the East San Narciso Freeway," an egregious paving over of history (95). The Mexican anarchist Jesús Arrabal—perhaps the one person in the novel with political consciousness—tells Oedipa that Pierce represents "the thing we fight" (120). Pynchon's representation of uneven development makes evident that the social and geographic effects are not just the massive accumulation of wealth and the construction of more suburbs, but kaleidoscopic and pluralized forms of inequality and alienation and multiplied geographies of withdrawal and immiseration that proliferate, popping up everywhere. Soja's "other spaces," of which there are too many "to be informatively described," are the spaces of the many Others in *Lot 49*.[63] "If San Narciso and the estate were really no different from any other town, any other estate, then by that continuity," Pynchon posits, "she might have found The Tristero anywhere in her Republic, through any of a hundred lightly-concealed entranceways, a hundred alienations, if only she'd looked" (179).

When Oedipa's quest deposits her in San Francisco, her search takes on added urgency in inverse proportion to her anxious and dispersed agency. Her fateful decision to abandon her car and "to drift tonight, at random" (to become literally a "drifter") through the city on foot is a turning point that tells us Oedipa will subject herself to the unexpected (109). Unlike the slummers we encountered in chapters 1 and 2 of this book, who ventured through the city at night on scripted tours with moonlighting police officers to gaze upon ethnic, racial, and sexual difference, Oedipa's nocturnal ramble has no set course and no guide. She does not know what she will find as she makes her way into a world that is utterly alien to her. Relinquishing a bourgeois need for control and order, she adopts the rootlessness of the urban lumpenproletariat who circulate through the city in search of shelter or work.

Oedipa's desperate decision to drift brings her into contact with almost every instance of urban difference; rather than reinforcing the superiority and sanctity of her privileged position, her sense of self slowly begins to crumble. She quickly finds herself pushed into a gay "bar called The Greek Way" with a group of tourists who are curious "to see the members of the third sex" (110). This inauspicious beginning is an exercise of voyeurism and sexual Othering, yet it nevertheless leads to unpredicted disclosures that ameliorate the crude fetishism of the sexual slumming tour. In the "fag joint" she learns that the muted post horn originally infiltrated Yoyodyne through one of its executives in "the corporate root-system" who was automated out of job by an IBM 7094 mainframe, a victim of an unremitting and technologically facilitated stress on efficiency (110, 113). After the executive's botched suicide attempt, he establishes Inamorati Anonymous, whose members renounce love. They are "a whole underworld of suicides who failed. All keeping in touch through that secret delivery system" (116). What perversely unites this "society of isolates"—and also keeps them from killing themselves—is a commitment not to be with each other (116). In this instance, WA.S.T.E. is less an alternative community than it is an anti-community, postmodern alienation at its most dire.

Like the Trystero conspiracy, W.A.S.T.E. never adds up, never accretes into an organized collectivity. The point is further illustrated on Oedipa's insomniatic flânerie, where the socioeconomic inequalities that have been occluded from her begin to surface into view. In quick succession, she stumbles upon homeless children playing in Golden Gate Park, walks among "delinquents" whose "gang jackets" sport the post horn as an insignia, rides "among an exhausted busful of Negroes going on to graveyard shifts all over the city," sees a mad night-watchmen eating soap, wanders the "Negro neighborhood" of the Fillmore and the Mexican barrio of the Mission, and discovers that "decorating each alienation, each species of withdrawal . . . was somehow always the post horn" (121–123). Here is a postmodern social geography of the racialized, the insane, the sexually minoritized, and the poor at its most kaleidoscopically surreal. Oedipa notices the putative underworld everywhere, yet her encounters come, it is crucial to note, as isolated incidents with individuals or small groups scattered throughout the city. Never merging into a collective experience or knowledge, the city, even after all of this exposure, remains for her at the level of fragments, a multiplication of geographically broken solitudes.

Pynchon lowers Oedipa through social and geographic space until she finally bottoms out in an extended encounter outside a rundown halfway house with a lonely, elderly sailor with a muted post horn on his hands that shake from delirium tremens. He pleads with her to mail a letter for him through the W.A.S.T.E. mailboxes under the freeway. The moment is a test to see if Oedipa can move beyond her conditioned reflexes, a test she fails. Pynchon characterizes Oedipa as a "voyeur and a listener," the first connoting unseemingly curiosity and the second empathy (123). He writes that the "old man . . . [shakes] with grief she couldn't hear" (125). Even though Oedipa is herself "shaking, tired," she cannot acknowledge their connection (125). Her nightlong wanderings in effect have made her indistinguishable from the other sad and impoverished souls who form Trystero. "Exhausted, hardly knowing she was doing," she takes him into her arms, but only to whisper "I can't help . . . I can't help" (126). Oedipa absolves her sense of guilt—and tries to restabilize herself—by offering him ten dollars. She leaves him on his urine-stained mattress and spends a dazed hour looking for the garbage can in which to drop his letter.

What, we might ask, is Pynchon's goal in subjecting his fictional creation to these terrible trials and tribulations, and what are the results? Pynchon endeavors to make Oedipa "sensitive," a word he deploys multiple times in reference to her ability to detect postwar America's "separate, silent, unsuspected world" (125). Early in the narrative he remarks that she is called "too sensitive" by her husband, then we are told later that she has been "sensitized" (12, 45). Still later Pynchon has her tested with Maxwell's Demon to see if she is a "Sensitive," and writes in another moment that she has been, yet again, "sensitized," this time to the existence of the Trystero (87, 91). Oedipa's experiences in L.A. and San Francisco result in her discovery of "a network by which X number of Americans" have chosen a "calculated withdrawal from the life of the Republic," an alternative nation of "drifters" and "squatters" living in "lean-tos behind smiling billboards along all the highways," sleeping in abandoned "Pullman cars" and in "junkyards in the stripped shells of wrecked Plymouths" (124, 170, 179, 180).

Repurposing the scraps of a modern culture of motion, the urban underworld fashions its own geography. But what they do not make is a space of resistance that might pose a threat to the Pierce Inveraritys of the world. In Pynchon's novel, the junked, wasted populations of capitalism may be connected to each other, linked through alternative flows of information, but they are never united. Their agency is exercised in their refusal to participate in the civic life of the nation, an antipolitical abandonment of ideological and territorial struggle: "It was not an act of treason, nor possibly even of defiance. . . . Whatever else was being denied them out of hate, indifference to the power of their vote, loopholes, simple ignorance, this withdrawal was their own, unpublicized, private" (124). This is the disinherited, unacknowledged legacy of America, and Oedipa forlornly ponders, "How had it ever happened here, with the chances once so good for diversity?" (181).

Oedipa cannot answer the very question she asks, for to answer it honestly would once and for all destabilize the ideological foundation of her middle-class life that permits her to function in the world. Her descent into the underworld unmoors all of her traditional pieties, and has placed her in a "void" where "nobody . . . could help her" (171). "Where am I," she asks in distress (153). She has "lost her bearings" and become disoriented in an urban space whose differences she cannot coalesce through any kind of totalizing vision (177). Instead of becoming more "sensitive," she ends up more paranoid, "out of [her] skull," and lost (171). There is no chance for Oedipa to return to her former life on her old terms. The suburbs surely will offer her no asylum, only a quieter form of madness. Her initial response to the exposure of socioeconomic inequality is fear and likely will be followed, if Mucho's experience is an indicator, by disgust, which ultimately will be replaced by paranoia. Mucho's former work as a used-car salesman, we learn, brought him into contact with "people poorer than him . . . Negro, Mexican, cracker" with "the most godawful of trade-ins: motorized, metal extensions of themselves" (13). For Mucho, the poor are conflated with their despoiled environment. Like modern versions of Riis's dirty tenement dwellers, the poor are inseparable from the filth surrounding them in their cars filled with cigarettes, coupons, help-wanted ads, "rags of old underwear," "a salad of despair, in a gray dressing of ash, condensed exhaust, dust, body wastes—it made him sick to look, but he had to look" (13, 14). In these broken vehicles, the litter of twentieth-century mass consumerism piles up, reeking of despair. As with all this junk, the poor and the working class are used up; every ounce of use-value squeezed out of them, they are traded in, exchanged like so many cars.

While Pynchon's catalog of immiseration grows longer and longer, Oedipa's horizon of vision constricts, her capacity for recognition, engagement, and individual and social transformation narrowing into a fearful, isolated protectionism in which she suspects that everyone is "her enemy" (183). In the whirlwind of these discoveries, paranoia, Patrick O'Donnell writes, "rearranges chaos into order."[64] It recenters and reconsolidates Oedipa's subjectivity in a landscape that is itself without a center. It writes her into the narrative of the nation by casting her—rather than the underworld poor—as the truly disadvantaged and besieged subject. At the novel's conclusion, she is immobilized, literally sitting down (124). She is unable to move past a bifurcated "either/or" conceptualization of the country, one of compartmentalized and mutually exclusive dualities and polarities. Pynchon delineates her options: "Another mode of meaning behind the obvious, or none. Either Oedipa in the orbiting ecstasy of a true paranoia, or a real Tristero. For there either was some Tristero beyond the appearance of the legacy [of] America, or there was just America and if there was just America then it seemed the only way she could continue, and manage to be at all relevant to it, was as an alien, unfurrowed, assumed full circle into some paranoia" (182).

Oedipa cannot comprehend the truth of her experience, cannot comprehend the contradiction that there is "just America" and in its injustice it also includes the realities she has witnessed. What truly links the manifold underclass populations of America, Pynchon suggests, is not, of course, an alternative network of garbage-can mailboxes, but the networks of capitalist power through which flow money, cheapened labor, technology, and information and out of which comes both new skylines, suburbs (and missiles to protect them), and more and more waste, tons of it. This is what Oedipa is incapable of discerning. The transformational vision that might have been ignited in her, however, is available to the reader who can see through the jittery paranoia in Oedipa's eyes. It would be a vision that would connect the suburban archipelagos of the nation to the unregulated sprawl of post-Fordist production and would link both to the urban geographies of homelessness and alienation. It would recognize that the accumulated wealth in Kinneret is made possible by the unevenly distributed profits of a postwar boom, which in turn made possible the "calculated withdrawal" not of the poor but of the middle class to their enclaves (124). In *The Crying of Lot 49*, the underworld is a real-and-imagined space where one retreats, a space of making do but not under the conditions of one's doing. This is where Pynchon leaves us. At the same time that Oedipa was looking for definitive proof of the Trystero conspiracy, a more radical vision of territorial politics, one beyond the limits of her imagination, was beginning to surface in the Los Angeles neighborhood of Watts. It is to that neighborhood I now briefly turn, following Pynchon's ongoing journey through the lower geographies of the city.

Exiting the Imperial Freeway: Pynchon's "A Journey into the Mind of Watts"

"The city burning is Los Angeles's deepest image of itself," Joan Didion claimed in 1968, an apocalyptic wish that was transformed into a sociological reality the year before *The Crying of Lot 49* was published.[65] "At the time of the 1965 Watts riots what struck the imagination most indelibly," Didion writes, "were the fires. For days one could drive the Harbor Freeway and see the city on fire, just as we had always known it would be in the end."[66] Didion's anonymous "one" who is mesmerized by the riot from the safety and privilege of a car on the freeway morphs with just a few words into a self-gratulatory, if mournful, "we" whose suspicions are confirmed. Neither this "one" nor this "we" are part of "them," the residents of the black South Central community who staged a nearly weeklong uprising that stunned the world. Edward Soja labels it "the most shattering challenge to the local regime of accumulation that had sustained fifty years of rapidly expanding industrial production in Los Angeles."[67] What began with the botched arrest in Watts of Marquette Frye for erratic driving soon spawned a rebellion of 35,000 people, which called for comparisons to Vietnam: black residents fired on LAPD helicopters and flights over LAX were diverted because "rioters were shooting at planes."[68] Thomas Sheridan of the McCone Commission, which was charged with uncovering the causes of the rebellion, commented that one reason it lasted so long was because Los Angeles is "so sprawling . . . a riot here is much harder to control."[69] The irony of ironies. By the time Watts was forcibly pacified by "16,000 National Guard, Los Angeles Police Department, highway patrol, and other law enforcement officers," at least thirty-four people were dead and "property damage was estimated at $200 million."[70]

In "A Journey into the Mind of Watts" from 1966, Thomas Pynchon takes the reader into the community that Oedipa never sees on her many travels on Los Angeles's freeways. He remarks: "The panoramic sense of black impoverishment is hard to miss from atop the Harbor Freeway, which so many whites must drive at least twice every working day. Somehow it occurs to very few of them to leave at the Imperial Highway exit for a change, go east instead of west only a few blocks, and take a look at Watts. A quick look. The simplest kind of beginning. But Watts is [a] country which lies, psychologically, uncounted miles further than most whites seem at present willing to travel."[71] I close with Pynchon's essay because it illuminates the racial contours of Oedipa's spatial imagination and because it returns us to the issues raised by urban redevelopment and geographical isolation in Los Angeles, which seemingly made inevitable this outburst of collective violence.

Most of the displaced inhabitants of the Bunker Hill neighborhood were pushed "to the west bank of the Harbor Freeway" and cut off from a future new downtown.[72] In 1964, the Community Redevelopment Agency, which was overseeing the large-scale renovations to the area, issued *Centropolis*, a comprehensive vision whose most radical proposal was a design to link major retail structures in downtown with "pedways," a network of interlocking streets suspended in the air above the homelessness and poverty beneath.[73] Tellingly, *Centropolis* was scrapped after the Watts uprising and after the McCone Commission predicted "that by 1990 the core of the Central City of Los Angeles will be inhabited almost exclusively by more than 1,200,000 Negroes."[74] Neither businesses nor white residents would want to be in the center of that, the commission implied.

"A Journey into the Mind of Watts" is a psycho-geographical exploration into the perceptions of violence from the perspective of Watts's residents. As a rebuttal to the "panoramic" view that only sees a phantasmagoria of black underclass deviancy, Pynchon attempts a narrative of descent that will not succumb to the voyeurism that is often the ideological baggage of such expeditions. The impetus of the essay was the 1966 killing of Leonard Deadwyler by the LAPD as he sat in his car with his pregnant wife, a sign that police brutality was alive and well a year after the riot. Pynchon remarks, "somehow nothing much has changed."[75] Like Oedipa who attempts, but ultimately fails, to glean "concealed meaning" behind the "astonishing clarity" of the San-Narciso sprawl, Pynchon tries to see past "the daytime's brilliance and heat" of Watts where "everything seems so out in the open."[76] "Underneath the mood in Watts is about what you might expect," he observes: "Feelings range from a reflexive, angry, driving need to hit back somehow, to an anxious worry that the slaying is just one more bad grievance, one more bill that will fall due some warm evening this summer."[77] Trying to read the city, Pynchon characterizes Watts in language that directly contrasts it with the fictional Kinneret and San Narciso of his novel: "all of it real, no plastic faces, no transistors, no hidden Muzak, or Disneyfied landscaping, or smiling little chicks to show you around."[78]

Instead of inviting the reader to inhabit the abstract, disembodied "one" who floats aloft over the city, Pynchon's essay seeks to imaginatively resituate the reader as "you," a victim of Watts's discriminations under the scopic eye of the police. "How very often the cop does approach you with his revolver ready . . . your life trembling in the crook of a cop's finger because it is dark," Pynchon writes.[79] With this tense encounter, the perspective of the "you" emerges and for the rest of the essay the daily life-and-death exchanges in Watts are viewed from the point of view of a resident. We should understand this grammatical elision not as another example of a white author's colonizing perspective, not as another effort to expropriate the experience of the marginalized subject. Such a charge would accuse Pynchon of conflating perspectives, when his aim actually is the opposite of this. In other words, we should understand it instead as an exposure of how race, class, and geography color the ways we see. Pynchon reverses the conventional positions in the unequal economy of vision. Instead of treating black urban life as a confusing spectacle to be gazed upon, he turns the gaze back onto the rest of white Los Angeles which is suddenly made strange: "From here, much of the white culture that surrounds Watts . . . looks . . . a little unreal, a little less than substantial. . . . It is basically a white Scene, and illusion is everywhere in it, from the giant aerospace firms that flourish or retrench at the whims of Robert McNamara, to the 'action' everybody mills along the Strip on weekends looking for, unaware that they, and their search which will end, usually, unfulfilled, are the only action in town. Watts lies impacted in the heart of this white fantasy."[80] What is seen "from here" is the invisible whiteness of a narcissistic middle-class culture of death. And in the heart of this culture is a fantasy of the black ghetto, an underworld of the poor, and a queer netherworld in city parks and street corners across America.

In the 1960s, Thomas Pynchon and John Rechy imaginatively inhabited this fantasy. In their writing, the real-and-imagined microcommunities of the underworld registered the first impacts of urban redevelopment, ramped-up police harassment, and the large-scale restructuring of the urban economy. Whereas Rechy's narrative gives us an intimate portrait of a queer underworld with great texture, Pynchon's novel provides an outsider's flawed perspective of an underworld that has multiplied and diversified in the postwar era. In the years that followed these texts, the effects of post-Fordist restructuring would be felt across the nation. The geographies of exclusion would proliferate until, as Don DeLillo would show in a novel I now turn to, the whole world seemingly had become the underworld.

5 / White Spaces and Urban Ruins: Postmodern Geographies in Don DeLillo's *Underworld*, 1950s–1990s

"It's the decade of crack and homelessness. It's the decade of the tunnels. . . . People've been down and out since the beginning of time, but we's the first to actually live in tunnels. There's been nowhere else to go. . . . There was too many of us": these words belong to Seville Williams, a recovering drug addict and twelve-year denizen of the underground who in the 1980s lived "under Track 100 in Grand Central Station" and was one of an estimated five thousand people scratching out a life in the grimy interstices of New York City's transportation network, according to Jennifer Toth in *The Mole People: Life in the Tunnels beneath New York City* (1993).[1] Thomas Pynchon's mid-1960s fantasia of an underworld of drifters and squatters huddled behind "billboards along all the highways" and railroad tracks has become, two and half decades later, "a crisis of our time" and a harbinger of the future, Toth writes in her popular, shocking, and controversial journalistic account of New York's underworld homeless (41).[2] Replete with photographic evidence, the voices of the tunnel dwellers themselves, and Toth's own precipitous narrative of hellish descent, *The Mole People* brings up to date Jacob Riis's *How the Other Half Lives* at the close of another century. Between 1890 and 1990, the poorest of the poor apparently exchanged their lightless tenement cellars for the toxic, rat-infested environment of dripping catwalks and electrocuting rails in the modern city's circulatory system.[3]

Within the subway network's rational, efficient underworld space, Toth offers images of people grouped around campfires "like prehistoric men against the elements," where atavistic primitivism resurfaces and human evolution slides backward into degeneration or into some future mutation in the human form itself (38). "Down here, man becomes an animal. Down here, the true animal in man comes out, evolves," claims Bernard, a leader of one of the city's main underground encampments whom Toth interviews (104). In his opposition to a national fallout shelter program in 1957, Robert Moses, New York's master builder, parks commissioner, and latter-day version of Baron Haussmann, expressed fear of a "mole life of the future," the devolution that would follow not from gamma rays but from confining oneself and one's family in a basement, a converted cistern, or a do-it-yourself backyard bomb-shelter during a nuclear winter.[4] Moses's human moles, unlike Toth's, were in the planned communities of suburban America where the white middle class was contemplating burying itself in its fenced-in lawns. With New York City's "mole people" of the 1980s and 1990s living in pockets in the transportation infrastructure that Moses himself had helped construct, Moses's fear was literalized to a degree he would have found inconceivable.[5]

The American underworld has refused to die, resurfacing periodically to belie a century of progressive political advance. The "too many of us" (to quote Seville Williams) living in the squalid realities of the underground point to the uncomfortable truth of deepening poverty in a new gilded age in a new fin de siècle. The underworld's uncanny recrudescence in books—such as Toth's journalistic account; or Margaret Morton's *The Tunnel* (1995), a collection of stunning black-and-white photographs of homeless communities living in an Amtrak tunnel on New York's West Side near the neighborhood of Hell's Kitchen; or films such as Marc Singer's *Dark Days* (2000), a documentary of men and women residing beneath Penn Station; or in urban spelunking societies that recently have popped up in major cities in the United States—speaks both to an enduring cultural fascination and to an attempt to understand the reconfigured intersections of cityspace, race, urban decay, and poverty in the post-Fordist or postmodern city.[6] At the center of this discourse is Don DeLillo's epic *Underworld* (1997), which I shall turn to shortly, a novel that has gone further than any other in its efforts to apprehend—and to make art out of—the profound disquietude that characterizes the social and spatial alterations of late twentieth-century urban life.[7] Coeval with the dominance of global capitalism in the postwar era, the postmodern city poses exceptional difficulties for novelists, scholars, and journalists because its geographies of inequality, immiseration, and uneven development are not only polarized but are also splintered and pluralized in

FIGURE 12. Subway tunnel encampment with kitchen. Courtesy of Margaret Morton, *The Tunnel* (Yale University Press, 1995).

ways that make representing them a significant challenge. One of the most notable features of the contemporary American city is its diverse inequalities, "the expansion and consolidation of distinct social forms, such as an underclass," as one sociologist has put it.[8] According to the geographer Edward Soja, socioeconomic inequality has only intensified as the century has ground to a close, a trend he has called "disturbing."[9]

Far from witnessing the elimination of the urban underworld as a potent locus of social anxieties, the contemporary period has seen its amplification. The specter haunts late twentieth-century writings on urban decay, renewal, and restructuring. In order to begin elucidating the function of the underworld in the contemporary urban imaginary—in order, that is, to understand how it has shaped responses to uneven social and geographical development in the 1980s and 1990s—I would like to return briefly to Jennifer Toth's *The Mole People*, which served as source material for DeLillo's *Underworld*.

Toth's work responds to recent urban crises—increased homelessness, crime, drug addiction, the physical deterioration of public architectures—by rehabilitating a nineteenth-century tradition of city-mystery writing and muckraking journalism that bifurcated the city into high and low, gaslight and shadow, rhetorically creating the differences it described. As did Jacob Riis before her, Toth shines a light on a "dark world" in an effort to illuminate a social and physical geography glimpsed by few outsiders (5). Riis's text mapped the geographies of class at a time when rapid industrialization was creating a mass urban lumpenproletariat living in the ash-strewn streets of lower Manhattan. Similarly, *The Mole People* navigates new social geographies at a time when post-Fordist restructuring—hastened by drastic cuts to the Department of Housing and Urban Development in the 1980s—left American cities flooded with unprecedented numbers of the homeless, including entire families. But unlike Riis, Toth is a late twentieth-century liberal writing in the context of multiculturalism whose foray into the hellish terrain of the city proceeds out of compassion, respect, and a humanizing impulse: "In describing the dangerous world of the underground homeless, I've sought to bring up to the reader not only their personal histories but also the sparks of friendship and caring that help light their dark world," she announces at the outset (5). From her descent in the subway tunnels, Toth "brings up to the reader" a reassuring sign: even underground the spirit of companionship and care cannot be snuffed out. Toth's admittance to this "world of outcasts" was gained by befriending members of the tunnel communities—such as graffiti writer Chris Pape—while she volunteered in a Harlem tutorial program as a graduate student at Columbia University (38). Her Virgil thus was an insider, one of the very subjects she had come to study, rather than an off-duty police officer or a slumming tour-guide operator, as was so often the case in the sensational literature and practice of nocturnal descents from earlier in the century.

As it anatomizes New York's underground, *The Mole People* presents a surreal geography that stretches the limits of plausibility, resulting in a city whose demography and secret spaces are even more unfathomable than originally imagined. Far from clarifying the reader's vision of the city, as is so often the stated purpose of underworld narratives, Toth's work, which draws heavily from folklore of hollow-earth societies and post-apocalyptic films of irradiated humans, may have the opposite effect. If Toth's ostensible aim is to spotlight the horrors of extreme poverty and the human costs of sociospatial exclusion, the phantasm of "the mole people" which she deploys to focus attention on these issues may end up obfuscating them behind a grotesque spectacle in which the animal nature of the poor is the greater worry.

One of the first things that Toth learns through Seville is that "tunnel life closest to the surface is the worst" because of rats, which are a danger but also a source of food (20). Yet "the further down you go," he declares, "the weirder people get, and I mean real weird. . . .There are people down there, man, I swear they have webbed feet" (21).[10] Seville is probably testing Toth's gullibility, misinforming the amateur urban ethnographer by countering her voyeurism and fear with his own inflated rumors that exceed her wildest nightmares. But reports of the devolution of humans back into an amphibious state are offset by Seville himself. He later tells her about underworld societies that are rebuilding civilization from scratch around a renewed commitment to fundamental values of sharing and hard work, unlike the greedy, rapacious world above. One such urban underworld, he reveals, is supposedly located in "'the Condos,' a kind of natural cavern . . . accessible from the tracks in Grand Central" "where over two hundred people lived. . . . 'Some were homosexuals, some straight'" (20, 21). With another homeless man named J. C. from Harlem, Toth visits this utopian, though fantastic, subterranean "'multicultural community'" that is outfitted with its own nurse, teacher, several children, and a "mayor" (J. C. himself) who lives in a tent with two bookcases "filled mostly with sociology, psychology, and philosophy texts and a sprinkling of the classics" (191, 198). J. C.'s community deep under the cement of Manhattan subscribes to "our 'human religion'" (196). Elaborating, he adds, "It's based on caring and protecting our brothers and sisters, on communication and love" (196). Rejecting the notion that they need any intervention on their behalf by Toth or any state agencies, J. C. remarks that "we are a clean and healthy community. . . . We don't allow drugs or hard liquor here. We're not crazy or insane. We're healthy individuals who have chose [*sic*] an alternative. We don't need . . . help . . . we are a superior people. We've purified ourselves" (199, 201). The residents of "the Condos" prefer to stay underground, finding their "alternative way of living" more free and more hospitable than life on the cold and violent streets (200). In this inverted world, hell is located above the sewer grates.

Typical of urban narratives of descent, *The Mole People* is filled with contradictory sentiments of curiosity and terror, attraction and repulsion, and a socially progressive mindset with an ethic of care and a retrenchment into self-interest and self-preservation. These contradictions reveal less about the idiosyncrasies of particular individuals than they do competing impulses that a modern capitalist society instills in its citizens. Like many of the stories of descent I have considered in this book, Toth's narrative tears itself in half. On the one hand, she is drawn to the underworld out of a desire to help publicize an unconsciable social problem, and on the other, she is driven from it out of fear for her own safety and the feeling that the homeless are "wild and frightening" (2). "If I had it to do again, I wouldn't," she forthrightly declares, "The sadness and the tragedies were overwhelming, and, in the end, the danger to myself was too great to want to relive" (5).

Taking a page from mythological journeys of descent in which the young hero comes face to face with the god of the underworld, *The Mole People* tells of Toth's (her name calls to mind the Egyptian underworld god Thoth) brief encounter with a psychically addled tunnel dweller with "fiery red" eyes who is known as the "Angel of Death" and who sleeps in a "coffin-shaped box" (166, 168). He is feared throughout the tunnels, and in Toth's chilling run-in with him, he hisses that she has "left the world of fairness and good" (168). The world she leaves by the end of the book is actually New York City. Stalked by another underground resident who threatens her life because he believes she has witnessed him committing a crime, she abandons her investigation once and for all.

The Ivy-league-educated Toth finishes her narrative with a testimony of her own survival that is meant to serve as a reason for hope for those she has left behind, despite the practically insurmountable differences between them: "As many tunnel people have told me, the line between them and people who live on the surface is very thin, much thinner than people on the 'topside world' like to realize. I felt I could step over that line. I could also escape, and I did. I hope some of them will escape, too" (246, 247). Toth's concluding remarks replace the politics of spatial poverty with the nonpolitics of "hope." Ignoring the racial and class privileges that have made her "escape" possible, Toth sets up her flight from the poor as a very model of inspiration for them to follow. As was true with nineteenth-century slumming narratives I discussed in chapter 1, Toth's descent began with the security that she could leave at a time of her own choosing, unlike the sub rosa populations on whom she reports. "Let us go home," Ernest Ingersoll once advised his nauseated sightseer after a nighttime ramble through the slums of lower New York, advice Toth gladly takes.[11] "I felt drained and hollow," she writes in her epilogue, her twenty-four-year-old life turned upside-down and haunted by memories of walking "into the tunnels clutching the can of mace my father gave me, . . . so frightened I could not turn back to look for the eyes I felt watching me" (252, 253).

In the end, we might ask if Toth's book is anything more than a bizarre variation on the perennial theme of the outsider's eye-opening experience in the big city. Or does this strange text offer us another kind of knowledge? I want to suggest that *The Mole People*, like one prominent strain of academic and popular discourse, calls for greater tolerance and appreciation of difference by championing the nation's forgotten or buried histories. In this sense, Toth's narrative, like Ralph Ellison's *Invisible Man*, John Rechy's *City of Night*, and as I will show, DeLillo's *Underworld*, is part of a cultural project to give voice to the spatially marginalized as compensation and succor for their suffering in the city's wastelands. Riis freely trafficked in ethnic caricatures and shut out the voices of "the Nether Half" from his text, which has the silence of a diorama of "picturesque filth and poverty."[12] Toth, however, allows "the mole people" to speak for themselves. Her dialogic chapters—"Seville's Story," "Mac's War," "Bernard's Tunnel," "J. C.'s Community"—individuate this invisible population and serve as a platform from which its members can speak up for their humanity. By definition, eliminating poverty would eliminate the poor, causing them, quite literally, to disappear from the streets and subways. But this radical goal is not Toth's, whose ambition is not to eradicate the social causations of poverty but to dignify the poor in spite of their immiseration and their continual denigration as social parasites. Toth's stated aim—at odds with the title of her book—is "to dismiss the myth of animal-like underground dwellers, so that you, the reader, can come to know that mole people don't exist beneath the surface of New York City, but people do" (x). Her method is to relay their "personal histories . . . the sparks of friendship and caring"; the "stories tell not only of their present lives in the tunnels and the communities they form but also of their communication networks, and of the encounters with government agencies, charitable programs, and nonprofit advocacy groups" (5).

The story that ultimately emerges from Toth's underground is a story of human endurance and creativity in the face of urban neglect, drug addiction, abuse, mental illness, and chronic poverty. This, too, is the story of *Underworld*, which ambitiously tells a national counternarrative that "lives in the spaces of the official play-by-play."[13] This "underhistory," as

DeLillo also calls it, is a record of situated practices that grow out of a consciousness of geography's effects, informal economies of barter that exist in the interstices of conventional systems of monetary exchange, and networks of resistance that link people in the postmodern city regardless of differences in race, ethnicity, or sexual orientation (791). For DeLillo, the second half of the twentieth century is littered with "trapped souls trying to emerge" from wasted urban terrains (621). His novel's title, without a definite or indefinite article, uncovers the underworld in almost every conceivable manifestation: the underclass ghettoes of Harlem and the Bronx; the secret world of subway tunnels where the queer graffiti artist Moonman 157 skulks; the criminal underworld of late-1940s Italian New York; mutant humans who in Sergei Eisenstein's fictitious sci-fi film *Unterwelt* live in crevices in the earth; and the forgotten history of the down-winders of Nevada and Utah who were unknowing test subjects in a vast government experiment with radioactive fallout (424). DeLillo imagines underworld spaces as locations of resistance, indigenization, historical and bodily memory (what he calls "muscle memory"), rupture, and national trauma which belie the dominant postwar liberal narrative in which historically marginalized subjects benefited not only from a growing economy but also from an expanded, more inclusive definition of civil rights and citizenship (27). DeLillo's many underworlds, we will find, are sites of locally rooted expressions of communal grief and outrage, as well as sites of ingenuity and coalition building through which neglected and exiled urban residents take possession of their own geographies, remaking them as a means of exercising power in the postmodern landscape.

Underworld's wide-ranging, branching narrative covers a lot of ground—from New York, to Arizona, to Kazakhstan—but its central line follows the peregrinations of the estranged brothers Nick and Matt Shay as they separately leave their decaying, impoverished Bronx neighborhood and by circuitous means wind up living in suburbs, where they work in the new insular architectures of the postmetropolis. In Phoenix, Nick works in a glassed-in, panoptic office tower for a waste management corporation with business partnerships in the former Soviet Union, while Matt is an engineer in an underground atomic weapons lab, before he quits to take a position at an NGO studying Third World poverty. Alongside the private, domestic dramas of the Shays, DeLillo weaves the life of Matt's chess mentor Albert Bronzini, who refuses to leave the Bronx even though it has fallen into a wasteland of drugs, disease, and homelessness, and even though his wife Klara Sax, who becomes an internationally famous artist, divorces him. Also in the Bronx are Sisters Gracie and Edgar, who minister to the broken community, and Ismael Muñoz (aka Moonman), an HIV-positive community muralist who paints the Bronx's dead children on a giant wall. A closeted, germophobic J. Edgar Hoover, along with Lenny Bruce, Frank Sinatra, and Jackie Gleason make appearances, as do several more characters—a young African American boy from Harlem named Cotter, his deadbeat father Manx, a paranoid baseball memorabilist Marvin Lundy, the ad executive Charles Wainwright, and a Russian trading executive Viktor Maltsev, among others. At the center of *Underworld* is the subject of the changing nature of cityspace and the imperiled status of marginalized individuals and communities suffering through nearly a half-century of urban crises. The historical period dramatized by DeLillo covers the rapid decline of the Fordist city and the emergence of a new, disorienting urban form that, as we began to see in chapter 4, has left sociologists, urban planners, and geographers reaching for a new vocabulary and another set of theoretical tools, and as we will see in this chapter, has left DeLillo's Nick Shay spinning with a "sense of displacement and redefinition" (786).

The ambition of DeLillo's longest, most complex novel to date is both to map forty-plus years of capitalist geography and to unearth capital's concealed logic, its contradictory production of fortified spaces of suburban wealth and quietude and their uncanny double, the geographies of gutted inner-city ruins. He does so by writing American history from the 1950s to the 1990s through the eyes of the urban poor, who have suffered from the breathtaking storm of globalization, and from the perspectives of the winners who imagine their successes to be unrelated to the impoverishment of others. DeLillo traces the polarities of the postmodern age further by tying them to the contradictory logic of multinational capitalism, which *Underworld* shows has been expressed through two interrelated countertendencies. On the one hand, the era is characterized by the derealization of urban space into a network of global referents and signs that float through contemporary culture without being rooted to any place, and on the other, it is defined by the production of spectacular urban decay and new fortified, gleaming corporate architectures. In social terms, the result of this logic has been the creation of an hourglass-shaped class structure with the expansion of a well-to-do population of information managers, venture capitalists, and high-tech workers at the top (such as the Shay brothers) and at the bottom, a growing body of low-wage, itinerant service workers mixed with those (such as Moonman and many others in the novel), who are either chronically unemployed or working in expanding black market economies.

DeLillo's "underhistory" of the postwar period is an attempt to orient us in a newly fragmented, kaleidoscopic, discombobulating physical and social geography. Intensely dialectical in its representations of city-life, *Underworld* dramatizes the contradictions of uneven development. DeLillo narrates urbanization's simultaneous erosion of spatial textures and histories, territorial communities, and the reconstitution of localities and geographically rooted identities. And by way of its central character, the upper-middle-class Nick Shay, DeLillo's novel illustrates how the sentimental bourgeois subject responds to its perceived losses by constructing mystifying narratives of the past. Even as he mourns over his childhood Bronx, which he believes African Americans and Hispanics have turned into an uninhabitable underworld, he profits from his own loss through managing a company whose slogan is "The Future of Waste" (282).

"This Latest Mutation in Space": Mapping the Postmodern City

Out of the urban crises and riots of the 1960s and out of the global recessionary economies of 1970s, the post-Fordist city rose like a phoenix. Phoenix, Arizona, where DeLillo's Nick Shay stands in the window of the hermetically sealed "bronze tower" of his waste management company, is *Underworld*'s primary post-Fordist geography (119). What Nick sees is this: "miscellaneous miles of squat box structures where you took your hearing aid to be fixed or shopped for pool supplies, the self-replicating stretch I traveled every day, and I told myself how much I liked this place with its downtown hush and its office towers separated by open space and its parks with jogging trails and its fairy ring of hills and its residential streets of oleanders and palms and tree trunks limed white—white against the sun" (85, 86). This sprawling white space is insular, compartmentalized (businesses separated from residences), and functionalist—you travel through it by car as a consumer or on foot as a jogger disciplining your body until it too is stronger and guarded. "I liked the way history did not run loose here. They segregated visible history," Nick states, his voice perhaps pausing on the word "segregated" (86). DeLillo's protagonist finds pleasure and empowerment in standing in his office tower amid the whir of computers, fax machines, voicemail, and email. He admires the Mondrian-like "linked grids," space reduced to pure geometry that establishes his masculine "sense of order and command" (89, 806, 810). Oedipa's hilltop vision in *The Crying of Lot 49* of southern California as a printed circuit card has been extrapolated in this instance across the globe through new information technologies that connect spaces in a vast matrix of fiber optics and wireless transmission. But whereas Oedipa was seeing the city with the eyes of a suburban innocent, Nick surveys it as a resident and a New York City transplant who tells himself through gritted teeth that he likes it here. The well-apportioned spaces and "downtown hush" are isomorphic with the psychic and bodily repressions that define him. One of the shrewd insights DeLillo makes in *Underworld* is that our identities are always geographically constructed. Nick forthrightly articulates his sense of self in spatial terms: "I've always been a country of one. There's a certain distance in my makeup" (275).

Nick's vision of himself as a solitary nation into which no one is permitted to trespass is rooted in sociopolitical, global realities that he cannot see from his window. But his most immediate reasons for this self-declaration are deeply personal. Following his father's suspicious disappearance (he's rumored to have been murdered) when Nick was an adolescent, Nick seems to reenact the crime. He shoots his friend and heroin junkie, George Manza, and is subsequently convicted as a juvenile of criminally negligent homicide. After reform school, Nick turns his back on the Bronx as it sinks into despair and drugs to remake himself as a successful executive in the West. Enforced discretion, personal privacy, and a willingness to defend personal space by violence if necessary are linked in *Underworld* to Nick's masculinity, race, and class position. In a discomfiting scene that I will return to, the thuggish Nick assaults a young black kid who dares to cross into the Italian quarter of the Bronx where DeLillo's protagonist lives. Years later, he says, "In the bronze tower I looked out at the umber hills and felt assured and well defended, safe in my office box and my crisp white shirt and connected to things that made me stronger," his whiteness blending in with Phoenix, which is "white against the sun" (119). For DeLillo, Nick is the main chord between the Bronx's fire-gutted geographies, where people "living in the ruins" form tight-knit communities, and the posturban spaces of skyscrapers where unwanted human interaction is guarded against (240).

DeLillo implies that the unnatural cleanliness and whiteness of Phoenix's postmodern sprawl have been made possible by the expulsion and containment of unruly differences by sociogeographic forces of which Nick's company, Waste Containment, plays a small part. To understand the meanings of his company's glass office tower, we might compare it to another famous skyscraper, the fortified Bonaventure Hotel by the architect John Portman, which the theorist Fredric Jameson, in one of the most-often cited readings of postmodernity, has argued is a totem of global spatiality in a highly condensed and confusing form. A multifaceted jewel, the shiny hotel presides over the decades-long redevelopment of the Bunker Hill neighborhood which, as I discussed in chapter 4, displaced many of the sexually minoritized, ethnic, and racial communities of downtown Los Angeles to the other side of the Harbor Freeway in the 1950s and 1960s. The Bonaventure's four symmetrical and identical mirrored towers of thirty-plus stories, its difficult-to-locate entrances, and its elevated walkways from the parking garage that keep one's feet off the street suggests it "does not wish to be a part of the city."[14] The "glass skin achieves a peculiar and placeless dissociation of the Bonaventure from its neighborhood"—the still grimy skid rows of downtown—while its elevators that shoot up the outside of the building allow a panoramic vision from a reassuring distance and height that turn the city into a hypnotic spectacle: "Los Angeles itself, spread out breathtakingly and even alarmingly before us."[15] The internal common spaces of the hotel, a mishmash of spiraling escalators, elevated jogging tracks, indistinguishable atriums, and a rotating cocktail lounge, however, offer no such visual clarity, thwarting at each step Jameson's attempt to articulate a narrative stroll through the building. Famously, he gets lost in its space. His effort to map the Bonaventure leaves him in "milling confusion."[16]

What Jameson wishes to make clear is that the Bonaventure is by no measure exceptional, is by no means simply the work of an architect toying with hotel guests who regularly were seen walking around in circles until directional signs were installed. Rather, the hotel is paradigmatic of the "latest mutation in space," a leading indicator, when it was built in 1976, of the advent of multinational finance capitalism that not only has erected citadels of power and commerce in the midst of so-called squalor but has also scrambled the relationship between different kinds of space in ways that trouble efforts to obtain perspective and critical distance.[17] If we cannot represent this discombobulating space to ourselves, how are we ever to change it?, Jameson seems to ask, The stakes are enormous: "My implication is that we ourselves, the human subjects who happen into this new space, have not kept pace with that evolution; there has been a mutation in the object unaccompanied as yet by any equivalent mutation in the subject. . . . . The newer architecture therefore . . . stands as something like an imperative to grow new organs, to expand our

FIGURE 13. The fortified Westin Bonaventure Hotel in downtown Los Angeles. Courtesy of Yves Rubin.

sensorium and our body to some new, yet unimaginable, perhaps ultimately impossible, dimensions."[18]

Jameson's language of mutated spaces and bodies draws upon, perhaps unwittingly, an older tradition of ecological determinism that in Toth's recent example imagines humans growing webbed feet in the murky tunnels of New York. Beneath the organic language of ecology and mutation is a deeper stratum of politics and ideology that *Underworld* endeavors to transform into art. The postmodern city tests one's capacity to read and understand it because the global flows of capital that shape life within it are either absent—displaced into other cities, regions, or nations—or mystified behind the hypnotic spectacles of media saturation and information overload that characterize the contemporary period. In the last third of the century, the scope of uneven geographical development has become global. In the post-1960s period in the United States, capital and labor steadily fled the Rustbelt—the Fordist urban centers of the Midwest and Northeast—and relocated to the non-unionized Sunbelt, with the rise of warfare and information technologies. Developing nations and former Soviet-bloc countries with weaker environmental and labor regulations similarly have become nodes of labor for decentered multinational corporations with headquarters, factories, and design teams strategically located in several different countries. The modern metropolis has become conceptually and materially unbound, dispersed, relocated somewhere in the global ether.[19] It is this representational challenge that greets DeLillo. And it is in the context of this rupturing of traditional boundaries that Nick asserts he is "a country of one" (275).

Underworld captures one of the difficult contradictions of the century's end. The decades-long trend toward greater urban sprawl has been complemented by a new movement toward urban recentralization and reconsolidation, a rebirth of urban centers for high-wage workers clustered in law, finance, marketing, and advanced-technology sectors. In terms of sheer numbers, the job growth in these areas has been far outpaced by another trend, a surge in low-wage employment and an expansion of underground economies that "escape official record keeping."[20] Once thought to be limited to developing nations, the informal sector is now seen by sociologists as a permanent feature of First World cities where a growing surplus population seeks "a means of survival at the margins of the modern economy."[21] The postmodern city is a fractal of global social and geographic unevenness. The "relatively stable mosaics of uneven regional development" of the prior era "have suddenly become almost kaleidoscopic."[22] The swirling transformations in work, technology, and urban space at the end of the twentieth century has been like a gyre turning in two directions simultaneously, a centripetal vortex drawing the rich and the poor into the city and a centrifugal whirlwind scattering money and labor across the globe. As a result, the contemporary world city that DeLillo narrates is an altogether new patchwork of discontinuous spaces filled with migratory peoples, bastions of culture and finance next to slums and tent cities, a tessellation of differentially empowered immigrant groups, urban subcultures, the indigent, and the extremely wealthy, all mixing.

For writers and visual artists, the new spatiality has precipitated a crisis of representation. As one pair of scholars of urban literature have recently stated, "the traditional metropolis has changed beyond recognition."[23] In response, Jameson has called for a new "aesthetic of *cognitive mapping*," something "much more complex" than the mental mapping that disoriented individual subjects use to situate themselves within the physical space of an unfamiliar city.[24] For Jameson, the art of "cognitive mapping" promises to coordinate "existential data (the empirical position of the subject) with unlived, abstract conceptions of the geographic totality."[25] This is to say, it aims to graft the sensorial experience of urban space to the knowledge that this "existential data" emerges from "local, national, and international class realities" that are produced by forces that are obscured, geographically absent, and decentered.[26] In this way, the "cognitive map" transforms perception into apperception, bridging the "alarming disjunction point between the body and its built environment" with knowledge that connects both to the spatiality of global capital.[27] The "cognitive map" will situate the individual within the space of the city and "in the global system" that, by definition, exceeds regional and national boundaries.[28] A critical geographical analysis sufficient to contemporary conditions must engender a new postmodern global consciousness by locating individuals in space and by unveiling ideology located in a newly globally fragmented, pluralized terrain. "The new political art (if it is possible at all)," Jameson concludes, "will have to hold to the truth of postmodernism, that is to say, to its fundamental object—the world space of multinational capital—at the same time at which it achieves a breakthrough to some as yet unimaginable new mode of represent[ation]"[29]

Underworld responds to this daunting challenge. It provides readers with a critical geographical description that mines the contradictory logic of multinational capital and the transformations it has wrought. *Underworld* is, of course, a novel, not a theoretical disquisition on space and economics. But in its post–cold war epilogue, tellingly labeled "Das Kapital," the novel voices some of the central propositions of recent theories of urban political economy. DeLillo posits that "capital burns off the nuance in a culture . . . making for a certain furtive sameness, a planing [*sic*] away of particulars that affects everything from architecture to leisure time to the way people eat and sleep and dream" (785, 786). "Foreign investment, global markets, corporate acquisitions, the flow of information through transnational media. . . . Some things fade and wane," DeLillo ponders, adding, "states disintegrate, assembly lines shorten their runs and interact with lines in other countries" (785). Acutely attuned to the nature of contemporary uneven social and geographical development, DeLillo as a postmodern cartographer observes how "instantaneous capital that shoots across horizons at the speed of light" links the smoking ruins of the Bronx and the sparkling city of Phoenix to "the great eastern reaches, endless belts of longitude, the map-projection arcs beyond the Urals and across the Siberian Lowland" (786, 787). "Difference itself, all argument, all conflict programmed out," he pessimistically writes, though the claim is belied by the novel itself, in whose pages the underworlds of global capitalism uncannily resurface with their resistant microhistories of community and struggle (826).[30]

DeLillo typographically registers uneven postmodern geographies and exposes their coded racial contours by splitting the title pages of *Underworld*'s several sections into two unequal parts: the top two-thirds of each page, which are white, bear down on the bottom third that is inked black. This typographic strategy is extended to DeLillo's narrative of Harlem in 1951, which centers on the Martin family—the young boy Cotter and his unemployed father Manx. Each new segment of the Martin storyline is introduced with a fully solid black page, and the segments themselves are spaced throughout the book's shuffled chronology. "You can actually see his [Manx Martin's] movement: when you look at the book you'll notice that the black pages create a little stream," DeLillo remarked in an interview, noting that "Manx Martin is one little chronological stream moving against the huge flow of the river in the rest of the novel."[31]

What sutures together the novel's black and white spaces—Harlem, the Bronx, Phoenix, and the clandestine military installations in the desert where Matt Shay works—is the polarizing logic of capital. Historically spaces of blight and wealth have been intertwined and interdependent, falling and rising in lockstep with each other. From the late 1970s to the mid 1980s, neighborhoods in DeLillo's New York City experienced large turnovers in population as part of a half-century-long movement of whites to the suburban periphery. New York City as a whole bled a half million jobs, many of which migrated with changes in manufacturing to emergent economies in edge cities and further in the New West.[32] The abstract movement of money and labor does not easily lend itself to narrative drama, but the human toll of it—told through the dysfunctional Martin and Shay families—does. DeLillo uses the flight of the Shay brothers out of the Bronx to represent the push of larger socioeconomic upheavals that have led the Shays to look for prosperity elsewhere and have left the Martins to struggle simply to survive, even if it means a father selling his son's prized possession, the home run baseball that Cotter has brought back from the ballpark. In following the peregrinations of each, DeLillo maps the movement of capital and power across the landscapes of America and beyond.

When DeLillo introduces Nick in Part 1 (set in 1992), the fifty-seven-year-old is speeding in a Lexus through the desert Southwest (63). Every aspect of this detail holds meaning. And every aspect of it carries with it the weight of a damaged past, even as it augurs a seemingly weightless future. The man with whom the reader henceforth will spend several hundred pages is tellingly first glimpsed in his car. Nick's luxury automobile signifies one of the main culprits that in the postwar period dramatically uprooted the older organization of urban life around the intimate unit of the pedestrian city block of local shops and familiar faces, which Nick mourns and whose destruction DeLillo will detail after Part 1, as his novel periodically leapfrogs back in time.

The change—a slow erosion of urban communities by drugs, crime, and demographic shifts—perhaps occurred nowhere more dramatically than in New York in the postwar period. The Bronx, in particular, was pinpointed as the center of a spreading urban crisis that needed to be urgently cauterized. In the 1950s and 1960s urban planners generally agreed that the problem could be addressed by the new federal Title I slum-clearance program, which subsidized demolition and rebuilding projects, and which, by additional highway construction, opened up and drained infected areas. Enter New York's legendary Parks Commissioner Robert Moses.[33] Moses does not show his face in DeLillo's *Underworld*, but his presence is felt on almost every page. As had Jacob Riis and Lewis Mumford, Moses insisted that New York's "traditional pattern of street-oriented, gridiron urbanism created unhealthy living conditions" and produced cancerous slums that needed to be eradicated through wide-scale redevelopment, rather than through targeted refurbishment of individual buildings or blocks.[34] The Federal Highway Program, which Moses helped to implement, "conceived of cities principally as obstructions to the flow of traffic, and as junkyards of substandard and decaying neighborhoods from which Americans should be given every chance to escape," the literary scholar and Bronx native Marshall Berman writes.[35] Thus it was under the banner of progress and a belief in the salubrious effects of highways that Moses plowed the seven-mile-long Cross-Bronx Expressway through the neighborhood where DeLillo, like Nick Shay, was born. When it was completed in 1963, its canyon-like ten-foot-high walls displaced, by one estimate, upward of 60,000 people: "apartment houses that had been settled and stable for twenty years [were] emptied out, often virtually overnight."[36] Moses literally parted the Bronx, quipping that "When you operate in an overbuilt metropolis, you have to hack your way with a meat ax."[37]

The parks commissioner attempted and largely succeeded in changing the fundamental structure of parts of the city by creating "a new superurban reality" of highways that integrated New York with the sprawling metropolitan and suburban region, facilitating, at least conceptually,

Nick's flight from the city.[38] The rapid decline of the Bronx—which was hastened after the construction of the expressway—is what quickens Nick's search for an exit. It is an exit that takes Nick beyond the constraints (historical, bodily, and ideological) of his neighborhood upbringing and on into what Moses described as a "unified flow" between urban, regional, and national geographies "whose lifeblood was the automobile."[39] "Cities are created by and for traffic. . . . The city that achieves speed achieves success," Moses declared.[40]

With hindsight we now recognize that Moses's construction projects fulfilled many of the mandates envisioned by Sigfried Giedion in his influential work *Space, Time and Architecture* (1941). Looking into the future, Giedion theorized that the city had to be remade to lubricate the flow of capital, commodities, and labor. "It is the actual structure of the city that must be changed," he asserted, adding, "There is no longer any place for the city street with its heavy traffic running between rows of houses; it cannot possibly be permitted to persist."[41] The dense layering of pedestrians, vehicular traffic, residences, and workplaces that characterizes New York had to be unpeeled to make a new space that catered to the modern spirit, a space for "the freedom of uninterrupted forward motion."[42] "The space-time feeling of our period," Giedion claimed "can seldom be felt so keenly as when driving."[43] While he spoke of "freedom" and the "restoration of liberty," his rhetoric often was shadowed by a fear of "the chaotic state of the cities" and "an almost physical revulsion" at the prospect of an "increase in urban population": "The enormous heaping up of human beings induces a horror of mankind."[44] By now the car is a required tool for navigating the dispersed geographies of almost all American cities, which the automobile itself has helped to create by unbundling home, work, and leisure. In separating out different spheres of life, the car makes for "a particularly good illustration of a putative globalization."[45] Hence, the outsized Moses was emblematic of something even bigger than any particular mode of transportation: he embodied "the latest mutation in space" itself.

The kind of car-centered urban spaces that Moses helped usher in were a precursor to a new postindustrial "space of flows," a space of motion untied to any geography, a postmodern liquidity of digitized capital and information that has increasingly superseded "the meaning of the space of places."[46] Both ideas are voiced by DeLillo's brooding protagonist: "This is a car assembled in a work area that's completely free of human presence," free of bodies that might gum up the process (63). The flatly uniform, uninterrupted geometries of the Southwest through which Nick's car is kicking up dust in Part 1 are a close equivalent to the unimpeded flows of global capital that have produced Nick's Japanese automobile. "My rented car was a natural match for the landscape I was crossing," he states (63). Contemplating capital's need for ceaseless circulation, its need to always move, expand, colonize, he finds poetry: "The system flows forever onward, automated to priestly nuance, every gliding movement back-referenced for prime performance. Hollow bodies coming in endless sequence" (63). Faster than any blacktop, the flows of "the system," DeLillo shows, dematerialize personal, urban, and national space where his characters once lived, breathed, fought, and had sex into an eternal present tense ("an endless sequence"), causing "states [to] disintegrate," and resulting in a vertiginous sense of continual motion and disorientation that Nick finds exhilarating and terrifying (785).

Fast forward to near the end of the novel, and we find Nick experiencing a vertiginous "sense of displacement and redefinition" while on a business trip with Brian Glassic to the former Soviet Union, whose disintegration has reshuffled every boundary in the world. In Moscow to negotiate a business deal involving the international trade, traffic, and disposal of waste, they sit in a club "on the forty-second floor of a new office tower filled with brokerage houses, softwear [*sic*] firms, import companies and foreign banks," as well as professional Lenin, Trotsky, and Marx look-alikes circulating through the crowd. Nick gazes about in wonder, contemplating the "random arrangement" (786). The postmodern global space of capitalism in the immediate post-Soviet years is a mash-up of historical quotations, ideological simulacra, information technologies, finance, foreign trade, and entertainment that scrambles the brain. In *Underworld*, the new postmodern geography lacks indigenous urban textures of "real" places and "real" history by which subjects locate themselves. "I didn't know where we were," Nick at another point and on another trip reveals, "it might have been Long Beach or Santa Monica or some blurry suburban somewhere" (325).

The crumbling inner cities—abandoned relics of older production processes—cannot be left for good, however, especially when one's character has been forged in them. And so, back in the desert in Part 1, Nick's car uncannily returns him to his past. As he is driving through the Southwest, "a New York taxi, impossible but true" appears as an "apparition" on the horizon (65). Driven by art students, the taxi leads Nick to the woman he has been searching for in vain. It takes him back in the past to Klara Sax, a famous artist who is painting decommissioned B-52 bombers as part of a post–cold war project, but whom Nick first knew as the woman he slept with when he was seventeen and she was married to Matt's chess mentor Albert Bronzini. "We're a long way from home," she tells Nick, but deep inside he knows better (73). Like everything about him, his response is haunted: "You know how certain places grow powerful in the mind with passing time. In those early morning dreams . . . there is one set of streets I kept returning to, one dim mist of railroad rooms, and certain figures reappear, borderline ghosts" (74). Throughout the novel, the discarded parts of the past in all of its forms—personal, familial, national—keep reappearing like apparitions, or keep surfacing like waste that refused to be disposed despite Nick's best intentions. "What we excrete comes back to consume us," Nick says much later, a pithy line that sums up so much of *Underworld*'s logic (791).

Nick himself, as we shall see, does not answer Jameson's call for a new cognitive map that peers into the realities of postmodern sublime. Instead, Nick provides the reader with an alienated and highly ideological map that reflects his own melancholia, sentimentalism, and sense of bourgeois entitlement. His relation to space and history is one of dispossession, but if anyone should feel this way, DeLillo implies, it should be Cotter and Muñoz, the novel's racialized and queer subjects who suffer the novel's greatest thefts. What *Underworld* offers in the end is a critical human geography of postwar space that lets us see how ideologically distorted responses to this "latest mutation in space" arise from class privilege that is blind to the underworlds it helps create.

"I Want Them Back, the Days When I Was Alive on the Earth": *Underworld* and Bourgeois Melancholy in an Era of Lost Connections

Laid end to end, American literary narratives of the underworld are a hidden tunnel through the time and space of the American canon. *Underworld* begins where Ralph Ellison's mid-century epic *Invisible Man* opens its cellar door to the world. The two works overlap seamlessly, their historical and geographic contexts soldered to each other, one underworld narrative welded onto the next, a blend of voices echoing between and across decades of American spatial impoverishment. Sitting in a basement apartment on the edge of Harlem in the early 1950s, Ellison's hero concludes *Invisible Man* with the question "Who knows but that, on the lower frequencies, I speak for you?"[47] Forty-five years later it is as if he hands the microphone to DeLillo, who opens his 1997 novel on October 3, 1951, with the affirmative answer that "He speaks in your voice, American, and there's a shine in his eyes that's halfway hopeful" (11). "He" is DeLillo's Cotter Martin, a "scrawny," "flat broke" fourteen-year-old from Harlem who jumps the turnstile at the Polo Grounds and winds up with Bobby Thomson's ninth-inning, two-out home run off the Dodgers' Ralph Branca, "The Shot Heard 'Round the World" that completes the improbable, come-from-behind playoff victory by the Giants (12). Cotter's possession of the home run ball—the best thing he will ever hold in his hands—comes only after he wrestles it from Bill Waterson, a white owner of a construction firm (a telling detail to be sure) who befriends Cotter during the game. As it flies out of the field and into the seats, Thomson's home run not only brings the game to the end, it pierces the illusory membrane around interracial camaraderie and good-natured rivalry. The ball immediately precipitates racial tensions over the right to property at a pivotal moment in history when the city is about to fall into a period of steep decline.

DeLillo symbolically condenses the era's interracial conflicts into the struggle between Waterson, with "a cutthroat smile," and his "buddy Cotter" for the ball (49, 53). Holding tight to what DeLillo labels an emblem of "the people's history," Cotter weaves his way through the streets toward the safety of his home in Harlem, all the while chased by Waterson, who alternately threatens him, accuses him of stealing, and offers to purchase the ball from him for a measly ten dollars (60). DeLillo remarks that "the nature of Thomson's homer . . . makes people want to be in the streets" regardless of skin color, but this deracialization of public cityspace is ephemeral (47). Once Waterson is "past the ballpark crowd," he nervously finds himself in "unmixed Harlem," where the "side streets" are "weary with uncollected garbage and broken glass, with the odd plundered car squatting flat on its axle and men who stand in doorways completely adream" (55, 57). The moment marks the entry into the novel of the entangled subjects of waste, race, urban neglect, and uneven geographical development, the last Bill the builder surely knows something about. If the "halfway hopeful" gleam in Cotter's eye is the utopian promise that he can speak for "you," the generalized, although American, reader, by the end of the prologue we are led to believe that he is more likely to wind up loitering in a doorway, more dazed than dreaming. Only for a magical moment does the "people's history" belong to a poor black teenager from a dysfunctional family, as the ball, stolen by his own father while his son sleeps, will soon drop into the hands of Wainwright, Lundy, and ultimately Nick Shay—three white men.

Cotter is a minor figure in *Underworld*, but he gets the ball rolling in DeLillo's novel. Using "The Shot Heard 'Round the World" as a launching pad, DeLillo follows the shifting ownership of the baseball and all of the stories that accrue around it through the decades of the cold war and into the post-cold war period. The paths of Cotter and Nick do not cross, but as residents of Harlem and the Bronx their fates are bound up with each other. When Waterson nervously trails Cotter into Harlem, the scuffle over who has rights to the Thomson homer grows into a question of who has the right to be in certain public spaces in the city. Likewise, the theft of the ball by Cotter's unemployed, often absent father Manx, who sells it to Wainwright for quick cash, $32.45 to be exact, exemplifies for DeLillo the fractures within the black family as a result of poverty and social isolation. For the adolescent Nick, who listens alone to the historic game with a radio on his building's rooftop, the home run marks a traumatic loss that later in life he will try to rectify by gaining possession of the coveted ball. The home run divides his history into "before" and "after" and seems to signal the beginning of the end for his Irish and Italian American community in the Bronx. When the baseball lands in Nick's hands decades later—sold to him by Marvin Lundy for $34,500—it has obtained the aura of a fetish. It gains in value the further the past recedes. Nick imagines it will take him back, as he says, to "the days of disarray, when I didn't give a damn or a fuck or a farthing" (806). He has suffused his entire adolescence into the ball's five ounces. Yet his ownership of it and the history that has congealed around it, DeLillo implies, has been made possible by the initial loss suffered by Cotter.

It is Nick, however, who speaks the language of what literary scholar Catherine Jurca has termed "sentimental dispossession," the ironic "affective dislocation by which white middle-class suburbanites begin to see themselves as spiritually and culturally impoverished by prosperity."[48] Despite his material spoils, in the bland suburbs Nick feels robbed of his past; but he does not merely look back in anger. His "sentimental dispossession" not only expresses his sense of entitlement but it is also a strategy for further capital accumulation for himself and for his Waste Containment corporation. The point is key to the critique that DeLillo makes again and again in *Underworld*, in which the underclass are appropriated of their voices (their rhetoric of aggrievement) as much as they are expropriated of the property pried from their hands.

Peering out of his office tower into the endless sun-baked stretches of

Arizona in the summer of 1992, Nick discloses how his company "used the rhetoric of aggrieved minorities to prevent legislation that would hurt our business. . . . We learned how to complain, how to appropriate the language of victimization" (119). To pump himself up for the dirty work of waste management, the CEO of Nick's company listens to "gangsta rap on the car radio every morning. Songs about getting mad and getting laid and getting even, taking what's rightfully ours by violent means if necessary" (119). Nick is self-consciously aware of the cynical strategy by which his company steals the rhetoric of justice and empowerment, which inner-city residents have used to protest not only their disenfranchisement but also their neighborhoods' treatment as dumping grounds for toxic garbage. Nick employs this rhetoric as well to voice his own personal grievances that he replays in a loop over and over in his mind. With sad resentment he declares, "I want them back, the days when I was alive on the earth, rippling in the quick of my skin, heedless and real. I was dumb-muscled and angry and real. This is what I long for, the breach of peace, the days of disarray when I walked real streets" (810). Nick does not hold responsible Cotter, whom he does not know, for his misplaced feelings of loss, but in one sense he does. DeLillo reveals that in the days following the 1951 Giants-Dodgers game, Nick had "defended" his territory "by violent means" on at least two occasions, both involving racist attacks on "black guys" in the Bronx (763). One unprovoked confrontation occurs when two African-American men are assaulted by Nick and his friend Grasso for entering the cherished working-class locales of a Bronx bowling alley and luncheonette. Grasso warns them, "It's better, you know, at night especially, if you stay where you belong" (762, 763). In the other ugly confrontation on a snow-white playground, Nick severely beats a young African American, after which Nick's friend JuJu smears "dog shit . . . into his hair and ears" (714, 715). He literally coats him with waste, soiling racial difference in the most foul of ways in order to keep his neighborhood clean and his own sense of whiteness pristine.

It has been argued that postwar suburbanization helped create through the construction of exclusionary spaces a "purified identity" by which ethnic Americans—such as the Shay brothers—could come to be known as white.[49] Matt Shay, who "back in the Bronx . . . looked a little everything. Mexican, Italian, Japanese even," becomes whiter when he relocates later in life to a "huddled enclave off the turnpike, situated to discourage entry" (211, 409). But in *Underworld*'s 1950s sections, the white sanctuary of childhood innocence is still inside the city—in the ethnic American Bronx in the days before it became a black and Puerto

Rican area. Nick tries to stave off this change by temporarily expelling the unwelcomed from the neighborhood.

The literary scholar Mark Osteen remarks that "Nick's underworld is internal."[50] He has built his entire life around containing his feelings of grief, guilt, and rage over the loss of his connection to the "real streets" of his neighborhood (streets he could "walk"), over his father's mysterious disappearance, and over his own "accidental" murder of George Manza. When George, strung out and wishing to die, hands the teenage Nick a sawed-off shotgun that he claimed is empty, Nick pulls the trigger. The moment marks him with an indelible stain, as well as reenacts what Nick imagines to have been the last moments of his father's life, who he believes was murdered by the Italian underworld in 1946 for a failure to follow through on bets he took as a bookie. Unable to control the chaos of his inner, psychic space, he vigilantly polices his outer space with his fists and racial invectives. His psychological underworld of pent-up rage and haunting memories erupts when he violently enforces the racial boundaries of his terrain. In the years since he left the Bronx, Nick's former neighborhood has become a surreal underworld, a medieval, plague-ridden, and burnt-out landscape through which monks in cloaks and nuns in veils gingerly step. The Bronx of the 1950s no longer exists, and when Nick transports his aged mother from her decrepit building to his air-conditioned nightmare of Phoenix (she quickly dies like a fish out of water), his last important connection is severed.

Nick responds to the loss of the spaces of his past by buying an imaginary, compensatory narrative. His purchase on the past is literally a purchase, one in which the sullen bourgeois male is turned into both the subject and object of four decades of American history that lands in his hands as a baseball he squeezes late at night in a cold sweat. In truth, the ball has been passed through the hands of Branca, Cotter, Manx, Charles and Chuckie Wainwright, Genevieve Rauch and her husband, and Marvin Lundy, but these temporary owners and contributors to the "people's history" are unrecognized in Nick's retelling that is centered on himself alone. In a desperate attempt to appropriate a missing past, Nick reconstructs the Bronx in his imagination as a space that is putatively "real," a Bronx that is white, working-class, male, and heterosexual, a Bronx of poolrooms, "the old streets, the street games, the street fights, the alley sex, the petty theft," and Klara's mattress (86). "I lived responsibly in the real. I didn't accept this business of life as a fiction," he declares, adding, "I did not stand helpless before it [history]" (82). It is important to recognize that Nick does not yearn for a sanitized, Rockwellesque image of the Bronx in which social conflict has been strenuously denied and airbrushed from memory (806). To the contrary, he longs for "the real," a term that is so freighted with racial, sexual, and gendered meanings and conflicts that it threatens to burst like the pent-up Nick himself. Nick's nostalgic rhetoric of "realness" obtains its charge by defining the contemporary residents of the Bronx—its populations of people of color, queer men, homeless kids, the HIV-positive—as a "surreal" and unbelievable underworld, a social inferno. One of the rationalizations for Nick air-lifting his mother from this Fort Apache is to save her from "the daily drama of violence and lament and tabloid atrocity and matching redemption," a description of the neighborhood that is itself derived from the language of sensational media (86). His nostalgia for the "days of disorder" is for a disorder of a smaller, manageable scale, a desire for a time and place where his individual masculine power—enacted through local sexual and physical conquests—was consequential.

Despite all of the ball's connecting work, Nick's link to the time when he was "heedless and real" is more willed than real, as the ball's status as "the authentic ball," its "absolute final documentation" as the "real" one cannot be confirmed (96, 97, 810). The ball is a broken link more than a sturdy connector, a fact that Nick cannot bear to acknowledge as true. Suffering a sense of disenfranchisement while still maintaining economic and political hegemony, the white, middle-class male responds in two ways, DeLillo suggests. One way is through a fascination with the putatively real and authentic. The other is through a search for origins. Nick's imaginary reconstruction of the past and to the past is, paradoxically, a means of empowerment in which the middle-class subject is the loser of the postwar era. For Nick, the baseball is not Thomson's winning homer, but Branca's bad pitch. It is a talismanic object "commemorat[ing] failure," the moment in Nick's mind when he began to lose power (97). Nick's narrative reconstruction creates an emboldened rhetorical position for him that justifies his privacy and conspicuous consumption as a repayment for losses imagined and real. In the final analysis, DeLillo's protagonist is able to obtain the ball for exactly the opposite reason—access to money—that Cotter is unable to hold on to it. This commodity permits Nick, in his own words, "To have that moment in my hand when Branca turned and watched the ball go into the stand—from him to me" (97). In contradistinction to the proliferating micronarratives of underworld life Nick counters with a direct line. The fantasy locates Nick in history; it is reparation for his sense of being lost in space. But when, as Jameson posits, "the city itself . . . has deteriorated or disintegrated to a degree surely still inconceivable in the early years of the twentieth century," this fantasy is attenuated and unsustainable, and Nick's desperation to hold on to it shows he will not lose his grip on his privileged position no matter what the cost.[51]

The "South Bronx Surreal": Touring the Wastelands of New York City in *Underworld*

"How urban squalor can be a delight to the eyes when expressed in commodification," Fredric Jameson ponders.[52] In the contemporary period, urban decay has assumed the status of a sublime ocular phenomenon that produces a "strange new hallucinatory exhilaration" in spectators.[53] In response to this general claim, we would do well to ask, "Who is looking?" If the history of slumming has taught us anything, it is that the answer to this question matters dearly. DeLillo's *Underworld* confirms Jameson's declaration and sees through it to revitalized possibilities for solidarity and coalition building among inhabitants of the so-called slums. In postmodern culture, extreme marginalization is often transformed into hypnotic tableaus that occlude the socioeconomic and spatial processes that have produced inequality. One has only to be reminded of the ghoulish "Hurricane Katrina—America's Worst Catastrophe" bus tours of New Orleans recently offered by Gray Line, as reported by Reuters's Ellen Wulfhorst, or of the tour packages sold by Reality Tours and Travel of Mumbai's Dharavi slum, or the Favela Tour company based in Rio de Janeiro which, as Eric Weiner described in the *New York Times* on July 31, 2008, carefully escorts vacationers through Brazil's shanty towns.[54] The social meaning of poverty tourism into the global underbelly is found in the way it reinforces the middle-class subject's privilege and in how it allegedly fosters an "entrepreneurial spirit" among the lumpenproletariat who sell souvenirs to the stupefied slummers who gaze upon them. Weiner reports of the indigent plying the slum tourists with dyes and fruits, rather than begging for money or food. Disaster capitalism mitigates the image of the slum as a place of squalor and extreme poverty, while doing little or nothing to eliminate the slums it has helped create except to encourage their residents to become capitalists themselves. According to one tour participant in Weiner's report, "Everybody in the slum wants to work, and everybody wants to make themselves better," and according to another, "I was shocked at how friendly and gracious these people were."

Closer to home—DeLillo's home to be exact—are the slums of New

York. The catastrophic decline of the Bronx from the 1960s onward was a result of global developments which found their expression in DeLillo's birthplace in ways that were very local. Perhaps no other American urban area was so laid to waste by the postwar period's uneven development as the Bronx. In fact, the entire historical geography of postwar capitalism, *Underworld* suggests, can be read in its "landscape of vacant lots filled with years of stratified deposits—the age of house garbage, the age of construction debris and vandalized car bodies, the age of moldering mobster parts" (238). Rather than clearing slums, Robert Moses's Cross-Bronx Expressway created more. The Bronx's deterioration was a result of numerous forces—deindustrialization, disinvestment, racist banking practices, federal and municipal policies that privileged Manhattan and the suburbs—but "more than any other project in New York City . . . it [the Cross-Bronx Expressway] became the vantage point for motorists to survey the 1970s urban crisis."[55] By the early 1980s the borough had degraded, Marshall Berman recalls, into "an international code word for our epoch's accumulated urban nightmares: drugs, gangs, arson, murder, terror, thousands of buildings abandoned, neighborhoods transformed into garbage- and brick-strewn wilderness."[56] To cover up the blight, New York City installed fake blinds and flowers in the windows of derelict buildings that peered over the expressway at the motorists looking up in shock and wonder.[57]

Using montage, staggered historical sequences, and a multiplicity of voices and points of view from older and newer residents, *Underworld* provides readers with a means of apprehending the Bronx's decline and fall. In the novel, the street is one of the fundamental spatial units for organizing daily life and for keeping the community relatively intact. The crumbling of whole blocks of inner-city New York in the 1970s and 1980s, DeLillo suggests, has profoundly disoriented his older characters who came of age with another "space-time feeling" in their minds and in their footsteps. In the 1950s sections (Parts 5 and 6) of the novel, however, the Bronx is a lively ethnic neighborhood, hardly the center of the epidemic of disease, drugs, violence, and urban failure that it would come to be for so many. In these sections, the teacher and mentor Albert Bronzini is frequently spotted walking through the streets, taking in his colorful, close-knit community. DeLillo writes that for Bronzini "walking [is] an art" by which he both fosters a connection to people around him and maps the space in which he lives and works as means of keeping tabs on life in his immediate environs (661). The philosopher Michel de Certeau, who also calls walking an "art" and a form of "writing," conceives of walking as a "spatial practice" by which individuals temporarily inhabit and appropriate the "geometrical space of urbanists and architects" in order to write "an urban 'text,'" a text different from the top-down perspectives that condemned large portions of the Bronx as a prelude to clearing them.[58] "Bronzini didn't own a car, didn't drive a car, didn't want one, didn't need one, wouldn't take one if somebody gave it to him," we are told, "Stop walking, he thought, and you die" (662). He is, quite simply, Nick's foil, just as Nick is his secret sexual rival. DeLillo shows Bronzini the day after the Giants-Dodgers game that opens the novel on one of his strolls watching girls "jumping double dutch," chatting with shopkeepers, and catching up with the local butcher who "called to people walking by. . . . with knowing references" (662, 667). Bronzini thus witnesses and participates in the microlevel intimacies that often go unnoticed beneath "the clear text of the planned and readable city."[59] By walking, he assembles a "poetic geography," a place of working-class masculine labor in which the sense of familiarity is such that locals are warmly referred to by their first name and occupation—"George the Waiter" and "George the Barber" (663, 664).[60] "Even in this compact neighborhood," DeLillo writes of this traditional, patriarchal community, "there were streets to revisit and men doing interesting jobs, day labor, painters in drip coveralls or men with sledgehammers he might pass the time with, Sicilians busting up a sidewalk, faces grained with stone dust" (661).

DeLillo, however, is not a nostalgist, and Bronzini—who cannot detect the troubles under his own roof—is not a reliable point of view. DeLillo exposes the fissures in the idyllic scene even before Moses's crew arrives, the conflicts—drugs, racial tension, violence, family instability—that are bubbling just under the surface. A "cloacal stink beginning to emerge," DeLillo writes; the sewer was bubbling up (770). For the most part Bronzini is unaware that there is a canker in the "rosebush[es]" that he admires in front of the "little frame houses" (677). When he casually asks in a chat with George who "used to sell ice cream on the beach": "Remember the drowned man?" he does not detect the source of his own allusion to the drowned Phoenician sailor in T. S. Eliot's *The Waste Land* (665).

By the "mid-1980s–early 1990s" the dripping paint from men in overalls has been replaced in DeLillo's text with a squalid impasto of "spray paint, piss, saliva, dapples of dark stuff that was probably blood" (211). DeLillo presents the decimated Bronx first (in Part 2), thus setting up the ironic portrait of the neighborhood that follows hundreds of pages later. The reader is confronted with the ruins of the postwar urban underworld, the wreckage of an older Fordist economy—the rapid obsolescence of forms of human labor and production now piled up as debris from the storm of history and progress. "Whole blocks leveled by arson, and there were buildings still burning in the distance. . . . Three or four buildings oozing lazy smoke. No sign of fire engines," DeLillo writes (395). By this time, Klara has divorced Bronzini and left the neighborhood, but her husband hangs on by teeth and cane. "Too rooted to leave," but also refusing to adapt or, in his own words, "to adjust," he resists the desertification of the Bronx (214). Inside the carceral architecture of an apartment building wrapped in cameras and fences, he "watches the ruin build around him" (211). "We complain," the long-suffering Bronzini reflects, "but we don't mourn, we don't grieve. There are things here, people who show the highest human qualities, outside all notice, because who comes here to see?" (214). DeLillo brings the reader "to see" the Bronx, whose devastation has to be understood—as the "Das Kapital" epilogue insists—within the context of global economic transformations that have uprooted all fixities into a revolutionary, hypnotic flux.

This kind of dialectical seeing and thinking which peers through the spectacle is not glimpsed by the voyeuristic tourists on the "South Bronx Surreal," which drives through the neighborhood (247). Its passengers stare out of over a landscape of junked cars, scavenging birds, and the poor. The postmodern slummers hop off the bus to snap photos of "boarded shops and closed factories" and "painted angels," and to buy "battery-run pinwheels" from the locals who have responded to the commodification of their misery by selling "brightly-colored" trinkets that mirror the garish "carnival colors" of the unseemly bus (247). While delivering food in this "terrain of torched buildings," Sister Gracie spots the tour bus and shouts after it, "It's not surreal. It's real, it's real. Your bus is surreal. You're surreal. . . . Brussels is surreal. Milan is surreal" (247, 395). Despite Gracie's protestation, the scale of devastation and of poverty and the multiple, overlapping temporalities suffused with memory, stretches the limits of the imagination and stymies one's ability to piece together a coherent narrative. Sister Edgar is more reflective and resigned: "She thought she understood the tourists," DeLillo writes, "You travel somewhere not for museums and sunsets but for ruins, bombed-out terrain, for the moss-grown memory of torture and war" (248).

Bronzini's own relation to the underworld is largely a determined nostalgia. He lives in a geography of memory, of "sweet-tasting time" and "tender reminiscence,"and his cane-assisted flânerie through the streets (now filled with Jamaicans, Malaysians, and Indians) is the stroll of a walking exile (233, 234). Visiting Bronzini as an adult, Matt Shay, for his part, feels like an estranged onlooker. "I've been walking around. It's a complicated thing. I find myself trying to resist the standard response," Matt tells him (213). The older man responds, "You saw your building. The squalor around it. The empty lot with the razor wire. . . . The men. Who are they, standing around doing nothing? Poor people. They're very shocking. . . . And these were your streets," his use of the possessive pronoun revealing his deep-seated feelings of dispossession (213).

At issue is who has the right to the city, who owns it, which streets are "yours" and which ones are or once were "mine." These are DeLillo's fundamental questions. In *Underworld* the voice of the street and the underworld below it primarily belongs to the graffiti writer Ismael Muñoz, DeLillo's example of the heroic artist who is still tethered to his imperiled community, who makes a redeeming art in bricolage fashion out of the ruined commodities and destroyed lives around him. Bronzini's role in the novel is that of the urban white ethnic caught in a neighborhood undergoing severe economic deterioration and demographic upheaval, while Muñoz stands as the underclass Hispanic who eventually will succeed him, inheriting the "mass of junked cars" and "garbage pits" that have been left behind (811, 812). In spite of, or perhaps because of, Muñoz's material impoverishment and his extreme social marginalization (he is queer and HIV-positive at the height of the AIDS panic), *Underworld* privileges his story, "the underhistory, . . . literally from under the ground," the story that is connected to "root reality" but which refuses to be buried (211, 791). In Part 4, "Cocksucker Blues: Summer 1974," which takes place before Muñoz becomes a sought-after artist and community organizer in the Bronx, DeLillo leads him into the underground. He links Muñoz's art with his burgeoning queer sexuality that is awakened when one day feeling lonely and prideful he makes his descent through "an emergency hatch in the sidewalk" and into the underworld of the city's tunnels where Toth's mole people reside (435). Toth's text appears to have opened an imaginative hole for DeLillo, which he explores in order to provide a back-story for one of the novel's central characters: "Ismael went down there, feeling sorry for himself" and discovered once when urinating that a "man held his dick and eventually sucked it" (436). He "went down there . . . fairly often after that," DeLillo laconically writes (436). Walking below the streets, rather than on them, he fathoms his budding intimacy with other men who reappropriate the degraded space "under the water mains and waste pipes, under the gas and steam and electric, between the storm sewers and telephone lines" to create a sexual underground, a clandestine queer territory in which his art will be made and from which it will surface (433).

Underworld reflects upon the discursive and geographical inscription of extreme material inequality through Muñoz who, while spelunking in the tunnels, discovers the strange and frightening existence of a whole underworld of the homeless who have left the streets for the warm, cave-like spaces along the subway tracks. In DeLillo's novel, the underworld homeless are associated with nightmarish urban phantasms that percolate just below the surface and haunt the imagination of city-dwellers. Taking a page from Toth's study, DeLillo writes that down in the tunnels Muñoz hears rumors of cannibalism and of a "rat man who lived in level six under Grand Central . . . and cooked and ate a rat a week—track rabbits, they were called" (440). But these dehumanizing legends, which have been a staple of New York City lore, are only part of the story. DeLillo's allusions are not only sociological and mythical but also literary. Like the specter haunting the basement in Ellison's *Invisible Man*, the tunnel residents in DeLillo's text poach on the dominant culture's spaces and power as a sign of their ingenuity and survival skills. They fashion a modicum of comfort and a tight-knit community in spite of their degraded social status and squalid living conditions. DeLillo writes: "they had bookshelves, some of them, and Christmas decorations. . . . They kept pets down there and ran clotheslines across the tunnel and stole electricity from the government" (436, 437).

What the space of the underground primarily breeds in *Underworld* is not crime and disease (or even mutated humans), but the art of everyday life built out of the scraps of consumer capitalism, art that repurposes commodities to offer a critique of the contemporary culture of easy disposability, and art that rebuts the pathologizing images of gay, poor, and ethnic Americans that circulated freely in an era of perpetual urban crisis. This is Muñoz's art. It is art that draws upon the harsh experience of underground life, as well as on one's illicit desires—"some habits you drop and others you come to rely on," Muñoz observes (437). Ismael alternates between a life above and a life below, all the while writing on trains, transforming them into a kinetic art that is a self-assertion in an overbearing city. His art connects both worlds—upper and under—in a rush of hurling metal that rides "the sky in the heart of the Bronx, over the whole burnt and rusted country," "over the garbagy streets and past the dead-eye windows of all those empty tenements" (440). It is in the subway tunnels that Muñoz learns of the underworld's codes, a kind of protective linguistic membrane that distinguishes insiders from unwanted outsiders: they "used half names and code names, tags like the writers would develop" (437). He later incorporates such strategies into his illegal graffiti writing. What the bricoleur Muñoz comes to understand from his time in the literal underground instills in him a commitment to art that underscores the agency and anger of the city's marginalized communities, a lesson that he will carry with him back to the Bronx later in the novel. "You can't *not* see us anymore, you can't *not* know who we are," declares Muñoz's "flickery jumping art of the slums and dumpsters" to all of the authorities that would deny the existence of his invisible community or deny its dignity by tagging it as degenerate, perverse, polluted, or diseased (440, 441).

Like Ellison's narrator, he eventually abandons his self-aggrandizing delinquent behavior—spray painting the city with his name—for the socially responsible role of the artist who is an activist on behalf of his or her community. DeLillo nominates Muñoz for this position when he has him help create "a memorial wall" that is a "six-story flank of a squatters' tenement" on which the platoon of runaway and abandoned kids he takes care of "spray-paint an angel every time a local child dies of illness or mistreatment" (811). This uncanny Wall stands in defiance of the canyons of Moses's expressway. Muñoz's team have charged themselves with preserving the neighborhood's tragic history in the face of their own systematic erasure and "the general sense of exclusion" in a "land adrift from the social order," which defines their sense of displacement and unease (239). Looming over the trashed area where "foragers and gatherers" are picking through vacant lots piled with garbage, it is a memoryscape that resists the desire to forget the neglected spaces and peoples of the putative underworld and in doing so, it rebuts the belief that urban development is always progressive and without casualties (242). Erased and written over time and again, the Wall can never be commodified into a static image, but rather is painted anew with each death. A communal wailing wall, it is symbol of their segregation, and a text that Muñoz's crew collectively writes in protest. It literally stops cars, causing traffic jams a blockage to the desire for a "unified flow" (247).[61]

From the ruins of urban decay, new life sprouts. Ecological regeneration is spied in the elegant "hawks and owls" that fly over DeLillo's world of "dumped objects" (238). One Catholic Brother even carries a guidebook to the trash lots to count plant species (240). DeLillo at times runs the risk of romanticizing the ghetto as an emerging urban pastoral that will heal itself if nature is allowed to take its course. But something else is growing in the cracks and fissures, too. For DeLillo, the large-scale abandonment of the urban poor to their misery at the end of the twentieth century is a catalyst for the construction of new informal economies, as well as new forms of social solidarity and social regeneration of which art is a catalyst. In no sense does this excuse poverty, DeLillo implies, rather it testifies to the way the new urban poor self-organize in order to continue breathing.

In his thirties, Muñoz is "an elder of the barrio" who, in addition to publicly memorializing the neighborhood, runs a "salvage operation" that involves collecting junked cars from around the city and selling them as scrap metal (439, 811). He subcontracts the labor of the Sisters, who spot abandoned automobiles for him while conducting community outreach (government assistance is seemingly nonexistent). He not only pays the nuns money for their work (money which is recycled back into their charity programs), but his crew also helps them distribute food to the needy. Left to their own devices, Muñoz's team adopts a do-it-yourself attitude, an entrepreneurialism motivated by necessity that is not that different from the poor selling trinkets to tourists vacationing in Third World slums. Muñoz's team mine a tiny profit from geographies that on the surface look depleted and then use them for altruistic purposes to ameliorate the urban blight in a way that benefits the community, rather than erases it. They also pirate cable TV and wire a World War II generator to a stationary bicycle which one of them peddles to crank out electricity. Neither a residual domain in which older modes of life can still be found nor a separate sphere, the postmodern underworld is integrated into the global economy as a marginal but important site of labor, resources, and consumption. Muñoz, who "loves the language of buying and selling," even speaks of taking his business on-line (814). He is thus at the center of an underworld economy that has long been associated with developing nations but which has become increasingly found in postindustrial First World cities, where itinerant labor has spread to all employment sectors. One of the ironies of Matt Shay's second career in a think tank that draws up "studies to help third world countries develop health services and banking facilities" is that the Third World is in his former backyard (198).

The most important networks Muñoz establishes are social—new communal formations that the economics of scarcity and neglect bring into being. Even though the nuns are skeptical of him, they laud the "sense of responsibility and self-worth" that he cultivates in the kids he takes under his wing (813). Together they cobble a makeshift, non-consanguineous family which DeLillo contrasts with the heteropatriarchical

Shay and Deming households, both of which are profoundly unstable and secretly perverse. Nick Shay's household maintains a veneer of normality, but is torn apart by the sexual affairs of Nick and his wife Marian, by the estrangement between Nick and his brother, and by Marian's heroin use. For their part, the Demings, whom DeLillo subjects to a withering satire of the 1950s, are as transparently normal and cloyingly sweet as the Jell-O that the housewife, Erica, compulsively serves to her "husband Rick" and her son Eric, who masturbates to Jayne Mansfield's breasts and who grows up to be a weapons engineer in the Pocket with Matt Shay (515). For the likes of the Shays and the Demings, the urban underworld is the spatial Other they can define themselves against. The private walls of their suburbs are erected as a rejection of community for the fortified insularity of bourgeois life, whose dirty laundry and sexual fantasies remain behind closed doors or "behind drawn fiberglass curtains" (514). In contrast, the Wall in the Bronx is not only a towering edifice; it is the name for the entire area where people live. The Wall of angels honoring the Bronx's dead children publicly records the tragic history of its community and its symbolic, if not its material, transcendence, for the residents of the monument.

Muñoz's underworld community exemplifies the coming to voice of new political actors—gay men, the HIV-positive, the working poor, ethnic and immigrant coalitions—in the contemporary political landscape at the century's end. Their community also signifies the reconstitution of localities at the very moment that the meaning of geography has eroded. In DeLillo's text, they stand as a recommitment to the space of the margins as the space of critique and the space of new forms of association, cultural adaptation, informal networks, and alternative identities that do not meet traditional definitions. All of these dialectically arise as a result of global uneven development, not in spite of it. DeLillo's mammoth novel dramatizes their emergence and ties it to post-Fordist restructurings on a geopolitical level which impact urban geographies in ways that have been underacknowledged. DeLillo's artist testifies to the struggle of people whose identities are constituted at the nexus of two conditions: "relative territorial immobility" at a time of increased "mobility of international capital."[62]

One byproduct of uneven geographical development is the production of heterotopical spaces. These are the so-called subterranean spaces of *Underworld*, spaces where differences are geographically condensed because of segregation, white flight, and disinvestment, spaces which, as we have seen in American literature of urban underworlds, are sites of new spatial movements that often demand justice and recognition in the face of erasure and neglect. Whereas Bronzini refuses to adjust to the new reality of the Bronx, Muñoz in contrast is supple, flexible, and improvisational. An entrepreneur, artist, father-figure, community organizer, gay, and Hispanic, his identities are combinatorial and situational. He has turned a position of weakness into one of assembly and creativity through which he builds projects that empower local residents. His crew does not engage in a traditional oppositional politics of place, a politics of sit-ins and demonstrations. Rather, theirs is a mischievous cultural politics whose greatest achievement may just be, I want to suggest, the production of empathy, what DeLillo labels a shared "single consciousness" (821). Such empathy is made possible by the global matrices that unite, as the scholar Peter Knight observes, "individuals and larger social and economic forms," an expanded sense of interconnectedness that Edward Soja and others term the "production of globality," "'the compression of the world and the intensification of consciousness of the world as a whole.'"[63]

As evidence for this claim of a moment of shared "single consciousness," let us turn to the conclusion of *Underworld*, where an image of Esmeralda, the young runaway girl who is raped and murdered in the Bronx, uncannily appears in a Minute Maid billboard advertisement that looms incongruously over the burnt-out landscape. The Sisters had been searching for the fleet-footed girl, whom DeLillo depicts as a feral sprite of the slums rushing through the weeds and trash, but she is always a step ahead of their outreach. News of her strange reappearance in the orange juice ad quickly spreads, and soon a few people, then a few dozen, and finally a few hundred gather on the expressway arches to watch what is understood to be a modern-day miracle. DeLillo makes plain the heterogeneity of the crowd who are lured by a moment of wonder in a desacralized age: "Working people, shopkeepers, maybe some drifters and squatters," Muñoz's gang, as well as the nuns, wait breathlessly for the moment when the headlights of a "commuter train" strike the sign, causing a ghostly apparition of the girl to illuminate behind a "vast cascade of orange juice pouring" into "a goblet" held by "the perfectly formed hand of a female caucasian of the middle suburbs" (820, 821). At that moment of illumination, the germophobic Sister Edgar "yanks off . . . [the] gloves" she has been wearing through the whole novel to protect her from disease, "finds Ismael and embraces him," "looks into his face and breathes the air he breathes and enfolds him in her laundered cloth" (822, 823). The crowd "sobs and moans" in an "unnameable painful elation" and "unstoppered belief" at a sign of redemption in a godforsaken landscape of violence and fear (821).

The sign has drawn together people from inside and outside of the Bronx, huddled them in a collective experience of grief and joy that might serve as a spark for coalitional politics that grows out of a striking instance of political illumination. In the one arresting heartbeat that the light hits the billboard, capitalism's wasted inner-city geographies and its affluent kingdoms of suburban domesticity merge into a surreal collage. Collapsing time and space, the juxtapositions of death and consumerism, and a girl from the Bronx and a white woman from a world away, exemplify *Underworld*'s aesthetics. On the palimpsestic square of the billboard, the Janus-faced logic of capital's polarized development at its most uncanny can be apprehended. The flare permits one to think in two directions at once, positively and negatively, grasping how the circuits of capital produce death and life, poverty and luxury, underworld and upper in a single gesture when the specter of the underclass girl emerges beneath a "perfectly formed hand."

DeLillo intimates, though never confirms, that this sudden eruption of the celestial may be a sneaky trompe l'oeil, more physics than metaphysics, an artfully staged spectacle by Ismael and his crew who have put to work their skill with trains and murals of the dead to craft something new and angelic. If this reading is correct, then it suggests something important about the role of political art at the century's end. "They control the language, you have to improvise and dissemble," DeLillo advises (444). Art that is going to be sufficient to the challenges of the postmodern era will have to interrogate the logic that constructs the commodified and official memories of our time and space and move beyond them into another kind of memory that is not wedded to a narrow definition of historical truth. Out of local memories, urban myths, consumer culture, and whatever other materials are available, it will surpass the crude world of statistics that document the ills of the city, by reintroducing the fantastical in the oddest of places and by means that are unpredictable. To those who either willfully ignore the ruins of the city or who write them into an "endless sequence" that narrates a linear history of development, Ismael counters with an image that fissures the calm veneer and disrupts the progressive storyline. The "commuters" gazing out their window will be momentarily confronted with a startling image whose affect is to make them ponder how the spaces and lives below them and the spaces and lives of the "middle suburbs" are linked by more than a train that snakes through the early evening light.[64]

The image does not entertain. It haunts. The moment is ephemeral, already on the cusp of being coopted by crass commercialism and shut down by the police as site of public disturbance. But its ephemeral nature is also part of its tactic of surprise. By the following night a "thousand people fill the area," a boy is injured in a hit-and-run, and an impromptu informal economy of vendors moves "along the lines of stalled traffic selling flowers, soft drinks and live kittens," and "police trail orange caution tape through the area" (823, 824). And then by "the next evening the sign is blank," and the spectacle is confined to collective memory (824). In place of Esmeralda are words that might be said to foreshadow the coming gentrification of even this hard-luck landscape, words that call out not just to advertisers, but also advertise to investors and future residents the undercapitalized geographies of the underworld: "Space Available" (824).[65]

To close this decades-long passage through the American underworld, I turn to the neglected figure of DeLillo's Marvin Lundy, the basement-dwelling widower, baseball collector, and all-around terribly lonely old man. Muñoz's gang is able draw people from across the city to peer beneath the white hand of the suburbs to see the eyes of a dead homeless girl caught in its grip. Lundy's "long journey" in search of Thomson's homer demonstrates that Muñoz's underworld is a fragment of a national geography of exclusion that stretches from coast to coast (175). His peregrinations thus tell a national "underhistory" (791). "Waste is the secret history," DeLillo states (791). Lundy's excavation of an unacknowledged present stands in contrast to Nick's reconstruction of an invented past. His obsessive pursuit takes him into the nooks and crannies and shadows of American life, in much the same way that Oedipa before him immersed herself in a zealous and increasingly urgent expedition through the post-Fordist geographies of California in search of W.A.S.T.E. "I said to myself a thousand times. Why do I want this thing? What does it mean? Who has it?" Lundy tells Glassic who hears the stories about the discarded lives that have been stitched into the ball (175). Lundy's quest for Thomson's homer inspires "people to tell him things, to entrust family secrets and unbreathable personal tales," which then become "exalted, absorbed by something larger, the long arching journey of the baseball itself" (318). The hunt for the baseball, thus, is DeLillo's red herring, as Pynchon's Trystero conspiracy was for Oedipa. Its meaning is not in the thing itself, but in the knowledge that is acquired from "the whole wandering epic" and in the sense of purpose that it lends to a life that is either routine, sad, or both. The real discovery in both DeLillo's and Pynchon's quest narratives is the so-called underworld of abandoned and broken citizens, a "fraternity of missing men" whose stories briefly surface when they are connected in some way to Branca's misplaced pitch (182).

Lundy's travels are some of *Underworld*'s most affecting passages, and what comes to light from them is the sheer heteronomy of America's down-and-out populations. In Part 3, Lundy tracks the ball as far back as Chuckie Wainwright and ventures to San Francisco to greet him at the dock where his steamer is scheduled to arrive. When Chuckie fails to show, Lundy finds himself distracted by a "stinkhole odor, barely detectable but odd in its emotional force," an olfactory trigger which recalls to memory (as the odor of the slum once did for Djuna Barnes's Matthew O'Connor in *Nightwood*) "old hotels and their toilets," "public toilets in railroad stations," and his own "shameful, . . . intense and deeply personal" smells (306, 309, 310). As the currents of capital flow through this novel's landscapes, they produce the smell of waste that trails them. His scented trail to the barge leads him past "a lone figure asleep in a mail sack," another nod to Pynchon's alternative mail route through which waste flows (311). Lundy's memories also are of places that connote motion and travel, signaling the uprootedness of postwar American life. The "unaccountable urge to follow [the odor] to its source" concludes with a graffiti-covered barge of toxic sludge sailing from country to country in search of a home (306, 307).

DeLillo uses Lundy's search for waste to bind individual existential realities—a fundamental baseness that DeLillo calls "a sorrowful human sewage"—to the material and geographical production of social waste, the lower classes, the sexually deviant, and the racialized (770). It is another slumming tour in a long history of them, but this is one is different: Lundy goes in search of his own waste—his shameful smell—and finds a nation that shares his secret. During their stay in San Francisco, his wife Eleanor says "I want you to show me the seamy underside" and soon enough they are both walking through the streets of the same city where Oedipa has her nervous breakdown, an area lined with flophouses, shops and cafes catering to sexual fetishists and conspiracy theorists, streets where men in raincoats are "looking at old copies of National Geographic," and a woman in rags pushes her belongings in a shopping cart (318, 320, 323). The walk through San Francisco fuels his geographical imagination and leads him to ponder: "Did people live unknown to us in the crawlspaces of the . . . infrastructure, down the tunnels and under the bridge approaches?" (323).

Through Lundy's search DeLillo excavates the plurality of American life that "lives in the spaces of the official play-by-play"; he unearths a diversity that is erased, paved over, disposed of, or pushed out of sight by the "single narrative sweep" of postwar history (27, 82). The narrative of American suburban affluence, the rise of the middle class, and the triumph over communism has no place for the voices that emerge from the woodwork when Lundy comes knocking to ask about the ball. By way of his "weary traipse," his "suitcase crawl through empty train stations, the bitter winter flights" to complete his collection of memorabilia, he finds himself collecting stories that are a kind of countermemory of the nation (175). In three separate lists, DeLillo enumerates who and what Lundy discovers on his peregrinations (176, 308, 317). The final one begins:

> 1. The mother of twins in what's that town.
>
> 2. The man who lived in a community of chemically sensitive people, they wore white cotton shifts [*sic*] and hung their mail on clotheslines.
>
> 3. The woman named Bliss, which he was younger then [*sic*], Marvin was, and maybe could have, with eyes as nice as hers, done a little something, in Indianola, Miss.
>
> 4. The shock of lives unlike your own. Happy, healthy, lonely, lost. The one-eighth Indian. Lives that are blunt and unforeseen even when they're ordinary.
>
> 5. Who knew a Susan somebody who spoke about a baseball with a famous past.
>
> Marvin forgets the tribe.
>
> 6. Stomach acting up again.
>
> 7. The chemically sensitive man, his whole body vibrated when somebody snapped a photo a mile and a half away.
>
> 8. And Chuckie Wainwright gone to sea, leaving a woman and a child behind, a hippie Christian cluster, barefoot with beads, and Marvin tracking him ship by ship. (317)

Is this not DeLillo's *Underworld* in miniature? Lundy's three paratactic lists overlap and repeat their elements in a litany, an encircling discontinuous narrative for the forgotten people whose voices are never braided into a larger story. Erupting without warning into the forward thrust of his search, they hauntingly emerge and fade without comment, remaining all the while syntactically untethered to the textual spaces around them. Internally, they are discontinuous as well, fragments of an atomized, diverse, and dispersed population in the small towns of America, in the cancer-filled landscapes of Utah, in the new "cities with no downtowns," and in the eviscerated urban dead zone of Detroit where Lundy sees "riots and fires in the distance" (176).

In attempting to track down the "lineage" of the home run ball, Lundy becomes an unwitting chronicler of the "people's history," one who is just as likely to walk through the streets sniffing out waste as he is to drive through the impoverished streets of the Bronx and the Lower East Side hunched over his steering wheel and deathly afraid to make eye-contact with "the wheelchair beggars," "the window washers, the flower sellers, the carjackers" (189, 192). Lundy, like Oedipa, is paranoid, and though their paranoias are of different magnitudes (Oedipa is almost catatonically distraught by the end), their etiologies are the same. Both are a reaction to the inadmissible truth of America's "lineage," or as Pynchon labels it, its "legacy" (192).[66]

The legacy of post-Fordism's social and geographic crises is the "lineage" exposed by DeLillo through *Underworld* (192). One response to that exposure is nostalgia, alienation, and paranoia, but another is what DeLillo on the last page calls "the *argument* of binding touch" (827; emphasis added). The phrase directs us to something related to, but different from the sudden embrace that Sister Edgar gives Ismael when she sees Esmeralda's image. Their physical bonding is heartfelt but limited in its reach, in a way that an argument that challenges, defends, convinces, and binds, when printed, circulated, and read is not limited. It is an argument that maps cognitively and physically our individual lived realities to global networks of capital and power, and allows us to see the connections to those we cannot see. *Underworld* opens with the declaration that a poor kid from a broken home in Harlem "speaks in your voice," and over eight hundred pages later it fades to black with a nearly page-long sentence that begins, "And you can glance out the window for a moment, distracted by the sound of small kids playing a made-up game in a neighbor's yard, some kind of kickball maybe, and they speak in your voice, or piggy-back races on the weedy lawn, and it's your voice you hear." "Fasten, fit closely, bind together," DeLillo instructs on *Underworld*'s final page (827). The labor of the novel is found in the way it ties "your voice" and Cotter's, braids them into a universalist grammar of the second person in which both voices exist intertwined, rather than conflated. This new subject position is not one of expropriation but one of incorporation. It incorporates "you," the reader, into the text but only on the condition that "you" have come "through the tunneled underworld" and through the uneven geographies of late twentieth-century capitalist development that DeLillo's text assiduously maps (826). In other words, the universal "you" that emerges at the end of *Underworld* has its roots in the experience of spatial marginality, its very definition arising from the specific originary contexts and moments of historical emergence by which we speak or are rendered silent.

In a passage of *Underworld* devoted to *Unterwelt*—the "lost" film about "people living in the shadows" and in "some netherland crevice"—what DeLillo says of Eisenstein's work could be said of his own: "All Eisenstein wants you to see, in the end, are the contradictions of being. You look at the faces on the screen and you see the mutilated yearning, the inner divisions of people and systems, and how forces will clash and fasten, compelling the swerve from evenness that marks a thing lastingly" (424, 430, 444). DeLillo's dialectical imagination perceives that capital's production of spatial unevenness spawns an urgent creativity and an insurgent politics. These in turn interrogate the exclusionary practices that simultaneously constrain and constitute the positions from which the putative underworlds of America speak, write, labor, and love. These are "the contradictions of being" that arise from "the inner divisions of people and systems," the fissures through which new subjectivities and new modes of thinking surface and through which "trapped souls [are] trying to emerge" (444, 621). Fredric Jameson urges us "to think the cultural evolution of late capitalism dialectically, as catastrophe and progress all together."[67] The "progress" that might emerge out of the "catastrophe" is what scholar, poet, and community activist bell hooks sees as "the shared sensibilities which cross the boundaries of class, race, gender, etc., that could be fertile ground for the construction of empathy—ties that would promote recognition of common commitments, and serve as a base for solidarity and coalition."[68] The "argument of binding touch" is the argument of *Underworld*. It challenges readers to recognize that their subjectivities are geographically constructed and that whether these geographies are the insular kingdoms of suburban wealth or the inner-city terrains of poverty, they are linked. Their very polarization is the logic that binds the "raw sprawl of the city" to "the solitary hills" across the nation and across the long century (827).

It all comes together in *Underworld* or, as DeLillo writes, "Everything is connected in the end," an axiom that is uttered multiple times in the novel (289, 408, 465, 826). Out of the tenement basements of Jacob Riis's netherworld, the cellars and sewers of Ralph Ellison and Richard Wright, and the subway tunnels of Toth and DeLillo surfaces a different story of the nation. Whether you call it, as Djuna Barnes once did in *Nightwood*, "the stories that do not amount to much. . . . that are forgotten in spite of all man remembers," or you call them, as Ellison did, America's "unwritten history," the "obscure alter ego" to the officially sanctioned narrative of the nation, the story is largely the same.[69] It is the story of besieged communities and individuals who, in moments of local and national panics over crime, immigration, or changing sexual or social mores, have found themselves castigated, excluded, and exiled, and have found that the communities in which they live—the Lower East Side, Greenwich Village, Harlem, Bunker Hill, Chicago's West Side, the Left Bank, the Bronx—have been deemed polluted and immoral.

In the course of this dirty century, the label "underworld" has been foisted on many populations—the immigrant poor, gays and lesbians, urban African Americans—and each time it has been used to create a new social and spatial formation, a real-and-imagined territorial culture that is a source of fascination and fear. The epithet has worked to congeal social anxieties whose sources are complex and difficult to pinpoint, and in doing so it has worked to localize these fears within the degraded, wasted geographies of American cities. Aiding and abetting this process at each moment have been the practices of segregation, urban renewal, punitive zoning, and policing. At the new fin de siècle when inequality and poverty surged (and continues to surge) to record levels, DeLillo's novel shows readers that the underworld is all around them in their heterogeneous society. And like so much of the literature of the American underworld, it writes out of marginality and immiseration a story that underscores the politics of space—of how spaces are made at the microlevel of everyday practices and at the macrolevel of what DeLillo calls "vast shaping strategies" (60). The making of human geographies is what *Urban Underworlds* has tried to make visible. The enforced segregations of urbanization, development, and exploitation have resulted in new concrete sites for urban political action and solidarity. And from these sites, a literature of the underworld has emerged and will continue to emerge so as to argue for dignity, justice, democracy, equality, and a right to the city even as globalization continues to destroy and rebuild the world under our feet.

Notes

An Overview and an Underview

1. Edgar Saltus, "New York from the Flatiron," in *Tales of Gaslight New York*, ed. Frank Oppel (Edison, N.J.: Castle Books, 2000), 201, hereafter cited by page number in the text.

2. Quoted in Thomas Bender, *The Unfinished City: New York and the Metropolitan Idea* (New York: New Press, 2002), 42.

3. Karl Marx, *Capital: A Critique of Political Economy*, trans. Samuel Moore and Edward Aveling (New York: Modern Library, 1906), 195.

4. Michel de Certeau, *The Practice of Everyday Life*, trans. Steven Rendall (Berkeley: University of California Press, 1984), 93, hereafter cited by page number in the text.

5. Fredric Jameson, *Postmodernism, or, the Cultural Logic of Late Capitalism* (Durham: Duke University Press, 1991), 33.

6. De Certeau, *Practice of Everyday Life*, 93. See George Chauncey, *Gay New York: Gender, Urban Culture, and the Making of the Gay Male World, 1890–1940* (New York: Basic Books, 1994), 201. See also Henri Lefebvre, *The Production of Space*, trans. Donald Nicholson-Smith (Oxford: Blackwell, 1991), 33.

7. James Weldon Johnson, *Black Manhattan* (New York: Knopf, 1930), 160, 169.

8. Max Nordau, *Degeneration*, trans. George L. Mosse (New York: Howard Fertig, 1968), 13.

9. Neil Smith, *Uneven Development: Nature, Capital and the Production of Space* (Malden, Mass.: Basil Blackwell, 1984), 155.

10. Marx, *Capital*, 709.

11. Karl Marx and Friedrich Engels, "The Eighteenth Brumaire of Louis Bonaparte," in *Selected Works*, Vol. 1 (London: Lawrence & Wishart, 1953), 257.

12. Ibid.

13. James Donald, "The Immaterial City: Representation, Imagination, and

Media Technologies," in *A Companion to the City*, ed. Gary Bridge and Sophie Watson (Malden, Mass.: Blackwell, 2003), 48.

14. Don DeLillo, *Underworld* (New York: Scribner, 1997), 791.

15. Norman Klein, *The History of Forgetting: Los Angeles and the Erasure of Memory* (London: Verso, 1997), 1.

16. Ralph Ellison, "Going to the Territory," in *Going to the Territory* (New York: Vintage, 1986), 124.

17. Djuna Barnes, *Nightwood* (New York: New Directions, 1961), 15.

18. Jacob A. Riis, *How the Other Half Lives* (New York: Penguin, 1997), 5.

19. Ernest W. Burgess, "The Growth of the City: An Introduction to a Research Project," in *The City Cultures Reader*, ed. Malcolm Miles, Tim Hall, and Iain Borden (London: Routledge, 2000), 25.

20. Ibid.

21. "Enright Blames Press for Crime," *New York Times*, November 11, 1920, 1.

22. Lewis A Erenberg, *Steppin' Out: New York Nightlife and the Transformation of American Culture, 1890–1930* (Chicago: University of Chicago Press, 1981), 76.

23. Burgess, "Growth of the City," 25.

24. Gunnar Myrdal, *An American Dilemma: The Negro Problem and Modern Democracy* (New Brunswick, N.J.: Transaction, 1996), 330.

25. Citizens' Housing and Planning Council, "Cellar Occupancy Attacked," *Housing News*, December 1952, 1.

26. Jennifer Toth, *The Mole People: Life in the Tunnels beneath New York City* (Chicago: Chicago Review Press, 1993), 5.

27. Roderick Ferguson, *Aberrations in Black: Toward a Queer of Color Critique* (Minneapolis: University of Minnesota Press, 2004), 16.

28. Ibid.

29. Chauncey, *Gay New York*, 1.

30. John D'Emilio, "Capitalism and Gay Identity," in *Powers of Desire: The Politics of Sexuality*, ed. Ann Snitow, Christine Stansell, and Sharon Thompson (New York: Monthly Review, 1983), 102.

31. Ibid.

32. John Rechy, *City of Night* (New York: Grove, 1990), 31.

33. Karl Marx and Friedrich Engels, *The Communist Manifesto*, trans. Samuel Moore (New York: Penguin Classics, 2002), 223.

34. Lewis Mumford, "Urban Degeneration and Congestion," in *Urban Crisis in Modern America*, ed. Robert L. Branyan and Lawrence H. Larsen (Lexington, Mass.: D. C. Heath, 1971), 9.

35. Barnes, *Nightwood*, 80.

36. Samuel Delany, *Times Square Red, Times Square Blue* (New York: New York University Press, 1999).

37. Edward Soja, *Thirdspace: Journeys to Los Angeles and Other Real-and-Imagined Places* (Oxford: Blackwell, 1996), 87.

38. Carlo Rotella, *October Cities: The Redevelopment of Urban Literature* (Berkeley: University of California Press, 1998); Catherine Jurca, *White Diaspora: The Suburbs and the Twentieth-Century American Novel* (Princeton: Princeton University Press, 2001); Betsy Klimasmith, *At Home in the City: Urban Domesticity in American Literature and Culture, 1850–1930* (Durham: University of New Hampshire Press, 2005).

39. Gary Bridge and Sophie Watson, "City Differences," in *A Companion to the City*, ed. Gary Bridge and Sophie Watson (Malden, Mass.: Blackwell, 2003), 251.

40. Rechy, *City of Night*, 99.

41. Ibid.

42. Lefebvre, *Production of Space*, 7.

43. Ibid., 29.

44. Ibid., 129.

45. Edward Soja, *Postmodern Geographies: The Reassertion of Space in Critical Social Theory* (London: Verso, 1989), 6.

46. Smith, *Uneven Development*, x; Soja, *Postmodern Geographies*, 105.

47. Henry James, *The American Scene* (New York: Penguin Classics, 1994), 74, 124.

48. Djuna Barnes, "Chinatown's Old Glories Crumbled in Dust" and "Greenwich Village as It Is," in *Djuna Barnes's New York* (Los Angeles: Sun and Moon, 1989), 125, 225.

49. Barnes, "Greenwich Village as It Is," 225.

50. Marshall Berman, *All That Is Solid Melts into Air: The Experience of Modernity* (New York: Penguin, 1988), 290.

51. Lefebvre, *Production of Space*, 51.

52. Sigfried Giedion, *Space, Time and Architecture* (Cambridge: Harvard University Press, 1941), 826.

53. Lefebvre, *Production of Space*, 48–51.

54. Ibid., 33.

55. Claude McKay, *Home to Harlem* (Boston: Northeastern University Press, 1987), 224, 225.

56. Soja, *Postmodern Geographies*, 170; Edward Soja, *Postmetropolis: Critical Studies of Cities and Regions* (Oxford: Blackwell, 2000), 114.

57. Soja, *Postmodern Geographies*, 173.

58. Michael B. Katz, "The Urban 'Underclass' as a Metaphor of Social Transformation," in *The "Underclass" Debate: Views from History*, ed. Michael Katz (Princeton: Princeton University Press, 1993), 4.

59. Although other studies of the underworld have preceded this one, none of them has satisfactorily synthesized the subject's discursive and material origins in modern urban political economy. The small but growing body of work on the underworld has been mytho-allegorical, such as Walter Strauss's *Descent and Return: The Orphic Theme in Modern Literature* (Cambridge: Harvard University Press, 1971); or focused on built environments, such as Rosalind Williams's *Notes on the Underground* (Cambridge: MIT Press, 1990); or centered on British and French literature, history, and culture, as is the case with Williams's aforementioned monograph and David Pike's trilogy, *Passage through Hell: Modernist Descents, Medieval Underworlds* (Ithaca: Cornell University Press, 1997), *Subterranean Cities: The World Beneath Paris and London, 1800–1945* (Ithaca: Cornell University Press, 2005), and *Metropolis on the Styx: The Underworlds of Modern Urban Culture, 1800–2001* (Ithaca: Cornell University Press, 2007). Scott Herring's *Queering the Underworld: Slumming, Literature, and the Undoing of Lesbian and Gay History* (Chicago: University of Chicago Press, 2007) and Robert Dowling's *Slumming in New York: From the Waterfront to Mythic Harlem* (Chicago: University of Illinois Press, 2007) are two studies of the underworld in American literature that are acutely attuned to the spatial experience of racial and sexual

marginality. They have been instrumental in my thinking on this subject. However, by organizing their investigations around the subject and practices of slumming, Herring and Dowling miss an opportunity to engage with a broader range of American underworld narratives. Focusing their investigations on the period before 1940, they leave most of the twentieth century's lower geographies unmapped.

60. Quoted in Frederick Jackson, *The Frontier in American History* (New York: Henry Holt, 1920), 1.

61. Riis, *How the Other Half Lives*, 191.

62. Henry James, *The American Scene* (New York: Penguin Classics, 1994), 149.

63. Ralph Ellison, *Invisible Man* (New York: Vintage, 1982), 7.

64. Soja, *Postmetropolis*, 140.

65. Soja, *Postmodern Geographies*, 222.

66. Rechy, *City of Night*, 231.

67. DeLillo, *Underworld*, 810.

68. Ibid., 785.

69. Riis, *How the Other Half Lives*, 14.

1 / Going Down

1. William B. Meloney, "Slumming in New York's Chinatown," in *Tales of Gaslight New York*, ed. Frank Oppel (Edison, N.J.: Castle Books, 2000), 229, hereafter cited by page number in the text.

2. Christopher Mele, *Selling the Lower East Side: Culture, Real Estate, and Resistance in New York City* (Minneapolis: University of Minnesota Press, 2000), 49.

3. Stephen Crane, *Maggie: A Girl of the Streets* (New York: Norton, 1979); Ernest Ingersoll, *A Week in New York* (New York: Rand McNally, 1891); Frank Moss, *The American Metropolis*, 3 vols. (New York: P. F. Collier, 1897); Jacob A. Riis, *How the Other Half Lives* (New York: Penguin, 1997); Henry James, *The American Scene* (New York: Penguin Classics, 1994).

4. Ned Buntline, *The Mysteries and Miseries of New York: A Tale of Real Life* (London: Milner, 1848); George G. Foster, *New York by Gas-Light and Other Urban Sketches* (Berkeley: University of California Press, 1990); Jose Vose, *Seven Nights in Gotham* (New York: Bunnell and Price, 1852); George Lippard, *New York: Its Upper Ten and Lower Million* (Cincinnati: E. Mendenhall, 1854).

5. Scott Herring, *Queering the Underworld: Slumming, Literature, and the Undoing of Lesbian and Gay History* (Chicago: University of Chicago Press, 2007), 4.

6. Robert M. Dowling, *Slumming in New York: From the Waterfront to Mythic Harlem* (Chicago: University of Illinois Press, 2007), 4.

7. Alan Trachtenberg, *The Incorporation of America: Culture and Society in the Gilded Age* (New York: Hill and Wang, 1982), 103.

8. Foster, *New York by Gas-Light*, 69.

9. Ibid., 92.

10. Dowling, *Slumming in New York*, 5. Dowling's book devotes a chapter to slumming literature written between 1850 and 1900, but it addresses a different cluster of narratives—the work of George Thompson, George Lippard, and John Vose—from those considered here.

11. Quoted in Frederick Jackson, *The Frontier in American History* (New York: Henry Holt, 1920), 1.

12. Ibid.

13. Dowling, *Slumming in New York*, 111.

14. Mario Maffi, *Gateway to the Promised Land: Ethnic Cultures on New York's Lower East Side* (New York: New York University Press, 1995), 68.

15. Trachtenberg, *Incorporation of America*, 118, 128.

16. Luc Sante, *Low Life: Lures and Snares of Old New York* (New York: Vintage, 1991), 32.

17. Lydia Morris, *Dangerous Classes: The Underclass and Social Citizenship* (London: Routledge, 1994), 62.

18. Ibid., 61.

19. Quoted ibid.

20. Roderick Ferguson, *Aberrations in Black: Toward a Queer of Color Critique* (Minneapolis: University of Minnesota Press, 2004), 16.

21. Ibid., 8.

22. Mele, *Selling the Lower East Side*, 43.

23. Betsy Klimasmith, *At Home in the City: Urban Domesticity in American Literature and Culture, 1850–1930* (Durham: University of New Hampshire Press, 2005), 5.

24. Ibid., 108.

25. Eleanor Hoyt, "Romances of New Americans" in *Tales of Gaslight New York*, ed. Frank Oppel (Edison, N.J.: Castle Books, 2000), 246.

26. Crane, *Maggie*, 6.

27. James, *American Scene*, 124, hereafter cited by page number in the text.

28. Dowling, *Slumming in New York*, 12.

29. David Pike, *Subterranean Cities: The World beneath Paris and London, 1800–1945* (Ithaca: Cornell University Press, 2005), 196.

30. William Sharpe and Leonard Wallock, "From 'Great Town' to 'Nonplace Urban Realm': Reading the Modern City," in *Visions of the Modern City: Essays in History, Art, and Literature*, ed. William Sharpe and Leonard Wallock (Baltimore: Johns Hopkins University Press, 1987), 3.

31. Dowling, *Slumming in New York*, 10, 11.

32. M. H. Dunlop, *Gilded City: Scandal and Sensation in Turn-of-the-Century New York* (New York: Harper Perennial, 2000), 135.

33. Mark Pittenger, "A World of Difference: Constructing the 'Underclass' in Progressive America," *American Quarterly* 49.1 (1997): 31.

34. Dunlop, *Gilded City*, 135, 136.

35. Sante, *Low Life*, 296.

36. Eric Schocket, "Undercover Explorations of the 'Other Half,' or the Writer as Class Transvestite," *Representations* 64 (Fall 1998): 109.

37. Sante, *Low Life*, 296.

38. Pittenger, "A World of Difference," 29, 30.

39. Mele, *Selling the Lower East Side*, 72.

40. Ibid., 73.

41. Ibid., 72.

42. Dunlop, *Gilded City*, 124.

43. Clyde L. MacKenzie Jr., "Biographic Memoir of Ernest Ingersoll: Naturalist, Shellfish Scientist, and Author," *Marine Fisheries Review* 53.3 (1991): 23.

44. Ingersoll, *A Week in New York*, 202, hereafter cited by page number in the text.

45. Moss, *American Metropolis*, 3:165, 166.

46. Ibid., vii.

47. Timothy Gilfoyle, *City of Eros: New York City, Prostitution, and the Commercialization of Sex, 1790–1920* (New York: Norton, 1992), 198, 313.

48. Ibid., 198.

49. Ibid.

50. Moss, *American Metropolis*, 2:357, 414; 3:160.

51. Foster, *New York by Gas-Light*, 92.

52. Michel de Certeau, *The Practice of Everyday Life*, trans. Steven Rendall (Berkeley: University of California Press, 1984), 93.

53. Ibid., 97.

54. Ibid., 98.

55. Ibid., 115, 116.

56. Ibid., 115.

57. Moss, *American Metropolis*, 2:416.

58. De Certeau, *Practice of Everyday Life*, 127.

59. Riis, *How the Other Half Lives*, 38, hereafter cited by page number in the text.

60. Quoted in Gilfoyle, *City of Eros*, 304.

61. Dunlop, *Gilded City*, 135.

62. Quoted in Morris, *Dangerous Classes*, 22, 29.

63. Ingersoll, *A Week in New York*, 206.

64. Stephen Chalmers, "The Park Bencher Derelict of Humanity," *New York Times*, November 13, 1904, SM7.

65. Karl Marx and Frederick Engels, *Karl Marx and Frederick Engels, Selected Works*, Vol. 1 (London: Lawrence & Wishart, 1953), 267, 42.

66. Quoted in Morris, *Dangerous Classes*, 22.

67. Ibid., 17.

68. Sante, *Low Life*, 30.

69. Edward S. Martin, "East Side Considerations" in *Tales of Gaslight New York*, edited by Frank Oppel (Edison, N.J.: Castle Books, 2000), 101.

70. Sante, *Low Life*, 30.

71. Ibid.

72. Jacob Riis, *The Peril and Preservation of the Home* (Philadelphia: George W. Jacobs, 1903), 79.

73. Richard E. Foglesong, *Planning the Capitalist City: The Colonial Era to the 1920s* (Princeton: Princeton University Press, 1986), 75.

74. Ibid.

75. Moss, *American Metropolis*, 2:358.

76. Critical engagements with *The American Scene* have situated it within the turn-of-the-century discourses of surveillance and coercion, have documented its affinities with William James's pragmatist writings and the anti-essentialist account of identity they tender, and have focused on its representation and negotiation of ethnic difference. See, respectively, Mark Seltzer, *Henry James & the Art of Power* (Ithaca: Cornell University Press, 1984); Ross Posnock, *The Trial of Curiosity: Henry James, William James, and the Challenge of Modernity* (New York: Oxford University Press, 1991); and Sara Blair, *Henry James and the Writing of Race and Nation* (New York: Cambridge University Press, 1996).

77. Quoted in F. O. Matthiessen, *The James Family* (New York: Knopf, 1947), 307, 308.

78. Henry James to William James, May 24, 1903, *The Letters of Henry James*, ed. Percy Lubbock. Vol. 1 (London: Macmillan, 1920), 425, 428,

79. Mele, *Selling the Lower East Side*, 72.

80. Pittenger, "A World of Difference," 36.

81. James, *Letters*, 425, 428.

82. Riis documented his participation in a violent "raid on the stale-beer dives," dramatizing it as a descent into the criminal underworld—"To the devil or the dives, same thing"—in which he literally goes down, groping a "half a mile . . . in the dark" and into the "tramps' burrows" (*How the Other Half Lives*, 58–60, 65).

83. Ibid, 5.

84. Henri Lefebvre, *The Production of Space*, trans. Donald Nicholson-Smith (Oxford: Blackwell, 1991) 33, 101

85. Ibid.

86. De Certeau, *Practice of Everyday Life*, 24.

2 / Degenerate Sex and the City

1. Djuna Barnes, *Djuna Barnes's New York* (Los Angeles: Sun and Moon, 1989), 301, 304, hereafter cited by page number in the text.

2. "Enright Blames Press for Crime," *New York Times*, November 11, 1920, 1.

3. Ibid.

4. Ibid.

5. Ernest Ingersoll, *A Week in New York* (New York: Rand McNally, 1891), 203.

6. Henry James, *The American Scene* (New York: Penguin Classics, 1994), 149.

7. George Chauncey, *Gay New York: Gender, Urban Culture, and the Making of the Gay Male World, 1890–1940* (New York: Basic Books, 1994), 227.

8. Christine Stansell, *American Moderns: Bohemian New York and the Creation of a New Century* (New York: Henry Holt, 2000), 281–290. See, for instance, Stansell's reading of Village resident Hutchins Hapgood's *The Spirit of the Ghetto* (1905) and *The Spirit of Labor* (1907).

9. Recent cultural histories of the period have celebrated the artistic, social, and sexual freedoms of residents of Harlem and the Village. See Stansell's *American Moderns*; Andrea Barnet, *All-Night Party: The Women of Bohemian Greenwich Village and Harlem, 1913–1930* (New York: Algonquin, 2004); and Ann Douglas, *Terrible Honesty: Mongrel Manhattan in the 1920s* (New York: Farrar, Straus, Giroux, 1995).

10. Scott Herring, *Queering the Underworld: Slumming, Literature, and the Undoing of Lesbian and Gay History* (Chicago: University of Chicago Press, 2007), 160.

11. Barnes's newspaper reporting has not received much scholarly attention, nor has it been adequately historicized. Her biographer Phillip Herring surveys a number of Barnes's reports, but ultimately dismisses them as of scant interest if Barnes had not been destined for greater things. See Phillip Herring, *Djuna: The Life and Works of Djuna Barnes* (New York: Viking, 1995), 81. Nancy Levine is attuned to the spatial dynamics of the social relations in Barnes's work, yet she does not fully contextualize the representation of these relations or account for the deep ambivalence that structures Barnes's portrait of social marginality. See Nancy Levine, "'Bringing Milkshakes to Bulldogs': The Early Journalism of Djuna Barnes," in *Silence and Power:*

A Reevaluation of Djuna Barnes, ed. Mary Broe (Carbondale: Southern Illinois University Press, 1991), 27–34. Justin Edwards provides a persuasive reading of Barnes's journalism within the "new subgenre of travel writing." Edwards observes that "As the first woman writer to fully explore this subgenre, Barnes frequently foregrounded its narrative and performative aspects so as to engage her audience in imaginary travelling across the abysses of class, ethnicity, race, gender, and sexual identity." See Edwards, "'Why Go Abroad': Djuna Barnes and the Urban Travel Narrative," *Journal of Urban History* 26.3 (2002): 7. Scott Herring argues in *Queering the Underworld* that Barnes's "antisapphic modernism fails to exhibit the history of a pathologized queer underworld. It obliquely illuminates how fantastic underworlds help nonnormative subjects escape this imperative to embrace a collective sexual history by putting a stranglehold on the pervasive ideal" (155).

12. Stansell, *American Moderns*, 250.

13. Djuna Barnes, *Nightwood* (New York: New Directions, 1961), 17, hereafter cited by page number in the text.

14. Claude McKay, *Home to Harlem* (Boston: Northeastern University Press, 1987), 225, hereafter cited by page number in the text.

15. Richard E. Foglesong, *Planning the Capitalist City: The Colonial Era to the 1920s* (Princeton: Princeton University Press, 1986), 201.

16. Ibid.

17. Benjamin C. Marsh, *An Introduction to City Planning: Democracy's Challenge to the American City* (Manchester, N.H.: Ayer, 1974).

18. Daniel H. Burnham and Edward H. Bennett, *Plan of Chicago* (Princeton: Princeton Architectural Press, 1993), 1.

19. Ibid.

20. Foglesong, *Planning the Capitalist City*, 201.

21. Christopher Tunnard and Henry Hope Reed, "The City Efficient," in *Urban Crisis in Modern America*, ed. Robert L. Branyan and Lawrence H. Larsen (Lexington, Mass.: D. C. Heath, 1971), 15.

22. Foglesong, *Planning the Capitalist City*, 214.

23. Quoted ibid., 224.

24. Frank Koester, "American City Planning—Part I," *American Architect* 102 (October 1912): 145.

25. Lewis A. Erenberg, *Steppin' Out: New York Nightlife and the Transformation of American Culture, 1890–1930* (Chicago: University of Chicago Press, 1981), xiii.

26. Ibid., 61.

27. Ibid., xiv, 61.

28. Ernest W. Burgess, "The Growth of the City: An Introduction to a Research Project," in *The City Cultures Reader*, ed. Malcolm Miles, Tim Hall, and Iain Borden (London: Routledge, 2000), 25.

29. Ibid.

30. Ibid.

31. Burgess, "Growth," 24.

32. David Sibley, "Border Crossings from *Geographies of Exclusion*," in *The City Cultures Reader*, ed. Malcolm Miles, Tim Hall, and Iain Borden (London: Routledge, 2000), 363.

33. Quoted in Erenberg, *Steppin' Out*, 80.

34. Ibid., 76.

35. Quoted ibid., 82. The reaction to the seemingly rapid erosion of "caste and convention" was increased regulation and licensing of popular entertainment, rather than outright prohibition. Wanting "a wider social morality based on the tenets of the restrained family and ascetic character, [these reformers] saw the need for the state to create proper public amusements" (63). The report "You Can Tango" (1913) in *Djuna Barnes's New York* bears out Erenberg's claims. Barnes notes "the absolute elimination of the old-style dance hall with its flickering gaslights and furtive faces," which has been replaced by new-style establishments (13). Sydney Cohen, treasurer of the Social Centers Corporation, proudly asserts to Barnes that "We are endeavoring to elevate the tone of dancing and to place the dance-hall business on a clean and wholesome basis" (15). His goals of increased social legibility and cleanliness in the "dance-hall business" were perfectly aligned with City Practical urban redevelopment plans that managed cityspace so as to elevate the social status and the ground rents of degraded geographies.

36. Caroline F. Ware, *Greenwich Village, 1920–1930: A Comment on American Civilization in the Post-War Years* (New York: Harper & Row, 1965), vi. Barnes, *Djuna Barnes's New York*, 225.

37. Ware, *Greenwich Village*, 13, 112.

38. George Chauncey, *Gay New York: Gender, Urban Culture, and the Making of the Gay Male World, 1890–1940* (New York: Basic Books, 1994), 23.

39. Ibid., 1, 201.

40. James D. McCabe, "From *Lights and Shadows of New York Life: or, the Sights and Sensations of the Great City*," in *The Greenwich Village Reader: Fiction, Poetry, and Reminiscences, 1872–2002*, ed. June S. Sawyers (New York: Cooper Square Press, 2001), 4.

41. Guido Bruno, "From *Fragments from Greenwich Village*," in *The Greenwich Village Reader: Fiction, Poetry, and Reminiscences, 1872–2002*, ed. June S. Sawyers (New York: Cooper Square Press, 2001), 201.

42. Floyd Dell, "Rents Were Low in Greenwich Village," in *The Greenwich Village Reader: Fiction, Poetry, and Reminiscences, 1872–2002*, ed. June S. Sawyers (New York: Cooper Square Press, 2001), 264.

43. Erenberg, *Steppin' Out*, 252, 253.

44. Phillip Herring, *Djuna: The Life and Works of Djuna Barnes* (New York: Viking, 1995), 66.

45. Ibid.

46. Ibid.; Timothy Gilfoyle, *City of Eros: New York City, Prostitution, and the Commercialization of Sex, 1790–1920* (New York: Norton, 1992), 214.

47. Ware, *Greenwich Village*, 15.

48. Chauncey, *Gay New York*, 147.

49. Ibid., 204; Burnham and Bennett, *Plan of Chicago*, 107.

50. Stansell has commented on the real-estate exploitation of Greenwich Village: "Downtown, wartime repression had occurred against the backdrop of a real estate boom and tourist influx, an efflorescence of commercial bohemia capitalized upon by landlords (who profiteered by subdividing row houses into 'artists' studios') and also by some Villagers who enacted their bohemian personae for the benefit of tourists" (334).

51. Douglas Messerli, foreword to *Djuna Barnes: Interviews*, by Djuna Barnes, ed. Alyce Barry (New York: Sun and Moon, 1985), 5.

52. Burnham and Bennett, *Plan of Chicago*, 1.

53. See John D'Emilio, "Capitalism and Gay Identity," in *Powers of Desire: The Politics of Sexuality*, ed. Ann Snitow, Christine Stansell, and Sharon Thompson (New York: Monthly Review, 1983), 100–113.

54. Lillian Faderman, *Odd Girls and Twilight Lovers: A History of Lesbian Life in Twentieth—Century America* (New York: Columbia University Press, 1991), 8, 9.

55. Scott Herring, introduction to *Autobiography of an Androgyne*, by Ralph Werther (New Brunswick: Rutgers University Press, 2008), xiv, xv, 75, 76.

56. Werther, *Autobiography of an Androgyne*, 63, 121.

57. Ibid., 121.

58. Ibid., 120, 129.

59. Ibid., 63, 89.

60. Ibid., 76.

61. Ibid.

62. Ibid., 143.

63. Quoted in Chauncey, *Gay New York*, 44.

64. Werther, *Autobiography of an Androgyne*, 143.

65. Kevin Mumford, *Interzones: Black/White Sex Districts in Chicago and New York in the Early Twentieth Century* (New York: Columbia University Press, 1997), 22, 23.

66. Edwards, "Why Go Abroad," 10.

67. Burnham and Bennett, *Plan of Chicago*, 107.

68. See Shari Benstock, *Women of the Left Bank: Paris, 1900–1940* (Austin: University of Texas Press, 1986).

69. Quoted in Douglas, *Terrible Honesty*, 109.

70. Benstock, *Women of the Left Bank*, 235.

71. David Pike, *Subterranean Cities: The World beneath Paris and London, 1800–1945* (Ithaca: Cornell University Press, 2005), 251.

72. Quoted ibid., 248.

73. Ibid.

74. François Loyer, "Haussmann's Paris," in *Paris: La ville et ses Projets*, ed. Jean-Louis Cohen and Bruno Fortier (Paris: Babylone, 1988), 156.

75. Ibid.

76. Michel de Certeau, *The Practice of Everyday Life*, trans. Steven Rendall (Berkeley: University of California Press, 1984), 94

77. Loyer, "Haussmann's Paris," 157.

78. Dianne Chisholm, "Obscene Modernism: Eros Noir and the Profane Illumination of Djuna Barnes," *American Literature* 69.1 (March 1997): 167–206.

79. Herring, *Queering the Underworld*, 155.

80. Brassaï's *The Secret Paris of the '30s*, trans. Richard Miller (London: Thames & Hudson, 1976) is unpaginated. The text surrounding the photographs was written by Brassaï in the 1970s. In this reminiscence, he reveals how he was "impelled by an inexplicable desire" to wander around Paris at night, sometimes with a friend (the novelist Henry Miller or the poet Jacques Prévert), sometimes with a bodyguard, but most often alone with his camera guiding him into "unsavory, ominous areas where I wouldn't dare go today."

81. Michel Foucault, *The History of Sexuality: An Introduction*, trans. Robert Hurley (New York: Vintage, 1978), 145.

82. Herring, *Queering the Underworld*, 174.

83. Quoted in Foglesong, *Planning the Capitalist City*, 204.

84. Max Nordau, *Degeneration*, trans. George L. Mosse (New York: Howard Fertig, 1968), 36.

85. Ibid., 35.

86. Ibid., 17.

87. Ibid., 21.

88. Ibid., 13, 538, 539. *Degeneration* developed an argument for the psychopathology of modern art. Nordau's cultural bugbears were Baudelaire, Zola, Nietzsche, Wilde, Ibsen, the Impressionists, and the Symbolist poets.

89. Lewis Mumford, "Urban Degeneration and Congestion," in *Urban Crisis in Modern America*, ed. Robert L. Branyan and Lawrence H. Larsen (Lexington, Mass.: D. C. Heath, 1971), 9.

90. William Laurence, "Women's Personalities Changed by New Adrenal Gland Operation," *New York Times*, October 28, 1935, 1.

91. George W. Henry, *Sex Variants: A Study of Homosexual Patterns* (New York: Paul B. Hoeber, 1948).

92. Ibid., xii, 1049.

93. Ibid., 1099.

94. Ibid.

95. Herring, *Queering the Underworld*, 179.

96. Pike, *Subterranean Cities*, 249.

97. Erenberg, *Steppin' Out*, 256.

98. Mumford, "Urban Degeneration and Congestion," 9.

99. Ibid.

100. Mumford, *Interzones*, 133.

101. Ibid., 155.

102. Ibid.

103. James Weldon Johnson, *Black Manhattan* (New York: Knopf, 1930), 160.

104. Ibid., 169.

105. Mumford, *Interzones*, 34.

106. Rudolph Fisher, "The Caucasian Storms Manhattan," in *The Portable Harlem Renaissance Reader*, ed. David Levering Lewis (New York: Penguin, 1994), 115.

107. Wayne Cooper, ed., *The Passion of Claude McKay: Selected Poetry and Prose, 1912–1948* (New York: Schocken Books, 1973), 29.

108. Carl Van Vechten, *Nigger Heaven* (Chicago: University of Illinois Press, 1999), 89, 90.

109. Mumford, *Interzones*, 145.

110. W.E.B. Du Bois, "Critiques of Carl Van Vechten's *Nigger Heaven*," in *Portable Harlem Renaissance Reader*, ed. David Levering Lewis (New York: Penguin, 1994), 106.

111. W.E.B. Du Bois, "Two Novels: Nella Larsen, *Quicksand* & Claude McKay, *Home to Harlem*," *Crisis* 35 (June 1928): 202.

112. Ibid.

113. Douglas S. Massey and Nancy A. Denton, *American Apartheid: Segregation and the Making of the Underclass* (Cambridge: Harvard University Press, 1993), 26.

114. Joseph Trotter, "Blacks in the Urban North: The 'Underclass Question' in Historical Perspective," in *The "Underclass" Debate: Views from History*, ed. Michael Katz (Princeton: Princeton University Press, 1993), 68.

115. Between 1917 and 1920, fifty-eight African-American houses were firebombed in Chicago, approximately one every twenty days. Massey and Denton, *American Apartheid*, 34, 35.

116. Douglas, *Terrible Honesty*, 311, 312.

117. Massey and Denton, *American Apartheid*, 9.

118. Claude McKay, *Harlem: Negro Metropolis* (New York: E. P. Dutton, 1940), 23.

119. Ibid.

120. Roderick Ferguson, *Aberrations in Black: Toward a Queer of Color Critique* (Minneapolis: University of Minnesota Press, 2004), 101.

121. Claude McKay, "A Negro Extravaganza," in *Voices from the Harlem Renaissance*, ed. Nathan Irving Huggins (New York: Oxford University Press, 1995), 132.

122. Douglas, *Terrible Honesty*, 74.

123. Robert M. Dowling, *Slumming in New York: From the Waterfront to Mythic Harlem* (Chicago: University of Illinois Press, 2007), 154.

124. Quoted in Foglesong, *Planning the Capitalist City*, 224.

125. David Levering Lewis, introduction to *The Portable Harlem Renaissance Reader* (New York: Penguin, 1994), xviii.

126. McKay, "A Negro Extravaganza," 132.

127. Douglas, *Terrible Honesty*, 74.

128. Johnson, *Black Manhattan*, 169.

129. McKay, *Home to Harlem*, 337.

3 / The Black Underground

1. Quoted in Gilbert Osofsky, *Harlem: The Making of a Ghetto, Negro New York, 1890–1930* (New York: Harper & Row, 1963), 128.

2. Claude McKay, *Harlem: Negro Metropolis* (New York: E. P. Dutton, 1940), 28.

3. Osofsky, *Harlem*, 127, 128.

4. Adam Clayton Powell Jr., "Powell Says Rents Too High," in *Harlem on My Mind*, ed. Allon Schoener (New York: New York Press, 1995), 138.

5. Osofsky, *Harlem*, 139.

6. Claude McKay, *Home to Harlem* (Boston: Northeastern University Press, 1987), 224, 225.

7. Ibid., 44.

8. See Richard Wright, "The Man Who Lived Underground," in *Eight Men*, 19–84 (New York: HarperPerennial, 1996); and Ralph Ellison, *Invisible Man* (New York: Vintage, 1982), hereafter cited by page number in the text.

9. Ralph Ellison, "Harlem Is Nowhere," in *Shadow and Act* (New York: Quality Paperback Book Club, 1994), 295, hereafter cited by page number in the text.

10. Ralph Ellison, introduction to *Invisible Man* (New York: Vintage, 1982), xv.

11. Harvey Warren Zorbaugh, *The Gold Coast and the Slum: A Sociological Study of Chicago's Near North Side* (Chicago: University of Chicago Press, 1929), 147.

12. Douglas S. Massey and Nancy A. Denton, *American Apartheid: Segregation and the Making of the Underclass* (Cambridge: Harvard University Press, 1993), 46.

13. Ibid., 32.

14. W.E.B. Du Bois, *The Souls of Black Folk* (New York: Bantam, 1989), 76.

15. James Baldwin, "The Harlem Ghetto: Winter 1948," *Commentary* 5.2 (1948): 165.

16. Powell, "Powell Says Rents," 138.

17. Ibid., 138, 139.

18. Zorbaugh, *Gold Coast*, 148.

19. Powell, "Powell Says Rents," 139.

20. Citizens' Housing and Planning Council, "The Cellar Menace," *Housing News*, May 1952, 3.

21. Ibid.

22. Citizens' Housing and Planning Council, "Cellar Occupancy Attacked," *Housing News*, December 1952, 1.

23. Ibid.

24. Ibid.

25. Jacob A. Riis, *How the Other Half Lives* (New York: Penguin, 1997), 14.

26. Ibid., 5.

27. Ibid.

28. "Troops Guard Harlem: Mayor Pleads for Peace," in *Harlem on My Mind*, ed. Allon Schoener (New York: New York Press, 1995), 132, 133.

29. *Complete Report of Mayor LaGuardia's Commission on the Harlem Riot of March 19, 1935* (New York: Arno Press and the New York Times, 1969), 3.

30. Adam Clayton Powell Jr., "Powell Says Men Can't Get Jobs," in *Harlem on My Mind*, ed. Allon Schoener (New York: New York Press, 1995), 137.

31. Alain Locke, "Harlem: Dark Weather-Vane," *Survey Graphic* 24 (August 1936), 457, 458, 462.

32. Ibid., 495.

33. Lawrence Jackson, *Ralph Ellison: Emergence of Genius* (New York: John Wiley & Sons, 2002), 289.

34. Dominic J. Capeci, *The Harlem Riot of 1943* (Philadelphia: Temple University Press, 1977), 127.

35. "195 Hurt, 500 Held in Looking," in *Harlem on My Mind*, ed. Allon Schoener (New York: New York Press, 1995), 175.

36. Ibid.

37. Ralph Ellison, "Eyewitness Story of Riot: False Rumors Spurred Mob," in *Reporting Civil Rights: Part One, American Journalism 1941–1963*, ed. Clayborne Carson, David J. Garrow, Bill Kovach, and Carol Polsgrove (New York: Library of America, 2003), 49, 51.

38. Ibid., 50.

39. Ibid., 51.

40. Locke, "Harlem," 458.

41. McKay, *Harlem: Negro Metropolis*, 206, 207.

42. Ibid., 23.

43. Ibid., 22.

44. Ralph Ellison, "Going to the Territory," in *Going to the Territory* (New York: Vintage, 1986), 131.

45. Zorbaugh, *Gold Coast*, 105, 147, 151, 159.

46. Ibid., 132.

47. Ibid., 151.

48. Gunnar Myrdal, *An American Dilemma: The Negro Problem and Modern Democracy* (New Brunswick, N.J.: Transaction, 1996), 330.

49. Ibid., 98, 376.

50. Zorbaugh, *Gold Coast*, 105, 128, 134, 141, 152.

51. Jackson, *Ralph Ellison*, 373.

52. Wright was a friend of Dr. Wertham, who after reading *Native Son* analyzed Wright using free association. See Michel Fabre, *The World of Richard Wright* (Jackson: University Press of Mississippi, 1985), 122.

53. Wright, "The Man Who Lived Underground," 19, hereafter cited by page number in the text.

54. David Pike, *Subterranean Cities: The World beneath Paris and London, 1800–1945* (Ithaca: Cornell University Press, 2005), 191.

55. Ibid.

56. David Pike, "Urban Nightmares and Future Visions: Life beneath New York," *Wide Angle* 20.4 (1998): 20, 21.

57. Citizens' Housing and Planning Council, "Cellar Occupancy," 1.

58. Michel de Certeau, *The Practice of Everyday Life*, trans. Steven Rendall (Berkeley: University of California Press, 1984), xiv.

59. bell hooks, *Yearning* (Boston: South End Press, 1990), 47.

60. Ibid.

61. Fabre, *World of Richard Wright*, 99.

62. Ibid., 97.

63. Zorbaugh, *Gold Coast*, 151, 152.

64. Ellison, "Harlem Is Nowhere," 297, 302.

65. Ibid., 301; "195 Hurt," 175.

66. Ellison, "Harlem Is Nowhere," 301.

67. Fabre, *World of Richard Wright*, 99.

68. Ibid.

69. Zorbaugh, *Gold Coast*, 126.

70. Pike, *Subterranean Cities*, 7.

71. Roland Barthes, "Semiology and Urbanism" in *The Semiotic Challenge*, trans. Richard Howard (New York: Hill and Wang, 1988), 195.

72. Taussig quoted in Pike, *Subterranean Cities*, 194.

73. Ellison, "Going to the Territory," 124; Djuna Barnes, *Nightwood* (New York: New Directions, 1961), 15.

74. Ellison, "Going to the Territory," 124.

75. Wright, "The Man Who Lived Underground," 47.

76. Ellison, *Invisible Man*, 460; Ellison, "Going to the Territory," 124.

77. Robert E. Park and Ernest W. Burgess, *Introduction to the Science of Sociology* (Chicago: University of Chicago Press, 1921), 136.

78. Robert E. Park, Ernest W. Burgess, and Roderick D. McKenzie, *The City* (Chicago: University of Chicago Press, 1967), 138, 139.

79. Jackson, *Ralph Ellison*, 146.

80. Richard Kostelanetz details Ellison's responses in *Invisible Man* to Washingtonian accommodationism, Garveyite pan-Africanism, and Communist class struggle. See Richard Kostelanetz, *Politics in the African-American Novel* (Westport, Conn.:

Greenwood, 1991). In *City of Words*, Tony Tanner offers a brief but insightful essay of *Invisible Man*'s major themes. Roderick Ferguson reads *Invisible Man* in terms of its representation of black homosexuality and its dialogue with canonical sociology's production of the racial and gender norms required for citizenship status. See Roderick Ferguson, *Aberrations in Black: Toward a Queer of Color Critique* (Minneapolis: University of Minnesota Press, 2004).

81. Paul Allen Anderson, "Ralph Ellison's Musical Lessons," in *The Cambridge Companion to Ralph Ellison*, ed. Ross Posnock (New York: Cambridge University Press, 2005), 92.

82. Ralph Ellison, "On Bird, Bird-Watching, and Jazz," in *Shadow and Act* (New York: Quality Paperback Book, Club, 1964), 228.

83. Ibid., 227.

84. Ibid., 225, 228.

85. Joe R. Feagin and Harlan Hahn, *Ghetto Revolts: The Politics of Violence in American Cities* (New York: Macmillan, 1973), 3.

86. Ralph Ellison, Whitney M. Young Jr., and Herbert Gans, *The City in Crisis* (New York: A. Philip Randolph Educational Fund, 1967), 8. Ellison's biographer adds, "In 1942, military authorities had begun a campaign of removing white women from Harlem, the rationale being to protect servicemen's morale. Such enforcement of rigid racial segregation and harassment had predictable consequences." Jackson, *Ralph Ellison*, 289.

87. Ronald Lawson, and Mark Naison, eds., *The Tenant Movement in New York City, 1904–1984* (New Brunswick: Rutgers University Press, 1986), 128, 129.

88. To an uncanny degree, the scene enacts what French philosopher Louis Althusser would later call the allegorical moment of "hailing," where the police officer's "Hey, you there!" causes the person on the street to turn around in acknowledgment, thus establishing him or herself as a subject of power. The moment "'recruits' subjects among the individuals," and "'transforms' the individuals into subjects," and the only way this can be undone, in Althusser's estimation, is through the Marxist "science" of historical materialism that can help liberate one's consciousness from domination. In *Invisible Man*, the exact reverse is true. See Louis Althusser, *Lenin and Philosophy and Other Essays* (New York: Monthly Review, 1971), 173, 174.

89. Ellison, "Introduction to *Invisible Man*," xv.

90. Ralph Ellison, "*An American Dilemma:* A Review," in *Shadow and Act* (New York: Quality Paperback Book Club, 1964), 316.

91. Ibid.

92. I owe this insight to Adam Bradley's paper "Rereading Ralph Ellison's *Invisible Man* through the Unpublished Second Novel Manuscripts," which he delivered on May 22, 2008, at the American Literature Association conference in San Francisco, California.

93. Ellison, "Introduction to *Invisible Man*," xii.

94. Ibid.

95. Myrdal, *American Dilemma*, 139.

96. Ellison, "Introduction to *Invisible Man*," xvi.

97. Ferguson, *Aberrations in Black*, 74.

98. Myrdal, *American Dilemma*, 23.

99. Ellison, "Going to the Territory," 128.

100. Ralph Ellison, "The Little Man at Chehaw Station," in *Going to the Territory* (New York: Vintage, 1986), 24.

101. Ellison, "Going to the Territory," 126.

102. Thomas Pynchon, *The Crying of Lot 49* (New York: HarperPerennial, 1990), 181.

4 / Wasted Dreams

1. William Wilcox Robinson, *Tarnished Angels: Paradisiacal Turpitude in Los Angeles Revealed* (Los Angeles: Ward Ritchie Press, 1964), 23, hereafter cited by page number in the text.

2. The brochure does not include page numbers.

3. Norman Klein, *The History of Forgetting: Los Angeles and the Erasure of Memory* (London: Verso, 1997), 55.

4. Ibid., 11.

5. Michel de Certeau, *The Practice of Everyday Life*, trans. Steven Rendall (Berkeley: University of California Press, 1984), 107.

6. Lillian Faderman and Stuart Timmons, *Gay L.A.: A History of Sexual Outlaws, Power Politics, and Lipstick Lesbians* (New York: Perseus, 2006), 145.

7. Klein, *History of Forgetting*, 53.

8. Quoted in Faderman and Timmons, *Gay L.A.*, 82.

9. Edward Soja, *Postmodern Geographies: The Reassertion of Space in Critical Social Theory* (London: Verso, 1989), 196.

10. Mike Davis, *City of Quartz: Excavating the Future in Los Angeles* (New York: Vintage, 1992), 230.

11. Soja, *Postmodern Geographies*, 216.

12. Ibid., 221.

13. Quoted in David Fine, *Imagining Los Angeles: A City in Fiction* (Reno: University of Nevada Press, 2000), 8. Fine is quoting historian Carey McWilliams. The "least heroic" quotation is from Charles Fletcher Lummis.

14. John Rechy, *City of Night* (New York: Grove, 1990), 87, hereafter cited by page number in the text.

15. Several American writers before Rechy—Raymond Chandler and John Fante, most famously—have depicted downtown Los Angeles, and Bunker Hill more specifically. See Fine, *Imagining Los Angeles*.

16. John Rechy, introduction to *City of Night*, xi.

17. Thomas Pynchon, *The Crying of Lot 49* (New York: HarperPerennial, 1990), 178, hereafter cited by page number in the text.

18. Thomas Pynchon, "A Journey into the Mind of Watts," *New York Times Magazine*, June 12, 1966, 84.

19. Soja, *Postmodern Geographies*, 210.

20. Lauren Berlant and Michael Warner, "Sex in Public," *Critical Inquiry* 24.2 (Winter 1998): 558. See also Jennifer Moon, "Cruising John Rechy's *City of Night*: Queer Subjectivity, Intimacy, and Counterpublicity," *disclosure* 15 (2006): 42–59. Moon's essay is one of the few extended assessments of Rechy's novel. She reads the text through the lens of Warner and Berlant's notion of a queer counterpublic, but is ultimately more concerned with the discursive context around the novel than with the spatial context, which I am asserting here.

21. Frank Mort, "The Sexual Geography of the City," in *A Companion to the City*, ed. Gary Bridge and Sophie Watson (Malden, Mass.: Blackwell, 2003), 307, 308.

22. Ibid., 307.

23. Ibid., 311.

24. Quoted in Charles Casillo, *Outlaw: The Lives and Careers of John Rechy* (Los Angeles: Advocate Books, 2002), 151.

25. Henry James, *The American Scene* (New York: Penguin Classics, 1994), 82.

26. When Rechy feels it is warranted, he even interrupts the fictive frame of the novel to directly address the reader: "'And this is Tiguh—' Miss Destiny went on. And Tiger (names, you will notice, as obviously emphatically masculine as the queens' are emphatically obviously feminine and for the same reason: to emphasize the role they will play)" (102).

27. Quoted in Casillo, *Outlaw*, 151.

28. Patrick O'Donnell, *Latent Destinies: Cultural Paranoia and Contemporary U.S. Fiction* (Durham: Duke University Press, 2000), 31.

29. Pat Califia, "The City of Desire: Its Anatomy and Destiny," in *Public Sex: The Culture of Radical Sex* (San Francisco: Cleis, 2000), 216, 218, 220.

30. Jon Binnie, "The Erotic Possibilities of the City," in *Pleasure Zones: Bodies, Cities, Spaces*, ed. David Bell, Jon Binnie, Ruth Holiday, Robyn Longhurst, and Robin Peace (Syracuse: Syracuse University Press, 2001), 104.

31. Steve Herbert, *Policing Space: Territoriality and the Los Angeles Police Department* (Minneapolis: University of Minnesota Press, 1997), 13.

32. Ibid., 175.

33. Faderman and Timmons, *Gay L.A.*, 82.

34. Ibid., 75.

35. Ibid., 103.

36. As Faderman and Timmons record in their history of gay Los Angeles, in the pre-Stonewall years some gay Angelinos responded to this climate of fear by organizing underground homophilic societies, such as the Mattachine, which employed elaborate Masonic-like rituals before its ceremonies and parties, and took its name from "medieval folk jesters who always wore masks when they performed in public" (111).

37. Gary Bridge and Sophie Watson, "City Differences," in *A Companion to the City*, ed. Gary Bridge and Sophie Watson (Malden, Mass.: Blackwell, 2003), 252, 253.

38. Ibid., 253, 256.

39. Henri Lefebvre, *The Urban Revolution*, trans. Robert Bononno (Minneapolis: University of Minnesota Press, 2003), 118.

40. Samuel Delany, *Times Square Red, Times Square Blue* (New York: New York University Press, 1999), 129.

41. Mark Sussman, "New York's Facelift," *TDR* 42.1 (Spring 1998): 39.

42. Walt Whitman, *Leaves of Grass*, ed. Sculley Bradley and Harold Blodgett (New York: Norton, 1973), 126. I owe insight into Whitman's poem to Dianne Chisholm, *Queer Constellations: Subcultural Space in the Wake of the City* (Minneapolis: University of Minnesota Press, 2005), 21, 22.

43. Berlant and Warner, "Sex in Public," 558, 562.

44. Mike Davis, *Dead Cities and Other Tales* (New York: New Press, 2002), 132, 136.

45. Davis, *Dead Cities*, 146, 147.

46. Fine, *Imagining Los Angeles*, 10.

47. Davis, *Dead Cities*, 133.

48. Larry Knopp, "From Lesbian and Gay to Queer Geographies: Pasts, Prospects, and Possibilities," in *Geographies of Sexuality*, ed. Kath Browne, Jason Lim, and Gavin Brown (Hampshire, England: Ashgate, 2007), 23.

49. John Rechy, "The Outlaw Sensibility: Liberated Ghettos, Noble Stereotypes, and a Few More Promiscuous Observations," in *Beneath the Skin: The Collected Essays of John Rechy* (New York: Carroll & Graf, 2004), 150.

50. The secondary critical literature on Pynchon is immense, though little of it has addressed the geographies of *The Crying of Lot 49*. For one notable exception, see Brian Jarvis, *Postmodern Cartographies: The Geographical Imagination in Contemporary American Culture* (New York: St. Martin's, 1998), 64. David Fine in *Imagining Los Angeles* and Richard Lehan in *The City in Literature* provide engaging, though brief, treatments of Pynchon's representations of Los Angeles. See Richard Lehan, *The City in Literature: An Intellectual and Cultural History* (Berkeley: University of California Press, 1998).

51. Djuna Barnes, *Nightwood* (New York: New Directions, 1961), 80.

52. Soja, *Postmetropolis*, 265.

53. Soja, *Postmodern Geographies*, 224.

54. Ibid., 196, 226.

55. Ibid., 2, 222.

56. Ibid., 222.

57. Soja, *Postmetropolis*, 283.

58. Betty Friedan, *The Feminine Mystique* (New York: Norton, 2001).

59. Mimi Sheller and John Urry, "The City and the Car," in *The City Cultures Reader*, ed. Malcolm Miles, Tim Hall, and Iain Borden (London: Routledge, 2000), 210.

60. Gerald Horne, *Fire This Time: The Watts Uprising and the 1960s* (Charlottesville: University of Virginia Press, 1995), 53.

61. Reyner Banham, *Los Angeles: The Architecture of Four Ecologies* (Berkeley: University of California Press, 2001), 5.

62. Lehan, *City in Literature*, 277.

63. Soja, *Postmodern Geographies*, 222.

64. O'Donnell, *Latent Destinies*, 11.

65. Joan Didion, *Slouching towards Bethlehem* (New York: Dell, 1968), 220. Didion here speaks in the aftermath of the Watts riot, but she is referencing Nathanael West's *The Day of the Locust.*

66. Ibid.

67. Soja, *Postmodern Geographies*, 216.

68. Quoted in Horne, *Fire This Time*, 66.

69. Ibid, 52.

70. Ibid., 3.

71. Pynchon, "Journey into the Mind," 78.

72. Davis, *Dead Cities*, 149.

73. Ibid., 150.

74. Ibid.

75. Pynchon, "Journey into the Mind," 35.

76. Ibid., 78.

77. Ibid.
78. Ibid.
79. Ibid., 35.
80. Ibid., 78.

5 / White Spaces and Urban Ruins

1. Jennifer Toth, *The Mole People: Life in the Tunnels beneath New York City* (Chicago: Chicago Review Press, 1993), 13, 14, hereafter cited by page number in the text.

2. See Thomas Pynchon, *The Crying of Lot 49* (New York: HarperPerennial, 1990), 180.

3. Some of Toth's claims about underground homelessness in New York's transportation system have been called into question. See, for instance, Joseph Brennan, "Abandon Stations" (2001). Available from: http://www.columbia.edu/~brennan/abandoned/mole-people.html.

4. Quoted in Kenneth Rose, *One Nation Underground: The Fallout Shelter in American Culture* (New York: New York University Press, 2001), 88.

5. Moses was hardly alone in expressing these concerns. "The 'mole' metaphor," historian Kenneth Rose writes, became ubiquitous in debates about the reliability (or even wisdom) of fallout shelters (88). The real possibility of life underground incited fears that Americans might physically and psychologically devolve. In "The Case against Shelters" (1962), Erich Fromm and Michael Maccoby wondered "is this troglodytic life the fulfillment of the American Dream?" (78). See Erich Fromm and Michael Maccoby, "The Case Against Shelters," in *No Place to Hide: Fact and Fiction about Fallout Shelters*, ed. Seymour Melman (New York: Grove Press, 1962). For their part, P. Herbert Leiderman and Jack H. Mendelson were troubled by a potential "atavistic return of man and his tribe to the recesses of the earth": "It is one matter for man to have evolved from living deep in a Paleolithic cave to the city apartment or the garden home in the suburb, but an entirely different matter to consider whether he can successfully return to the cave. The question of whether an abrupt return along this evolutionary path is psychologically possible will hopefully remain a metaphysical issue." See P. Herbert Leiderman and Jack H. Mendelson, "Some Psychiatric Considerations in Planning for Defense Shelters," in *The Fallen Sky: Medical Consequences of Thermonuclear War*, ed. Saul Aronow (New York: Hill and Wang, 1963), 52.

6. See *Dark Days*, VHS, directed by Marc Singer (New York: Wide Angle Pictures, 2000); Margaret Morton, *The Tunnel: The Underground Homeless of New York City* (New Haven: Yale University Press, 1995).

7. Postmodern American literature more generally has shown a pronounced interest in underworld waste, which it uses as a pungent metaphor for residual history and subjectivity in the context of consumer culture's decadent excesses. Paul Auster's *The New York Trilogy* (1987) and *In the Country of Last Things* (1987) both prominently feature the collecting, sorting, and classifying of garbage as essential to understanding urban decay. In DeLillo's *White Noise* (1985), Jack Gladney with fascinated horror picks through his suburban home's trash compactor, which presents him with a spatially condensed, sedimented history of his family's everyday life. In Thomas Pynchon's *V.* (1963), Benny Profane hunts alligators in the New York City sewer system, bringing to life an urban legend whose moral is that what we flush down the toilet can come back to eat us.

8. Saskia Sassen, "Economic Restructuring and the American City," *Annual Review of Sociology* 16 (1990): 467.

9. Edward Soja, *Postmetropolis: Critical Studies of Cities and Regions* (Oxford: Blackwell, 2000), 265.

10. For a fuller reading of the representation of underground New York City in recent films (and to a lesser extent, recent literature), see David Pike, "Urban Nightmares and Future Visions: Life beneath New York," *Wide Angle* 20.4 (1998): 9–50.

11. Ernest Ingersoll, *A Week in New York* (New York: Rand McNally, 1891), 217.

12. Jacob A. Riis, *How the Other Half Lives* (New York: Penguin, 1997), 73, 191.

13. Don DeLillo, *Underworld* (New York: Scribner, 1997), 27, hereafter cited by page number in the text.

14. Fredric Jameson, *Postmodernism, or, the Cultural Logic of Late Capitalism* (Durham: Duke University Press, 1991), 40.

15. Ibid., 42, 43.

16. Ibid, 43.

17. Ibid, 44.

18. Ibid., 38, 39.

19. Soja, *Postmetropolis*, 218.

20. Alejandro Portes and Saskia Sassen-Koob, "Making It Underground: Comparative Material on the Informal Sector in Western Market Economies," *American Journal of Sociology* 93.1 (1987): 30.

21. Ibid., 36.

22. Edward Soja, *Postmodern Geographies: The Reassertion of Space in Critical Social Theory* (London: Verso, 1989), 172.

23. Bart Keunen and Bart Eeckhout, "Whatever Happened to the Urban Novel? New Perspectives for Literary Urban Studies in the Era of Postmodern Culture," in *Postmodern New York City: Transfiguring Spaces*, ed. Günter H. Lenz and Utz Riese (Heidelberg: University of Heidelberg Press, 2003), 58, 59.

24. Jameson, *Postmodernism*, 51.

25. Ibid., 52.

26. Ibid.

27. Ibid., 44.

28. Ibid., 54.

29. Ibid.

30. For DeLillo's paranoid Hoover, the primary threat to America's hegemony is not the Soviet Union, but the conspiratorial undervoice that undermines the nation from within. Peter Knight has argued that *Underworld* reimagines and reconfigures conspiracy theory for a new global age where the "bomb-induced fears" of the cold war are replaced by "newer anxieties resulting from the fragmentation of . . . former geopolitical certainties," which are a result of "the gradual transition from a Fordist to a post-Fordist economy" (291–293). Peter Knight, "Everything Is Connected: *Underworld*'s Secret History of Paranoia," in *Critical Essays on Don DeLillo*, ed. Hugh Ruppersburg and Tim Engles (New York: G. K. Hall, 2000), 282–301.

31. Maria Moss, "Writing as a Deeper Form of Concentration: An Interview with Don DeLillo," *Sources* (Spring 1999): 86.

32. Portes and Sassen-Koob, "Making It," 46.

33. Operating from 1949 to 1960, "Title I provided deep federal subsidies for

clearance of slum areas in order to stimulate their reconstruction by private developers," according to Hilary Ballon. As a result of Moses's will power and innovation in "capturing federal funds," "New York won more Title I aid than any other city." See Hilary Ballon, "Robert Moses and Urban Renewal: The Title I Program," in *Robert Moses and the Modern City: The Transformation of New York*, ed. Hilary Ballon and Kenneth T. Jackson (New York: Norton, 2007), 94.

34. Ibid., 96.

35. Marshall Berman, *All That Is Solid Melts into Air: The Experience of Modernity* (New York: Penguin, 1988), 307.

36. Ibid., 293.

37. Quoted ibid., 290.

38. Ibid., 307.

39. Ibid.

40. Quoted in Robert Fishman, "Revolt of the Urbs: Robert Moses and His Critics," in *Robert Moses and the Modern City: The Transformation of New York*, ed. Hilary Ballon and Kenneth T. Jackson (New York: Norton, 2007), 125.

41. Sigfried Giedion, *Space, Time and Architecture* (Cambridge: Harvard University Press, 1941), 832.

42. Ibid., 825.

43. Ibid., 826.

44. Ibid., xxxiv, 822, 832.

45. Mimi Sheller and John Urry, "The City and the Car," in *The City Cultures Reader*, ed. Malcolm Miles, Tim Hall, and Iain Borden (London: Routledge, 2000), 202.

46. Quoted in Soja, *Postmetropolis*, 214.

47. Ralph Ellison, *Invisible Man* (New York: Vintage, 1982), 568.

48. Catherine Jurca, *White Diaspora: The Suburbs and the Twentieth-Century American Novel* (Princeton: Princeton University Press, 2001), 7.

49. See Richard Sennett, *The Uses of Disorder* (New York: Vintage, 1970), 71.

50. Mark Osteen, *American Magic and Dread: Don DeLillo's Dialogue with Culture* (Philadelphia: University of Pennsylvania Press, 2000), 237.

51. Jameson, *Postmodernism*, 33.

52. Ibid.

53. Ibid.

54. Ellen Wulfhorst, "Bus Line Debuts Tour of Stricken City," *Reuters*, January 5, 2006. Available from: http://www.redorbit.com/news/general/348774/bus_line_debuts_tour_of_stricken_city/index.html.

55. Ray Bromley, "Cross-Bronx Expressway," in *Robert Moses and the Modern City: The Transformation of New York*, ed. Hilary Ballon and Kenneth T. Jackson (New York: Norton, 2007), 219.

56. Berman, *All That Is Solid*, 290.

57. Bromley, "Cross-Bronx Expressway," 220.

58. Michel de Certeau, *The Practice of Everyday Life*, trans. Steven Rendall (Berkeley: University of California Press, 1984), 93, 100, 101.

59. Ibid., 93.

60. Ibid., 105.

61. Berman, *All That Is Solid*, 307.

62. John Friedmann, quoted in Soja, *Postmetropolis*, 221.

63. Knight, "Everything Is Connected," 297; Soja, *Postmetropolis*, 192.

64. For an extended consideration of the relation between memory and dilapidated inner-city spaces, see Tim Edensor, *Industrial Ruins: Spaces, Aesthetics and Materiality* (Oxford: Berg, 2005).

65. For more on the gentrification of New York City's ethnic neighborhoods in the 1990s, see Neil Smith, *The New Urban Frontier: Gentrification and the Revanchist City* (London: Routledge, 1996).

66. Thomas Pynchon, *The Crying of Lot 49* (New York: HarperPerennial, 1990), 178.

67. Jameson, *Postmodernism*, 47.

68. bell hooks, *Yearning* (Boston: South End Press, 1990), 27.

69. Djuna Barnes, *Nightwood* (New York: New Directions, 1961), 15; Ralph Ellison, "Going to the Territory," in *Going to the Territory* (New York: Vintage, 1986), 124.

Index

About the Author

Thomas Heise lived in San Francisco and New York City before moving to Montreal, Quebec, where he is an assistant professor of English at McGill University. He is the author of *Horror Vacui: Poems* (2006). His poetry and essays have been published widely.